GW00994852

DEATH RITES AND RIGH

Death has diverse religious, social, legal, and medi
the main areas in which medicine and the law intersect. In this volume, we
ask: What is the meaning of death in contemporary Britain, and in other
cultures, and how has it changed over time? The essays in this collection
tackle the diverse ways in which death is now experienced in modern society,
in the process answering a wide variety of questions: How is death defined
by law? Do the dead have legal rights? What is one allowed to have and not
have done to one's body after death? What are the rights of next of kin in
this respect? What compensation exists for death and how is death valued?
What is happening to the law on euthanasia and suicide? Is there a human
right to die? What is the principle of sanctity of life? What of criminal
offences against the dead? How are the traditions of death still played out
in religion? How have customs and traditions of the disposal of bodies and
funerals changed? What happens to donated bodies in the biomedical setting
where anatomical education is permitted? What processes are employed by
police when investigating suspicious deaths? What of representations of
death? These and other questions are the subject of this challenging and
diverse set of essays.

Death Rites and Rights

Edited by

BELINDA BROOKS-GORDON
FATEMEH EBTEHAJ
JONATHAN HERRING
MARTIN H JOHNSON
MARTIN RICHARDS

For the Cambridge Socio-Legal Group

·HART·
PUBLISHING

OXFORD AND PORTLAND, OREGON
2007

Published in North America (US and Canada) by
Hart Publishing
c/o International Specialized Book Services
920 NE 58th Avenue, Suite 300
Portland, OR 97213-3786
USA
Tel: +1-503-287-3093 or toll-free: (1)-800-944-6190
Fax: +1 503 280 8832
E-mail: orders@isbs.com
Website: www.isbs.com

Hart Publishing, 16C Worcester Place, Oxford, OX1 2JW
Telephone: +44 (0)1865 517530 Fax: +44(0)1865 510710
E-mail: mail@hartpub.co.uk
Website: http://www.hartpub.co.uk

British Library Cataloguing in Publication Data
Data Available

ISBN: 978-1-84113-732-2

Typeset by Compuscript Ltd, Shannon
Printed and bound in Great Britain by
TJ International Ltd, Padstow, Cornwall

Acknowledgements

This book is the sixth in a series by the Cambridge Socio-Legal Group and is a product of a three-day workshop held in Cambridge in September 2006.

We are grateful for a grant in support of the workshop from the John Hall Fund of the Faculty of Law, University of Cambridge, and we thank the Institute of Criminology for hosting the event, especially Joanne Garner and Caroline Edwards, who were most helpful.

We would like to acknowledge the contributors for their participation in this stimulating project, the discussants for their insightful comments, and Frances Murton for her careful sub-editing of the whole manuscript.

The Editors
Cambridge
April 2007

Contents

Notes on Contributors

Hazel Biggs is Professor of Medical Law at Lancaster University and the Lancaster Centre for Bioethics and Medical Law. Previously she was Director of Medical Law at the University of Kent. The focus of her research is medical law and ethics, with the main emphasis being end-of-life decision-making, human reproduction and clinical research. She is the author of *Euthanasia, Death with Dignity and the Law* (Hart, 2001) and is currently on the editorial boards of *Medical Law Review* and *Research Ethics Review*.

Antje du Bois-Pedain is a Lecturer in Law at the University of Cambridge, Faculty of Law. Her main research interests are in the fields of criminal law and procedure, medical law, legal theory and transitional justice. With JR Spencer, she has recently co-edited *Freedom and Responsibility in Reproductive Choice* (Hart, 2005).

Belinda Brooks-Gordon is a Reader in Psychology and Social Policy at Birkbeck College, University of London, where she is Programme Director of the Family and Systemic Psychotherapy Courses. Belinda's research interests address psychological and social policy questions on sexuality, gender, and the law. She has written and produced five volumes for the Home Office Offending Behaviour Programmes Unit and has completed four systematic reviews for the Department of Health. Recent publications include *The Price of Sex: Prostitution, Policy and Society* (Willan Publishing, 2006) and *Law and Psychology: Issues for Today* (co-edited with M Freeman, Oxford University Press, 2006).

Caragh Brosnan is a PhD Candidate in the Faculty of Social and Political Sciences at the University of Cambridge. Her doctoral research is in the sociology of medical education and examines medical students' experiences of learning reproductive medicine in a 'traditional' and an 'innovative' medical curriculum. Her primary research interests are in the sociology of health, illness and the body, gender, professions, and the work of Pierre Bourdieu.

P-L Chau is a staff research scientist at the Pasteur Institute, Paris. He read medicine, and did research in physics and pharmacology at the University of Cambridge. He was a research fellow at the Departments of Pharmacology and Biochemistry, and a supervisor in physiology and pharmacology at New Hall, Cambridge, for seven years. Currently his main research interest is biomolecular recognition. He collaborates with Jonathan Herring on research at the interface of biology, medicine and law.

Claudia Downing is a Wellcome Trust Postdoctoral Fellow based at the Centre for Family Research, University of Cambridge. Her research focuses on becoming and being parents in families facing late-onset genetic disorders as new options present for resolving uncertainty about genetic risk and for reproduction.

Fatemeh Ebtehaj is an associate member of the Centre for Family Research, University of Cambridge. Her research focuses on Iranian migrants and exiles, with a particular interest in issues related to gender, self and identity, narrative and discourse analysis. Her current research highlights the impact of migration on ageing and on the care of the elderly. She has been a contributor and co-editor of an earlier Socio-Legal Group volume, *Kinship Matters* (Hart, 2006).

Loraine Gelsthorpe is Reader in Criminology and Criminal Justice at the Institute of Criminology, University of Cambridge, and a Fellow of Pembroke College. Her interests revolve around gender, crime and social justice, youth justice and, more generally, concepts of crime and criminal justice in late modernity. She has written extensively on these and related issues. Recent publications include *The Handbook of Probation* (Willan Publishing, 2007). She is also a psychoanalytical psychotherapist.

Sarah Webster Goodwin is Professor of English at Skidmore College in Saratoga Springs, New York. She is the author of *Kitsch and Culture: The Dance of Death in Nineteenth-Century Literature and Graphic Arts* (Garland, 1988) and the co-editor with Elisabeth Bronfen of *Death and Representation* (Johns Hopkins, 1993), as well as co-editor of a number of other volumes eg *The Scope of Words* (Peter Lang, 1991); *Feminism, Utopia and Narrative* (University of Tennessee Press, 1990). Her current work is concerned with the relationship between poetry and the law of testaments and property in post-Revolutionary England and Germany.

Elizabeth Hallam is Senior Lecturer in Social Anthropology at the University of Aberdeen. She has researched and taught in the fields of anthropology and cultural history at the University of Kent and the University of Sussex. Her publications include *Cultural Encounters: Representing Otherness* (edited with B Street (Routledge, 2000)), *Beyond the Body: Death and Social Identity* (with J Hockey and G Howarth (Routledge, 1999)) and *Death, Memory and Material Culture* (with J Hockey (Berg, 2001)). She is currently writing *Anatomy Museum. The Body, Death and Display* for Reaktion Books. Her research and publications focus on the historical anthropology of the body; death and dying; visual and material cultures; histories of collecting and museums. She is also involved in collaborative museum, exhibition and digitisation projects.

Steve Hedley is Professor of Law at University College, Cork. He is author of *Tort* (5th edition) (Oxford University Press, 2006) as well as other books and articles in obligations and commercial law. His most recent book is *The Law of Electronic Commerce and Internet in the UK and Ireland* (Routledge-Cavendish, 2006).

Jonathan Herring is a fellow in law at Exeter College, University of Oxford. He is author of *Medical Law and Ethics* (Oxford University Press, 2006); *Criminal Law: Text, Cases and Materials* (2nd edition) (Oxford University Press, 2006); *Family Law* (3rd edition) (Pearson, 2007); and *Criminal Law* (5th edition) (Palgrave, 2007).

Emily Jackson is Professor of Medical Law at Queen Mary, University of London. She is a Member of the Human Fertilisation and Embryology Authority and sits on the Ethics Committees of, among others, the British Medical Association, the Royal College of Pathologists and the Royal College of Physicians. In 2002, her book *Regulating Reproduction* (Hart, 2001) won the Society of Legal Scholars Annual Book Prize. Her textbook, *Medical Law*, was published in 2006 (Oxford University Press).

Martin H Johnson is Professor of Reproductive Sciences in the Department of Anatomy at the University of Cambridge. He was a Distinguished Visiting Scholar at the Law School at La Trobe University, Melbourne (2005–06) and a member of the Human Fertilisation and Embryology Authority (1993–99). He is the Annual Ver Heyden de Lancey Lecturer in Medical Law at the Law School, University of Cambridge (2007). In 2004 he was elected a scientific Fellow of the Royal Society of Obstetricians and Gynaecologists. He is author of *Essential Reproduction* (6th edition) (Blackwell Science, 2007), co-editor of *Sexuality Repositioned* (Hart, 2004) and has authored over 230 papers on reproductive science, ethics, law and medical education.

Peter C Jupp is a United Reformed Church minister and Golders Green Foundation Research Fellow in the Department of Theology and Religious Studies, University of Durham. He was Director of the National Funerals College project, 1992–97. He was a founding co-editor of the journal *Mortality* and has co-edited a number of books in death studies, including *Interpreting Death* (Cassell, 1997) and *Death in England: An Illustrated History* (Manchester University Press, 1999). His *From Dust to Ashes: Cremation and the British Way of Death* was published in 2006 (Palgrave). He is Chairman of the Cremation Society of Great Britain.

Judith Middleton-Stewart lectures on late-medieval art, architecture and church history in the Continuing Education Departments of the University of Cambridge and University of East Anglia, although her original training was in physiotherapy, working in London, East Anglia and Northern Rhodesia. Her book *Inward Purity and Outward Splendour; Death and Remembrance in the Deanery of Dunwich, Suffolk 1370–1547* (Boydell, 2001) examined testamentary bequests to medieval churches, and at present she is preparing Mildenhall's late-medieval churchwardens' accounts for publication.

Daniel Miller is Professor of Material Culture at University College London. His most recent books include *The Cell Phone: an anthropology of communication* (with H Host Berg, 2006) a study of the impact of mobile phones on low income families. Also *Materiality* (ed), (Duke University Press, 2005), and *Clothing as Material Culture* (ed. with S Küchler), (Berg, 2005). He is currently writing a book on the experience of au pairs in London with Zuzana Burikova, and another on material culture and loss with Fiona Parrott. He is starting a new project on how separated families maintain long term relationships in 2007.

Frances Murton is an associate member of the Centre for Family Research, University of Cambridge, and has worked on a number of studies on the psychosocial aspects of genetic and reproductive technologies. She was formerly a social worker specialising in work with children and families, and a family mediator. She has assisted the editors of earlier Socio-Legal Group volumes.

Fiona Parrott is an AHRC funded doctoral student in the Department of Anthropology at University College London. She has published her work with patients in a secure psychiatric hospital: '"It's not forever"—The Material Culture of Hope' (2005) 10 *Journal of Material Culture* 245, and has a forthcoming publication in *Ethnologie Française* on the materiality of memory in South London homes.

David Price is Professor of Medical Law at the De Montfort University School of Law in Leicester. He is author of *Legal Aspects of Organ Transplantation* (Cambridge University Press, 2000) and has recently had an edited work, *Organ and Tissue Transplantation* (Ashgate, 2006) in the *International Library of Medicine, Ethics and Law* series. He is a member of the editorial board of the *Medical Law Review* and the *International Review of Law, Computers and Technology*, and is the United Kingdom Editor of the Medical Law volume of the *International Encyclopaedia of Laws*, which was first published in 2002 (Kluwer Law International). He is a member of the Leicestershire Clinical Ethics Committee.

Martin Richards is Emeritus Professor of Family Research at the Centre for Family Research, University of Cambridge. His research is focused on psychosocial aspects of new genetic and reproductive technologies. He has been a member of the Human Genetic Commission and the Law and Ethics Committee of the Human Fertilisation and Embryology Authority. He has been a contributor and co-editor of earlier Socio-Legal Group volumes: *What is a Parent?* (Hart, 1999); *Body Lore and Laws* (Hart, 2002); and *Children and their Families* (Hart, 2003). He co-edited *The Troubled Helix* (Cambridge University Press, 1996) with Théresa Marteau. He also has historical interests in this field: 'Perfecting people: selective breeding at the Oneida Community 1869–1879 and the eugenic movement' (2004) 23 *New Genetics and Society* 49.

Graham Scambler is Professor of Medical Sociology in the Centre for Behavioural and Social Sciences in Medicine at University College London. He is editor of the leading textbook *Sociology as Applied to Medicine* (Saunders, 2003) now in its sixth edition, and the four-volume *Medical Sociology* (Routledge, 2005), featured in the Routledge Major Themes Series. Recent sole-authored books include *Health and Social Change* (Open University Press, 2002) and *Sport and Society* (Open University Press, 2005). He is currently writing a book on *Social Exclusion* for Polity Press. He is a founding co-editor of the international journal *Social Theory and Health*, published by Palgrave.

Francis Woodman is Staff Tutor for Art History and Architecture at the University of Cambridge Institute for Continuing Education, having previously been a Research Fellow at Christ's College Cambridge and lecturer in Art History at the University of East Anglia. A Fellow of the Society of Antiquaries, he lectures widely on Architecture from the Roman period to the Reformation, and on topics as varied as Medieval Women and collapsing structures. He has published widely, including monographs on Canterbury Cathedral and on King's College Chapel.

Anji Wilson is a member of the Centre for Family Research at the University of Cambridge. Her academic background is in biology, anthropology and psychology. She has been involved with research examining attitudes to tissue donation, lay understanding of inheritance and most recently social development in school-age children.

Joanne Wilton is currently the Clinical Anatomist at the University of Cambridge, and a Fellow of St Catharine's College. Prior to this she was Director of Anatomy at the University of Birmingham. Her major area of activity is in the development of relevant and stimulating anatomy courses for medical students and in encouraging the retention of functional anatomy in modern medical curricula.

1

Introduction: Death Writes

MARTIN RICHARDS AND MARTIN H JOHNSON

BENJAMIN FRANKLIN FAMOUSLY remarked 'in this world nothing can be said to be certain, except death and taxes'.[1] While death may come to us all,[2] its circumstances, the manner and timing of its coming vary, and these and our social institutions and how we deal with the resulting corpse are the subjects of this book. Two related tensions run through almost all of our discussions. The first is between the perception of death as a discontinuity that marks a sharp divide between two fundamentally different states, and death as simply part of a continuing process. These different perspectives affect, for example, how we treat corpses, our attitudes to suicide, euthanasia and martyrdom, and whether we 'avoid' death or face it constructively. A second, related tension is that between a personal or idiosyncratic response to a corpse and social attitudes to it. Managing these tensions lies at the core of many of the debates—how we treat the corpse legally, what we do with it medically, and how we treat it socially and ethically. Against this background, three broad questions are addressed in the three sections of the book. The first section asks: How, when and where do we, or should we, die? The second: What are the rituals and practices of death? And the third: How do we deal with the resulting corpse?

THE HOW, WHEN AND WHERE OF DYING

How do we know if someone is dead? One might think that biology provides a simple answer, but not so. Our living dynamic bodies are in a constant state of a life and death flux. Worn cells die and are replaced with new ones. We reshape and jettison tissues throughout life, starting during our earliest foetal development, when we first produce and then actively kill the cells that make up our tail, the webs between our fingers and toes,

---

[1] In a letter to Jean Baptiste le Roy, 13 November 1789.
[2] Some radical biologists have begun to argue that, in principle, we may become able to live forever but this would not seem to be an immediate prospect.

gills in our neck and the primitive genitalia of both sexes of which (usually) only one set survives. In this way, a process involving cellular death partly recapitulates the evolutionary process by which we arrived here, recalling our watery hermaphroditic origins. This process of recapitulation and development also reminds us that we are here by virtue of the massive and truly terminal death of the many extinct species that did not adapt successfully to their changing environments. And this may also remind us just how precarious is that survival. At birth we discard a placenta, a scaffold no longer required for our survival as liver, lungs and kidneys take over its functions. This habit of tissue littering persists throughout life as our milk teeth, nail clippings, uterine lining and virtually all the eggs, sperm and embryos we produce are doomed to an early death. In the midst of life, there is indeed much death.

However, all this dying is highly regulated and organised, and the systems of our material body retain an integrity and structure throughout life which is only lost in the process of the whole organism dying. Then breathing ceases, the heart stops and the blood no longer circulates and consciousness is lost. Irreversible changes begin to take place in all the tissues of the body as necessary metabolic processes cease. Traditionally, as Pak-Lee Chau and Jonathan Herring describe (chapter two), the indicator of death has been taken to be the loss of the more obvious vital signs—breathing and the pulse. However, modern medicine can maintain these functions mechanically so that loss of vital signs may now follow the switching off of a ventilator. This capacity of medicine to arrest death, albeit temporarily, has encouraged new uses for 'dead' bodies as sources of living transplants, as well as new medical practices. It has also led the law to defer to medicine and thereby encouraged new definitions of death. If a transplant is to be successful, the organ for transplantation must be removed before the irreversible changes of tissue-death take place. The point is well illustrated by the evidence that the living donation of a kidney is more likely to be successful because it is in better physiological shape than one from a corpse. So, for post-mortem removal of organs for transplant, death has been redefined in terms of failing brain activity. Now, a body can be 'brain dead' but breathing on a respirator awaiting the transplant surgeon's removal of the (living) organs destined for transplantation. And, when the surgeon begins that process of removal, a curious after-death practice may occur in which the (brain) dead body is anaesthetised to ease the removal of these organs.

Chau and Herring advance the view that death is more a process than an event, made up of a series of smaller death-like moments, each with its own significance (emotional, spiritual, practical, legal) for those around the dying person. The 'process view' of death sits more easily with ideas of continuity that are seen, not only in the biological continuity between successive generations, but also in developmental continuity at the beginning of life (Johnson, 2006) and the in vitro continuity that biopsied cell cultures

(Landecker, 2007) and even embryonic stem-cells promise. This idea of continuity can also be taken to a more personal level with the survival across death of aspects of identity and bodily integrity. This is already achieved with human face transplants and is conjectured by Chau and Herring for brain transplants. These authors also ponder on the likelihood of medical science providing immortality of whole organisms; a prospect that has already excited the imagination of social scientists (Turner, to be published 2007) and bio-ethicists (Harris, 1998).

The intrusion of medical practices and technology into the process of dying and its legal definition is also influenced by the fact that, as compared with a century ago, contemporary death has different causes and a significantly different place in the life span. In the 19th century, infectious diseases of childhood were major killers with almost a quarter of all deaths occurring in infancy. Now we live longer,[3] the deaths of children are rare in the West, and for most death has become a 'natural conclusion' to life in old age. Most of us will die from the 'slow' deaths of the more chronic diseases of later life: heart disease, stroke and cancer. The rarity of deaths of young children has made childhood deaths more shocking and anomalous in a way that is not true in cultures where many do not live to reach adulthood (Scheper Hughes, 1992). This changing demography of death has also encouraged the demand for transplants to replace worn parts and help individuals to conform to 'the social expectations of death age'. But it is particularly ironic that some of these living donations may be supplied by the poor from countries where life expectancy remains short.

Accompanying all these medical changes is a shift in the location of death, which, like birth, has moved to the institution of the hospital or hospice for most. So, paradoxically, the hospital becomes simultaneously the place of hope and the feared charnel house—patients enter hoping for the transplant to sustain them but fearing that MRSA will carry them off together with their transplant. Along with this change in the location of death, the hands on the body have also changed. Preparation of the corpse for the funeral and disposal is no longer carried out by the kin and the priest, but is now entrusted to a bevy of professionals that may include doctors, nurses, the police, medical students and the undertaker.

While family members may well be at the hospital bedside at the time of death, it is often suggested that we have become more distanced from death and that it has moved into a more public space and thereby a less personal sphere. The commonplace images of death in our culture have changed. Each day we can witness a mass of fictional deaths on television and in films, while the media also record the real dead on one or other of the world's battlefields, in a crashed car in a Parisian underpass or in an

---

[3] Global life expectancy at birth is 66 years but the range is wide; from 34 years in Sierra Leone to 82 years in Japan. See Scambler, ch 10).

exhibition of corpses in an art gallery. But there is more caution in allowing us to see more personal deaths. For example, at the execution of Saddam Hussein, the moments of his dying were excluded from clips shown on British television.

Doctors are perceived as playing different roles in this modern drama of death, with their actions determining the timing of death through such means as giving heavy sedation or withholding potentially life-prolonging treatments. Indeed, it has been suggested that the timing of a majority of deaths is now controlled by the actions of doctors (Ariès, 1983; see Jackson, chapter 3). But perhaps sometimes we also retain some influence over the timing of our own deaths. There is certainly a widespread belief that we may sometimes postpone our deaths until after some important event or social occasion. This idea has been put to an empirical test in an American study of Jewish and non-Jewish deaths before and after the Jewish holiday of Passover. It was found that death may indeed take a holiday (Phillips and King, 1988). Amongst Jewish people, but not in other comparison groups, deaths were significantly lower in the week before Passover and higher in the following week. The effect was found to be stronger when Passover coincided with a weekend and would be celebrated by more people.[4]

The more obvious case of someone taking control over ending a life is, of course, suicide. Until the 1961 Suicide Act, this was a criminal offence and those who killed themselves were stigmatised by exclusion from funeral and burial rites. But today, while suicide is legal, it is an offence in the United Kingdom to assist someone to kill themselves, though assisted suicide and medical euthanasia are legal in a few other jurisdictions. There appears a paradox here in that the law passes the buck to doctors in defining death and distress (see chapter fourteen by Hedley and chapter two by Chau and Herring) but does not trust them sufficiently to administer it (see chapter three by Jackson).

Three chapters in the book address aspects of the contentious issue of assisted death. Emily Jackson analyses the link between attitudes to the legalisation of euthanasia and trust in doctors, suggesting that rather than euthanasia reducing trust in doctors, it is only when such trust is high that voluntary euthanasia becomes generally acceptable. She argues that legalised euthanasia would result in fewer and more humane and peaceful deaths than the current situation, in which doctors are already shortening the lives of many of their patients. Hazel Briggs (chapter four) examines the legal position of carers and others in the context of suicide and where they may accompany someone abroad who is seeking voluntary euthanasia. And there is a broader principle at stake here, as Antje du Bois-Pedain (chapter five) asks, 'Is there a human right to die?'

---

[4] It is, of course, possible that doctors may collude with their patients and act in ways that contribute to death's holiday.

RITUALS AND PRACTICES OF DEATH

The burial of the dead is a particularly human social activity that is not seen in any of our primate relatives. While we can speculate whether goods in early human graves are an indication of a belief in an afterlife and were intended to aid the dead person on some further journey, or whether they had some other social function, the act of burial represents a social marking and recognition of the ending of a life. Societies in which Christian belief in an afterlife held a strong grip traditionally have viewed this life-ending as simply a transition, often to a better life, that could be prepared for and facilitated (see chapter six by Jupp and chapter seven by Woodman and Middleton-Stewart). Such beliefs may complicate life and funeral practices in modern societies. In contemporary Britain, some of the Pakistani Muslim community are buried in special areas in local cemeteries with their heads facing Mecca, but others, especially men, are returned to their village of origin in the Pakistani homeland to be buried alongside their biradari (clan) members. Relatives there can see the body and pay respects before burial, and blessings will accrue to the deceased person's account with God through the prayers of kin who visit the grave, which will be weighed up on the day of judgement. However, these benefits are to be set against the necessary delay in burial. Muslims should be buried as soon as possible after death because the soul remains in the body and continues to suffer at least until burial, although, again, such pain and suffering can be relieved through the prayers of others (Shaw, to be published 2008). Such beliefs and practices may cause difficulties should a post-mortem be required.

Even in our modern more secular world the metaphor of life's journey continuing beyond death remains in popular culture. And there is a tension here between the continuing resonance in popular culture of songs about the journey to an afterlife and the more retrospective character of most funeral services. An example is a Christian song from the age of steam, which remains popular on both sides of the Atlantic in several genres of popular music: *Life's Railway to Heaven*.

Life is like a mountain railroad, with an engineer that's brave,
We must make the run successful from the cradle to the grave;
Watch the curves, the fills, the tunnels, never falter, never fail,
Keep your hand upon the throttle and your eye upon the rail.
Chorus
Blessed saviour, thou will guide us till we reach the blissful shore,
Where the angels wait to join us in thy praise for ever more.

As you roll up grades of trial you will cross the bridge of strife;
See that Christ is your conductor on the lightening train of life;
Always mindful of obstructions, do your duty, never fail,
Keep your hand upon the throttle and your eye upon the rail.
Chorus

As you roll across the trestle, spanning death's dark swelling tide,
You behold the union depot into which your train will glide;
There you'll meet the superintendent, God the Father, God the Son,
With a hearty joyous plaudit, weary pilgrim, welcome home.
Chorus.[5]

It is the social common place that people deserve a 'good send off' (a decent funeral and burial or cremation) and should then be allowed to 'rest in peace'. What, however, characterises many of our contemporary funeral rites—whether religious or secular—is that they tend to be retrospective, usually focusing on a celebration of the life of the now irredeemably dead person, and are centred physically on the disposal of the body with its emphasis on the ending. Perhaps that is another reason why the death of a child or young person has become so difficult to handle: it is easier to be retrospective when older people die (an expected death after a 'good innings'), whereas more challenging when a life ends early and so there is less 'achievement' to record and the loss is more palpable because most of the life lost can only be imagined.

The ceremony may be held to lack completion if a body has not been found to dispose of and so bring finality to the life lived. Considerable effort may be expended to collect remains of bodies crushed or exploded and to DNA type them for secure identification. But how much body is enough for closure? The answer to this question may be highly contingent. Thus, any portion seems to help if the alternative is none, yet it was the absence of a relatively small, but perhaps particularly significant part (brain or heart) from an otherwise intact child's corpse that sparked the outcry that led to the Human Tissue Act 2004[6] (Maclean, 2002; and Kennedy, 2001).

Another feature that may characterise contemporary ceremonies and rituals is how very varied and idiosyncratic they can be. Thus, while burials may be marked by tombstones or trees, cremations, which account for some 70 per cent of United Kingdom disposals, may not be. Ashes may be simply scattered or buried in a place associated with the dead person with no permanent marker.[7] Where death is sudden, the site of the accident, or killing, may be marked by placing flowers, soft toys, messages, photos and other objects to commemorate the life lost. This individualisation of death

---

[5] This is from the version first copyrighted in 1890 by Ernest Thompson. But it closely follows an earlier poem, 'Old hayseed's railroad idea of life' by William Shakespeare Hays (1895). See Cohen, 1981.

[6] Following this scandal of the retention of body parts of dead children in some hospitals, some parents chose to have further funerals at which rediscovered pathology slides, and preserved tissue samples were reunited in the grave with the rest of their child's body.

[7] Or, more provocatively, ashes may be snorted a la cocaine by a relative, according to recent press reports. Indeed, decorative sociology seems to have missed an obvious opportunity here and has yet to analyse the many adventures and misfortunes that may befall ashes stored in tea caddies or in potting sheds.

rituals reflects, perhaps, the more materialist society that we now inhabit and the increased emphasis on individual rather than social ethics. The issue of place may have particular salience and can raise social dilemmas for those, for example, in immigrant communities as we have already noted. Others have managed to achieve being in two places at once by dividing their remains. Thomas Hardy's ashes are interred in Westminster Abbey in the Poet's Corner. But his heart was removed prior to cremation and is buried in a church in his beloved Dorset. These themes of the rituals of death and the dead are developed in the chapters by Peter Jupp (chapter six), Graham Scambler (chapter ten) and Daniel Miller and Fiona Parrott (chapter nine).

The second section of the book begins with a chapter by Peter Jupp, who provides an historical survey of the interaction between Christian doctrine and funeral practices. These include beliefs in the resurrection of the body and immortality of the soul, burial and the role of Purgatory. It concludes with a discussion of the legacy of the Reformation and the theological move from a prospective towards a more retrospective view of death that has become more evident with increased secularisation. Frank Woodman and Judith Middleton-Stewart (chapter seven) also provide historical analysis based on a firmly prospective view of death. They focus on the medieval pre-Reformation ideas of Purgatory and the attractive notion of 'heavenly dry cleaners' of the soul. The tombs and post-mortem arrangements of Richard Beauchamp, Earl of Warwick are compared with those of John Baret of Bury St Edmunds. Both shared the belief in the life hereafter and the time in Purgatory, which lies behind the actions of both men, but they differed in how they saw their anticipated route to and place in this glorious afterlife, based largely on the life each had lived on earth. Sarah Goodwin (chapter eight) explores the relationship between law and literature in a discussion of Wordsworth's poem *Tintern Abbey,* in which she sees the poet shifting the role of a poem from the status of a monument to a more inter-subjective and dynamic model for the modern poetic response to death.

Daniel Miller and Fiona Parrott (chapter nine) are concerned with contemporary deaths and present a study of ritual and material culture of death in a street in South London. They describe how material culture is used as a way of mediating a relationship with the dead and how ad hoc rituals using these materials are constructed, which complement the more formal rituals of religious and secular traditions. Particularly powerful is their evidence that, in immigrant families, death can provide a powerful stimulus to the living not only to place the dead one in relation to their life, but also to re-evaluate and thereby 'find their own place' in the world. The section concludes with Graham Scambler's chapter ten, which sets the earlier discussion in a more theoretical framework to provide a sociological analysis of post-modern death.

THE CORPSE

In the final section we turn to the corpse itself, which may not be simply buried or cremated with due ceremony and ritual. Indeed, the corpse can represent a major provocation to us socially and personally. The disposal may be preceded by a post-mortem to establish the cause of death (Herring, chapter thirteen) or perhaps for research purposes related to the condition that caused the death, or a police enquiry into criminal actions that may have caused the death. Corpses may be used for other purposes; a source of organs for transplantation (Chau and Herring, chapter two) or as an object for dissection for the instruction of medical students (Wilton, chapter fifteen; and Hallam, chapter sixteen).

There is a general belief that the dead should be treated with due respect. A rationalist might claim that following death we will not have any interest in our mortal remains and so how we treat corpses is immaterial. However, it is more commonly argued that the dead are worthy of respect for a variety of reasons, including concerns for their living relatives, respect for religious or personal beliefs about the relationship between the deceased person and their corpse, and the view that to treat corpses disrespectfully somehow demeans human dignity generally and the dignity of the corpse itself in particular (Bostrom, 2005). The post-mortem desecration of bodies and tombs of the 'enemy' illustrates this last point powerfully—corpses used to 'dehumanise' groups by religion, race, gender, sexuality etc. Reflecting these concerns, there is an impressive list of crimes that can be committed against a corpse, ranging from issues connected with burial, through prevention of lawful burial, to sexual acts with the dead, as Jonathan Herring describes. However, what is perhaps striking is that there is no general legal concept of a crime against a corpse, but rather a set of apparently rather ad hoc laws resulting in some obvious gaps.

David Price (chapter twelve) takes this discussion further in considering whether the dead might have 'rights' in the sense of some continuity of the rights of the living extending into death. The possible post-mortem survival of the rights and interests of the dead person raises potential conflict with the rights and interests of the surviving next-of-kin. This potential for conflict has become particularly acute with the passing of the Human Tissue Act 2004, which places at its heart the consent of the predeceased person about what happens to their body after death—a good example of a legal protection surviving death and for the corpse. However, anatomist Joanne Wilton (chapter 15) challenges the reality of this primacy of pre-mortem consent in her description of what actually happens between death and the arrival (or not) of a body in the dissecting room. The potential for conflict between the consent of the person donating their body for use in medical research and the desires of the surviving relatives can make a nonsense of the primacy of the consent, and in reality the relatives' interests will trump those of the corpse. Herein lies the problem, discussed also by Price, of trying to tie down your post-mortem fate: your rights may expire with your death whatever provisions you put in place. This expiration of rights also extends legally to compensation for death and the value of death under tort law as Steve Hedley considers (chapter fourteen). Again, the corpse is a weak player legally compared, for example, with the claims for assessment of damages by living relatives and other potential claimants.

The Human Tissue Act 2004 in England and Wales, and the Human Tissue (Scotland) Act 2006 in Scotland—which have brought major changes in practice to areas as diverse as post-mortem pathology analysis, dissection of bodies by medical students, regulation of tissue and organ transplants, and handling of human remains by museums—were themselves a legislative response to an emotional reaction to the perceived disrespectful treatment of corpses. The Acts followed public concern at the way in which human tissue and organs had been retained, especially from children, at Alder Hey Hospital and elsewhere (Redfern, 2001; Kennedy, 2001; and Maclean, 2002). That this legislative response may have been disproportionate to the problem it set out to solve is suggested not only in Wilton's chapter fifteen, but also in that of anthropologist Elizabeth Hallam (chapter sixteen). She explores the social and cultural life of a body as it moves into the dissecting room and its redefinition as it re-emerges for burial or cremation in rituals and memorialisation in which the anatomists and medical students participate. Strong themes in both these chapters are the respect and affection that the students may express towards their 'silent teachers'.

Death may, at least for the time being, remain a certainty, but the ways in which we mark it and deal with the material remains are likely to remain complex and often inconsistent as the chapters of this book testify.

REFERENCES

Ariès, P (1983) *The Hour of Our Death* (Harmondsworth, Penguin).

Bostrom, N (2005) 'In defence of posthuman dignity' 19 *Bioethics* 202–214.

Cohen, N (1981) *Long steel rail: The railroad in American folksong* (University of Illinois Press, Urbana, Illinois).

Harris, J (1998) *Clones, genes and immortality* (Oxford, Oxford University Press).

Hays, WS (1895) *Poems and songs* (Louisville, KY, CT Dearing).

Johnson, MH (2007) 'Escaping the tyranny of the embryo? A new approach to ART regulation based on UK and Australian experiences' 21 *Human Reproduction* 2756–2765.

Kennedy, I (2001) *Learning from Bristol: The report of the public inquiry into children's heart surgery at the Bristol Royal Infirmary 1984–1995* Cm 5207 (Norwich, The Stationery Office).

Landecker, H (2007) *Culturing life. How cells become technologies* (Cambridge, MA, Harvard University Press).

Maclean, M (2002) 'Letting go ... parents, professionals and law of human materials after post-mortem' in A Bainham, SD Sclater and M Richards (eds), *Body lore and laws* (Oxford/Portland OR, Hart Publishing Ltd) 79–90.

Phillips, DP and King, EW (1988) 'Death takes a holiday: Mortality surrounding major social occasions' ii *The Lancet* 728–732.

Redfern, M (2001) *Report of the Royal Liverpool Children's Inquiry: Summaries and Recommendations* (Norwich, The Stationery Office).

Scheper Hughes, N (1992) *Death Without Weeping. The Violence of Everyday Life in Brazil* (Berkeley, CA, University of California Press).

Shaw (to be published 2008) *Negotiating Risk: British Pakistani Experiences of Genetics* (Oxford, Berghahn).

Turner, BS (to be published 2007) 'Piety, prolongevity and perpetuity: The consequences of living for ever' Lecture delivered to the conference on the Sacred and Medicine (Canberra, Australian National University).

Part 1

When and How We Die

2

The Meaning of Death

P-L CHAU AND JONATHAN HERRING

I. INTRODUCTION

OUR ATTITUDES TOWARDS death have changed in recent years. In the past death was simply something that happened to us and had to be accepted. However, with technological developments it has become possible to exercise greater control over our dying (Jackson, chapter three this volume). Many people now want to organise their death so that it can be quiet, peaceful and controlled (du Bois-Pedain, chapter five this volume; and Battin, 1998). Cryogenic freezing and remarkable medical advances have even meant that it is possible to consider seriously the possibility of immortality (Harris, 2004). The advances in life support technology have meant that there is a sense in which dying has become a fragmented occasion and can be more controlled. It can even be claimed that deaths are timed to fit into the convenience of the hospital and/or the patients' families. One study from California found that among patients with Jewish surnames there was a reduction in deaths the week before Passover and an excess in the following week (Phillips and King, 1988). Whether this is explained as death taking place at a time of convenience to the hospital or whether it is rather the effect of dying patients willing themselves to keep alive until after an important or religious or social event is unclear (Lee and Smith, 2000). Further, the more public nature of death, or at least the facility for intervention by the state over the timing and moment of dying, has meant that dying can become a site of conflict between the interests of the individual and the state. The state's interests in obtaining organs for transplantation and controlling the cost of expensive life-preserving treatment have rendered the moment of death a point of public interest. In some ways, the debate over the moment of death is reminiscent of the continuing debate over the status of the embryo in relation to personal identity ('When does life begin?' 'When can and cannot an embryo be killed?'). Technological advances in fertility and embryo research have rendered the status of the embryo a matter of public interest too (Johnson, 2006).

In this chapter, we will analyse some of the definitions of death which have been promoted by, among others, lawyers, philosophers and doctors. The benefits and disadvantages of each definition will be discussed. We will argue that death carries multiple meanings. It is best understood as a process during which in different ways and for different purposes a person may be considered to be dead. We suggest that the main issue is not what death is, but rather what one should or should not be able to do to a person at different stages during the dying process.

II. WHAT IS DEATH?

Defining death is controversial and problematic (Lizza, 2006; Veatch, 2005; and Schapiro, 1999). The issue raises fundamental questions about our humanity: What is it to be a person? What are the essential elements of life?

Usually, there are no difficulties in deciding whether a person is dead or not, even if there is disagreement over when death occurred. In the absence of medical intervention, the process of death is relatively simple and quick. As people age, the cells of their body show a reduced capacity to proliferate (Takahashi and others, 2000; and Maedler and others, 2006), and so tissues show impaired cellular regeneration in response to normal 'wear and tear' or to injury (Jejurikar and others, 2006) and indeed cells are also more likely to die (Mammone and others, 2006). With fewer and fewer cells, organs such as kidneys, heart or liver ultimately fail and the person dies 'naturally'. In the case of disease, a specific major organ system fails, and its cells and tissues start to die (Borutaite and others, 2003; and Qiao , 2005). In both aging and in disease, the final common pathway is that cells of an organ die in quick succession, leading to other organ systems failing, eg heart failure quickly leads to kidney failure. Death of the whole organism is concomitant with massive cellular death in major organs.

Consider the disease progression of one of the commonest causes of death in affluent societies: death due to the failure of the cardiovascular system. A blood clot may come to block one of the coronary arteries, and parts of the heart muscle suffer a restricted blood supply (ischaemia) and become starved of oxygen and nutrients. This leads to increases in the acidity of the tissue (lowering of pH), the potassium levels around the heart cells, and the calcium levels within them, all of which lead to electrical instability of the heart, and so to an irregular heart beat (cardiac arrhythmia: Mehta and others, 1997; and Zipes and Wellens, 1998) or even cessation of beating, both of which prevent effective pumping of blood round the body. The tissues of the body are therefore also starved of oxygen and nutrients, and their cells begin to die, their membranes disintegrating and their genetic material, the DNA, degrading. For example, in the case of nerve cells, isch-aemia leads to damage and then death within half an hour of total heart failure (Hayashi and Abe, 2004). In the kidney a restriction in blood supply leads to cell death (Padanilam, 2003), so the excretory function is severely compromised. General ischaemia caused by cardiac insufficiency thus leads to massive cell death in all tissues. The patient can no longer maintain physiological functions such as digestion or excretion, and dies.

What we have described above is the process of death in the absence of any medical intervention. However, the matter becomes more complicated if medical procedures are applied. For example, if the heart fails, restriction of blood flow in the brain will set in within a matter of minutes, and after about 15 minutes a large proportion of cerebral cortical neurons will have died. Should the patient be resuscitated before total brain death occurs, the brainstem (which controls breathing, blood pressure and body temperature) can remain functional when the cerebral cortices are dead. These patients are in a 'persistent vegetative state' ('PVS') (Multi-Society Task Force on PVS, 1994a and 1994b). A PVS patient is unaware and insensate, cannot self-feed and has lost all language capabilities, but is capable of some degree of movement and is not comatose. However, even with medical intervention, the cerebral cortices and the brainstem might both die. In this case, the patient is defined as 'brain-dead', but the other major organ systems of that individual can be intact, since the brain is one of the most sensitive organs to interruption of blood flow. The difference between PVS and brain death is that, in the former, the patient is 'awake' and can execute some motions, although lacks consciousness, but in the latter, the patient is comatose.

PVS patients present a major challenge to the notion of death. The cerebral cortices of PVS patients are not functioning, so their personalities are totally absent; they have no consciousness. They can often breathe spontaneously, their blood pressure is under physiological control, but they have to be fed and exercised by carers. In brain-dead patients, they can be kept alive (often for years) but only with total parenteral nutrition (where food is usually given to the patients through their veins), artificial respiration and special medical procedures to prevent pressure ulcers and muscle degeneration.

This ability to 'keep alive' people who, in the past, would have died causes problems in defining death. And this problem will only get worse when looking to the future if even more remarkable medical procedures should become available. Transplants of bone marrow (Mathé and others, 1963), kidneys (Merrill and others, 1956), livers (Starzl and others, 1968; and Calne and Williams, 1968), hearts (Barnard, 1968), lungs (Hardy and others, 1963), hands (Dubernard and others, 1999), or even faces (Spurgeon, 2005) are now possible. And this list may well expand. The most challenging organs to keep alive in this respect are probably the head and brain. Although human brain transplants are not yet possible, animal head transplants have been performed for some time with variable survival rates and with evidence of functional brain activity such as pupillary light reflexes, noise-responsive eye winking, facial movements on electrical stimulation of the motor-sensory region of the cerebral cortices and breathing, sleeping, biting and eating (Heymans, 1912; Chute and Smyth, 1939; and Demikhov, 1962). These experiments have shown that, under appropriate conditions, it is possible to keep even the head of a higher mammal alive for a prolonged period of time.

Machines that replace parts of the human body are also becoming increasingly common. Dialysis techniques can replace the human kidney to some extent (Alloatti and others, 2000); liver dialysis can replace some functions of the liver on a very short-term basis (van de Kerkhove and others, 2004); and artificial hearts have been placed in humans (Gray and Selzman, 2006). With further scientific progress, it would not be inconceivable that any part of a human being could be kept alive using machines for the course of its cells' natural lives. What, then, is the meaning of death under those circumstances?

III. THE LEGAL DEFINITION OF DEATH

It is surprising that the legal definition of death has received very little attention from the courts (Herring, chapter thirteen this volume). Rarely has the judiciary felt the need to pronounce on the issue. In *Airedale NHS Trust v Bland*,[1] Lords Brown-Wilkinson, Goff and Keith accepted that brain stem death was the definition of death for the purposes of medicine and law. Lord Keith in *Bland* held:

In the eyes of the medical world and of the law a person is not clinically dead so long as the brain stem retains its function.

Tony Bland, although suffering PVS, was not brain stem dead and so was still alive. In *re A*,[2] Johnson, J held that a child who was on a ventilator and certified as brain stem dead was also legally dead. This was in line with the medical expert opinion, even though the parents took the view that the boy was still alive.

Perhaps the safest statement to make is that at present the legal definition of death is taken to coincide with the medical one. Traditionally, death is equated with failure of the heart (Harvey, 1653: 81–82) and the cessation of breathing (Lancisi, 1707), and this concept of cardiopulmonary death was widely used as a medical definition of death all over the world until the 1960s. Pattinson has argued that

---
[1] *Airedale NHS Trust v Bland* [1993] 1 All ER 821 (HL) **Page 859.**
[2] *Re A* (1992) 3 Medical Law Review 303 (**Family Division**).

the term 'death' is not restricted to the absence of any biological life, but used as shorthand for the legal acceptability of certain conduct (Pattinson, 2006: 422),

but cites no cases to support this proposition, and it is not clear that such cases exist! In the *Bland* case, for example, the easy route would have been to declare Tony Bland dead, thereby to justify turning off the life support machine—not the line of reasoning taken by the judges. That said, what *might* be appropriately claimed, is that the legal definition of death is so fluid that it is open to manipulation by a judge to achieve the desired result. In fact, in the few cases where the issues arise, a court is very likely to follow the expert medical opinion (Skegg, 1985: chapter nine; and Bennion, 1994). Section 26(2) of the Human Tissue Act 2004 authorises the Human Tissue Authority to issue codes of practice that will set out how it will be determined whether a person has died in cases involving transplantation. None has been produced yet, but an early publication from the Human Tissue Authority (Human Tissue Authority, 2006: 29) suggests that brain stem death will be the test.

So, lawyers may seek to pass the hot potato of defining death over to the doctors. The problem is that it there is some disagreement over what the medical definition of death is. More significantly, it is far from clear that the definition of death is entirely, even predominantly, a medical issue. The next section will consider some of the definitions of death that have been used.

IV. BRAIN STEM DEATH

A. Defining Brain Stem Death

As already indicated, brain stem death is widely accepted in the United Kingdom and many other European countries as the medical definition of death (Pallis and Harley, 1996). The brain stem is the most caudal or lowest part of the brain, and connects the spinal cord with the rest of the brain. It contains the medulla oblongata, midbrain and pons. These structures are responsible for general wakefulness, controlling blood pressure, body temperature and breathing. Normal spontaneous breathing will be impossible if the brain stem is injured.

Before the advent of mechanical ventilators and associated techniques to keep immobile patients from muscle wasting, pressure ulcers etc, a patient with brain stem death would be unable to breathe, and would thus die within a matter of minutes. Advances in mechanical ventilators and related methods made it possible for patients suffering from brain stem death to survive, and in this way these patients could be kept alive for the natural course of their lives. The problem thus arises of whether these patients are dead or not, because they cannot sustain life on their own, but are obviously not dead provided the machines are working.

In the late 1950s and early 1960s, clinicians began to use electro-encephalography (EEG) as a diagnostic tool to decide if the brain of a patient was dead (Jouvet, 1959; and Schwab and others, 1963). The EEG records electrical activity from the outside of the skull, and cessation of EEG activity was interpreted to mean that the patient was brain-dead. Around the same time, organ transplantation was making rapid progress. Less invasive surgical techniques and more effective immunosuppressive drugs were making transplantations safer. The first kidney transplantation was performed in 1954, albeit between genetically identical twins (Merrill and others, 1956). The first successful liver transplant was performed in 1967 (Starzl and others, 1968; and Calne and Williams, 1968); the same year witnessed the first successful heart transplant (Barnard, 1968).

The success in human organ transplantation meant that there was a demand for viable cadaveric organs. Notably, one month after the first successful heart transplant, a committee was convened at Harvard Medical School to study the problems of the hopelessly unconscious patient, and concluded that irreversible coma should be the criterion of death of such patients (Harvard Medical School, 1968). It is hard to avoid the suspicion that ensuring that organs could be used for transplantation played an important part in their deliberations. In the United Kingdom, brain stem death was recommended as a criterion for death (Royal College of Physicians Working Group, 1995).

At present the Department of Health's *A Code of Practice for the Diagnosis of Brain Stem Death* (Department of Health, 1998) sets out in detail its definition, which outlines three requirements that must be met before a doctor makes a diagnosis of brain death: first, it must be concluded that the coma is not due to reversible causes, such as a drug overdose; secondly, it must be demonstrated that the several components of the brain stem have all been permanently destroyed (significantly, this includes the respiratory centre); and thirdly, it must be proved that the patient is unable to breath spontaneously. The code suggests that two medical practitioners who have been registered for more than five years and are both specialists in the field should agree that there is brain death, before pronouncement.

B. The Justification for Brain Stem Death

The primary justification for using brain stem death as the decisive criterion is that a person whose brain stem is dead has ceased to live in anything but a mechanical way (Dubois, 2002). The 'integrative unity' of body and mind has come to an end (Potts, 2001). The reasons for preferring the brain stem test as opposed to the whole brain test are: first that without the brain stem, the patient will be rendered comatose; and secondly, that clinically, it is easier to ascertain brain stem death than total brain death.

C. The Objections to Brain Stem Death

A fundamental attack on the concept of brain death is that it elevates the brain to being the sole component of personhood—too narrow a view (Shewmon, 1998; Potts and others, 2000; and Russell, 2000). Veatch imagined a time in the future in which it would be possible to give a person a brain transplant (Veatch, 1989: 41). He suggested that if a brain stem test were used, this would lead to such a person being classified as dead, even though they would patently be alive. One response to this argument, though, is that we can say that the body is not dead but the person is dead. His example also raises the issue, in the case of a head transplant: Who now exists? Is it the person who had the head, or the person who had the body, or both?

It has also been objected that under the brain stem criterion, a person can be classified as dead, even though their body is warm and breathing (Evans, 2002). This creates too big a gap between the legal meaning of death and its understanding by people on the street (Byrne and Rinkowski, 1999: 42). Shewmon states that homeostasis (maintenance of the internal environment of the living organism, for example, energy balance, wound healing, fighting off infections, development of a febrile response), successful gestation of a fetus, sexual maturation, and proportional growth are all capable of occurring in people who are 'brain-dead' (Shewmon, 2001: 467–8).

Others have expressed concerns about the reliability of the tests used to determine brain stem death (Karakatsanis and Tsanakas, 2002; Mejia and Pollack, 1995; and Wang and others, 2002). If it is not possible to provide a reliable test of brain stem death, then doubt is created over the efficacy of it as a criterion of death.

V. THE END OF CONSCIOUSNESS

A. Definition of End of Consciousness

This approach is based on a person's capacity for consciousness (DeGrazia, 2004): once that is lost irreversibly then the person should be regarded as dead. Sometimes this is known as 'higher brain death'. Note that brain stem death is different from higher brain death. In the former, usually only the brain stem and the rest of the brain is dead, but in the latter, only the cerebral cortices are dead. Its use would mean that PVS patients would be regarded as dead, and so Engelhardt is able to refer to the permanently unconscious as 'biologically living corpses' (Engelhardt, 1999).

B. Justification of End of Consciousness

To some commentators the definition of death should depend on what we understand it is to be human (Rich, 1997). To some people this is a consciousness of one's self or others and an ability to interact with other people. Supporters of such an approach would argue that a person who has permanently lost the ability to communicate or relate to other people and/or a person who has permanently lost a conscious awareness of themselves and their surroundings has lost what is essential to being a human and should therefore be regarded as being dead. As Savulescu puts it, 'it is our mental life which constitutes who we are, not the machine that supports it' (Savulescu, 2003: 130). Indeed, this view has led some commentators to suggest that we should see a difference between biological death (of the organism) and the death of the person (the permanent loss of consciousness). It is the latter that matters in moral terms, supporters argue (Engelhardt, 1999).

C. Objections to Loss of Consciousness

A loss of consciousness criterion for death would lead to a far wider classification of death than used at present. Most directly, those suffering from PVS would be regarded as dead. Even more dramatically it could classify as dead (or at least non-human) large numbers of people with severe mental illness or disability. However, it may well be argued that most people with severe mental disability have some form of self-awareness and are not therefore categorised as lacking consciousness. That said, the possibility that there is a question mark hanging over whether a very mentally ill person is dead, may lead one to doubt the wisdom of the approach.

An alternative critique of an approach emphasising consciousness is to challenge that concept itself. Neurophysiological progress is making us realise that what is uniquely human is shared by many other species, and that what in the past we thought to be metaphysical can be explained by biology. Many people think that there is a mind-matter duality, and that the seat of consciousness could not be located in the brain. Over the years, neurophysiology shows us that thinking, learning, emotions and other kinds of complex behaviour are most probably changes in the brain state. For example, people who train at spatial recognition tasks have a larger right hippocampus (Maguire and othesr, 1997), while other parts of the brain are involved in motor sequence learning (Toni and others, 1998). Changes in brain activity are related to emotions (Keightley and others, 2003; and Phan and others, 2004) and psychiatric diseases (Harvey and others, 2005; and Hugdahl and others, 2004). It is not inconceivable that our feeling that there is an external existence outside of our body which is 'us' (religious people would probably call it the soul) is an illusion our brain cells gives us, so that we think there is something called 'us' outside our bodies, when there is not. In short, science may be coming to the view that we humans are a form of very complex physiological machine, like many other animals. In that case a more mechanistic definition of death than that based on consciousness may be appropriate.

VI. THE ENDING OF CARDIAC FUNCTION

A. Definition of Ending of Cardiac Function

If the heart stops beating irreversibly, then this definition concludes that the patient is dead. It is important to stress the irreversibility of this definition, because the heart can stop but the patient be resuscitated; clearly it would be nonsensical to define a person as dead every time his or her heart stops.

B. Justification of Ending of Cardiac Function

One prominent supporter of the loss of cardiac function test is the Danish Council of Ethics, which preferred it to brain death (Shewmon, 2001; Shewmon 2004; and Kamm, 2001). The Council took the view that the definition of death is not a technical question, but must be decided in terms of how the community as a whole understands death. It argued that the person in the street would view the stopping of the beating heart as the criterion for death because the heart is widely seen as a symbol of life (Truog, 1997). So, even if the notion of the beating heart as the key to life is not logically or philosophically justifiable, it is intuitively felt to be the essential mark of life.

C. Objections to Using End of Cardiac Function

One difficulty with using the cessation of the heartbeat as the criterion for death is that even if a patient's heart has stopped beating, medical intervention may still enable their resuscitation. This requires the 'end of cardiac function' criterion to rely on the concept of an irreversible end of breathing. That is problematic because, in respect of a particular patient, it might not be known whether the cessation of cardiac function is irreversible until further medical intervention has been used. Another difficulty is that it is also now clear that the stopping of the heart does not immediately lead to an end of brain activity (Mason and others, 2006: 466). This, then, could lead to a person being treated as dead even though there is some form of consciousness.

VII. THE END OF THE ORGANISM

A. Definition of End of Organism Approach

If the body is seen as a 'working organism' with various functions then it might be possible to define death as when that organism ceases to achieve those functions (Lamb, 1987). The functions of the body might include metabolism, reproduction, sensation and locomotion. Only when all of these functions are no longer being performed should the body be said to have died.

B. Justification of End of Organism Approach

This approach is supported by those who criticise the brain death criterion because it elevates the brain over the rest of the body. It would argue that a human being performs many functions, some of which, but not all, relate to the brain. Using the end of the organism as the criterion for death recognises that bodies are made up of many parts and perform many functions. The brain and its functions are only part of what the body does.

C. Objections to End of Organism Approach

To opponents of this view, it treats the body like a piece of machinery, and yet most people regard their bodies as more than an organism that, for example, simply takes in and expels air. Such an approach overlooks what most people regard as most important about their bodies: feelings, thoughts, emotions and the like. The counter-argument is that, as far as we know, our feelings, thoughts and emotions are correlated with changes in the state of the brain. In short, we are a machine that eats, sleeps, feels, and thinks—though an extremely elaborate one—so to view our body as a machine is quite acceptable.

The other problem with this approach is that, as we have seen, in due course it should be possible to replace some of our organs with artificial ones, including the brain. The patient then could be defined as living until all the original parts and replacement parts fail. Ultimately, we might end up with a living patient having none of the body parts from the original person, but who is defined as dead!

VIII.   DEATH OF EVERY CELL

A. Definition of 'Death of Every Cell' Approach

An extreme view would declare that a person has not died until every cell in the body has ceased functioning. This would place the point of death at the state when the body has begun to putrefy.

B. Justification for 'Death of Every Cell' Approach

This approach could be the 'safest'. If you believe that treating a live body as if it were dead is an appalling evil, then one would seek to avoid that at all costs. If you believe that one cannot be certain when death occurs, then this has the benefit of being the point in time at which we can be sure the person is dead.

C. Objection to 'Death of Every Cell' Approach

The practical implications of this approach are its main difficulties. It would mean that bodies could not be disposed of until they are 'some kind of smelly porridge' (Kennedy, 1988: 10). Until then they would need to be treated as live bodies. It would be an approach very much out of tune with the understanding of death of the person in the street. It is unlikely to be regarded as an acceptable notion by most people, especially those for whom religious belief or cultural practice require burial soon after death (see Jupp, chapter six this volume). Pattinson explains that it would involve

diverting finite health care resources, extending the grieving process, undermining health care staff morale, and preventing the use of any human organ or tissue for virtually all beneficial purposes from transplantation to teaching and research (Pattinson 2006: 423).

IX.   DESOULMENT

A. Definition of Desoulment

For those of a religious persuasion death is often defined as the moment the soul leaves the body and moves on to the afterlife (desoulment). The concept of a 'soul' is not easy to define. Roughly speaking the soul is the spiritual essence of a person that continues after death (Eberl, 2005). The Catholic Encyclopaedia suggests:

The soul may be defined as the ultimate internal principle by which we think, feel, and will, and by which our bodies are animated (Hughes, 1947), although the definition of the soul is a matter of heated and complex debate among theologians (see, eg Moreland and Rae, 2000).

B. Justification for Desoulment

If the soul exists and if it is what is our essence, our eternal essence and is what makes a body a person, then its presence its crucial. Hence, in many theological circles the entry of the soul into the body is the start of life and its departure is the end in the sense that it marks the point in time when the individual's life in their body ends and their afterlife begins.

C. Objections to Desoulment

Of course such a definition will be rejected by those who deny the existence of a soul. Even if the existence of a soul is accepted, there is the problem that the moment of desoulment is not apparent to humans. It cannot therefore readily provide a basis of a legal or medical test. Eberl argues that once a body is brain stem dead the soul cannot function and leaves it. He therefore supports a brain stem death test, albeit from a desoulment perspective (Eberl, 2005).

X. DEATH AS A PROCESS

A. Definition of Death as a Process

All the approaches defined so far have sought to indicate the point in time at which death occurs. An alternative approach argues that death is better seen as a process that occurs over time (Halevy, 2001). Occasionally there will be a clear instant of death, where, for example, a person is destroyed physically in an accident. But otherwise there is no easy cut-off point at which we can mark the line between a person who is alive and a person who is dead. As one dying patient put it, 'death keeps taking a little bit of me' (see Kafetz, 2002: 536).

B. Justifications of Death as a Process

The argument in support of this approach is that at different points in time a person can be regarded as dead according to some understandings of that concept, but not according to others. Death is therefore better regarded as a process during which different aspects of death may be apparent. We can be sure by the time of putrification that a person is now dead, but to select one point of the process as the moment of death is artificial.

C. Objections to the 'Death as a Process' Approach

Although there is much to be said in favour of this approach biologically, it is not a practical one. Aries has argued:

Death in the hospital is no longer the occasion of a ritual ceremony, over which the dying person presides amidst his assembled relatives and friends. Death is a technical phenomenon obtained by a cessation of care ... Indeed in the majority of cases the dying person has already lost consciousness. Death has been dissected, cut to bits by a series of little steps, which finally makes it impossible to know which step was the real death, the one in which consciousness was lost or the one in which breathing stopped. All these little silent deaths have replaced and released the great dramatic act of death, and no one any longer has the strength or patience to wait over a period of weeks for a moment which has lost part of its meaning (Aries, 1974: 88).

The law, relatives and professionals require a clear point at time at which someone has died (Stanley, 1987). Proponents of seeing death as a process could, however, suggest that a person could be treated as dead for different purposes at different times. There could be one point in time in the process where a person is declared dead for the purpose of removal of organs for transplant, but another where they are dead for the purposes of burial or cremation.

XI. NO DEFINITION

A. Definition of 'No Definition'

This approach argues that to seek to define death is an impossibility. We are better off not seeking to do so. It is more profitable to focus on particular questions: At what point is it appropriate to authorise burials of bodies? When can organs be removed from a body for transplant to another? When can a person whose body is being artificially ventilated have the machine switched off? It would be possible to have different answers to these questions (Younger and Arnold, 2001).

B. Justification for 'No Definition'

This approach is based on the notion that we cannot define the moment of death. There is no 'correct' answer. It is the kind of question to which one can answer 'death means whatever you want it to mean'. Disputes over what death means are likely to lead to high-minded disputes between theologians, philosophers, lawyers and medical scientists, which are, to be frank, likely to get nowhere. Better to focus the mind on the more concrete questions specified in the previous paragraph (Zamperetti and others, 2003).

C. Objections to 'No Definition'

To many people there is a fundamental difference between a dead person and one who is not. We are willing to treat dead bodies in a way that would be utterly unacceptable were the body alive. Morally, the loss of personhood is a fundamental change of status (Veatch, 2005). It is of crucial importance to relatives and medical staff that we can declare a point of death. It is impractical not to define death. For lawyers too, a definition of death is used in the way the criminal and medical law is structured. That said, it would not be impossible for the law to dispense with the notion of death. It would be possible, for example, for the law to list what can or cannot be done to a body demonstrating certain characteristics, without having to declare whether that body is dead or not.

XII.   CHOOSING BETWEEN THE DEFINITIONS

We will now highlight some of the differences between the definitions, and summarise the key issues which have lead people to define death in such different ways.

A. Safety First?

In choosing between these different definitions, consider the claim by Lamb: 'It is as wrong to treat the living as dead as it is to treat the dead as alive'(Lamb, 1994:1028). The argument here is that it is as important not to put the point of death too early, as to put it too late. But not everyone will agree with Lamb's suggestion. Treating a dead person as alive may be a waste of resources or may delay improperly the grieving process for the family; but is it really as serious as burying a person who is alive?

B. Death of the Body or Death of the Person

The different definitions of death tend to group into two categories: those that emphasise life as being about conscious awareness and those that understand the body as a living organism. The problem is that many people regard both understandings of our bodies and lives as valid (Holland, 2003: 75). One solution could be to accept that we die twice: once when we lose consciousness and once when our biological organism comes to an end. This solution would be supported by those who argue that we are not just minds, nor are we just bodies, we are 'embodied minds' (McMahan, 2002: 426). McMahan suggests:

An organism dies in the biological sense when it loses the capacity for integrated functioning. The best criterion for when this happens is probably a circulatory respiratory criterion ... What it is important to be able to determine is when we die in the non-biological sense—that is, when we cease to exist. If we are embodied minds, we die or cease to exist when we irreversibly lose the capacity for consciousness—or, to be more precise, when there is irreversible loss of function in those areas of the brain in which consciousness is realized. The best criterion for when this happens is a higher-brain criterion—for example, what is called 'cerebral death' (MacMahon, 2006: 48).

C. The Perspective of Death

Another difference between the definitions may be the viewpoint from which death is appreciated: the dying person or his or her carers. Arguably brain stem death will be the point at which the dying person will lose all appreciation of their life, but cessation of breathing will be the point at which the person will appear to have died to an on-looker. However, it should be noted that the stopping of breathing is the most common cause for the brain stem function to cease (Pallis, 1990). Indeed, Mason and others suggest it would be wrong to see brain stem death and non-breathing as two competing definitions of death. They prefer,

to visualise the brain, the heart and the lungs as forming a 'cycle of life' which can be broken at any point; looked at in this way, there is no need to speak of two *concepts* of death—that is, cardiorespiratory death or brain death; it is simply that different criteria, and different tests, can be used for identifying that the cycle has been broken (Mason and others, 2006: 466).

Similarly, the American Uniform Determination of Death Act 1981 states that

[a]n individual who has sustained either irreversible cessation of circulatory and respiratory functions, or irreversible cessation of all functions of the entire brain, including the brain stem, is dead.

The advantage of this viewpoint is that it does reflect the biology of death. Different parts of the body cease to function irreversibly at different times, so having a cycle of death would allow lawmakers to decide at what point organs can be harvested, and at what point the person is no longer considered to be in control of his or her higher faculties, etc.

D. Is Death a Medical, Philosophical or Legal Question?

A further key issue is who should define death. As already mentioned, so far the English courts have in recent times tended to follow the medical definition of death. Although this is approved of by some lawyers (Kennedy, 1969), others have argued that the philosophical and moral arguments must also be taken into account and therefore the courts should not slavishly follow medical opinion (Skegg, 1974; and Lizza, 2006).

For some scholars, death must be regarded as a basic biological phenomenon. J Bernat argues :

Accepting that death is a biological phenomenon neither denigrates the richness and beauty of various cultural and religious practices surrounding death and dying, nor denies societies their proper authority to govern practices and establish laws regulating the determination and time of death. But death is an immutable and objective biological fact and not fundamentally a social contrivance (Bernat, 2006: 39).

E. The Relevance of Practicality?

In producing a legal definition of death it is necessary to consider not only philosophical considerations, but also whether it is 'usable', and acceptable, ie in accordance with the general public's understanding of death. In other words, it may be that the philosophically most desirable definition of death is not usable because it cannot be transformed into a clear and practical test. But should convenience affect the definition of such a fundamental concept?

F. The Problem of Irreversibility

For many definitions there is a problem concerning irreversibility (Lizza, 2005; and Hershenov, 2003). Do the definitions require that the condition in question be 'irreversible'? Let us take, by way of example, the suggestion that loss of consciousness be the definition of death. If there is no need for this to be an 'irreversible' state, then whenever people temporarily lose consciousness they die and are then brought back to life. This seems implausible. However, if we insist that the condition be irreversible, this is problematic. We have already outlined earlier the experiments in which separate body parts (including the head) were kept alive with appropriate technology. Another example would be patients apparently suffering from PVS who have been aroused from that state with the use of drugs (Clauss and Nel, 2006). Using irreversibility as a criterion would mean that the boundary is constantly changing, so any socio-legal definition would have to update itself frequently. Further, it raises the question of whether the condition can be reversed by the use of any available technology. If so, if a person is in a state of unconsciousness and there is somewhere in the world a piece of machinery which could revive consciousness, then that person is not dead, even though it is implausible that the machinery could be used in their case. Or what about the freezing of bodies, in the hope that at some point in the future technology will have advanced to allow their revival?

G. Religion

We suggest that there is no getting away from the interconnection of religious belief and the definition of death. If there is a God or Gods, then a plausible definition of a person is 'a human being recognised as such by God'. The value and meaning of life depends on God's or the Gods' perspective, which may include criteria not observable to humans, or not valued by them. By contrast, if there is no God then the value and meaning of life depends only on what we can experience of the material world. Atheists tend, therefore, to be attracted by those views that emphasise the connection between an individual and the observable: namely, consciousness or the functions of organisms. Believers in God or Gods, however, might accept that a person is recognised as alive by God even though there is no way for that individual to relate to the world. They may prefer a definition of death which focuses on the death of the whole body (Jones, 1999) as a point at which it might be assumed that even God or the Gods cannot regard there to be life in the body. There is no easy reconciliation between such approaches. One solution may be to allow the deceased and or their relatives to select their own definition of death (Appel, 2005). This approach has been adopted in Japan. One author has written of the right to choose which concept of human death will be applied to 'our' death (Morioka, 2001). A difficulty with this approach is whether a patient should be entitled to insist on highly expensive treatment, keeping them 'alive' when they are in fact 'dead' according to the generally accepted medical standard (Evans, 2002). Another solution is to declare that the law cannot be based on unverifiable religious beliefs and we must reach the answers on the best scientific evidence available. The problem is that it is not clear that science provides us with a clear answer anyhow.

H. The Role of Policy

It can be difficult to separate out the issue of defining death and the controversial ethical issues which can arise as a result, especially concerning

euthanasia and organ transplantation (Kerridge and others, 2002). Bernat
suggests:

Some scholars have gone astray by not attempting to capture our consensual
concept of death and instead redefining death for ideological purposes or by
overanalyzing death to a metaphysical level of abstraction—thereby rendering it
devoid of its ordinary meaning (Bernat, 2006: 36).

Although it is tempting to suggest that a particular definition of death is
unacceptable because the costs of adopting it would be too high for the
National Health Service, surely a far more honest way of addressing the
issue would be to determine the definition of death and then determine
whether the spending of money on this patient is appropriate?

I. Public Opinion

How important, if at all, is it that the definition of death matches that understood by the general public? Some commentators insist that any acceptable
definition of death must accord with the general understanding of death.
This has formed part of the criticism of those approaches that regard PVS
patients or severely mentally disabledpeople as dead (Bernat, 2006).

XIII. CONCLUSION

It is interesting that defining the exact moment of death has become such
a topical issue for lawyers and doctors. Death in the absence of medical
intervention can be seen as a relatively straight-forward biological process.
Untreated, the failure of major organ systems will lead to death quickly. For
example, if the circulatory system is compromised by ventricular fibrilla-
tion, there will be widespread cellular death, and within a few minutes, the
subject will be dead. Respiratory collapse due to, for example, drowning,
will also cause widespread cellular death in a few minutes. However, with
medical intervention, the situation becomes much more complex. Medicine
has made progress in keeping part(s) of the body alive for long periods
of time. Indeed, it is not inconceivable that in the future most body parts
will be able to be kept alive well beyond the 'natural' course of their lives.
Furthermore, the possibility of organ donation and concern about expense
have generated greater public interest in the exact timing of death.

   We have attempted in this chapter to outline a variety of ways of seeking to define death and to outline their advantages and disadvantages.
An attempt has been made to indicate some of the key issues that need to
be addressed in seeking to reach a definition. We suggest that to produce
a single definition of death with medical intervention is impossible and

perhaps undesirable. One could see a justification for each of the foregoing definitions. There is much truth in the claim that death occurs as a process, with death occurring at different times and in different ways, and is experienced and understood differently by the various parties to the process. The search for a definition for a point of death is, we suggest, futile. The best we can do is to point out as clearly as possible the different ways in which, in a different sense, we die. Certainly in the process of death there are some significant milestones: the disappearance of higher neural functions, the cessation of breathing and the death of the body as a whole organism.

The question of when a person dies might, therefore, not be a useful one. It might be preferable, rather than asking when does a person die, to ask a series of different questions. How is it appropriate to treat the body of a person who is in a PVS? How is it appropriate to treat the body of a brain stem dead person? When should relatives be informed that a person is dead and the body treated as a dead body? These questions are no easier to answer than asking what death is, but they make clear the reasons for which we are asking the question. They may bring out more clearly the medical, philosophical or theological questions than asking what death is in the abstract. They also recognise that death is not a straightforward event, but a process. Death, like life, can be a long journey.

REFERENCES

Publications

Alloatti, S, Manes, M, Paternoster, G, Gaiter, AM, Molino, A, Rosati, C (2000) 'Peritoneal dialysis compared with hemodialysis in the treatment of end-stage renal disease' 13 *Journal of Nephrology* 331–342.

Appel, J (2005) Defining death: when physicians and families differ 31 *Journal of Medical Ethics* 641–642.

Aries, P (1974) *Western attitudes towards death* (London, John Hopkins University Press).

Barnard, CN (1968) 'What we have learned about heart transplants' 56 *Journal of Thoracic and Cardiovascular Surgery* 457–468.

Battin, M (1998) 'Physician-assisted suicide: safe, legal, rare?' in M Battin, R Rhodes and A Silvers (eds), *Physician Assisted Suicide* (London, Routledge) 63–72.

Bennion, F (1994) 'Legal death of brain damaged persons' 44 *Northern Ireland Law Quarterly* 269–283.

Bernat, J (2006) 'The whole-brain concept of death remains optimum public policy' 34 *Journal of Law, Medicine and Ethics* 36–39.

Borutaite, V, Jekabsone, A, Morkuniene, R and Brown, GC (2003) 'Inhibition of mitochondrial permeability transition prevents mitochondrial dysfunction, cytochrome c release and apoptosis induced by heart ischemia' 35 *Journal of Molecular and Cellular Cardiology* 357–366.

Byrne, P and Rinkowski, J (1999) '"Brain death" is false' *Linacre Quarterly* 42–49.

Calne, RY and Williams, R (1968) 'Liver transplantation in man. Observations on technique and organization in five cases' 4 *British Medical Journal* 535–540.

Chute, AL and Smyth, DH (1939) 'Metabolism of isolated perfused cat's brain' 29 *Quarterly Journal of Experimental Physiology* 379–394.

Clauss, R and Nel, W (2006) 'Drug induced arousal from the permanent vegetative state' 21 *NeuroRehabilitation* 23–28.

DeGrazia, D (2004) 'Biology, consciousness, and the definition of death' in T Shannon (ed), *Death and dying* (Lanham, Rowman and Littlefield)1–8.

Department of Health (1998) *A Code of Practice for the Diagnosis of Brain Stem Death* HSC 1998/035 (London, Department of Health).

Demikhov, VP (1962) *Experimental transplantation of vital organs* (trans B Haigh) (New York, Consultants Bureau).

Dubernard, JM, Owen, E, Herzberg, G, Lanzetta, M, Martin, X, Kapila, H, Dawhara, M and Hakim, S (1999) 'Human hand allograft: report on first 6 months' 353 *The Lancet* 1315–1320.

Dubois, J (2002) 'Is organ procurement causing the death of patients?' 18 *Issues in Law and Medicine* 21–39.

Eberl, J (2005) 'A Thomist understanding of human death' 19 *Bioethics* 25–48.

Engelhardt, T (1999) 'Redefining death' in S Younger, R Arnold and R Schapiro (eds), *The definition of death* (Baltimore, John Hopkins University Press) 319–331.

Evans, H (2002) 'Reply to: Defining death: when physicians and families differ' 28 *Journal of Medical Ethics* 28–94.

Gray, N and Selzman, C (2006) 'Current status of the total artificial heart' 251 *American Heart Journal* 4–10.

Halevy, A (2001) 'Beyond brain death?' 26 *Journal of Medicine and Philosophy* 493–501.

Hardy, JD, Webb, WR, Dalton, ML and Walker, GR (1963) 'Lung homotransplantations in man' 186 *Journal of the American Medical Society* 1065–1074.

Harris, J (2004) 'Intimations of immortality' in M Freeman *Current Legal Problems* (Oxford, Oxford University Press) 65–97.

Harvard Medical School (1968) 'A Definition of Irreversible Coma. Report of the Ad hoc Committee of the Harvard Medical School to Examine the Definition of Brain Death' 205 *Journal of the American Medical Association* 85–88.

Harvey, PO, Fossati, P, Pochon, JB, Levy, R, LeBastard, G, Lehericy, S, Allilaire, JF and Dubois, B (2005) 'Cognitive control and brain resources in major depression: an fMRI study using the n-back task' 26 *Neuroimage* 860–869.

Harvey, W (1653) *The anatomical exercises of Dr William Harvey, concerning the motions of the heart and blood* (London, Richard Lowdnes) 81–82.

Hayashi, Tand Abe, K (2004) 'Ischemic neuronal cell death and organelle damage' 26 *Neurological Research* 827–823.

Hershenov, D (2003) 'The problematic role of 'irreversibility' in the definition of Death' 17 *Bioethics* 89–100.

Heymans, C (1912) 'Survival and revival of nervous tissues after arrest of circulation' 30 *Physiologcal Reviews* 375–391.

Holland, S (2003) *Bioethics* (London, Polity).

Hugdahl K, Rund, BR, Lund, A, Asbjörnsen, A, Egeland, J, Landro, NI, Roness, A, Stordal, K, Sundet, K and Thomsen, T (2004) 'Brain activation measured with fMRI during a mental arithmetic task in schizophrenia and major depression' 161 *American Journal of Psychiatry* 286–293.

Hughes, P (1947) *The Catholic Encyclopaedia* (New York, Encyclopaedia Press).

Human Tissue Authority (2006) *Removal, Storage and Disposal of Human Organs and Tissue* (London, Human Tissue Authority).

Jejurikar, SS, Henkelman, EA, Cederna, PS, Marcelo, CL, Urbanchek, MG and Kurzon, WM Jr (2006) 'Aging increases the susceptibility of skeletal muscle-derived satellite cells to apoptosis' 41 *Experimental Gerontology* 828–836.

Johnson, MH (2006) 'Escaping the tyranny of the embryo? A new approach to ART regulation based on UK and Australian experiences' 21 *Human Reproduction* 2756–2765.

Jones, D (1999) *The UK Definition of Death* (London, The Linacre Centre).

Jouvet, M (1959) 'Diagnostic électrosouscorticographique de la mort du système nerveux central au cours de certains comas' 3 *Electroencephalography—clinical neurophysiology* 52–53.

Kafetz, K (2002) 'What happens when elderly people die' 95 *Journal of the Royal Society of Medicine* 536–538.

Kamm, F (2001) 'Brain death and spontaneous breathing' 30 *Philosophy and Public Affairs* 297–332.

Karakatsanis, K and Tsanakas, J (2002) 'A critique of the concept of "brain death"' 18 *Issues in Law and Medicine* 127–142.

Keightley, ML, Wincour, G, Graham, SJ, Mayberg, HS, Hevenor, SJ and Grady, C, (2003) 'An fMRI study investigating cognitive modulation of brain regions associated with emotional processing of visual stimuli' 41 *Neuropsychologia* 585–596.

Kennedy, I (1969) 'Alive or dead' 22 *Current Legal Problems* 102–136.

Kennedy, I (1988) *Treat me right* (Oxford, Oxford University Press).

Kerridge, IH, Saul, P, Lowe, M, McPhee, J and Williams, D (2002) 'Death, dying and donation: organ transplantation and the diagnosis of death' 28 *Journal of Medical Ethics* 89–94.

Lamb, D (1987) *Death, brain death and ethics* (London, Routledge).

—— (1994) 'What is death?' in R Gillon (ed), *Principles of health care ethics* (London, John Wiley & Sons). 1027–1040.

Lancisi, G (1707) *De subitaneis mortibus* (trans PD White and AV Boursy) (1971) New York, St. John's University Press).

Lee, P and Smith, G (2000) 'Are Jewish death dates affected by the timing of important religious events?' 37 *Social Biology* 127–34.

Lizza, J (2005) 'Potentiality, irreversibility and death' 30 *Journal of Medicine and Philosophy* 45–64.

—— (2006) *Persons, humanity and the definition of death* (Baltimore, John Hopkins University Press).

Maedler, K, Schumann, DM, Schulthess, F, Oberholzer, J, Bosco, D, Berney, T, and Donath, M. (2006) 'Aging correlates with decreased cell proliferative capacity and enhanced sensitivity to apoptosis' 55 *Diabetes* 2455–2462.

Maguire, EA, Frackowiak, RSJ and Frith, CD (1997) 'Recalling routes around London: activation of the right hippocampus in taxi drivers' 17 *Journal of Neuroscience* 7103–7110.

Mammone, T, Gan, D and Foyouzi-Youssefi, R (2006) 'Apoptotic cell death increases with senescence in normal human dermal fibroblast cultures' 30 *Cell Biology International* 903–909.

Mason, JK, McCall Smith, A and Laurie, G (2006) *Law and medical ethics* (Oxford, Oxford University Press).

Mathé, G, Amiel, JI, Schwarzenberg, L, Cattan, A and Schneider, M (1963) 'Haematopoietic chimera in man after allogenic (homologous) bone-marrow transplantation' 2 *British Medical Journal* 1633–1635.

McMahan, J (2002) *The ethics of killing* (Oxford, Oxford University Press).

—— (2006) 'An alternative to brain death' 34 *Journal of Law, Medicine and Ethics* 44–48.

Mehta, D, Curwin, J, Gomes, JA and Fuster, V (1997) 'Sudden death in coronary artery disease: acute ischemia versus myocardial substrat' 96 *Circulation* 3215–3223.

Mejia, R and Pollack, M (1995) 'Variability of brain death determination practices in children' 274 *Journal of the American Medical Association* 550–553.

Merrill, JP, Murray, JE, Harrison, JH and Guild, WR (1956) 'Successful homotransplantation of the human kidney between identical twins' 160 *Journal of the American Medical Association* 277–282.

Moreland, JP and Rae, S (2000) *Body and soul* (Downers Green, Intervarsity Press).

Morioka, M (2001) 'Reconsidering brain death: A lesson from Japan's fifteen years of experience' 31 *Hastings Center Report* 41–46.

Multi-Society Task Force on PVS (1994a) 'Medical aspects of the persistent vegetative state (1)' 330 *New England Journal of Medicine* 1499–1508.

—— (1994b) 'Medical aspects of the persistent vegetative state (2)' 330 *New England Journal of Medicine* 1572.

Padanilam, BJ (2003) 'Cell death induced by acute renal injury: a perspective on the contributions of apoptosis and necrosis' 284 *American Journal of Physiology—Renal Physiology* F608–F627.

Pallis, C (1990) 'Return to Elsinore' 16 *Journal of Medical Ethics* 10–14.

Pallis, C and Harley, DH (1996) *ABC of brain stem death* (London, BMJ Books).

Pattinson, S (2006) *Medical law and ethics* (London, Sweet and Maxwell).

Phan, KL, Fitzgerald, DA, Gao, KX, Moore, GJ, Tancer, ME and Posse, S (2004) 'Real-time fMRI of cortico-limbic brain activity during emotional processing' 15 *Neuroreport* 527–532.

Phillips, D and King, E (1988) 'Death takes a holiday: mortality surrounding major social occasions' 24 *The Lancet* September 728–732.

Potts, M (2001) 'A requiem for whole-brain death' 26 *Journal of Medicine and Philosophy* 479.

Potts, M, Byrne, P and Nilges, R (eds) (2000) *Beyond brain death: The case against brain based criteria for human death* (Dordrecht, Kluwer).

Qiao, X, Chen, X, Wu, D, Ding, R, Wang, J, Hong, Q, Shi, S, Li, J, Xie, Y, Lu, Y and Wang, Z (2005) 'Mitochondrial pathway is responsible for aging-related increase of tubular cell apoptosis in renal ischemia/reperfusion injury' 60 *Journals of Gerontology Series A—Biological Sciences and Medical Sciences* 830–839.

Rich, B (1997) 'Postmodern personhood: A Matter for consciousness' 11 *Bioethics* 206–216.

Royal College of Physicians Working Group (1995) 'Criteria for the diagnosis of brain stem death' 29 *Journal of the Royal College of Physicians of London* 381–382.

Russell, T (2000) *Brain death: Philosophical concepts and problems* (Aldershot, Ashgate).

Savulescu, J (2003) 'Death, us and our bodies: personal reflections' 29 *Journal of Medical Ethics* 127–130.

Schapiro, R (1999) *The Definition of death: Contemporary controversies* (Baltimore, John Hopkins Press).

Schwab, RS, Potts, F and Bonazzi, A (1963) 'EEG as an aid in determining death in the presence of cardiac activity (ethical, legal and medical aspects)' 15 *Electroencephalography—clinical neurophysiology* 147–148.

Shewmon, DA (1998) '"Brain stem death", "brain death", and death' 14 *Issues in Law and Medicine* 125–146.

—— (2001) 'The brain and somatic integration: Insights into the standard biological rationale for equating "brain death" with death' 26 *Journal of Medicine and Philosophy* 457–478.

—— (2004) 'The "critical organ" for the organism as a whole: Lessons from the lowly spinal cord' 550 *Advances in Experimental Medicine and Biology* 23–42.

Skegg, P (1974) 'Irreversibly comatose individuals: alive or dead?' 33 *Cambridge Law Journal* 130–152.

—— (1985) *Law, ethics and medicine* (Oxford, Oxford University Press).

Spurgeon, B (2005) 'Surgeons pleased with patient's progress after face transplant' 331 *British Medical Journal* 1359.

Stanley, J (1987) 'More fiddling with the definition of death?' 29 *Journal of Medical Ethics* 41–44.

Starzl, TE, Groth, CG, Brettschneider, L, Penn, I, Fulginiti, VA, Moon, JB, Blanchard, H, Martin, AJ Jr and Porter, KA (1968) 'Orthotopic homotransplantation of the human liver' 168 *Annals of Surgery* 392–398.

Takahashi Y, Kuro-o, M and Ishikawa, F (2000) 'Aging mechanisms' 97 *Proceedings of the National Academy of Sciences USA* 12407–12408.

Toni, I, Krams, M, Turner, R and Passingham, RE (1998) 'The time course of changes during motor sequence learning: a whole-brain fMRI study' 8 *Neuroimage* 50.

Truog, R (1997) 'Is it time to abandon brain death?' 27 *Hastings Centre Report* 29–31.

Van de Kerkhove, MP, Hoekstra, R, Chamuleau, RAFM and van Gulik, TM (2004) 'Clinical application of bioartificial liver support systems' 240 *Annals of Surgery* 216–230.

Veatch, R (1989) *Death, dying and the biological revolution* (New York, Yale University Press).

—— (2005) 'The death of whole-brain death' 30 *Journal of Medicine and Philosophy* 353–378.

Wang, MY, Wallace, P and Gruen, JB (2002) 'Brain death documentation: Analysis and issues' 51 *Neurosurgery* 731–735.

Youngner, SJ and Arnold, RM (2001) Philosophical debates about the definition of death: Who cares? 26 *Journal of Medicine and Philosophy* 527–537.

Zamperetti, N, Bellomo, R and Ronco, C (2003) 'Defining death in non-heart beating organ donors' 29 *Journal of Medical Ethics* 182–185.
Zipes, DP and Wellens, HJ (1998) 'Sudden cardiac death' 98 *Circulation* 2334–2351.

Legislation

Human Tissue Act 2004.
Uniform Definition of Death Act 1981.

3

Death, Euthanasia and the Medical Profession

EMILY JACKSON

I. INTRODUCTION

IN THIS CHAPTER, I challenge three interrelated consequentialist arguments against the legalisation of euthanasia. These are, first, that legalisation would have a negative impact upon the doctor-patient relationship because patients' trust would be compromised by the knowledge that their doctors could lawfully kill them. Secondly, that few doctors would want to, effectively, specialise in death. And, thirdly, that legalisation would hamper efforts to improve palliative care because euthanasia would tend to be cheaper and more convenient than providing high quality care to terminally ill patients. These consequentialist arguments are not concerned with whether the legalisation of euthanasia would be *right* or *wrong*, but with whether the consequences would, overall, be *better* or *worse* than the status quo. This is necessarily a *comparative* judgement: we need to ask whether legalised euthanasia would have better or worse outcomes than are the case under conditions of illegality.

My central argument is that people who invoke consequentialist arguments against the legalisation of euthanasia often do so from an inaccurate and improbably optimistic understanding of the status quo. Three assumptions are key to the consequentialist case against euthanasia: first, that fairly high levels of trust currently exist between doctors and patients which might be damaged by the legalisation of euthanasia; secondly, that doctors do not already deliberately end their patients' lives, making legalisation a radical and unwelcome new step; and, thirdly, that there is already good access to palliative care which might be threatened if the easier and cheaper option of euthanasia were available. All three assumptions are, in my view, unwarranted.

In this chapter, I will argue for greater realism when invoking consequentialist arguments in the euthanasia debate. I will suggest that if we start instead from the position that there is not perfect trust between doctors and their patients, and we recognise that doctors are already routinely involved in ending their patients' lives, and that palliative care in the United Kingdom is far from perfect, some of the consequentialist arguments against euthanasia start to look rather different.

The next strand of my argument is, it must be admitted, rather circular. I will argue that it is impossible to divorce our attitudes towards the legalisation of euthanasia from our attitudes towards the medical profession. I draw on evidence from countries which have legalised different methods of assisted dying, as well as comparisons with countries which have not, in order to back up my claim that the causal link between damaged doctor-patient relationships and legalised euthanasia in fact works in the opposite direction from that which tends to be assumed in the consequentialist case against legalisation. In my view, where relationships between doctors and patients are already damaged and mistrustful, the legalisation of euthanasia becomes difficult, if not impossible. The obverse is that when patients have very high levels of trust both in their doctors and in the healthcare system in general, many of the arguments against legalising euthanasia fall away.

It is, I argue, worth noting that in both the Netherlands and Belgium, where euthanasia has been legalised, the communities' level of trust in the medical profession is extremely high. In the US State of Oregon, only physician-assisted suicide ('PAS') has been legalised, and it is this model that appears to appeal to some parliamentarians in the United Kingdom. One of the reasons for the distinction between these two models might, I argue, be traced to differences in the standing of, and trust in doctors.

I will further argue that the legalisation of euthanasia would not mean that some doctors would have to 'specialise in death'. I draw attention to evidence which suggests that two thirds of all deaths are now caused by a medical decision, either as a result of giving high doses of analgesics or through the withdrawal or withholding of life-sustaining treatment. Legalised euthanasia would result in far fewer deaths, and often more humane and peaceful ones, than either of these common medical practices through which doctors—who certainly do not view themselves as 'specialising in death'—routinely shorten their patients' lives. There is, of course, a difference between acts and omissions, but I will argue that, in relation to assisted dying, the law places too much reliance upon a distinction which Lord Mustill famously, and in my view rightly, described as 'morally and intellectually misshapen' (*Airedale NHS Trust v Bland*[1]).

The circularity in my argument is that compromised doctor-patient relationships might make the legalisation of euthanasia difficult in practice, and yet it is impossible to achieve improved levels of trust while euthanasia continues to be practised 'underground'. Could legalisation be

---

[1] *Airedale NHS Trust v Bland* [1993] AC 789 (HL).

a 'driver' for more open and transparent consultations between doctors and their terminally-ill patients? Perhaps, but laying out a blueprint for law reform is not my purpose in this chapter. Rather, I have the much less ambitious goal of explaining why consequentialist arguments against euthanasia, which rely upon misrepresentations of the status quo, must be rejected.

II. TRUST IN THE MEDICAL PROFESSION

It is often said that legalising euthanasia would damage the doctor-patient relationship by making it very difficult for patients to trust their doctors (Kass and Lund, 1996). The argument goes something like this: from the point of view of patients, knowing that their doctors could legally kill them would make them nervous and mistrustful, particularly if they are elderly and/or terminally ill. And, from the point of view of doctors, if 'killing' were to become a treatment option, the ethical foundations of the medical profession would be undermined, and this in turn would reduce patients' willingness to trust their doctors. The General Medical Council took this view in their evidence to the House of Lords Select Committee on Assisted Dying:

[A] change in the law to allow physician-assisted dying would have profound implications for the role and responsibilities of doctors and their relationships with patients. Acting with the primary intention to hasten a patient's death would be difficult to reconcile with the medical ethical principles of beneficence and non-maleficence (Assisted Dying for the Terminally Ill Committee, 2005: 42).

Of course, as I shall explain later, it is not just the prospect of being deliberately killed by their doctor that might make it difficult for patients to trust their doctors. Patients in the United Kingdom might fear having the phrase 'do not attempt resuscitation' recorded in their notes, or may be concerned that high-cost interventions, such as expensive cancer drugs, might be withheld or withdrawn on the grounds of cost. Perhaps more compelling still, patients might fear *over-treatment*, and being subjected to invasive interventions which might unnecessarily prolong the dying process.

In any event, as I hope to establish in this paper, the consequentialist argument against legalisation of euthanasia based upon the damage it might do to doctor-patient relationships is a red herring for a number of interrelated reasons. In the next two sections, I look at evidence from the Netherlands and Belgium before turning to the need for a comparative approach to the benefits or otherwise of legalisation.

III. EVIDENCE FROM THE NETHERLANDS

Although a statute specifically legalising euthanasia was not introduced in the Netherlands until 2001, since 1973 the Dutch courts had gradually been developing exceptions to the express prohibitions on active voluntary euthanasia and assisted suicide in the Dutch Penal Code. Through a series of court decisions, a set of guidelines had emerged which—if followed— served to protect doctors from criminal liability. The Termination of Life on Request and Assisted Suicide (Review Procedures) Act (2001) amended the Code in line with court practice. While euthanasia and assisted suicide continue to be criminal offences, exceptions exist if the physician fulfils the 'due care' criteria set out in the Act. The physician must, for example, believe that the patient's request is voluntary and well considered, and that his or her suffering is lasting and unbearable, and the physician must have consulted at least one other independent physician to confirm that the patient's circumstances warrant access to euthanasia.

To ask whether the legalisation of euthanasia in the Netherlands has diminished levels of trust in the medical profession is to get the question the wrong way round. The evidence appears to indicate that it was precisely because the Dutch have so much confidence in their doctors that legalisa- tion was possible. Griffiths, Bood and Weyers point out that 'the Dutch seem comfortable with the idea that doctors can be trusted with the discre- tion to perform euthanasia', and they trace this, in part, to 'an important characteristic of Dutch society', namely 'the level of confidence in public institutions and in professions' (Griffiths, Bood and Weyers, 1998: 304). This claim is backed up by a survey cited by the House of Lords Select Committee on Assisted Dying, which found that out of 11 European coun- tries, including the United Kingdom, the Dutch had the highest regard for and trust in their doctors (Assisted Dying for the Terminally Ill Committee, 2005: 41).

Euthanasia in The Netherlands is done in the *context* of the doctor- patient relationship. Most commonly, the doctor who administers the lethal injection is the patient's general practitioner. (Assisted Dying for the Terminally Ill Committee, 2005: 187). In his evidence to the House of Lords Select Committee, Dr Kimsma, who sits on one of the five regional assess- ment committees said that

> there is an absolute condition that [euthanasia] can only be done by the treating physician. It cannot be any other physician. We do not want to advertise 'eutha- nasia tourism'. What we insist on is that it only takes place within a meaning- ful medical relationship. That is an absolute condition (Assisted Dying for the Terminally Ill Committee, 2005: 175).

It is worth noting that despite the legalisation of both euthanasia and assisted suicide, it is euthanasia which has from the outset been more common in the Netherlands (Nys, 1999: 236). Again, this may offer evidence of the high level of confidence the Dutch have in the medical profession. Doctors can end patients' lives more effectively than the patients themselves, who might, for example, fail to ingest all of the prescribed dose and be left both alive and severely damaged by partially ingesting a lethal substance. Indeed, is noteworthy, but not surprising, that a study of clinical problems with the performance of euthanasia and assisted suicide in the Netherlands found that complications (such as vomiting) and problems with completion (such as a failure to induce coma) were much more common in cases of assisted suicide than they were when doctors performed euthanasia (Groenewoud and others, 2000). In 18 percent of cases where the intention was that the doctor would assist the patient's suicide, the doctor in fact decided to administer the lethal medication him- or herself, thus converting these assisted suicides into cases of euthanasia (Groenewoud and others, 2000). These decisions were generally taken because the patients were unable to take all of the medication themselves.

If assisted suicide is more likely to go wrong, preferring it to euthanasia is justifiable only if there is some residual fear that doctors might not be acting in accordance with the patient's wishes. In Oregon, the only US State to have legalised assisted dying, the prevailing view is that legalising assisted suicide is preferable to euthanasia because it provides an additional safeguard. Dr Nick Gideonse, a general practitioner in Oregon, said that

[t]he fact that the patient self-administers in a way that is not easy to do, drinking ounces of a bitter liquid, provides a final piece of clear evidence that this is completely volitional and self-administered (Assisted Dying for the Terminally Ill Committee, 2005: 146).

Similarly, Barbara Coombs Lee, from 'Compassion for Dying', maintained that

Having that last firewall, if you will, of having very clear self-administration, in this society, in this state, at this time is important to people, to have that reassurance that it really is a volitional act that a patient must take (Assisted Dying for the Terminally Ill Committee, 2005: 146).

Of course, it is also possible that the prospect of litigation might lead to a preference for assisted suicide. Nevertheless, evidence from Oregon undoubtedly impressed the House of Lords Select Committee, and, as a result of their recommendation, Lord Joffe's second Assisted Dying Bill would, if passed, have legalised only assisted suicide. Perhaps then, if assisted dying is ever legalised in the United Kingdom, as in the United States, this extra 'firewall' might be required in order to compensate for a lack of trust in the medical profession. If, instead, there is a high level of trust in doctors, and euthanasia is viewed as a legitimate medical procedure, the reasons for preferring assisted suicide fall away. I will return to this point later.

IV. EVIDENCE FROM BELGIUM

Belgium formally decriminalised euthanasia in 2002 (*Loi relative à l'euthanasie* (Euthanasia Act) 2002). To be eligible, patients must be over the age of 18, competent and conscious, and their requests for euthanasia must be explicit, unambiguous, repeated and durable. The patient must be in a hopeless situation, experiencing persistent and unbearable pain or distress that cannot be alleviated, and must be suffering from a serious and incurable mental or physical disorder. It is the patient who determines whether her suffering is persistent and unbearable, the physician is simply charged with certifying that the patient herself finds her suffering unbearable. The physician must give the patient full information about her condition and the possibilities of palliative care. A second doctor must consult the patient's medical file, examine the patient and confirm that the patient finds her suffering unbearable, and that it cannot be alleviated. If the patient is not terminally ill, two additional requirements are imposed: first, the physician must consult two colleagues, one of whom must assess whether the request is voluntary, considered, and repeated; and secondly, at least a month must elapse between the request and the performance of euthanasia.

The physician must fill in a registration form and deliver it within four working days to a national commission, consisting of 16 members, eight of whom are doctors, four are lawyers and four 'from groups charged with the problem of incurably ill patients'. If the commission is satisfied that any of the criteria were not met, the file will be sent to the public prosecutor. The commission reports biannually to Parliament on the implementation of the legislation. In 2004, 347 cases of euthanasia were reported (Assisted Dying for the Terminally Ill Committee, 2005: 74).

It is important to bear in mind that the legalisation of euthanasia in Belgium took place within a context in which there is a strong emphasis upon the provision of palliative care, and where the first response to a request for euthanasia will always be extensive investigation of other palliative options (Gastmans and others, 2004: 216). A request for euthanasia triggers concerted attempts to find ways other than euthanasia to relieve the patient's distress. Euthanasia is very definitely a 'last resort', and the comprehensive palliative care framework, which includes home care, support teams in hospitals and nursing homes, as well as specialist palliative care units, means that euthanasia will be used only when all these options are exhausted. In effect, there is a palliative filter upon access to euthanasia.

The decision-making process in Belgium does not just involve the patient and their doctor. On the contrary, nurses and the patient's family also play an important role. The legislation specifies that where a nursing team has had regular contact with the patient who has requested euthanasia, the physician must discuss the patient's request with the nursing team (Euthanasia Act 2002, Art 3). Even where a nursing team is not already involved, following a patient's request for euthanasia, palliative care nurses will spend time with him or her in order identify the reasons for the request (Dierckx de Casterlé and others, 2006). Finding out why a patient wants his or her life to be brought to an end helps the nurse to work out what palliative response might be able to deal with the suffering that underlies the patient's request for euthanasia (Dierckx de Casterlé and others, 2006). Of course, this sort of open discussion of all the options open to terminally ill patients, including euthanasia, is possible only because it has been legalised. I shall return to this point below.

Dierckx de Casterlé and others point to the high level of trust, and even intimacy, that exists in nurse-patient relationships (Dierckx de Casterlé and others, 2006). The palliative care nurse will visit the patient on a daily basis, providing constant care, which means they gain considerable insight into the patient's individual circumstances and particular concerns and anxieties. They also get to know the patient's relatives, which can be important in deciding upon a palliative care plan, but which also means that they can play a critical role in supporting the patient's family after the patient dies, whether naturally or as a result of euthanasia. It is also worth noting that Belgium only legalised euthanasia: assisted suicide remains a crime. As mentioned earlier, in the Netherlands both are legal but euthanasia is much more common. Again it seems likely that in Belgium, there is little fear that doctors will misuse their power to end their patient's lives, and so the 'firewall' provided by requiring the patient to perform the final act themselves is unnecessary, and instead the greater clinical effectiveness of doctor-administered euthanasia is preferred.

Indeed it could even be argued that allowing *only* euthanasia provides a different sort of control over the practice. It is commonly said that one of the benefits of assisted suicide is that it enables a patient to obtain a prescription for a lethal dose of drugs as a sort of 'comfort blanket' or 'insurance policy', so that they know they will be able to end their suffering when it becomes unbearable. Many, perhaps even most, patients will never actually take the drugs, but find it very reassuring to know that they have the means to end their lives if their quality of life deteriorates. In Oregon, from 1997 until the end of 2003, 265 prescriptions were written under the Death with Dignity Act, while only 117 people chose to take them. This statistic could be read in two ways. First, it is clear that patients who request assisted suicide, and get as far as obtaining a prescription under the Act (and it should be remembered that this is a tiny minority of those who initially request assistance with dying) feel under no obligation to go ahead and end their lives. Opponents of legalisation commonly suggest that vulnerable people will be pressurised into ending their lives prematurely. The fact that few people who express an interest in PAS in Oregon die as a result of assisted suicide suggests that terminally-ill patients do not, in practice, feel under pressure to end their lives. Secondly, 148 prescriptions were issued which were never used for their intended purpose, and while most of these were probably never obtained from the pharmacy, it is of course possible that a prescription could be filled but not used by the patient. Legalising euthanasia *alone* rules out the possibility that lethal drugs could be given to a patient but not used by them, which would raise the concern that they might fall into the hands of someone else who has not gone through the rigorous assessment procedure That this latter concern does not outweigh the importance of the 'firewall' provided by assisted suicide suggests that in places like Oregon—and perhaps the United Kingdom too—doctors may be trusted *less* than patients themselves.

V. THE RELATIONSHIP BETWEEN PALLIATIVE CARE AND ASSISTED DYING

The legalisation of euthanasia in Belgium rests upon the assumption that high quality palliative care may be able to obviate many but not all requests for euthanasia. There are those who would dispute this, and argue that good quality palliative care should mean that no terminally-ill patient should ever have to experience unbearable suffering. On this view, if all patients were to be given optimum treatment at the end of life, none would request euthanasia or assisted suicide, and the question of its legalisation would become redundant. This is, to some extent, an empirical argument, which depends upon evidence that all suffering at the end of life can be adequately relieved by palliative care.

It is undoubtedly true that a great deal of pain can now be controlled by analgesic drugs, but it would be a mistake to believe that modern drugs have effectively eliminated the possibility of unbearable pain. In a United States study of terminally-ill patients, 50 percent reported having suffered from severe or moderate pain in the previous four weeks (Weiss and others, 2001). And it is also important to remember that analgesic opioids themselves have some very unpleasant side effects, such as constipation and mental confusion, which patients find extremely distressing, and which might mean that they do not always take the drugs with which they have been supplied (Weiss and others, 2001).

Clearly too, there are other side effects of bodily degeneration, such as the inability to swallow or difficulties in breathing, which cannot be relieved by conventional analgesics, and instead the only way to relieve suffering is to sedate the patient into a coma (sometimes described as terminal sedation). From the patient's point of view, causing death and inducing unconsciousness from which the patient is not expected to recover might be said to be indistinguishable (Battin, 1994).

Furthermore, pain is seldom the principal reason for patients' requests for euthanasia. On the contrary, patients more frequently cite fear of indignity, loss of control and dependency as their reasons for wanting to be helped to die. The Remmelink study (van der Maas, 1992) into euthanasia in the Netherlands found that loss of dignity was a much more common reason for requesting euthanasia than unbearable pain.

In Oregon there were fears that PAS would be chosen by patients who did not have health insurance and could not afford high-quality palliative care, but the evidence does not bear this out. The overwhelming majority of patients who have sought PAS are middle class, well educated, and have access to health insurance (Dahl and Levy, 2006). In 2002, 92 per cent of the patients who sought PAS were already enrolled in hospice care (Dahl and Levy, 2006). The patients who request PAS in Oregon are, on average, younger than most terminally-ill patients (Oregon Department of Human Services, 2002). They do not choose PAS because of any lack of access to medical care and social support mechanisms, or from any sense that they have become a burden, either emotionally or financially (Miller and others, 2004). The most frequently reported reasons for choosing PAS under the Death With Dignity Act are 'loss of autonomy' (87 per cent); 'loss of the ability to enjoy the activities that make life worth living' (84 per cent) and 'loss of dignity' (80 per cent). All of the evidence suggests that factors that can be alleviated by high-quality palliative care are not the principal reasons for patients requesting PAS in Oregon. Interestingly, 'fear of excruciating pain' was a factor in only 22 per cent of cases (Dahl and Levy, 2006). There have been no cases in which pain was the only reason for requesting assisted suicide (Battin, 2005).

While optimum palliative care may be able to minimise physical pain, it is less clear that it can eradicate the helplessness and mental anguish that many people experience as a result of the progressive deterioration of their bodies. Certainly, the House of Lords Select Committee on assisted dying found that

[t]here was a general consensus among our witnesses as regards the limitations of palliative care in relieving patient suffering. The VES [Voluntary Euthanasia Society] took the view that 'no amount of palliative care can address some patients' concerns regarding their loss of autonomy, loss of control of bodily functions and loss of dignity' ... The BMA echoed this view, observing that 'there are patients for whom even the best palliative care is not dealing with their pain', adding that 'in spite of excellent palliative care, the position is not necessarily one which those patients regard as beneficial to them' (Assisted Dying for the Terminally Ill Committee, 2005: 88).

In Oregon, it also seems that since legalisation of PAS, the quality of palliative care that is available to patients has actually improved (Dahl and Levy, 2006). Since legalisation, death from PAS has been rare and there are higher standards of care for terminally-ill patients. In one study of all the physicians eligible to prescribe drugs under the Act, 30 per cent had increased their referrals to hospice care and 76 per cent reported that they made efforts to improve their knowledge of pain medication for the terminally ill (Ganzini and others, 2001). 69 per cent reported that they had sought to improve their recognition of psychiatric disorders, such as depression. Certainly, the House of Lords Select Committee found that Oregon 'had good end-of-life care with high enrolment in hospice programmes' (Assisted Dying for the Terminally Ill Committee, 2005: 154). Of course, it is not necessarily the case that the legalisation of PAS has *caused* the provision of palliative care to improve in Oregon, but the evidence is clearly not there to suggest that legalisation undermines attempts to enhance care for the dying. (Ganzini and others, 2001).

There is also evidence from Oregon that the doctors who do agree to issue prescriptions under the Act do so on the basis of a long relationship with the patient. Typically they will be the patient's

primary care physician, whom they have known and worked with for a long time where they feel they know a great deal about the patient, not only from a medical standpoint but from a behavioural standpoint (Evidence from Mr Jim Kronenberg, Chief Operating Officer of the Oregon Medical Association, Assisted Dying for the Terminally Ill Committee, 2005: 159).

As the Oregon Department of Human Services points out,

[w]hile it may be common for patients with a terminal illness to consider physician assisted suicide, a request for a prescription can be an opportunity for a medical provider to explore with patients their fears and wishes around end of life care, and to make patients aware of other options. Often once the provider has addressed patients' concerns, they may choose not to pursue physician assisted suicide. The availability of assisted suicide as an option in Oregon also may have spurred Oregon doctors to address other end of life care options more effectively (Ganzini and others, 2001).

VI. LEGALISATION VERSUS ILLEGALITY

It is important to remember that the illegality of doctors deliberately ending their patients' lives does not mean that it does not happen. Rather, it means that it happens under conditions of secrecy and concealment. In a comparative study of end-of-life decisions (including treatment withdrawal, giving doses of painkillers which could hasten death, and euthanasia) in six

European countries, at a time when euthanasia could be practised openly in only one of them (the Netherlands), van der Heide and others found that, for both competent and incompetent patients, end-of-life decisions were discussed openly most frequently in the Netherlands (van der Heide and others, 2003). For competent patients in the Netherlands, the end-of-life decision was not discussed with the patient in 5 per cent of cases, in Italy the figure was 52 per cent and in Sweden 53 per cent. Where the patient was now incompetent, the decision had not been discussed with the patient or relatives in 12 per cent of cases in the Netherlands, and 58 per cent in both Italy and Sweden. Shockingly, then, when Italian and Swedish doctors take steps that will result in a patient's death, this is kept both from the patient him- or herself and their relatives in the *majority* of cases. Far from being indicative of a high level of trust between patients and doctors, which might be damaged by the legalisation of euthanasia, these statistics indicate that levels of transparency and openness in the doctor-patient relationship are, in fact, poorest in countries where euthanasia is illegal. If I thought that my doctor might end my life without discussing it with me first, my trust in the medical profession would surely be inevitably compromised.

Van der Heide and others' study also revealed that Italian and Swedish doctors were very unlikely to consult other caregivers. In Italy, only 18 per cent of doctors consulted another doctor before making an end of life decision, and only 12 per cent consulted nursing staff. In contrast, in The Netherlands, 43 per cent discussed the decision with another doctor and 36 per cent discussed it with nursing staff (van der Heide, and others, 2003). Of course van der Heide's study did not confine itself to cases of euthanasia, although it is worth noting that they found that the both the administration of drugs with the explicit intention of hastening death and the ending of life without an explicit request from the patient are 'practised everywhere'.

It is, as Magnusson points out, crucially important to remember that the two possible scenarios are not: (a) euthanasia is illegal and never happens, and (b) euthanasia is lawful and does happen. Instead our choice is between (a) euthanasia is illegal but happens in secret, and (b) euthanasia is lawful and happens occasionally. We have to acknowledge that the illegality of euthanasia will not mean that doctors never end their patient's lives (Magnusson, 2004). For example, Kuhse and others' confidential survey of 3000 Australian doctors found that non-voluntary euthanasia is five times more common in Australia, where euthanasia is illegal, than it is in the Netherlands (Kuhse and others, 1997). Australian doctors were far less likely than their Dutch counterparts to discuss the decision to hasten a patient's death with the patient him- or herself, or to seek their consent. And in their study of six European countries, van der Heide and others found that non-voluntary euthanasia was more than twice as common in Denmark as it was in the Netherlands (van der Heide and others, 2003).

Cuttini and others' study of neonatal end-of-life decision-making found that *more* neonatal physicians in France (73 per cent) had administered drugs with the purpose of ending life than in the Netherlands (47 per cent). If, in the absence of an explicit request, patients' lives are ended with similar or even greater frequency in countries which have *not* legalised euthanasia, it is far from clear that the legalisation of euthanasia in the Netherlands has *caused* any propensity to engage in non-voluntary euthanasia.

Furthermore, the evidence appears to indicate that the illegality of euthanasia does not mean that doctors never comply with their patients' requests for euthanasia. Obviously, because doctors who admit to performing euthanasia in countries where it is illegal might be charged with murder, it is virtually impossible to gather accurate information about their participation in life-shortening practices. However, anonymous surveys consistently show that it is not unusual for doctors to be asked for assistance in dying, and that a significant minority of doctors have complied with such requests. A survey published in the *British Medical Journal* in 1994 found that 45 per cent of doctors had been asked to take active steps to hasten death, and of these, 32 per cent had complied with such a request (Ward and Tate, 1994). Four years later, 300 General Practitioners were interviewed by the *Sunday Times*, and 15 per cent admitted to having helped their patients die (Norton, 1998).

From the point of view of the patient, might not the evidence that a minority of doctors has performed illegal euthanasia with no safeguards—such as the need for a second opinion—be more damaging to their trust in the medical profession than legalised, and hence relatively controlled euthanasia?

I agree with Magnusson that we need to be more realistic about the inevitability of 'underground' euthanasia, and factor this in to our assessment of the benefits or otherwise of legalisation. And I would make a further plea for realism. Even in countries where euthanasia or assisted suicide is legal, it is a very unusual way to die. In the Netherlands, three per cent of patients die as a result of euthanasia; in Belgium, the figure is much lower; and in Oregon it is lower still. In 2004, there were 37 assisted suicides in Oregon (0.12 per cent of all deaths) (Oregon Department of Human Services, 2004). In contrast, we now have evidence from many countries and from many sources, that *most* deaths in developed countries are preceded by a medical decision—most commonly to withdraw or withhold life-prolonging treatment, or to give doses of analgesics, such as opioids, in doses which are likely to hasten the patient's death. Clive Seale's postal survey of 857 United Kingdom medical practitioners attempted to estimate the frequency of different end-of-life decisions (ELDs) in medical practice in the United Kingdom (Seale, 2006). The proportion of *all* United Kingdom deaths involving an ELD were:

- alleviation of symptoms with possibly life shortening effect = 32.8 per cent

- non-treatment decisions = 30.3 per cent
- ending of life without an explicit request from patient = 0.33 per cent
- voluntary euthanasia = 0.16 per cent
- physician-assisted suicide = 0.00 per cent.

Roughly a third of *all* deaths therefore follow treatment withdrawal, and nearly a third follow the giving of life-threatening doses of drugs. This means that only one in three of us will now die spontaneously, without any medical involvement in ending our life.

It is critically important to remember that both treatment withdrawal and the giving of large doses of drugs are not dependent upon any prior patient request. On the contrary, both are standard medical practices that are routinely justified as being in the best interests of patients who lack capacity to express their own views. Elderly or vulnerable patients might with good reason be more distrustful of doctors knowing that they can withhold life-prolonging treatment or give them life-threatening doses of drugs without their consent, should they become incapacitated, than they would if they knew that it was possible for doctors, under certain strict conditions, to provide euthanasia. Compared with legalised euthanasia, non-treatment decisions and the giving of potentially fatal doses of pain-killing drugs are comparatively unregulated. 'Do not attempt resuscitation' orders, for example, are commonly made without any consultation with the patient.

Much here turns on the acts/omissions distinction, but in my view the law places unwarranted weight upon whether a particular course of conduct can be described as an omission rather than an action (Jackson, 2004). Treatment withdrawal indubitably involves doctors *doing* something and, if the patient wants to go on living, maliciously withdrawing life support might be an act and the doctor might be guilty of murder. Describing what the doctor does as an omission does not, by itself, prove that she is morally blameless. Rather, because treatment withdrawal could also be described as an *action*, it is by taking into account the surrounding circumstances, such as the patient's condition or her request that treatment be withdrawn, and not by labelling what the doctor does as an *omission*, that we can ascertain whether her conduct is acceptable.

Interestingly, I think one of the most eloquent and thoughtful opponents of legalised euthanasia, John Keown, would agree with me that treatment withdrawal—where the intention is to bring about the patient's death—is morally equivalent to euthanasia (Keown, 2005). This leads him to conclude that treatment withdrawal, where the intent is to end the patient's life, should be unlawful. In contrast, my view that treatment withdrawal and euthanasia are morally equivalent leads me to the opposite conclusion, namely, that if it can be right to deliberately end a patient's life by treatment withdrawal, we should seriously consider the possibility that it might, in certain circumstances, be right to produce death by a lethal injection.

Analogously, Keown has argued that respecting competent refusals of treatment, where the patient's intention is suicidal, is morally equivalent to assisting their suicide (Keown, 2000). He would distinguish between treatment refusals motivated by a desire to be free from burdensome treatment, and treatment refusals motivated by a desire to die. Of course, it is likely that many patients who wish to refuse life-prolonging treatment will have both motivations simultaneously, and in any event, it would be extremely difficult for doctors both to identify the patient's primary motive, and to be forced to treat a competent patient who wants to die against his or her wishes (Price, 2001: 629). I disagree with Keown that we should only honour treatment refusals where the patient wants to be free from the burdens of treatment, and disregard those motivated by a desire to die, but I think there is some force in Keown's view that assisting suicide by an omission (treatment withdrawal) is morally equivalent to assisting suicide by an action (prescribing a lethal dose of drugs). This would, however, lead me to conclude that there might be times when assisted suicide is justified, in contrast to Keown's conclusion that treatment withdrawal, where the intent is to cause death, should be against the law (Keown, 2002).

It is also important to remember that the patient's own preferences are not necessarily taken into account when doctors invoke the doctrine of 'double effect' in order to justify giving a potentially fatal dose of painkillers. The focus is primarily upon the doctor's judgement that this patient's pain cannot be relieved without also threatening his or her life. The doctor is not under any obligation to investigate whether the patient shares his or her belief that relieving pain is more important than prolonging life, the doctrine of double effect permits doctors to make much more paternalistic quality of life judgements than would be possible if voluntary euthanasia were to be legalised. The lack of transparency and openness about decisions justified by the doctrine of double effect—where death is, perhaps disingenuously, described as an incidental *side-effect* of pain relief, when in reality death may be the *means* to alleviate pain—is much more likely to threaten patient trust and confidence than the set of clear and rigorous legislative criteria which would have to be satisfied before a patient could receive a lethal injection (Tur, 2002: 227).

Not even included in Seale's list of end-of-life decisions will be cases when treatment is withheld for *economic* reasons. Non-treatment decisions would generally only be described as 'end-of-life' decisions where the treatment to be withheld or withdrawn is a life-prolonging treatment such as Artificial Nutrition and Hydration ('ANH') or mechanical ventilation. A refusal to prescribe an expensive new cancer drug might mean that someone dies earlier than they would otherwise, but this is not categorised as a non-treatment decision for these purposes.

A condition such as haemophilia can be extremely expensive to treat and, in recent years, there has been interest in the question of when, if ever, it might be legitimate to withhold life-saving treatment, such as an expensive clotting agent, on the grounds of cost (Schonfield and Reid, 2002). Some haemophiliacs are categorised as 'high-cost' patients. These are individuals whose treatment can cost several hundred thousands and even millions of pounds *each* within the space of a few days or weeks. Where the patient has significant co-morbidities (additional life-threatening conditions), low life-expectancy and a poor quality of life, it has been suggested that there might be times when it would not be appropriate to start a course of treatment which might end up costing several hundred thousand or millions of pounds (Pan Thames Haemophilia Consortium Expert Advisory Group, 2006). There are, of course, good reasons for ensuring that the National Health Service does not spend so much of its resources on a handful of patients that it compromises its capacity to offer adequate care to the rest of the community. But it is important to recognise that this sort of decision can be taken without consulting the competent adult patient.

VII. CONCLUSION

If patients in general do not trust their doctors, legalising assisted dying will be more difficult than if there are already high levels of openness and transparency, as well as trust, between doctors and their patients. Placing the power of life and death in untrustworthy hands might leave vulnerable, and perhaps even not especially vulnerable patients in danger. And of course it is true that in the United Kingdom the legacy of the Harold Shipman affair casts a long shadow (Shipman Inquiry, 2004). There are those who would argue that the legalisation of assisted dying would make it harder to protect patients against any future Harold Shipmans. This is, in my view, another red herring. Shipman's massive breach of his patients' trust took place in a country where euthanasia is illegal, so we cannot plausibly argue that the illegality of euthanasia is necessary to prevent murderously inclined doctors from killing their patients. Indeed the protections that might surround legalised euthanasia, such as a requirement that at least two doctors should approve the patient's request, and perhaps, too, that the patient be assessed by an independent psychiatrist, and has to make their request for euthanasia several times in writing, would offer more protection to patients than the rules which currently govern United Kingdom doctors' access to potentially lethal drugs.

The important impact of the Shipman case on the euthanasia debate is not, in my view, that it serves as a warning to those who would argue in favour of legalisation that abuse is inevitable, but rather it has inevitably damaged, to some extent at least, some patients' confidence in the medical profession. In a number of recent court cases, there has certainly been evidence of compromised trust between patients and doctors. In *R (on the application of Burke) v General Medical Council*, [2] Leslie Burke challenged GMC guidance on the grounds that it would permit the withdrawal of ANH even where he had previously requested that it should continue. This, he argued, would breach his rights under the Human Rights Act 1998. Mr Burke succeeded at first instance but lost on appeal. In *Glass v United Kingdom*[3], the applicant believed that the doctors were intending, through the provision of diamorphine and 'Do not resuscitate' orders, to 'euthanase' her son covertly. Relations between the medical staff and the mother were extremely poor, but the hospital did not make an application to the court to resolve the question of the child's treatment. The European Court of Human Rights found that treatment in defiance of the parent's objections, without the authorisation of a court, amounted to an interference with the child's right to respect for his private and family life, and thus violated Article 8. Other cases might be mentioned, such as the prolonged litigation in the *Wyatt v Portsmouth NHS Trust*,[4] in which relations between the parents and the hospital where Charlotte Wyatt was being treated, had reached such a low ebb that the parents had reported the Trust's medical staff to the police for alleged assaults on Charlotte, and for significant periods of time the parents were only allowed onto the ward to visit Charlotte whilst accompanied by security personnel.

Taken together, these cases are not necessarily representative of any trend towards less productive relationships between patients and doctors at the end of life, but they should give us pause for thought when we claim that it is legalised euthanasia that poses a risk to trust within the doctor-patient relationship. After all, these cases all involved doctors engaged in *lawful* end-of-life decision-making.

Doctors can already end their patients' lives with very little scrutiny provided that death is caused by treatment withdrawal, as it is in around a third of all deaths in the United Kingdom. This, as I argued earlier, places unwarranted emphasis upon the acts/omissions distinction. Andrew McGee argues that there is a moral distinction between acts and omissions:

[T]he moral relevance of the distinction can therefore be put in this way: *euthanasia interferes with nature's dominion*, whereas withdrawal of treatment *restores* to nature her dominion after we had taken it away when *artificially* prolonging the patient's life (McGee, 2005:).

But while 'letting nature take its course' may be easier for doctors (and judges), because it does not force them to confront the question of when

---

[2] *R (on the application of Burke) v General Medical Council* [2005] EWCA Civ 1003.
[3] *Glass v UK* (Application No 61827/00) [2004] 1 FLR 1019 (ECHR).
[4] *Wyatt v Portsmouth NHS Trust* [2005] EWHC 2293 (Fam).

killing might be the kindest thing to do, it also implies, disingenuously in my view, that 'natural' deaths are necessarily morally preferable to 'man-made' deaths. We should remember, as Tom Campbell points out, that natural deaths can be extremely nasty (Campbell, 2006: 454).

If a 'natural' death involves suffocation, dehydration or starvation, might it be possible to argue that a 'man-made' death might sometimes be preferable? To say that 'nature taking its course' is better than 'interfering with nature' in order to end suffering might, if taken to its logical conclusion, also outlaw the provision of painkilling drugs to terminally ill patients.

Being 'allowed to die', by the withdrawal of treatment can, as Rachels explains 'be relatively slow and painful, whereas being given a lethal injection is relatively quick and painless' (Rachels, 1975: 78). It is perhaps odd that we accept that it is legitimate for the medical profession to cause death by starvation, dehydration, suffocation and infection (by withholding or withdrawing ANH, ventilation or antibiotics), but that we see achieving a quicker and more peaceful death by lethal injection as contrary to the ethical foundations of the medical profession. I would agree with Rachels' robust and stark criticism of the status quo:

> The doctrine that says that a baby may be allowed to dehydrate and wither, but may not be given an injection that would end its life without suffering, seems so patently cruel as to require no further refutation (Rachels, 1995: 79).

BIBLIOGRAPHY

Publications

Assisted Dying for the Terminally Ill Committee (2005) *First Report* (London, The Stationery Office).

Battin, MP (1994) *The least worst death: Essays in bioethics on the end of life* (Oxford, Oxford University Press).

—— (2005) *Ending life: Ethics and the way we Die* (Oxford, Oxford University Press).

Campbell, T (2006) Euthanasia as a human right in *First do no harm* SAM McLean (ed), (Aldershot, Ashgate) 447–459.

Cuttini, M, Nadai, M, Kaminski, M, Hansen, G, de Leeuw, R, Lenoir, S, Persson, J, Rebagliato, M, Reid, M, de Vonderweid, U, Lenard, HG, Orzalesi, M and Saracci, R (2000) 'End-of-life decisions in neonatal intensive care: physicians' self-reported practices in seven European countries' 355 *The Lancet* 2112–2118.

Dahl, E and Levy, N (2006) 'The case for physician assisted suicide: how can it possibly be proven? 32 *Journal of Medical Ethics* 335–338.

Dierckx de Casterlé, B, Verpoort, C, De Bal, N and Gastmans, C (2006) 'Nurses' views on their involvement in euthanasia: a qualitative study in Flanders (Belgium)' 32 *Journal of Medical Ethics* 187–192.

Ganzini, L, Nelson, HL, Lee, MA, Kraemer, DF, Schmidt, TA and Delorit, MA (2001) 'Oregon physician attitudes about and experiences with end-of-life care since the passage of the Death With Dignity Act' 285 *Journal of the American Medical Association* 2363–2369.

Gastmans, C, Van Neste, F and Schotsmans, P (2004) 'Facing requests for euthanasia: a clinical practice guideline' 30 *Journal of Medical Ethics* 212–217.

Griffiths, J, Bood, A and Weyers, H (1998) *Euthanasia and law in the Netherlands* (Amsterdam, Amsterdam University Press).

Groenewoud, JH, van der Heide, A, Onwuteaka-Philipsen, BD, Willems, DL, van der Maas, PJ and van der Wal, G (2000) 'Clinical problems with the performance of euthanasia and physician-assisted suicide in the Netherlands' 342 *New England Journal of Medicine* 551–556.

Jackson, E (2004)'"Whose death is it anyway?" Euthanasia and the medical profession' 57 *Current Legal Problems* 415–442.

Kass, LR and Lund, N (1996) 'Physician-assisted suicide, medical ethics and the future of the medical profession' 35 *Duquesne Law Review* 395–425.

Keown, J (2000) 'Beyond *Bland*: a critique of the BMA guidance on withholding and withdrawing medical treatment' 20 *Legal Studies* 66–84.

 —— (2002) 'The case of Ms B: Suicide's slippery slope' 28 *Journal of Medical Ethics* 238–239.

—— (2005) 'A futile defence of *Bland*: A reply to Andrew McGee' 13 *Medical Law Review* 393-402.

Kuhse, H, Singer, P, Baume, P, Clark, M and Rickard, M (1997) 'End-of-life decisions in Australian medical practice' 166 *Medical Journal of Australia* 191–96.

Magnusson, RS (2004) 'Euthanasia: above ground, below ground' 30 *Journal of Medical Ethics* 441–446.

McGee, A (2005) 'Finding a way through the ethical and legal maze: withdrawal of medical treatment and euthanasia' 13 *Medical Law Review* 357–385.

Miller, LL, Harvath, TA, Ganzini, L, Goy, ER, Delorit, MA and Jackson, A (2004) 'Attitudes and experiences of Oregon hospice nurses and social workers regarding assisted suicide' 18 *Palliative Medicine* 685–91.

Norton, C (1998) 'Doctor, will you help me die?' *The Sunday Times* November 15 1998.

Nys, H (1999) 'Physician involvement in a patient's death: a continental European perspective'. 7 *Medical Law Review* 208–46.

Oregon Department of Human Services (2002) *Fifth Annual Report on Oregon's Death with Dignity Act* (Portland, OR, Department of Human Services).

Oregon Department of Human Services (2004) *Seventh Annual Report on Oregon's Death with Dignity Act* (Portland, OR, Department of Human Services).

Pan Thames Haemophilia Consortium Expert Advisory Group (2006) personal communication.

Price, D (2001) 'Fairly Bland: an alternative view of a supposed new "death ethic" and the BMA guidelines' 21 *Legal Studies* 618–643.

Rachels, J (1975) 'Active and passive euthanasia' 292 *New England Journal of Medicine* 79–80.

Seale, C (2006) 'National survey of end-of-life decisions made by UK medical practitioners' 20 *Palliative Medicine* 3–10.

Shipman Inquiry (2004) *Fifth Report—Safeguarding Patients: Lessons from the Past—Proposals for the Future*:
http://www.the-shipman-inquiry.org.uk/fifthreport.asp
Tur, R (2002) 'Just how unlawful is euthanasia?' 19 *Journal of Applied Philosophy* 219–232.
van der Heide, A, Deliens, L, Faisst, K, Nilstun, T, Norup, M, Paci, E, an der Wal, G and van der Maas, P (2003) 'End-of-life decision-making in six European countries: descriptive study' 362 *The Lancet* 345–350.
van der Maas, PJ (1992) *Euthanasia and other medical decisions concerning the end of life* (Amerstad, Elsevier).
Ward, BJ and Tate, PA (1994) 'Attitudes among NHS doctors to requests for euthanasia' 308 *British Medical Journal* 1132.
Weiss, SC, Emanuel, LL, Fairclough, DL and Emanuel, EJ (2001) 'Understanding the experience of pain in terminally ill patients' 357 *The Lancet* 1311–1315.

Legislation

Loi relative à l'euthanasie (Euthanasia Act) (2002).
Termination of Life on Request and Assisted Suicide (Review Procedures) Act (2001).

4

Criminalising Carers: Death Desires and Assisted Dying Outlaws

HAZEL BIGGS

I. INTRODUCTION

THE LAW HAS always had an interest in the interface between life and death. For example, it has long concerned itself with the regulation of the disposal of the body and the allocation of assets and belongings after death, as well as the attribution of guilt and punishment in relation to unlawful killing (Hedley; Herring; Jackson; Price, chapters fourteen, thirteen, three and twelve, all this volume). Modern medicine has developed the potential to prolong and extend life even in the face of extreme illness and disability and, given the emphasis placed on the successes of medicine, death has sometimes been regarded as a failure of medical intervention—or, as Illich claimed more than a quarter of a century ago, death may be regarded as 'the ultimate form of consumer resistance' (Illich, 1975: 149). In reality though, death is inevitable and, regardless of medical intervention, in the end we are all going to die. What concerns most of us is not so much the fact that we may one day be dead but the fact that we will die and that the dying process may be unpalatable.

The increased emphasis on respect for individual autonomy in medical law and ethics has been instrumental in a number of high-profile legal cases concerning end-of-life decision-making in recent years. *Pretty v United Kingdom*,[1] *Re B (Adult: Refusal of Medical Treat ment)*[2] and *R (on the application of Burke) v General Medical Council*[3] all involved individuals who sought to influence the manner of their dying. Their cases concerned very different aspects of the dying process. Diane Pretty hoped to change the law so that she might lawfully be assisted to commit suicide; Ms B simply wanted her refusal of life-supporting treatment to be upheld; and

---

[1] *Pretty v United Kingdom* (2002) 35 EHRR 1.
[2] *Re B (Adult: Refusal of Medical Treatment)* [2002] EWHC 429.
[3] *R (on the application of Burke) v General Medical Council* [2005] EWCA Civ 1003.

Leslie Burke fought to have his wish for artificial feeding and hydration to continue until he died naturally respected. Of the three, only Ms B was granted the court order she sought.

In line with these outcomes, there remains no right to assisted dying in the United Kingdom and autonomy and choice over medical decisions at the end of life only extends as far as permitting treatment refusal (see further Du Bois-Pedain, chapter five this volume). It is also not legitimate to demand that specific medical interventions be instigated or continued if the treating clinicians do not regard it as clinically indicated (*Re J (A Minor) (Child in Care: Medical Treatment)*[4]). Cases like these, together with initiatives such as the Assisted Dying for the Terminally Ill Bill 2005 and the Mental Capacity Act 2005, have helped to raise public awareness of the significance of personal choice and control over medical treatment at the end of life. Raising awareness in this way is likely to have had a profound effect on the attitudes of some people suffering from chronic and debilitating conditions, and those who care for them. It may also have influenced the decisions and actions of many. Therefore, drawing upon specific examples of situations where care-givers have been potentially criminally implicated in the end-of-life decisions of those they cared for, this chapter will explore the precarious nature of the care relationship in this context.

II. CONTEXT—DEATH DESIRES

It is apparent that some people are prepared to go to extraordinary lengths in order to retain control over their dying and avoid what they perceive as undignified or protracted dying. Their stories are often harrowing. For example, the death of 80 year-old Sir Derek Bibby was reported in the national press (*The Guardian* 29 November 2002). Rather than wait to die of the leukaemia and prostate cancer from which he suffered, he sat in his home sauna and inhaled a highly toxic vapour of aluminium phosphide produced by pouring rat poison over the coals. He left a note advising his daughter to call the emergency services but not to enter the sauna. She followed his advice and, although still alive when rescued by fire fighters, he was dead on arrival at hospital where concerns about toxicity resulted in the emergency department being closed for around 12 hours. His desire to ensure that he would not survive his suicide attempt led him to select an extreme method that threatened the health and well being of others around him.

Perhaps less drastic is the example of people who opt to commit suicide before they need to, due to fears that leaving it too late will mean they become too physically debilitated to take their own lives (Stenager and Stenager, 2000). Others decide to travel to jurisdictions outside of the

---

[4] *Re J (a minor) (child in care: medical treatment)* [1993] Fam 15 (CA).

United Kingdom where assisted suicide is legally available, while yet others seek active intervention from those charged with their care, by requesting euthanasia. These are not new phenomena. Nor, as Ronald Dworkin explains, are they limited to particular jurisdictions:

Every day, rational people all over the world plead to be allowed to die. Sometimes they plead for others to kill them. Some of them are dying already ... Some of them want to die because they are unwilling to live in the only way left open to them (Dworkin, 1993: 179).

For many this is a logical, practical choice, albeit born of an extreme situation where the options are inherently limited. Often, however, those who make such choices require assistance from others because their intellectual autonomy is compromised by physical infirmity. But those who agree to assist may unwittingly be exposing themselves to criminal liability.

Depending on the circumstances, the person called upon to help may be either a professional or an informal care-giver. If they give the assistance sought and criminal culpability is demonstrated, the law will make scant distinction between them. In the much heralded words of Glanville Williams, in active mercy killing cases the law does not 'leave the issue in the hands of doctors; it treats euthanasia as murder' (Williams, 1983: 580). However, professional care-givers such as nurses and doctors are not the main focus of this chapter. Unlike informal, voluntary carers, they have the benefit of training, experience and professional support, which can be expected to inform their understanding of the legal implications of their actions. They will also have access to colleagues, advisors and counsellors to support them in their professional role, while an informal care-giver, typically a spouse or family member, will generally have no such recourse (Commission for Social Care Inspection, 2005). In addition, the care relationship occupied by informal carers is frequently premised upon bonds of affection and love. Not only does this make informal carers vulnerable to pressures that professional carers might reasonably be expected to resist, it can also generate a sense of obligation that may encourage a carer to comply with the will of the cared for person (Biggs and Mackenzie, 2006). In this way it is possible that a carer may act upon the wishes of the person they care for by assisting their suicide, for example. In this case it is highly probable that the carer would take such action intending and believing that they were simply giving effect to that person's autonomy, but this would be unlikely to provide a legal justification that would absolve them from criminal responsibility. Furthermore, informal caring responsibilities are often physically and emotionally demanding (Hirst, 2005), financially disadvantageous (Carers UK, 2006) and relentless, which may affect the carer's judgement and cause her or him to actively participate in the death of the cared for person. Frequently, however, informal carers who are charged with murder in these circumstances are able to successfully rely on the defence of diminished responsibility, in recognition of the strain that many such carers experience (Firth, 2005; and Brooke, 2006). In effect, their conduct is excused on the basis that they were, at the time, overcome with exhaustion or sometimes depression or other mental infirmity (Greenhill, 2006).

Of course when discussing carers' participation in end-of-life practices, such as assisted dying, it must be acknowledged that not all will act with beneficent motives. It is easy, for example, to discover reports spanning many years that illustrate the prevalence of physical, psychological and financial elder abuse (House of Commons Health Committee, 2004). And, as with all human relations, the relationship between carer and cared for is complex, encompassing a variety of power dynamics. It should therefore also be recognised that in some circumstances it can give rise to the carer being exploited or succumbing to pressure from their charge to take action that might be against their own judgement (Ungerson, 1987; and Baldock and Ungerson, 1994). Within that, whilst appreciating that valorisation of carers may sometimes be misplaced, this discussion is concerned only to address issues relating to those care-givers who act from compassionate motives and at the request of those they care for, to assist in their deaths, and later find themselves subject to the criminal law. It will not deal with complicity in the suicide of a person in their care. Specifically, it will assess how far a carer may be involved in helping their charge to take their own life before incurring criminal liability. How, for example, should a carer respond when their charge acts on a settled wish to commit suicide and insists that no medical assistance be summoned? Similarly, what is the legal position of a family member who accompanies a dying person to Switzerland for assisted suicide? The discussion will also address some specific issues associated with the failed Assisted Dying for the Terminally Ill Bill (2005), in the context of the expected role of informal carers. In particular, given the likelihood that a similar Bill will be introduced at some time in the future, it will assess some mechanisms that will help to ensure that carers obtain immunity from prosecution if they actively assist in suicide.

III. CRIMINALISING CARERS—ASSISTED DYING OUTLAWS

A. Actively Assisting in the Suicide of Another

Under section 1 of the Suicide Act 1961, suicide is no longer an act that can be punished under the criminal law. The law was changed in 1961 in recognition of the fact that generally those who opted to take their own lives but survived were deserving of compassion, rather than punishment. However, helping a person to commit suicide is regarded much less favourably. In a provision clearly designed to deter those who may act with malevolent motives, section 2 of the Act states that

[a] person who aids, abets, counsels or procures the suicide of another, or an attempt by another to commit suicide, shall be liable on conviction on indictment to imprisonment for a term not exceeding fourteen years.

This was the provision that Diane Pretty fought against in her quest for an assisted death. She was prevented from taking her own life by her physical incapacity associated with motor neurone disease, so she sought help from others. Having failed to persuade her doctors to assist her to end her life, her husband agreed that he would accede to her wishes. However, Mrs Pretty soon discovered that this could result in criminal liability, and sought assurances from the Director of Public Prosecutions ('DPP') that if her husband were to help her he would not face prosecution. Unfortunately, despite having discretion not to prosecute under section 2(4) of the Suicide Act 1961, the DPP took the view that giving such assurances would far exceed the authority of the office, not least because the powers of that office relate primarily to actions taken after a crime has been committed rather than in relation to speculative events (Tur, 2003). Hence, her claim was destined to fail. Further, even if the DPP agreed prospectively to waive the right to prosecute, any such decision could later become the subject of a judicial review by the courts, so it would be impossible to guarantee that prosecution would be avoided. The reasons why Brian Pretty agreed to help his wife to kill herself, and why Diane Pretty brought her legal challenge and was prepared to take it through the domestic courts and all the way to the European Court of Human Rights, are of particular interest here.

At the time the case was before the courts, Brian Pretty's motivation was easy to see. His concern and compassion for Diane was such that he was prepared to assist in her quest for a peaceful death at the time of her choosing despite the fact, as this excerpt from a BBC interview with David Frost illustrates, that he did not want to lose her:

DAVID FROST: Well would, if, if in the end you win in the courts the day when you help Diane to end her life, will that be just the saddest day of your life but in, or in terms of her liberation as it were, will it be the gladdest day of your life?
BRIAN PRETTY: ... it will be the saddest day of our life because I'm not losing a wife or a partner I'm losing part of me. And in Diane's case, yes it will be the gladdest day of her life because she will be free of a body what has restricted her from doing things that she'd love to do in the past (BBC, 2002).

Diane Pretty's primary intention was obvious in as much as she wanted to be enabled to exercise her autonomy by receiving the help she needed to commit suicide. The reason she doggedly pursued her case through the courts was rather different, however. She did not only want to die, she wanted to die without breaking the law and knowing that her husband would not be implicated in her death, arguing:

I want my family to remember me as someone who respected the law, and asked in turn that the law respected me (Dyer, 2002).

In the event, Diane Pretty suffered the death she had striven to avoid and Brian was not prosecuted because she died of natural causes. Others have been less fortunate. In 1988 George Beecham was convicted under section 2 of the Suicide Act 1961 after his 35-year-old daughter had committed suicide (Horder, 1988). She suffered from multiple sclerosis and cervical cancer and died of asphyxiation having passed a pipe from the exhaust to the interior of her car and settled down inside with the engine running. Her father had walked with her to the car, helped her to connect the pipe and checked on her every 15 minutes. Immediately after she was dead, he called the police. Beecham received a 12-month prison sentence, suspended for 12 months. Such incidents are reported with monotonous regularity and, as with any criminal case, the outcome is uncertain, but more recently the trend seems to be that those who have assisted are acquitted or receive suspended or non-custodial sentences in recognition of the fact that they acted compassionately and that there is little to be gained from imprisoning them (BBC News, 2006a; and BBC News, 2006b). The trauma and upset caused by having to mount a defence in a criminal court cannot be underestimated, however, especially where the defendant is recently bereaved; a trauma that must be further compounded in cases of 'death tourism', where the carer also has to make arrangements, inter alia, to repatriate the body.

B. Death Tourism

While assisted suicide remains unlawful in England, other jurisdictions, including Oregon, The Netherlands and Switzerland, have legislated to permit assisted suicide in carefully controlled circumstances. The vast majority of the states that permit assisted suicide limit it to their own residents, but Switzerland is a notable exception in that it permits foreign nationals to visit and avail themselves of facilities offering assisted suicide. 'Dignitas' is the main organisation providing this service, and to date estimates suggest that around 100 Britons have travelled to its clinic in Zurich to die. In 2003, the case of Reginald Crewe was the first case of so-called death tourism to be publicised in the United Kingdom, although he was in fact the second person to make the trip. He travelled to Switzerland accompanied by his wife and daughter and a television crew, all of whom were theoretically liable for assisting his suicide. The Crown Prosecution Service ('CPS') deliberated about whether to prosecute for eight months after his death before finally deciding that in the circumstances prosecution would be contrary to the public interest. To date, no other prosecutions have been brought either, but in the absence of clear guidance from the CPS or the DPP the uncertainty remains.

In this climate, carers and those they care for continue to support assisted suicide and to seek it out, especially by travelling to Switzerland. Different issues were raised in 2004 by the case of *Re Z (Local Authority: Duty)*.[5] Mrs Z became aware of the availability of assisted suicide in Switzerland and decided to travel there for assistance after she had tried unsuccessfully to take her own life. She lived at home with her husband but required extensive support from her local authority due to disabilities associated with cerebellar ataxia. Once his wife had made clear that it was her settled wish to travel to Switzerland for an assisted suicide, Mr Z informed the local authority of their plans. However, because Mrs Z was regarded as a 'vulnerable adult', the authority sought, and obtained a High Court injunction restraining Mr Z from committing a criminal offence by removing his wife to Switzerland. The Official Solicitor was engaged to act on behalf of Mrs Z and subsequently a psychiatric assessment of her legal capacity was ordered to be provided as evidence at a further hearing.

The scope of the local authority's duty towards Mrs Z was assessed at that hearing and Hedley, J confirmed that they owed a duty of care to Mrs Z because of her alleged vulnerability. He also made it clear that the duty extended to establishing whether she possessed the mental capacity to make the decision to seek assisted dying, and if so, whether her decision had been unduly influenced. The psychiatric report found Mrs Z to be mentally competent, so it was held that, like any other competent adult, she had the right to decide for herself. Therefore, in spite of any vulnerability or susceptibility to abuse, as a mentally competent individual her right to self-determination took precedence over any protective action proposed. Also, providing the decision was demonstrably her own, the duty of the authority was to enable her to lawfully give effect to her choice. Hedley, J also explained that where there were grounds to suspect that a criminal offence might be committed, the authority had a duty to draw that to the attention of the police, and here Hedley, J observed that 'by making arrangements and escorting Mrs Z on the flight, Mr Z will have contravened Section 2(1)'.[6] Ultimately the injunction was lifted and Mr and Mrs Z did travel to Switzerland, where she died with the assistance of 'Dignitas'.

Without the assistance of her husband, or somebody like him, Mrs Z would have been unable to exercise her choice. The fact that the judgment held that the local authority was obliged to enable her to exercise her choice is interesting, given that it also recognised the potential criminal liability of her husband. From the point of view of criminal liability, one wonders what

---

[5] *Re Z (local authority: duty)* [2004] EWHC 2817 (Fam).
[6] *Re Z (local authority: duty)* [2004] EWHC 2817 (Fam) [14].

kind of action the authority would need to take before its enabling might be construed as assisting within the terms of the Suicide Act 1961. No criminal action was brought against Mr Z, but the case demonstrates the vulnerability that carers and the cared for face in relation to the uncertainties of the legal process. The apparent reluctance to prosecute those who assist in death tourism is at odds with the experience of others, like George Beecham who assist in suicide, suggesting that, at least in some circumstances, the law enforcement authorities are sympathetic to the plight of those who seek to exercise a legitimate choice to travel to be assisted in suicide, and those who help them. However, even if prosecution and conviction is justified where the assistor has actively participated in the suicide—for instance by providing drugs or other some other intervention—what is the legal position where the carer deliberately fails to take action that may save a life?

C. Failing to Act

R v Anderson[7] is indicative of the kinds of situations that voluntary carers might confront through failing to take action. Jill Anderson was charged and eventually acquitted of manslaughter after declining to call the emergency services when her husband took a fatal overdose of morphine. He had previously attempted suicide and been hospitalised at least twice as a result. On this occasion, at his request and knowing that he had taken the pills, she had stayed with him all night and cared for him as he died. When he finally stopped breathing she cleaned and tidied the house before calling the doctor two hours later. Rather than assisted suicide, Jill Anderson was originally charged with murder, presumably because the prosecuting authorities were concerned that she may have deliberately engineered his death. The charge was later reduced to manslaughter by gross negligence.

Ordinarily the criminal law does not impose liability in cases involving failure to act unless a legal duty exists between the defendant and the victim, which requires the defendant to take action. Therefore, for Jill Anderson to be convicted it would have to be shown that she had a legal duty to take action in the circumstances that arose. Such a duty will arise in a range of distinct situations, including where there is a special relationship between those concerned and where one party has voluntarily assumed a duty to care for another, both of which are relevant here. Once it is established that a duty exists, whether or not any breach of that duty amounts to gross negligence capable of being characterised as a crime, is a matter of fact for the jury to decide (*R v Adomako*[8]). In other words, it would have to be demonstrated that her culpability was so great that it would be justifiable to impose criminal liability.

---

[7] *R v Anderson* (unreported) Leeds Crown Ct, 27 April 2005.
[8] *R v Adomako* [1994] 3 All ER 79 (HL).

The specific circumstances under which it is appropriate to impose such liability have been the subject of many years of legal debate (Glazebrook, 1960; Williams, 1987; Ashworth, 1989; and Norrie, 2001, and see also a number of cases (*R v Pattmore*,[9] *R v Nicholls*,[10] *R v Instan*,[11] *R v Gibbins and Proctor*,[12] *R v Bonnyman*,[13] *R v Stone and Dobinson*,[14] *R v Smith*[15]). The position was finally clarified in 1994 in the case of *R v Adomako*[16] and, following that, dicta in *R v Misra and Srivastava*[17] suggested that no further uncertainty should exist:

The hypothetical citizen, seeking to know his position, would be advised that, assuming he owed a duty of care to the deceased which he had negligently broken, and that death had resulted, he would be liable to conviction for manslaughter, if, on the available evidence, the jury was satisfied that his negligence was gross.

But it seems unlikely that an untrained carer who, like Jill Anderson, had voluntarily assumed responsibility for the care of her partner would be aware of the extent of her legal responsibility (Biggs and Mackenzie, 2006). Arguably, a hypothetical citizen like her would not be inclined to seek to know her position unless and until she was in a position to need to know it. Prior to that, it seems probable that Jill Anderson would be operating according to rather different imperatives, especially given her comments after her husband's death,

I searched my conscience and the act I did that night was for him, not me, he wanted to go ... what I did that night was an act of love and an act of kindness it was very difficult to face a prosecution for loving someone, because that's all I did that night (BBC News, 2005).

Realistically then, by the time a citizen like her sought to find out her legal position she would already potentially be liable.

The Andersons' case also raises an important question about how far a carer should be expected to intervene to override the wishes of the person they care for. Paul Anderson had apparently deliberately taken an overdose with the intention of ending his life and asked his wife not to interfere. In these circumstances did Jill Anderson have a legal obligation to step in and take action to save her husband or was she justified in failing to act, out

[9] *R v Pattmore* (1789) QB Sessions Papers 214 (Crown Court).
[10] *R v Nicholls* (1874) 13 Cox 75 Crown Court).
[11] *R v Instan* [1893] 1 QB 450 (Crown Court).
[12] *R v Gibbins and Proctor* (1918) 13 Cr App R 134 (CA).
[13] *R v Bonnyman* (1942) 28 Cr App R 131 (CA).
[14] *R v Stone and Dobinson* [1977] QB 354 (CA).
[15] *R v Smith* [1979] Crim LR 251(Crown Court).
[16] *R v Adomako* [1994] 3 All ER 79 (HL).
[17] *R v Misra and Srivastava* [2004] EWCA Crim 2375, 328 (CA) at 348.

of respect for his decision? Authorities demonstrate that legal liability has been imposed in similar situations in a number of cases. In *R v Nicholls*, the first case that decided such a duty could arise in the absence of a contractual relationship, Brett, J directed the jury that

> if a grown up person chooses to undertake the charge of a human creature help-less either from infancy simplicity or other infirmity, he is bound to exercise that charge without (at all events) wicked negligence; and if a person who has chosen to take charge of a helpless creature lets it die by wicked negligence, that person is guilty of manslaughter.[18]

The direction was followed in an array of subsequent cases (*R v Instan*[19]; *R v Hall*[20]; *R v Chatterway*[21]) establishing that a duty may arise in these circumstances without clearly specifying the parameters of when the duty arises and how far it extends. More recently, in *R v Smith*,[22] it was confirmed that a husband did have a duty to care for his wife's health. When he failed to summon medical help when she was gravely ill, Smith was found to have acted with a 'reckless disregard' for the duty of care he owed to his wife even though she had expressed a reluctance to be seen by a doctor.

Like Smith, Jill Anderson was aware that there was a serious risk to her husband's life if she failed to get help but she still acceded to his wishes and allowed him to die. In the determination of whether she had a duty to act according to the case law, three further points are relevant. First, was Paul Anderson a helpless human creature within the terms of the judgment above? Secondly, was Jill Anderson guilty of 'wicked negligence' as described in *R v Nicholls*? And finally, what was the status of his statement of intent to refuse medical care?

With regard to his physical condition, Paul Anderson did not seem to be so debilitated at the time of his suicide as to be dependent on his wife. He was being treated for chronic fatigue syndrome or ME, which was debilitating but not immediately life limiting. Clearly, then, he would not have been helpless at the time he took the overdose and refused medical care, but this would change once he lapsed into unconsciousness. At that time he would obviously become helpless and Jill Anderson could have taken action had she not preferred to abide by his wishes. The judge in *R v Smith*[23] questioned whether a person who has objected to medical treatment ought always to be regarded as a helpless creature if they become dangerously ill. However, this is a question of fact to be left for a jury to decide, based on

---

[18] *R v Nicholls* (1874) 13 Cox 75 (Crown Court) per Brett, J at 88.
[19] *R v Instan* [1893] 1 QB 450 (Crown Court).
[20] *R v Hall* (1919) 14 Cr App R 58 (CA).
[21] *R v Chatterway* (1922) 17 Cr App R 7 (CA).
[22] *R v Smith* [1979] Crim LR 251 (Crown Court).
[23] *R v Smith* [1979] Crim LR 251 (Crown Court).

the evidence and with particular regard to whether the deceased person had the mental capacity to decide to refuse treatment.

Whether or not Jill Anderson was guilty of 'wicked negligence' in her continuing failure to summon help once her husband became unconscious depends on her intention at the time. This, in turn, is largely determined by her own understanding of the status of his treatment refusal. For the purposes of criminal law it is significant that she must have foreseen that death was at least possible, but that does not necessarily mean that she deliberately failed to act in order to bring it about. On the assumption that no malice was intended, it is conceivable that she was simply acceding to what she saw as the autonomous wishes of her husband in an environment where the value of living wills and recent cases upholding the rights of patients to refuse treatment have been well publicised. It is now settled law that a competent adult has an absolute right to have their health care decisions respected, even if those decisions are irrational or unreasonable (*Re T (adult refusal of medical treatment)*,[24] *Re C (adult refusal of medical treatment)*,[25] *Re MB (medical treatment)*,[26] *Re B (Adult Refusal of Medical Treatment)*[27]). So if, in similar circumstances, he had been admitted to hospital while conscious and mentally competent, and refused medical intervention to save him, his refusal should have been respected. The same would apply under common law if he had made a valid advance directive refusing treatment (*Re C (adult refusal of medical treatment)*). Of course several points would need to be clarified, not least that he actually had refused treatment and was of 'sound mind' and so had the mental capacity to make such a decision. Further, the status of a verbal advance decision made known only to his wife and not otherwise verifiable would be dubious, particularly once the Mental Capacity Act 2005—which insists that advance decisions refusing life sustaining treatment should be written and witnessed—is fully implemented in 2007.

Without additional knowledge, it is difficult to assess Paul Anderson's actual psychological state. However, perhaps more significant here is his wife's understanding of his views and respect for his decision. Even if a legal duty could not categorically be constructed, with the benefit of hindsight and detachment from the situation we might recognise a moral imperative to call the emergency services. Ultimately, however, the jury must have decided that it could not be proven beyond a reasonable doubt that she had been wickedly negligent, because they acquitted her. It is essential that the state protects the interests of vulnerable people who are unable to look after themselves, and generally a charge of manslaughter by neglect is an

---

[24] *Re T (adult refusal of medical treatment)* [1992] 4 All ER 649 (CA).
[25] *Re C (adult refusal of medical treatment)* [1994] 1 All ER 819 (Fam Div).
[26] *Re MB (medical treatment)* [1997] 2 FLR 426 (CA).
[27] *Re B (Adult: Refusal of Medical Treatment)* [2002] EWHC 429 (Fam Div).

appropriate mechanism through which to achieve this. Similarly, where a non-professional carer has intentionally caused the death of a vulnerable person in their care through calculated omission, such as in *R v Sogunro*,[28] where the victim was locked in a room by the defendant and deliberately not fed. A murder charge may even be appropriate where there is evidence of premeditated and malicious failure to act (*R v Gibbins and Proctor*[29]). However, the hypothetical citizen who fails to obtain assistance for a person in her care because she is responding to what she perceives as a moral obligation to observe the desires of her charge may be unjustly held criminally liable for it. One way to avoid such injustice would be to introduce legislation such as the Assisted Dying for the Terminally Ill Bill discussed below, to define circumstances within which assisted dying might be permissible and absolve carers of criminal responsibility.

D. The Assisted Dying for the Terminally Ill Bill 2005

The Assisted Dying for the Terminally Ill Bill 2005 (ADTI, 2005) was originally presented to Parliament as a House of Lords Private Members Bill in the wake of the Diane Pretty case in 2003. It was revised extensively after Parliamentary debate and represented in 2004. That presentation led to the setting up of a special House of Lords Select Committee to examine the issues before deciding whether it should proceed further through the Parliamentary process. The Select Committee decided that it should proceed. After more revisions it was debated in the House of Lords in May 2006 but its prospects of further progress were effectively blocked for the foreseeable future. In many respects however, despite its failure, the Bill did represent a workable approach to assisted suicide and as such there is little doubt that a similar Bill will be presented to Parliament at some time in the not too distant future. In these circumstances, it therefore seems appropriate to consider some of its possible implications for voluntary carers.

Underpinning each version of the Assisted Dying for the Terminally Ill Bill has been the central premise that assisted dying is an option that some terminally-ill people favour. Certainly the evidence from recent case law and the numbers of people opting for death tourism suggests that this is an accurate assessment. In addition, there is an assumption that the safest and most effective method of organising the regulation of assisted suicide is to ensure that it is conducted by health care professionals. Based on this, the Bill was designed to provide immunity from prosecution to those who assist a suicide within the parameters it described. Accordingly, if such a Bill were to make it through the Parliamentary process and onto the statute book it

---

[28] *R v Sogunro* [1997] 2 Cr App R (S) 89 (CA).
[29] *R v Gibbins and Proctor* (1918) 13 Cr App R 134 (CA).

would permit only mentally competent, terminally-ill adults to be assisted to die. Their request for assisted dying would have to be voluntary, enduring and appropriately witnessed for the professional carers who assisted them to receive immunity from prosecution. In practice, however, for reasons that will be explained, it seems inevitable that informal unqualified care-givers will also be involved in assisting the dying process. As a result it is vitally important to assess the potential criminal liability of these carers and determine what safeguards might be constructed to help avoid their exposure to criminal prosecution.

Every incarnation of the Assisted Dying for the Terminally Ill Bill has included safeguards to ensure that the interests of the dying person would be protected. In order to meet the qualifying criteria, for example, the person would need to be adult and demonstrably mentally competent (ADTI 2005, clause 2(2)). They would be required to make a formal, written declaration of their desire to be assisted to die, which would have to be independently witnessed to ensure it was free from coercion and undue influence (ADTI, 2005, clause 4(3) and (4)). Two doctors would need to be involved in the process of making the declaration, one of whom would need to be independent of the clinical team caring for the patient. Once made, a declaration of intent to use the ADTI provisions could not be acted upon for 14 days and, if not implemented within six months, it would automatically lapse and become invalid. A requirement that alternatives to assisted dying should be discussed with the patient was also included in the Bill to ensure that the patient would be properly informed of all available options and not feel pressurised into assisted dying. In order to be fully informed, a patient would also need to know details of their specific condition, their own prognosis and the process involved in being assisted to die.

All versions of the Bill envisaged that once the formalities were completed, a terminally-ill patient seeking assisted dying would be prescribed medication, most likely to be a form of a barbiturate, which they would administer to themselves. Clearly this is necessary to avoid the possibility of abuse where patients might be deliberately poisoned or overdosed by their carers, and to distinguish assistance under the Bill from active euthanasia. This is where the legal implications for carers require careful consideration in relation to the practicalities involved.

Terminally-ill patients are not a homogenous group. It is to be expected that different people will be afflicted with a great many different medical conditions and that their physical ability to participate in the process of assisted dying will be very variable. They might, for instance, be cared for at home rather than in hospital, where some might simply need to be provided with a prescription for drugs, which they could collect and then administer themselves. Here the only assistance they would need would be the provision of a prescription and the dispensing of the drugs. Others, however, might be physically incapable of collecting a prescription from the chemist, even if well enough to be cared for at home. They may also not be able to ingest a drug orally or be too physically debilitated to put the cup to their mouth in order to drink it. Given that a great many terminally-ill people are primarily under the care of voluntary care-givers, it is at this level of application that it becomes apparent that legislation permitting assisted suicide would require precise drafting and meticulous attention to detail if such carers are to be adequately protected. Indeed it seems more likely that a comprehensive code of practice would need to be drafted to cover the practicalities associated with the implementation of a statute permitting assisted dying.

A close examination of some of the provisions of the most recent ADTI Bill (2005) will help to provide a little more detail on the practical implications for carers. For example, clause 8 outlined the protections available for health care professionals and other persons. It specifically referred to 'A physician who assists a qualifying patient to die' (clause 8(1)) and to

a member of a health care team who works in conjunction with a physician who assists a qualifying patient to die (clause 8(2)),

and stipulated that they would 'not be guilty of an offence or in breach of any professional oath or affirmation' (clause 8(4)) by acting under the terms of the legislation. It was, however, silent as to the position of voluntary carers who are highly likely to be involved in the kinds of activities described above. And, on the face of it, if a person who was not a part of the health care team were to assist in the suicide of a person who qualified for assistance under the statute, they would not be protected from prosecution.

A suggested way around this would be to categorise these voluntary carers as part of the health care team, providing that, like other members of the team, they were acting in accordance with the provisions in the legislation and 'in conjunction with a physician' (clause 8(2)). In some ways this would provide a solution, but it would also raise further concerns. What, for example, would be the extent of the obligations of these informal team members? And how would they be accountable for their actions? Clearly, if they overstepped their role in relation to assisting the suicide the ADTI Act, as it would then be, would impose criminal sanctions as for any other member of the team in similar circumstances. But what exactly would be the role of the informal care-giver and how would it be regulated? Also, and perhaps more importantly for the carer, clause 8(5) precludes assistance from any member of the health care team who has grounds to believe

that he will benefit financially or in any other way, except for his proper professional fees or salary, as a result of the death of the patient.

This, surely, will exclude many, if not the majority, of family members from acting in this capacity. Since it is they who are most likely to be visiting the chemist, mixing up and presenting the medication to the patient, especially where the patient is not in hospital, this is not a workable solution. As it stands, therefore, for the voluntary carer the proposed legislation adds little, leaving them almost as exposed to prosecution as they currently are.

IV. CONCLUSION

Much of the debate about assisted suicide has centred on whether or not it should be permitted, and if so, how the law might be reformed to facilitate it while protecting the interests of those who might seek to use it. High levels of public support are consistently recorded in opinion polls with a recent survey indicating that 80 per cent of the public support assisted dying for the terminally ill, despite the fact that assisted suicide is not lawful (Paterson, 2007; *The Telegraph*, January 24 2007). In the absence of permissive legal reform, however, those who would seek assisted dying seem to have few options. Some soldier on until nature takes its course. Some decide to take their own lives, with varying degrees of success, and an increasing number are travelling abroad to jurisdictions that can offer assisted dying. All of these options have the potential to expose carers to criminal sanction if they assist a person to commit suicide. Up-to-date statistics are difficult to obtain, as cases frequently take many months to progress but in 2003 it was reported that '38 cases of aiding and abetting a suicide were presented at magistrates' courts in the period 1990–2001' (VES, 2003: 14). More than three-quarters of these resulted in conviction.

Aiding and abetting, counselling and procuring the suicide of another is prohibited by the Suicide Act 1961 in order to protect the vulnerable from harm, but it is questionable whether justice is served by prosecuting those who have apparently acted out of compassion for a loved one (Horder, 1988). The Suicide Act 1961 could be regarded as a compassionate statute. It decriminalised the act of suicide (section 1(1)) and, in recognition of the fact that prosecution may not always be in the public interest, it allows the DPP to exercise discretion over whether to prosecute and permits discretion over sentencing. However, these discretionary provisions are just that—discretionary—so carers who act in contravention of the Act must run the gauntlet of the criminal law before they can discover whether or not compassion will be exercised. Moreover, given the number of convictions reported between 1990 and 2001, it seems plausible that at least some courts are still taking the view expressed by the judge in Beecham's case that '[o]ffences of this nature must in all circumstances be met with a term of imprisonment' (Horder, 1988: 309).

Potentially a provision such as the ADTI Bill tabled in 2005 would have helped Diane Pretty and Mrs Z by enabling their doctors to assist them to commit suicide, had it been enacted in time. It is unlikely that it would

72   *Hazel Biggs*

have altered the position of Jill Anderson, since she was not charged under the Suicide Act 1961. Arguably, however, as currently envisaged, such an Act would also offer little additional protection to voluntary carers generally, as they would seem to be excluded from its scope, although it seems probable that the DPP would exercise the available discretion and decline to prosecute if the other requirements for assisted dying had been satisfied. What carers require most of all in these situations is legal certainty. This will not be provided by trying to manipulate existing legal concepts such as the duty of care so that they can be moulded around emergent social problems like assisted dying. Instead it is necessary to recognise that assisted dying is fast becoming a social need, and to fashion an appropriate criminal law response. Perhaps the best way to achieve this would be through the implementation of new legislation like the ADTI Bill to introduce formal procedures permitting assisted dying, combined with the development of new principles of justification that would provide a defence in recognition of compassionate actions taken in pursuance of assisted dying. In this way, benevolent conduct could be recognised and absolved from responsibility (Ashworth, 1989: 437), but without such reform carers will continue to be outlawed.

BIBLIOGRAPHY

Ashworth, A (1989) 'The scope of criminal liability for omissions' 105 *Law Quarterly Review* 424–458.
Baldock, J and Ungerson, C (1994) *Becoming consumers of community care: households within the mixed economy*. (York, Joseph Rowntree Foundation).
BBC (2002) Breakfast with Frost interview: Richard Stein, Ms B's lawyer and Brian Pretty, 24 March 2002.
BBC News (10 May 2005) 'Widow's 'no regrets' over death' http://news.bbc.co.uk/1/hi/england/north_yorkshire/4534857.stm (last visited 3 February 2007).
BBC News (2006a) 'Man freed after helping wife die' Friday 1 September 2006 http://news.bbc.co.uk/1/hi/england/humber/5305964.stm (last visited 29 January 2007).
BBC News (2006b) 'Assisted suicide man walks free' 19 October 2006 http://news.bbc.co.uk/1/hi/england/southern_counties/6065836.stm (last visited 29 January 2007).
Biggs H, and Mackenzie, R (2006) 'End of life decision-making, policy and the criminal justice system: Untrained Carers Assuming Responsibility [UCARes] and their uncertain legal liabilities'2 *Genomics, Society and Policy* 118–128.
Brook, C (2006) 'Mercy for husband who killed Alzheimer's wife neglected by hospital' *Daily Mail* April 27 2006, 29.
Carers UK (2006) *Carers UK Welcomes White Paper* (London, Carers UK).
Commission for Social Care Inspection (2005) *The State Of Social Care In England 2004–05* (London, Commission for Social Care Inspection).
Dworkin, R (1993) *Life's dominion* (London, Harper-Collins).

Dyer, C (2002) Pretty's legal battle for dignity in death. *The Guardian* May 13 2002, 3.

Firth, M (2005) 'Man who killed terminally ill wife "as act of love" is spared jail' *The Independent* September 3 2005, 6.

Glazebrook, P (1960) 'Criminal omissions: the duty requirement in offences against the person' 56 *Law Quarterly Review* 386–411.

Greenhill, S (2006) 'Spared jail, the husband who killed his wife to end her suffering' November 4 2006 *Daily Mail*, 23.

Hirst, M (2005) 'Carer distress: a prospective, population-based study' 61 *Social Science and Medicine* 697–708.

Horder, J (1988) 'Some reflections on Beecham's case' 52 *Journal of Criminal Law* 309–316.

House of Commons Health Committee (2004) *Elder Abuse: Second Report of Session 2003–04* (HC 111–1) (London, The Stationary Office).

Illich, I (1975) *Medical nemesis: The exploration of health* (Delhi, Rupa).

Norrie, A (2001) *Crime reason and history: a critical introduction to criminal law* (Cambridge, Cambridge University Press).

Paterson, S (2007) '80% Favour mercy killing by doctor' January 24 2007 *The Herald*: http://www.theherald.co.uk/news/news/display.var.1142176.0.0.php.

Stenager, EN and Stenager, E (2000) 'Physical illness and suicidal behaviour' in K Hawthorn and K Van Heeringen (eds), *The international book of suicide and attempted suicide* (Chichester, Wiley) 405–420.

The Telegraph (editorial) 'Euthanasia' (January 24 2007), http://www.telegraph.co.uk/news/main.jhtml?xml=/news/2007/01/24/nclass424.xml.

Tur, R (2003) 'Legislative technique and human rights: the sad case of assisted suicide' [2003] *Criminal Law Review* 3–12.

Ungerson, C (1987) *Policy is personal: sex, gender and informal care* (London, Tavistock Press[?]).

VES (2003) *The quality of mercy* (London, VES).

Williams, G (1983) *Textbook of criminal law*, 2nd edn (London, Stevens).

—— (1987) 'What should the code do about omissions?' 7 *Legal Studies* 92–118.

Legislation

Assisted Dying for the Terminally Ill Bill.
Mental Capacity Act 2005.
Suicide Act 1961.

5

Is There a Human Right to Die?

ANTJE DU BOIS-PEDAIN

I. INTRODUCTION

THE LAW REGULATES the consequences of death with confidence. Dying, by contrast, seems not so much a legal matter as a personal, even intimate, experience, affected by bodily conditions, human relationships and social and medical practices. Those who think that people ought to be able to die differently, and particularly that one should have a decisive say in when, how, where and with whose help one dies, increasingly point to human rights in support of their claims. Human rights arguments are brought into play in these debates both defensively, as a demand for keeping the state from prying into the death chamber over dying people's bedsides, and proactively, as a claim for the creation of structures that enable people to die as they choose. In this chapter, I provide an overview of the rights and freedoms claimed by those who want to exercise greater control over their own deaths. I argue that while human rights law does indeed constrain the state in important ways in its regulation of dying, it is unhelpful to conceptualise these distinct legal entitlements as aspects of an overarching 'right to die'.

The structure of my argument is as follows. In the main part of this chapter, I break the alleged 'right to die' down into different and distinct components: non-interference by the state when a mentally competent individual decides to bring about his or her own death then and there, including with the help of others; the power to regulate prospectively, and with binding legal effects on others, matters that impact directly on the time and manner of one's own death (for instance by means of advance treatment refusals); and other 'enabling' measures, such as lasting powers of attorney and the like. I draw on examples from different jurisdictions to develop a realistic appreciation of the manifold ways in which human rights law impacts on the dying. In conclusion, I consider the difficulties involved in framing concerns to ensure humane dying in terms of a 'right to die', and suggest that the legal debate benefits from its current re-orientation towards a right to die with dignity.

But before I begin, I must put in place a reminder that is in some ways also a disclaimer. This is a chapter about the *legal* rights people have in respect of their own death. I am not concerned with the *philosophical* question of whether people have a 'right to die' (and I put to one side the *political* question of whether rights-talk and rights-based claims offer helpful or unhelpful focal concepts around which to structure the debate over the legal regulation of dying) (see further Lewis, 2001: especially 69–98). While philosophy can tell us what rights people should have if we want to order our communal life justly and fairly, it cannot make us *have* those rights. In order to have rights, there must be some authoritative setting that brings them into existence *as law*. An enforceable right must have a legal source. (I use the term 'human right' for rights enshrined in an international legal instrument that aims to create—or 'recognise'—rights that all people enjoy by virtue of their being human, and I use the term 'fundamental right' for rights contained in the constitution of an independent state).

It follows from the legal nature of rights that rights-claims are inevitably contingent propositions with clear temporal and spatial boundaries. It makes no sense to ask, from a legal perspective, the general question of whether 'people have a right to die as they wish'. One has to tie the question to a particular time and place. Legal debates of the 'right to die' are thus naturally structured around the sources of law in a particular jurisdiction. The arguments made do not always transfer easily or travel well. For instance, legal discussion of the 'right to die' in the United States focuses on the US constitution, where the 'Equal Protection Clause' and the 'Due Process Clause' compete as possible sources of a 'right to die' (eg compare *Vacco v Quill*[1] with *Washington v Glucksberg*[2] and see generally Meisel and Cerminara, 2004). While this is an appropriate way of formulating the legal issue that arises under US constitutional law, it cannot be matched with a parallel argument under the European Convention on Human Rights (ECHR). In the latter context, a 'right to die' may either arise under the right to privacy (Article 8) 'pure and simple' or under Article 8, read in conjunction with the right to non-discrimination (Article 14). It cannot arise 'either under Article 8 or under Article 14' (see *Pretty v United Kingdom*[3]).

Legal rights establish commitments that a community has already made, with binding effect. Herein lie both their specific value and their specific limitations. The binding effect of rights gives power to the right-holder. This is of crucial importance in the doctor-patient relationship, which—even in its ideal case where it is founded on trust—is *also* a power relation in which

---

[1] *Vacco v Quill* 521 US 793, 799 (1997).
[2] *Washington v Glucksberg* 521 US 702, 735 (1997).
[3] *Pretty v United Kingdom* [2002] 35 EHRR 1.

patients need to be protected from egregious violations of their physical integrity and moral autonomy (see Jackson, chapter three this volume). At the same time, the susceptibility of all law to change through appropriate legislative mechanisms means that commitments enshrined in law are not in any way 'eternal'. The denomination of certain legal rights as 'human' or 'fundamental' cannot displace their essential dependency on continuing authoritative stipulation.

II. BREAKING DOWN THE RIGHT TO DIE

When people claim a 'right to die' as an existing legal right, they usually want to assert the legal validity of one or more of a variety of distinct legal propositions. The first cluster of propositions concerns what can loosely be termed 'rights to non-interference in choices concerning dying and death'. I start with propositions concerning the right to refuse life-saving treatment, the validity of advance treatment refusals, the right to commit or attempt to commit suicide and the right to receive assistance in suicide. The latter issue leads to more general considerations of rights to assistance that a dying person might wish to claim. This, in turn, connects the discussion to the question whether the debate about the right to die has any implications for the rights of permanently incompetent persons who are incapable of personal choices in respect of their dying and death.

A. The Right to Refuse Life-saving Treatment

In almost every jurisdiction where the question has arisen, the courts have accepted that competent adult patients have the right to refuse further live-saving or life-sustaining medical treatment, even if the foreseen and desired consequence of the exercise of that right is death. In the United States, this was held in *Cruzan v Director, Missouri Department of Health*[4]; in England and Wales, this was established in *B v An NHS Hospital Trust*[5]; and in Germany, this was decided in *BGH NJW 1988, 1532*[6]. Somewhat more restrictive is the position in France, for which see *Pech*[7] and *Garnier*[8] (now superseded by Article 16-3 of the *Code civil* as amended; see further Lewis, 2006) and in Israel (see the Patient's Rights Act 1996 and Gross, 2005). Some differences remain with regard to the extent to which such a right is recognised in respect

---

[4] *Cruzan v. Director, Missouri Department of Health* 497 US 261, 278 (1990).
[5] *B v An NHS Hospital Trust* [2002] 1 FLR 1090 (Fam).
[6] *BGH NJW 1988, 1532* (Bundesgerichtshof).
[7] *Pech*, Conseil National de l'Ordre des Médicins, Section Disciplinaire, 23 avril 1980; reversed Conseil d'État, 6 mars 1981, (1981) Rec. des Décisions du Conseil d'État 133.
[8] *Garnier*, Conseil d'État, 29 juillet 1994, no 146.978.

of competent minors, and in relation to the question whether or not individual medical staff members are entitled to exercise a 'conscientious objection' against participating in treatment withdrawals which cause death (see for England and Wales *B v An NHS Hospital Trust* and for Germany, *BGH NJW 2005, 2385*[9]). The legal consequences of a violation of the right—civil or criminal—also differ. But the core guarantee is there.

That core of clarity notwithstanding, many issues concerning the practical exercise of the right to refuse live-saving treatment remain difficult and uncertain. Can relatives who, at the behest of the patient, switch off a life-sustaining machine, when prosecuted, rely on the fact that the patient chose this route to exercise his or her right to refuse further treatment? (see *LG Ravensburg MedR 1987, 196*,[10] discussed in Roxin, 1987). Or is the only way to exercise the right against unresponsive medical staff through a court order? Can patients insist that they want to leave hospital and die at home, and hence refuse not so much any possible treatment as any treatment that requires their continued hospitalisation? Can relatives be stopped from taking patients home, in adherence to their wish, if this would cause a predictable health crisis for the patient, which would be difficult to manage? Or do patients, conversely, even have a right to be assisted by medical staff to return home so that they can die there? These questions are not answered by merely pointing to the recognised absolute right of the competent adult patient to refuse any treatment he or she does not wish to receive. They require further legal analysis and discussion in the light of the particular facts of each case. What can be said in general terms, however, is that prima facie all these entitlements can arguably be based on the right to refuse unwanted treatment, if in the circumstances they are necessary to enable the patient to exercise this right without undue burdens or delay.

B. The Right to Refuse Life-saving Treatments in Advance

A related aspect concerns advance treatment refusals, variously referred to as 'living wills', 'advance decisions' or 'advance directives'. These are decisions to refuse certain types of treatment, which are made by a competent patient in anticipation of a future loss of competence. The time at which the treatment refusal is exercised is not concurrent with the time at which the refusal is expressed. The withholding or withdrawing of treatment in accordance with the advance decision will, if at all, only occur at a later stage when the patient can no longer be consulted about it.

The law concerning advance treatment refusals has recently been put on a statutory footing in England and Wales, where the power to make

---

[9] *BGH NJW 2005, 2385* (Bundesgerichtshof).
[10] *LG Ravensburg MedR 1987, 196* (Landgericht Ravensburg).

such decisions (of a binding nature for medical staff) has been restricted to competent adult patients. Thus, 'competent minors' are excluded from the right to put a legally-binding living will in place, although the definition of 'competence' for adults follows the general test for competence in medical decision-making which, in theory, mature minors can also meet (Mental Capacity Act 2005, sections 24–26). In Germany, advance treatment refusals in anticipation of a future loss of competence are seen simply as part and parcel of the patient's right to refuse treatment: legally binding expressions of the patient's will that restrict what doctors may do to them, without any need for separate statutory authority (see Bottke, 1995; Sternberg-Lieben, 1985; and Enquete-Kommission Ethik und Recht der modernen Medizin, 2004). The difficulty with the latter position is that there is a clear difference between, on the one hand, 'actual' or 'concurrent' treatment refusals (where the patient faces the consequences of his or her refusal in the immediate treatment situation) and, on the other hand, 'advance' refusals which take effect only in a future treatment context (when by definition 'the person making the refusal' can no longer be 'reached'). The problem is not so much that the advance decision may not be clear. As with wills and last testaments, possible uncertainties can be resolved in the process of interpretation, either by adopting a reading that is 'biased' towards the preservation of life or through a reading which is neutral towards life's preservation (see Michalowski, 2005). The problem is that even if an advance decision is clear and unambiguous, there is potential for real uncertainty about whether the balance of reasons points towards honouring the advance decision or not. Such uncertainty arises when the same individual who deemed certain treatments unacceptable when he or she was competent because he or she 'did not want to live like that', now (though incompetent) appears quite happy to receive the treatment and 'live like that' (see further Dworkin, 1993: 218–37). Should we in such a case really prioritise the interests of the autonomous person they once were over those of the non-autonomous person they are now? If we are to do that, we need a justification that goes beyond a counterfactual equation of the interests of the non-autonomous person they are now with the interests of the autonomous person they used to be.

Ronald Dworkin approaches this task by drawing a distinction between 'critical' and 'experiential' interests (Dworkin, 1993: 201–8). Experiential interests are interests we have in experiences we enjoy. We have an interest in doing things which give us pleasure and in avoiding things which give us pain. We judge the former activities as worthwhile doing because of the satisfaction involved in doing them. This is what gives them value. Some of these activities and experiences can be flitting and momentary: the pleasure of watching a tennis game on TV or a sunset. Others may require sustained application of effort: the writing of a book or the making of a dress. But even in respect of the latter, the enjoyment we get from them (perhaps overall or on balance) is what gives us an 'experiential interest' in engaging in the activity. However, there are also other interests, interests which (as Dworkin, 1993: 202 puts it) 'represent critical judgments rather than just experiential preferences'. Dworkin calls these interests 'critical interests'. They are interests in something we have judged as morally good and worth striving for, and which we strive for because we have judged it as morally good independent of our striving. The type of work we do, ideally, reflects both an experiential interest and a critical interest. On balance, we enjoy what we do, and we have also judged our occupation as an intrinsically worthwhile thing to do; worthwhile irrespective of the pleasure it gives us. Our specific critical interests are instances of an overarching critical interest in having our life go well according to our set of considered value-judgements.

The notion of a 'critical interest' enables Dworkin to identify a type of interest which persists even after a person has lost all experiential interests. A person in an irreversible coma no longer has experiential interests, but if this person during their conscious life formed a conception of a good life in the light of their considered value judgements, and thus developed 'critical interests', these interests can survive a complete loss of experiential interests. A person who is beyond experiencing their own death may thus have a present 'critical interest' in having what they would have considered a good or fitting death (Dworkin, 1993: 208–13).

This helps us to see why a genuine moral dilemma can arise in some situations where we are confronted with the question whether or not to honour an advance treatment refusal: a patient's critical and experiential interests may diverge. The advance refusal represents the critical interest this patient has in controlling the manner of her death. The very fact that the patient took the trouble to put an advance decision in place is evidence of the fact that she judged this matter an important aspect of making sure that her end would be in accordance with key value judgements she had made about a good life and a good death. This critical interest does not evaporate with the loss of the competence which is required to form critical interests. But if the now incompetent patient can still enjoy some activities and experiences, she now has experiential interests in having life with such experiences continue that contradict her critical interest in having the trajectory of her life over time reflect her considered value-judgements, as encapsulated in the advance treatment refusal (Dworkin, 1993: 218–37).

I do not at this point want to enter the philosophical debate of which interest ought to prevail. I merely want to draw attention to the fact that some legal systems are more sensitive than others to the fact that advance treatment refusals raise moral questions which treatment refusals made concurrent with their execution do not raise. As a matter of law, this is reflected in the diverging positions we often find within the same jurisdiction in respect of actual and advance treatment refusals. Legal systems which recognise a fundamental human right to self-determination and bodily integrity all agree that this right is violated when a competent adult patient's *actual* or *concurrent* treatment refusal is not adhered to. By contrast, they disagree about the extent to which *advance* treatment refusals should be accorded binding legal force (see, eg Antoine, 2004). The former case concerns the core exercise of a liberty right, whereas the latter falls into its penumbral regions where different solutions can justifiably be reached.

C. The Right to Appoint a Proxy Decision-maker

Differences between legal systems also persist in respect of the question whether the right to appoint a proxy decision-maker is one possible exercise of the patient's right to self-determination, and what follows from that for the powers of the proxy. When appointing a proxy decision-maker, the patient effectively says: 'I want *this person* to make the decision for me'. The reason the patient wants *this person* to be the proxy is that the patient's present self is happy to abide by the judgements the proxy will make about what is to happen to the patient's future incompetent self. The patient wants the proxy to have the power to decide 'what the proxy thinks is best', which is not necessarily identical with what is (in some objectified, generalised sense) in the 'best interests' of the patient. The patient's aim in appointing the proxy is that the proxy will decide matters concerning the patient, just like the proxy decides matters concerning herself: as she sees fit. The intention is to ride with the views and judgements of the proxy.

If this is the aim behind the patient's appointment or nomination of a proxy decision-maker—and I will assume for the purposes of this discussion that it is—then some people might argue that the patient bumps up against an absolute logical barrier in trying to give this kind of power to the proxy. To attempt to put the proxy into a position where the proxy will decide for me as he or she thinks fit, with other people having no more right to question the proxy's decision than they would have to question mine is, so the argument might run, like trying to sell one's future incompetent self into slavery, and that is something that one's present competent self cannot do. Our liberty rights do not reach far enough to empower us to destroy our future liberty (see Mill, [1859] 1956: 173). But the argument (even if it works for 'voluntary' slavery, which I am not entirely convinced it does) certainly does not work against proxy appointments, because the two situations are non-analogous. In the slavery example, the agent is indeed attempting to create a situation where (though he would, as a matter of fact, still be capable of making decisions for himself) this capacity will no longer be recognised in law. In the proxy example, by contrast, a competent individual strives to provide for a possible future situation where he will have lost the mental ability to determine the course of his life. One may well think that it is part of our right to self-determination that, while we still have decision-making capacity, we can provide in the best way we can for a future state of affairs in which we have lost that capacity. This gives us *more* influence over what will happen to us over the course of our lives than the contrary position, which simply prevents us from providing for our non-autonomous future existence in this way. Hence, empowering people to appoint proxy decision-makers engages their right to self-determination. Restrictions on what the appointed proxy may decide are therefore much harder to justify than it appears at first sight. They are not merely restrictions on the proxy. Instead, they restrict what the right-holder of the right to individual self-determination can do. Arguably, the Mental Capacity Act 2005 is too restrictive, in that it effectively ties proxy decision-makers appointed by the patient down to decisions that any 'best interest' analysis would reach (see Mental Capacity Act 2005, section 9(4)).

D. The Right to Commit/Attempt to Commit Suicide

A different and even more contentious set of questions surrounds attempted and assisted suicide. If we define suicide as death resulting from a person's wilful self-destruction that involves introducing a new agent of death (see Otlowski, 1997: chapter 2), the question arises whether, and against whom, individuals can assert a right to non-interference with this process. The first aspect of this right might be a right 'not to be saved' when a suicide attempt is discovered. Assuming that the person who is in the process of committing suicide has not put any advance decisions in place as regards the treatment required to save her life, is it possible to argue that this person has 'a right not to be saved' that prevents others (chance bystanders, relatives and friends, medical practitioners) from intervening?

As a matter of existing law, the answer in all legal systems I am familiar with is 'No'. Anybody discovering someone, in the standard attempted suicide situation, has by law a *right* to intervene. What these legal systems differ in is the extent to which they also impose a *duty* to intervene on all or some of the individuals mentioned. At the same time, none of these systems at present criminalises the person who attempts to kill herself. In some jurisdictions (for instance in Britain), the decriminalisation of suicide appears to be based both on the pragmatic consideration that individuals desperate enough to attempt to take their own life are unlikely to be effectively deterred from doing so by a legal prohibition, and on concerns that such persons may not be fit subjects for a criminal trial in the same way that children are not. In other legal systems (such as Germany), however, the decriminalisation of suicide reflects a legal judgement that choosing to kill oneself is one possible exercise of a person's right to self-determination that would be unjustifiably restricted by criminalising the right-holder for a suicide attempt. In the latter case, giving third parties the right to intervene in a suicide attempt appears prima facie to conflict with the right of the individual to take his own life. Can this apparent contradiction be disentangled?

It can be disentangled, in my view, if one bears in mind that limitations to the exercise of our liberties can come in 'from the side'—because the possible interference with our liberty does not, in the circumstances, provide a good enough reason to stop the other person from doing what she is doing. When a person 'happens upon' another who is engaged in an attempt to commit suicide, she is faced with a conflict between what she sees as her moral duty (as a medical professional, next-of-kin, friend, guardian, or mere compassionate 'bystander and neighbour') to try and save the person concerned, and her respect for the other person's choice (see Biggs, chapter four this volume). She must not only 'in the abstract' decide which value should prevail over the other—whether she should give priority to 'saving a life' or to 'respecting another's personal choice'. She may also be uncertain about whether she is indeed confronted with another person's considered personal choice. If the suicide attempt is not motivated by such a choice, the attempt to save the person's life does not engage (let alone violate) that person's liberty rights. The fact that in this situation—where moral duty appears to pull the agent either way—the state does not prohibit the well-meaning person from trying to save the person attempting suicide is not a 'restriction' on that person's right to determine the course of her life. It is, instead, a recognition of the fact that the would-be saviour does *not act wrongly* when she tries to help in a situation where there is a reasonable possibility that the suicide candidate is simply a person in need, and not a thwarted sage. There would be no moral justification for criminalising someone who is trying to save another's life in circumstances where it is uncertain whether the other person has competently and deliberately chosen to bring about her own death. This is why, in the standard suicide case, the interests of the saviour must prevail over the interest of the saved. To put it bluntly: when we try to kill ourselves, we have to live with the risk that a well-meaning person will try to save us, not believing that we really want to die. We cannot demand that the state criminalise those who try to save us.

The standard suicide situation—where there is room for genuine uncertainty about whether the person who is trying to kill herself has indeed arrived at a considered decision to die—is different from a case in which a patient has made an advance decision to refuse certain types of life-saving treatments. If the advance decision is clear and unambiguous, we can be reasonably certain that at least at the time when the decision was reached, the person concerned made a deliberate choice, which rationally expressed his or her long-term preferences. Of course, it is possible for a discrepancy to exist between the preference expressed in the advance decision, and what appears to be the now incompetent patient's current best interest. But it is at least possible to argue coherently, by drawing on Dworkin's notion of critical interests, that the patient also has a present interest in having his advance decision complied with, and that this interest is strong enough to allow us to prefer it over what might look like conflicting interests. If, in light of this fact, the law imposes a *duty* on third parties *not to* 'save' this individual in ways that conflict with a competently made advance treatment refusal, this does not impose an unacceptable burden on those forced to comply with the advance directive. Neither is it unacceptable for some form of legal liability to be imposed for the breach of an advance directive. Under German law, criminal liability for battery may well arise (Sternberg-Lieben, 1985). The Mental Capacity Act 2005, in section 26(2) and (3), creates explicit exemptions from liability for (a) the continuation of treatment incompatible with an advance decision, unless the decision-maker knew that the decision was valid and applicable to the treatment, and (b) the discontinuation of treatment based on a reasonable belief in the existence of a valid and applicable treatment refusal.

My analysis treats the 'right to commit/attempt suicide' as a 'protected liberty' rather than as a claim-right. This best reflects its legal status in a number of legal systems where the 'right to commit/attempt suicide' is seen as rooted in a fundamental right. That a person has a legal liberty means that this person is under *no duty* towards others *not to act* in the way that the liberty allows her to act. It does *not* mean that others have a duty to refrain from all interference with the exercise of the liberty by the right-holder (Hohfeld, 1923). A simple legal liberty is a freedom granted by statute or customary law. It can be restrained or taken away by legislation. However, if the exercise of a particular legal liberty at the same time engages a fundamental or human right of the right-holder, this legal liberty amounts to a protected liberty (see Alexy, 1996: 187–210; and Alexy, 2002). What this means is that legislation restricting the liberty must pass muster as a legitimate limitation of the fundamental right which is engaged by the exercise of the liberty.

The fundamental right engaged when a person tries to commit suicide is the right which protects personal autonomy, and generally the interest in living life according to one's personal choices, convictions and preferences. Different legal systems protect this interest under differently named rights. Within the framework of the ECHR, this interest is protected not by Article 2, the right to life, but by Article 8, the right to respect for one's private life (for details see *Pretty v United Kingdom*[11] and Pedain, 2003). I will address the question what limitations this right allows for when discussing a possible right to receive assistance in suicide. In the present context, I merely want to point out that to criminalise the person who attempts to commit suicide,

---

[11] *Pretty v United Kingdom* (2002) 35 EHRR 1.

with a view to scaring vulnerable persons away from suicide attempts, would go beyond the scope of permissible limitations. Notwithstanding the fact that the objective of protecting vulnerable persons against themselves may be a legitimate one, it is clearly counter-productive to hang the threat of prosecution over every unsuccessful attempt to commit suicide. It is also difficult to justify, in general terms, the criminalisation of someone who is merely trying to harm himself. The very point of our liberty to take our own life away is that we owe our life to no one; no other person has the right to demand of us that we stay alive. The criminalisation of the person who attempts to take her own life strikes at the very heart of this liberty by, in effect, creating a legal duty to stay alive. This would be unjustifiable.

A more difficult problem is posed by the tension between, on the one hand, the recognition of a right to attempt suicide, and, on the other hand, the imposition of a *duty* on others to take steps to save the person attempting to commit suicide. There are, in my view, cases where a *duty* to save someone who is trying to commit suicide is incompatible with the legal recognition of a right to attempt suicide. A legal order which insists that we *must* interfere with what we recognise or believe to be a considered choice by a competent person to take her own life, is inherently contradictory. If we accept that there are indeed cases where the person trying to commit suicide acts on the basis of a considered personal choice that ought to be respected as an exercise of her fundamental right to self-determination, the contradiction can only be resolved by releasing third parties from any *duty* to save that person. I also agree with Biggs (chapter four this volume) that it is, in principle, inappropriate to hold guardians and others legally liable for their non-intervention in a suicide attempt in cases where their decision not to help is motivated by an honest belief that the person who attempts suicide has made a considered choice to take her own life that it is not for them to disrespect.

E. The Right to be Helped to Commit Suicide

When considering the question whether people who want to commit suicide also have a right to draw on the assistance of willing others, we reach an intersection between rights to non-interference and rights to assistance. In one version of the argument, the right to receive 'assistance in suicide' amounts to a positive 'right to assistance', which falls into a different legal category from the 'negative' right not to be prevented from committing suicide unaided. In another version of the argument, the right to receive assistance in suicide, including assistance from one's doctor, is merely an emanation of the right not to be prevented from taking one's own life. If I can decide for myself whether or not to take my own life, then I can also insist that willing others be allowed to help me in exercising my choice to die. These different ways of thinking about the 'right to be helped to commit suicide' are evident in the regulation of assisted suicide in different European jurisdictions.

In Germany, assistance in suicide is not a criminal act. By contrast, killing another person at his or her request is prohibited as a special, less serious form of homicide (under section 216 of the German Penal Code, the StGB), and mercy killings in the absence of any request by the victim are seen as standard homicide offences (under section 212 of the StGB). The absence of criminal liability for a person who assists the suicide of another does not mean that the law approves of such assistance, or that helping another person to kill herself is seen as morally right. It simply reflects the fact that killing oneself is not a criminal wrong, and hence (by extension) helping another person to kill herself—where that person remains fully responsible for the outcome—does not engage the helper in a wrongful endeavour either (see Schreiber, 2006; and Neumann and Salinger, 2006).

Switzerland, likewise, does not criminalise people who assist others to commit suicide, provided the helper acts unselfishly (section 115 of the Swiss Criminal Code). In creating liability for those who assist another person's suicide from selfish motives, Swiss law is in fact stricter than German law. At first sight it is therefore surprising that Switzerland, rather than Germany, has become home to a private institution which takes the opportunity to provide others with assistance in dying to its logical conclusion: the non-profit organisation 'Dignitas', whose purpose it is to help its members to die a chosen death. But on reflection, perhaps we should not be surprised. By limiting criminal liability to those who assist another person's suicide from selfish motives, the Swiss legislator can be seen to have taken a clear position that 'assisting suicide is only morally wrong if done for selfish reasons'. Swiss law thereby gives clearer guidance than the German law on when assisted suicide is considered morally right, and when it is considered morally wrong. Unlike German law, which sends mixed signals at best, Swiss law does not 'reserve the right' to turn around and hold the people who assist another's suicide criminally liable for 'failing to try to save them'.

England persists in the criminalisation of assistance in suicide (Suicide Act 1961, section 2(1))—a criminalisation that was accepted as a permissible limitation of the right to private life by the European Court of Human Rights (*Pretty v United Kingdom*[12]). At the other end of the scale, Belgium and The Netherlands have de-criminalised physician-assisted dying in the form of active voluntary euthanasia (see Jackson, chapter three this volume). A similar variety of legal solutions can be found in different United States jurisdictions (see Meisel and Cerminara, 2004). What this suggests is that everywhere, the human and fundamental rights relied on in the legal debate are too indeterminate to be prescriptive of a particular outcome.

---

[12] *Pretty v United Kingdom* (2002) 35 EHRR 1.

They require of legislators that they pay attention to the fact that the right to autonomy/self-determination is engaged by the criminalisation of assisted suicide and euthanasia, and that this right calls upon them to give as much freedom to the individual as they think is consistent with the need to protect vulnerable persons. But the actual legislative outcome varies, in line with the legislature's margin of appreciation, which all human rights instruments accept. Extensive parliamentary debate in England met Lord Joffe's Assisted Dying for the Terminally Ill Bill (2003, reintroduced, 2004). The Bill was defeated, but no doubt other attempts will be made to reform the law (Branthwaite, 2005; and George, Finlay and Jeffrey, 2005).

F. A Right to Die the Least Worst Death?

What looms over the debate of the right to assistance in suicide is a concern that people might want to claim a right to be killed by their doctors. We should be able by now to see that such concerns are unfounded. No law can impose on one person a *duty to actively kill* another person: such a law would violate the personal freedoms of those who would be forced to kill other human beings.

But it is worth considering to what extent different legal systems may in fact be recognising a right to die 'the least painful death available', which kicks in when the dying process has begun. Morally, I think we recognise such a right—it underlies the practice of terminal sedation, as well as many other medical choices that alleviate suffering but hasten death. Legally, we hesitate to say that these practices are accepted because people have a right to die the least-worst death. But, indirectly, the legal defence of the wide-spread practice of terminal sedation must be based on the legal recognition of precisely such a right. It is generally accepted that a doctor who does an act that shortens his patient's life, knowing that this will happen, would be guilty of murder if his actions were not justified. Such a justification can only arise from a legal duty to provide the patient with pain-relief even if that step hastens the patient's death. This is so because, while doctors have both the right and the duty to treat their patients appropriately, their right to treat their patients only exists within the confines of other laws which may set limits on permissible treatments. It cannot justify doing something as part of the treatment that is forbidden by law. Only a legal *duty* can form the basis of doing something that would (in the absence of this duty) violate the law. So it must be the case that it is a doctor's *duty* to enable their patients to die the least-worst death that overrides the legal prohibition against killing in cases of terminal sedation.

The Netherlands and Belgium have taken the right to the least-worst death even further by empowering doctors to end, in appropriate circumstances, a patient's life. As Jackson (chapter three this volume) rightly reminds us, this extraordinary power given to doctors requires extraordinary trust in their personal integrity, and in the soundness of their medical judgement. But this should not stop us from recognising that this power, where it is given to doctors, is given to them not in their own interest, in order to grant them rights, but in an attempt to give the strongest possible legal recognition to the patient's right to the least-worst death.

Of course this discussion does not even begin to exhaust the specific rights which people may want to claim in respect of their own death, and/or the rights that others may want to claim on their behalf. A line of recent cases (*R v Portsmouth Hospitals NHS Trust, ex parte Glass*[13] and *Portsmouth NHS Trust v Wyatt*[14]) has put the problem of power relations between relatives and medical staff on the table. If medical staff believe that for a particular patient home care would amount to a neglect of his medical needs, whereas his relatives believe that his continued presence in an over-crowded hospital ward is in itself a situation to be avoided at almost all costs, who's judgement on where the patient is better off should prevail? Again, there is no doubt that in an ideal world the issue would not even arise: reasonable doctors would reach agreement with reasonable relatives on the best way forward for the patient. But in the real world, conflict persists and so power becomes an issue. It is not difficult to predict that cases where distressed relatives have become victims of institutional insensitivity and medical bullying will be the driving forces behind the next set of dying-related rights.

III. CONCLUSION

The scattered and somewhat co-incidental protection of aspects of a possible 'right to die' that we find in most jurisdictions is explained by the fact that the law at present does not recognise, as a value or interest worthy of legal protection, the desire we might rationally have to control the time and manner of our own death. To the extent that the law supports propositions which could be construed as aspects of a 'right to die', the rationale behind their acceptance is not the legal recognition of legitimate interests concerning one's own *death*, but the recognition of some *other* interest such as privacy, bodily integrity or self-determination, whose legal recognition has the incidental effect in question. Thus, the right to bodily integrity protects end-of-life choices where a treatment refusal does not merely stop a resented interference with one's physical self, but also speeds up death; and the construction placed on the value of patient autonomy explains our willingness to respect advance refusals of life-saving treatments. Only very recently have legal instruments begun to recognise that to be able to choose

---

[13] *R v Portsmouth Hospitals NHS Trust, ex p Glass* [1999] 2 FLR 905 (Admin).
[14] *Portsmouth NHS Trust v Wyatt* [2004] EWHC 2247 (Fam).

one's own death might be, in and of itself, an important interest worthy of legal protection. But the proper way of formulating a corresponding legal right is a matter of continuing concern.

When the legal debate is framed in terms of a 'right to die', the claimed right is invariably associated with the exercise of an autonomy right. This tends to exclude from the scope of this right those who cannot make a meaningful decision, or form a personal preference, about the manner and time of their own death. Of course, the law's conception of an autonomous choice is much less ambitious than what many philosophical readings of the concept would require. The law's concern is with individual liberty and self-determination, and with what Robert Nozick terms self-ownership (Nozick, 1973). Legal autonomy rights thus also protect the freedom to choose of those who choose unwisely, who lack certain capacities for full understanding, who are affected by irrational fears and beliefs, etc. In order to make a choice that falls within the scope of protection of an autonomy right, only the ability to form preferences and make choices in an every-day practical sense is required. Ambitious philosophical conceptions of autonomy have a place in guiding those of us who desire such guidance to lead morally better, and personally fuller, lives. But they give us no license to enforce morally-wise choices on others, and therefore they have no place in law (see Pabst Battin, 2005; and Spriggs, 2005).

Nevertheless, there are many patients for whom the claimed right to die would be of no consequence, because they do not pass even the law's low autonomy threshold. When the human right claimed is framed in terms not of a right *to die*, but of a right to *die with dignity*, this changes. As a legal concept, dignity is best understood as the space needed to lead life in accordance with one's critical interests. A right to die with dignity may well have implications for the dying process of those who are not, and never (again) will be, competent enough to form a personal preference or make a meaningful decision about their own life. If the debate gets refocused as a debate about a legal right to die with dignity, an argument about the possible right of relatives to be present at the bedside of a dying person becomes an argument not about their right, perhaps as parents to be with their child, but about the dying person's rights in relation to her own death (a right to have 'significant others' present, for instance). The reformulation shifts the focus away from the legitimate interest that some persons (those who are at least minimally choice-competent) have in *controlling* their own death, to giving legal effect to notions and convictions of what is a *good* and a *bad death*.

An attempt to reframe the legal debate as centred around the notion of a good death, a right to die with dignity, is apparent in the separate concurring opinion of Judge Stevens in *Washington v Glucksberg*[15]. The majority opinion in this case insists on distinguishing, as situated in separate liberty

---

[15] *Washington v Glucksberg* 521 US 702, 735 (1997).

rights, the right to refuse even life-saving medical treatment, on the one hand, and the right to commit suicide with the assistance of willing others, on the other. Stevens wants to connect these two dying-related liberty interests under the same concept of a possible liberty interest in hastening death, an interest which may at times not only be legitimate but also entitled to constitutional protection. In this reframing, the possible liberty interest can only be invoked by persons for whom the choice is 'not ... whether to live only how to die'—whether they can still know that or not.

This reframing of the issue seems, to me, a step in the right direction. It focuses our attention on those whose interests we are concerned about when we argue in its favour: people who, as Judge Stevens put it, might conceivably have a liberty interest in hastening their own death. It also gives renewed vigour to arguments that implicate states under the right to be free from torture or other inhuman or degrading treatment or punishment when the law blocks avenues which people might otherwise opt for to secure a less distressing death (Coggon, 2006)—whether the death concerned is the suffocation, from muscle failure, of a mentally aware and competent patient like Diane Pretty, or the slow starvation of an individual without any capacity for consciousness or sensate experience, like Tony Bland (*Airedale NHS Trust v Bland*[16]).

In considering how the law can do right by people who have reached this point in their lives I want to draw on Drucilla Cornell's explanation of why, philosophically, there is a 'right to die'. Cornell reminds us that any dying person, and any person attempting death, places us in an ethical relation towards them.

We do not choose to be 'ethical'—we can do good, we can do bad, but we cannot decide to be in [an] ethical relation. We are always with others and how we are with others is what shapes us, indeed constitutes us, if I may risk the word. The other presents a demand on us and never more powerfully than at the hour of her death ... The social conjecture is that, given our vulnerability, we all need assistance at the moment of our death, yes, but also throughout our experience of dying. We are together in 'our dying' and so let us face that, and have that fated togetherness recognised by the state as a matter of right (Cornell, 2003: 18).

It seems to me that the conviction that the ethical nub of the issue is our moral right to 'die in togetherness with the other' is what underlies many of the attempts to reframe the 'right to die', as an asserted or emerging legal right, in terms of a right to die with dignity. The way in which the state recognises 'that fated togetherness' is by accepting that for a person's dying moments it prescribes at its peril what may for *this* person, *this* death, *this* act of assistance be the morally wrong thing to demand. It does not only reflect persisting political disagreement about the question of what rights

---

[16] *Airedale NHS Trust v Bland* [1993] AC 789 (HL).

people ought to have in relation to their own death if, as I said in the beginning, the law treads carefully when it regulates dying. This carefulness, this 'backing off', is a requirement of justice.

This does not mean that the dying process must remain 'free of law'—indeed, it cannot mean that: one way or the other, legal propositions impinge upon it. But it means that the rights we create to govern this process must, first and foremost, enable people to do what is morally right. These rights cannot precisely map 'the ethical choice' in their prescriptions—there is no one ethical answer that fits all cases. The rights we grant must instead protect and preserve the freedom necessary to enable people to do what is, ethically, required of them. That we all have a moral right to 'die in togetherness with the other' is the starting point for what legal rights should strive to achieve.

BIBLIOGRAPHY

Publications

Alexy, R (1996) *Theorie der Grundrechte*, 3rd edn (Frankfurt am Main, Suhrkamp).
—— (2002) *A theory of constitutional rights* (Oxford, Oxford University Press).
Antoine, J (2004) *Aktive Sterbehilfe in der Grundrechtsordnung* (Berlin, Duncker & Humblot).
Bottke, W (1995) 'Strafrechtliche Probleme am Lebensbeginn und am Lebensende' in Deutsche Sektion der Internationalen Juristen-Kommission (ed), *Lebensverlängerung aus medizinischer, ethischer und rechtlicher Sicht* (Heidelberg, CF Müller Verlag) 35–128.
Branthwaite, MA (2005) 'Time for change' 331 *British Medical Journal* 681–683.
Coggon, J (2006) 'Could the right to die with dignity represent a new right to die in English law?' 14 *Medical Law Review* 219–237.
Cornell, D (2003) *Who bears the right to die?* (Paper presented at the Conference on Sovereignty and the Right to Death, Cleveland-Marshall College of Law, Cleveland, Ohio, 17–18 October 2003).
Dworkin, R (1993) *Life's dominion. An argument about abortion and euthanasia* (London, Harper Collins).
Enquete-Kommission Ethik und Recht der modernen Medizin (2004) *Zwischenbericht Patientenverfügungen vom 13 September 2004* (Berlin, Deutscher Bundestag, BT-Drucks 15/3700).
George, RJD, Finlay, IG and Jeffrey, D (2005) 'Legalised euthanasia will violate the rights of vulnerable patients' 331 *British Medical Journal* 684–685.
Gross, ML (2005) 'Treating competent patients by force: the limits and lessons of Israel's Patient's Rights Act' 31 *Journal of Medical Ethics* 29–34.
Hohfeld, WN (1923) *Fundamental legal conceptions as applied in judicial reasoning* (New Haven, Yale University Press).
Lewis, P (2001) 'Rights discourse and assisted suicide' 27 *American Journal of Law and Medicine* 45–98.

—— (2006) Assisted dying in France. The evolution of assisted dying in France: a third way? 14 *Medical Law Review* 44–72.

Meisel, A and Cerminara, K (2004) *The right to die* (3rd ed) (New York, Aspen Law and Business).

Michalowski, S (2005) 'Advance refusals of life-sustaining medical treatment: the relativity of an absolute right' 68 *Modern Law Review* 958–982.

Mill, JS ([1859] 1956) *On Liberty* (CV Shields (ed) (Indianapolis, Bobbs-Merrill).

Neumann, U and Salinger, F (2006) 'Sterbehilfe zwischen Selbstbestimmung und Fremdbestimmung—Kritische Anmerkungen zur aktuellen Sterbehilfedebatte' 2006 *Höchstrichterliche Rechtsprechung im Strafrecht (HRRS)* 280-288, available at: http://www.hrr-strafrecht.de.

Otlowski, M (1997) *Voluntary euthanasia and the common law* (Oxford, Oxford University Press).

Pabst Battin, M (2005) *Ending life: Ethics and the way we die* (Oxford, Oxford University Press).

Pedain, A (2003) 'The human rights dimension of the Diane Pretty case' 62 *Cambridge Law Journal* 181–206.

Roxin, C (1987) 'Die Sterbehilfe im Spannungsfeld von Suizidteilnahme, erlaubtem Behandlungsabbruch und Tötung auf Verlangen. Zugleich eine Besprechung von BGH NStZ 1987, 356 und LG Ravensburg NStZ 1987, 229' 7 *Neue Zeitschrift für Strafrecht* 345–350.

Schreiber, HL (2006) 'Das ungelöste Problem der Sterbehilfe—zu den neuen Entwürfen und Vorschlägen' 26 *Neue Zeitschrift für Strafrecht* 473–479.

Spriggs, M (2005) *Autonomy and patients' decisions* (Lanham MD, Lexington Books).

Sternberg-Lieben, D (1985) 'Strafbarbeit des Arztes bei Verstoß gegen ein Patienten-Testament' 38 *Neue Juristische Wochenschrift* 2734–2739.

Legislation

Assisted Dying for the Terminally Ill Bill (2003, reintroduced 2004)
Deutsches Strafgesetzbuch (German Penal Code)
European Convention for the Protection of Human Rights and Fundamental Freedoms 1950
Family Law Reform Act 1969
Mental Capacity Act 2005
Patients' Rights Act 1996 (Israel)
Schweizerisches Strafgesetzbuch (Swiss Penal Code)
Suicide Act 1961

Part 2

Rituals and Practices of Death

6

Religious Perspectives on the Afterlife: Origin, Development and Funeral Rituals in the Christian Tradition

PETER C JUPP

I. INTRODUCTION

IT IS OFTEN claimed, as by the anthropologist Bronislaw Malinowski, that religion owes its origin to the fact of death (Malinowski, 1954). The first section of this chapter asserts that this critique applies neither to Judaism nor Christianity. There is, of course, far more to be said for a different claim: that religions in part owe their powers of attraction to their interpretation of death and their offers of post-mortem salvation. This claim would be more true, in the West, of Christianity and Islam but it is not the explicit theme of this chapter.

The main part of the chapter focuses upon the Christian religion, emphasising the centrality of beliefs about the death and resurrection of Jesus. The chapter offers a historical survey of the process whereby issues and tensions in beliefs about life after death were resolved in the interaction between developing doctrines and funeral practices. With reference to Britain, it surveys developments from the Reformation until the present day. It discusses the contemporary 'open market' in beliefs about life after death in a society characterised by secularity, multi-culturalism and consumerism.

II. DEATH AND THE ORIGINS OF RELIGION

Malinowski wrote in 1925: 'of all sources of religion, the supreme and final crisis of life—death—is of the greatest importance' (Malinowski, 1954: 47). The origins of neither Judaism nor Christianity may be so characterised. With Judaism, Bowker and Bremmer have summarised the arguments for holding that beliefs in a satisfying existence beyond death come relatively late in that religion's development (Bowker, 1991; and Bremmer, 2002). In the Jewish Bible there is no explicit reference to the hereafter and the concept only takes shape when Graeco-Roman culture takes hold of the Jewish homeland (Cohn-Sherbok, 2003: 456). By contrast, Christianity was a new religion born out of Jewish stock. It sprang from the life and ministry of Jesus, whom Christians believed to have been raised from the dead by God and whose death they understood as sacrificial. True, Judaism and Christianity are two of the three major Western religions that have survived into the modern era. Islam will be briefly surveyed a little later. A comparative study of how those European religions that failed to survive into the modern era both interpreted death and ritually organised the disposal of the dead would pay dividends but is beyond the scope of this chapter.

If human life is to be lived to the full, the prospects of death and of the process of dying must be incorporated within it. For most of the 20th century, British culture seemed to be influenced by a sort of taboo about death, a taboo partially lifted over the last 20 years by increased media and scholarly attention. One response to the taboo was to assert that death was part of the natural process of life, with no necessary supernatural character. The naturalness of death can be emphasised in a number of ways. For fertility experts like Lord Winston, there would be no need for death at all if it were not for sexual reproduction. Young put it in a sociological context:

death ensures that the multiple connections over time between one generation and another are not too close. If they were, the adaptability of human beings, and all other forms of life, would be greatly weakened (Young, 1988: 255).

For Thomas death is not only natural but as such is part of God's creation and God's gift (Thomas, 1997); he enjoins Christians to interpret death without reliance upon the myth of the Garden of Eden. Since the era of the Higher Criticism of the Bible began, death—as *contra* St Paul (1 Corinthians 15) and John Milton (*Paradise Lost*)—has not been part of the Fall or consequent upon the 'sin of disobedience' by our 'first parents'.

We do not yet know what our earliest ancestors believed. But from archaeological and anthropological study we are learning more about how our forebears faced the fact of death, and organised themselves to comprehend it and learned to contain its social and spiritual impacts. Three observations (at least) emerge. First, there is wide diversity of ways in which communities and individuals have dealt with death and loss. This diversity suggests there is no simple connection between death and the origins of religion. Secondly, while, in any given society, death rituals tend to be stable, they do undergo change and development and the social context of change reveals the connections between mortality and social life. Thirdly, many funeral rituals are as much death-defying or denying as death-accepting (Huntington and Metcalf, 1979; and Bloch and Parry, 1982). Earlier I phrased the connection in this way:

> When someone dies, personal and communal worlds are disturbed, even shaken, in proportion to the social role played by the one who died. If so vital, so necessary a person has died, we say, what is there that can abide? Can nothing last? Individual deaths, therefore, challenge survivors to identify and to articulate the values and relationships that survive death, undefeated. Thus death, in exposing transience, effects an affirmation of what is permanent (Jupp, 2001: 21718).

In addition, whilst there will always have been a few who believed that nothing survives death, the vast majority of our ancestors believed that something survived death, that some trace remained. In conversation with Piers Vitebsky, shortly after the publication of his *Dialogues with the dead* (Vitebsky, 1993), I commented that Protestants do not pray for the dead. He responded, 'Then you are a minority among the world's religions'. For the majority of the world's populations, the dead not only have a life, but exercise an agency, a (revived) aspect of contemporary British life recently investigated by Hallam *et alii* (Hallam, Hockey and Howarth, 1999). While funerary rituals place the dead at a distance, they also leave room for interaction: in particular, constraining malevolence and providing channels for benevolence. The history of the Reformation in Britain shows how imposed orthodoxies can cause sub-cultural heterodoxies to flourish in, for example, controversies about witchcraft (Thomas, 1973) and disputes over the existence of ghosts (Bennett, 1987).

Today, we all still have to face death and dying, attend funerals and write meaningful letters of sympathy. A challenge for religious professionals and believers concerns the appropriate funeral rituals for those contemporary British families for whom neither the person who has died, nor their next of kin, has any religious beliefs. A 1995 survey (Davies and Shaw, 1995) revealed that 30 per cent of people believed that death was the end. Such people wish the attitudes towards life and death held by them during life to be honoured at their funerals. This need is increasingly being met in the United Kingdom by Humanist celebrants (Pearce, 2006) and by the new organisation, Civil Celebrants. 'If death is the end, what is the meaning of life?' is a question needing discussion by believers and non-believers together. Beliefs and practices surrounding death and disposal are so diverse around the globe as to make it certain that no single explanation will be able to eliminate all others and emerge as a single and sufficient and complete account. What can Christianity contribute to this debate?

III. THE JEWISH ORIGINS OF CHRISTIAN ATTITUDES TO THE AFTERLIFE

This section, which draws on Bowker's 1991 study, shows how Judaism's increasingly positive, though contested, concept of a life beyond death provided a legacy for the Christian religion. The Jewish people understood themselves to be brought into being by the creative act of God and to be sustained by His promises for the future. Of the major elements in Jewish theology, two stand out for our purpose. Historically, it was God's act in rescuing His people from captivity in Egypt in the 12th century BC (further developed in the promise of an everlasting kingdom to David and his descendants in the 10th century BC) and the deliverance from Babylonian captivity in the 6th century BC which constituted them and reconstituted them as a unique people (Psalms 147, v 20). Theologically and in the context of mythological origins, they were a people descended from the first man, Adam. His disobedience (the Fall) triggered a downward slope for humankind from which the obedience of Abraham began the upward journey (Davies, 1965).

The covenants with Abraham, Moses and David were part of a series by which God confirmed His loyalty to the Jews. They involved vocation and identity, land and the law. By contrast with Christian concepts in which from the start the guarantee of a good life beyond death was based upon the death and resurrection of Jesus, for Jews it was the nation that was assured of a good future, an assurance based on God's past blessings and future promises. Whilst the Covenants provided no precedents for post-mortem hopes, there were isolated visions, like that of Ezekiel in the valley of dry bones (Ezekiel 37) or of Daniel (7, v 13–14), and the conviction of the Wisdom of Solomon (2, v 24–3, v 8) that 'the souls of the righteous are in the hands of God'. Yet for much of the Biblical period (eg Job 10, vv 20–22; Psalms 6, v 4; and Isaiah 38, vv 18–19), the dead go to *Sheol*. *Sheol* is not complete oblivion; some memory lingers, but earthly status counts for nothing (Isaiah 14, vv 9–11). Nothing significant survived death. The Old Testament view of man was a creature made of dust and animated by God's breath (Genesis 2, v 7). At death, the breath returns to the air or to God. In later Judaism, beyond the Old Testament, that basic anthropology was extended either by giving to the 'animating breath' a more enduring status (an independent self or soul) or by God's deliberate recreation of the original person, body and breath. The soul pre-existed the body, since it came from God.

Whilst a number of Biblical passages suggested some hope of an afterlife, there is no indication of a well-defined concept (Cohn-Sherbok, 2003: 456). Yet, as daily experience continued to prove that the righteous were not automatically rewarded nor the unrighteous punished, the Rabbis' tentative concepts were reinforced and spurred, 160 years before the birth of Jesus, by the theological and practical issues raised by the Maccabaean war of independence (165–163 BC). The war experience stimulated more hopeful responses to the ethical question of God's attitude towards those martyred in His cause. The war experience made salient and urgent the question: If there was no decent life beyond death for the individual, what then was the individual's reward for virtue, for keeping God's law? It was the virtuous Jews, those rebels who lay down their weapons on the Sabbath, who were slaughtered by their enemies who held no such Sabbath scruples.

The Orthodox Bible books 2 and 4 Maccabees, written as commentaries upon the Maccabaean revolt, represent an acceleration of belief in a personal life beyond death. In 2 Maccabees there is a reward for the righteous, which includes the resurrection of the body (2 Maccabees 6 and 7). Thus, the guarantee of an earthly future based on the covenant relationship of God with the nation developed an individual extension, a reward for the righteous individual in the form of a resurrected body.

There is a socio-political context here: the extension of Greek culture in a Mediterranean world where Greek and Roman cultures held successive and parallel sway. Once the Hebrew language has been translated into Greek and, for example, the Hebrew words *nephesh* (life) and *ruach* (breath) were being translated into Greek (*psuche* and *pnuema*), there arose the conditions for speculation that the soul or spirit might be a self-sufficient reality which might be detached from and later reconnected with its body for its full expression. 4 Maccabees, as distinct from 2 Maccabees, says that the mode of a continued life for the individual with God is not the resurrection of the body but the immortality of the soul. The Patriarchs receive the souls of the faithful at death (eg 4 Maccabees 5, v 7) and these souls are then rewarded in the presence of God (4 Maccabees 9, v 8).

The difference between 2 and 4 Maccabees reminds us that these new views of the afterlife were both different and contested. The Sadducees would not go beyond scripture. Their disbelief in a resurrection is recorded in the New Testament in Matthew 22, v 23 and Acts 23, vv 6–9. From the 1st century AD, Judaism had first to cope with the rise of Christianity and then with the destruction of its geographical and spiritual capital Jerusalem (in 70 AD). In the face of such threats, the Rabbis reorganised Judaism with scrupulous attention to the law and its interpretation. In relation to life beyond death, they opted for resurrection, rather than for immortality, for the former was less inconsistent with the Biblical tradition (Cohn-Sherbok, 2003).

IV. THE CENTRALITY OF CHRIST'S DEATH AND RESURRECTION FOR
CHRISTIAN ATTITUDES TO THE AFTERLIFE

Christianity inherited the new Jewish hope in an afterlife, but the key difference was the centrality in its religion of the death of Christ (understood as sacrificial) and His resurrection as the guarantee of a future life for Christians. This centrality is, above all, to be seen in Christian worship. In funerals, Christians bury their dead 'in sure and certain hope of the resurrection to eternal life in Jesus Christ our Lord'. Christian weddings note that marriages should last 'until death do us part' for in Heaven there is neither marriage nor giving in marriage. At baptism, Christians are marked with the sign of the cross, as persons for whom, long before conception or birth, Christ has already died. In the Eucharist Christians consume, at Christ's command, the symbols of His body and blood and recall His words and actions on the evening before His crucifixion. Christians are called to live as persons conscious both that they are mortal and that Christ has guaranteed life beyond death. Christ's death and resurrection lie behind the architecture of churches and burial places (Colvin, 1991; Curl, 1993; and Morris, 2005).

Paul's Epistles provide the earliest statement of Christian beliefs. These include: his personal experience of the risen Jesus on the Damascus road; Christ's death as a means of dealing with human sin; Christ's resurrection as a guarantee of life after death for Christians; the Adam narrative as a model for interpreting Christ's death and resurrection; and that the physical resurrection of all of the dead will be a communal event at a time of God's choice. Paul's Epistles outline concepts about Christian eschatology whose tensions have never yet been reconciled. The earliest Christian churches had to face the problem raised by those Christians who died before the expected second coming of Christ, of which a later version was the problem of the salvation of those in countries where the Gospel had not yet been preached.

A second issue concerned the destiny of those saints of the Old Testament who were clearly Godly men and women, some of whom had prophesied Christ's coming. This issue of 'fairness all round' was part of the origin of the belief about Christ's descent into Hell (1 Peter 3; and John 5). This was largely rejected by later theologians but was a popular theme of medieval mystery plays and was revived briefly in the 19th century when underpinning was sought for new views of the universality of Christ's redemptive work.

Thirdly, when the first generations of Christians realised that their resurrection after death would not be immediate, the problem arose of what happened to the individual Christian in the interval between death and resurrection. As the Christian faith spread into the Roman and Hellenistic world, into a context very different from its Jewish roots, it spread into a world which believed in an immortal soul (Bremmer, 2002). A tension between two Christian concepts of the mode of life after death, principally understood as the resurrection of the body and the immortality of the soul, has persisted ever since (Jupp, 2005). It has underlain, for example, attitudes to the body and sexuality; to funeral rituals and practices; to burial and cemeteries; to the deaths of martyrs and of heretics; and to the quandaries about the bare minima for resurrection. Motifs of restored body parts appear in Christian art until the 13th century (Bynum, 1995: 195). Bynum's survey shows how, from Irenaeus through Augustine to Aquinas, Christian theologians addressed the whole range of human resurrection concerns from cut hair and finger-nails to missing limbs and aborted foetuses. An awareness of such patristic and medieval analyses might have informed debates about the significance of missing body parts not only when cremation was proposed in the late 19th century but also the 1990s controversies about retained body organ practices at the Bristol and Alder Hey hospitals.

V. THE DEVELOPMENT OF CHRISTIAN BELIEF AND PRACTICE IN THE PATRISTIC PERIOD

How did Christian theology and funeral practice impact upon each other? The first Christians had been Jews and followed Jewish precedents. Given the Middle Eastern climate, burials followed death quickly and burial grounds were usually located outside towns. So the procession from home to grave was already an important part of funeral ritual. Dead bodies were seen as polluting to Jews so graves were whitewashed as a hazard warning. Dead bodies were not seen as polluting for Christians: they were, after all, the shape of the post-mortem future. After the funeral there was a series of mourning periods. With no guaranteed afterlife, Jewish mourning rituals were more self-reflexive but their staged mourning rites offered a model for Christian rites of commemoration looking forward to incorporation in the communion of saints. Christians soon developed their own funeral liturgies. Rowell pointed out that information about early Christian funeral rites is incomplete as burial rites were then not controversial matters (Rowell, 1977: 19). Furthermore, the precarious political situation for Christians meant that their funerals were more likely to be discreet affairs: the very catacombs could provide an appropriate place for Christian worship.

Meanwhile, as Christian churches spread around the Mediterranean littoral, further pagan influences were encountered. Roman funerals included cremation, although reasons for the progressive dominance of burial over cremation in the Empire are not yet clear. Of significance was the concept of 'the dying breath', to be caught by a relative so that the departed soul was kept 'in the family'. Christians had been baptised—symbolising dying and being raised with Christ—so, thus reborn, Christians were members of a new family (2 Corinthians 5, v 14) whose Father was God, and in which Jesus Christ, as the first born from the dead, a sort of eldest brother. At funerals Christians expressed their resurrection hopes by joyful singing and not by the lamentation featured in pagan funerals. Saint Cyprian had discouraged the wearing of dark clothes by mourners praying for the dead who were already wearing their white garments in Heaven, but black eventually won the day. The *viaticum* ritual—a coin placed in the mouth or food on the grave—was to nourish the dead soul on its journey. Christians recycled this practice by offering the Eucharist ('the medicine of immortality') to dying Christians, but there were tensions over the practice of offering the Eucharist to those who had already died.

Before the first generation of Christians had themselves died, there was some expectation of Jesus's second coming (Glasson, 1980). Many in the early Church anticipated resurrection in the near future. When these hopes were disappointed, concepts of communal resurrection in a distant future took their place, gradually developing into concepts of the 'four last things': death, Judgement, Heaven and Hell. The concept developed of the soul as setting off on a journey while the body 'slept' awaiting the general resurrection when souls would be reunited with bodies for Judgement. Dangerous journeys need guides, like angels, and also prayers, among which the 'Proficiscere'—'Go forth upon Thy journey, Christian soul' (8th century AD)—is the most renowned (Lampard, 2005). The state of the dead is ambiguous: they are no longer with us but they are not yet with God, so our prayers might benefit them. Given the widespread belief in evil spirits and witchcraft, such fears are not surprising.

Julian the Apostate (Emperor 360-62 AD) sought unsuccessfully to put the clock back to pagan times. He is reported to have said that the way the Christians treated their dead was one of the reasons for the conversion of the Christian Empire (Rowell, 1977: 18). The period after Constantine saw the development of the cult of relics whose veneration provided a vital channel of communication with the next world (Brown, 1981). Martyrs were believed—though this was contested—to have passed straight to Heaven upon death. On the martyrs' tombs, the Eucharist was customarily celebrated. The cult developed over succeeding centuries, partly accelerated by the decision of the council of Nicaea (787 AD) that no church might be consecrated unless some relic of its patron saint was buried beneath its altar. Relics could provide miracles of healing and encouraged pilgrimage until the Reformation brought the practice to an end (Duffy, 1992). In parallel with the rise of the Papacy and the development of the feudal system, the Christian Church buried Christian Emperors with the social status that the maintenance of the political system deserved. The Church buried its leading clergy neither in cemeteries nor churchyards but beneath the altars where they had celebrated the Eucharist during their earthly ministry. Wherever Christianity became an established religion, Christian funerals came to reflect the dual status of the status quo and the status promised. Saint Augustine, observing the tension between religious rites and social status, wrote:

The care of the funeral arrangements, the establishment of the place of burial, the pomp of ceremonies, are more of a solace for the living than an aid for the dead (St Augustine, no date. [1940]).

VI. THE ADVENT OF ISLAM

Whilst neither Judaism nor Islam will be included within the major thrust of this chapter, a reference to Islam is appropriate at this point. Islam sprang suddenly into existence in the 7th century AD. Because the *Quran* is held

to consist entirely of the words of the Divine to Mohammed, it both constituted Islam and defined Muslim belief from the beginning, so that the
processes of doctrinal development that have characterised Judaism and
Christianity have not at all had a comparable effect within Islam. Death is,
for Muslims, as with Judaism and traditional Christianity, the creation of
God, yet its emphasis on the event of death as being supremely the will of
God is far more intensely held by individual Muslims.

All deaths for Muslims are at God's decree, so mourning should not be
excessive because it denies the acceptance of God's will. The dead body is
to be respected because it is to be resurrected, so burial has always been
universal for Muslims. Resurrection is followed by Judgement and then
by the stark alternatives of Heaven and Hell (the 'Garden' and the 'Fire').
Death in the service of God (especially by martyrdom) brings reprieve from
post-mortem interrogation, and guarantees privileged places in the Garden.
Muslim doctrines about the afterlife are presented with far greater detail
and emphasis than those of Christianity; the *Quran*'s descriptions are taken
as literal and not as metaphorical, and give added power to the prospects of
the afterlife. Islam has its own tradition of Purgatory and, from the beginning, devotional and charitable practices for the remembrance and aid of
the dead. On the Day of Judgement, God will intercede and also permits
all the prophets to do so. As in Calvinist Christianity, God has total control
over the destiny of the dead. Muslims do not accept any participation of the
person of Jesus in the salvation of the living or the dead, nor do they accept
that He was raised from the dead.

There have thus existed for 15 centuries, almost side by side in Southern
Europe and around the Mediterranean shores, two evangelistic religions
with opposing beliefs and ideologies. Islam represents for Bowker: 'the
understanding of death, in the western religious history and tradition, at its
furthest extreme of formalisation' (Bowker, 1991: 127). For Judaism and
Christianity, two different concepts of scripture and tradition have permitted courses of development whereby it has been possible for groups and
individuals to question (sometimes radically) the received concepts, and
details of death, and the afterlife without abandoning either their faith or
religious identity (see eg McDannell and Lang, 2001). That process would
be far more problematic in Islam.

VII. THE BIRTH OF PURGATORY

In Lesslie Newbigin's phrase (c.1978), the advent of Islam shut Christianity
up into a box, sealing it from the South and from the West, until the ages
of Marco Polo and Christopher Columbus widened European horizons.
We need to leap some centuries, by which time Christianity had become
the dominant religion of Europe. Within England, from the 9th to 10th

centuries, a spreading network of parish churches meant that increasing numbers of people had a local churchyard in which to be buried. By the 11th century this was the norm (Daniell and Thompson, 1999: 75). The Christianisation of Europe continued apace but, as Le Goff has described, the growth of established Christianity exacerbated the problem of virtue and the monitoring of behaviour (Le Goff, 1984). An awareness steadily grew of the need for a purgatorial process after death so that the Christian dead might be fit for Heaven.

Le Goff dated the final elaboration of the purgatorial process as a place and not just a process to his discovery that, after 1170, all saints had to pass through Purgatory on their way to Heaven, no matter how crystal-clear their virtue. Le Goff also suggested that this development paralleled the complexity of the urban class structures developing during the Middle Ages. For Bremmer, the final cementation of the purgatorial process within a specific location was occasioned by the Church's reaction to the Cathar movement (Bremmer, 2002). The Cathars had taught that only their sacrament for the dying would guarantee that the faithful would reach Heaven without going to Hell.

Purgatory and Judgement dominated the medieval Church until the Reformation. Woodman and Middleton (chapter seven this volume) strikingly describe the roles that Purgatory fears could play at local and domestic levels, particularly because of its economic and philanthropic implications. The effect upon ordinary Christian believers was that the moment of death became increasingly important. Themes of the Judgement and of wrath began to overwhelm the earlier themes of hope and joy. These are exemplified by the *Dies Irae* in the early 13th century. The increased penal aspect of death was emphasised by rites and offices for the dying and the dead. These were developed in a monastic context where there were more full-time religious professionals to 'watch and pray'. Medieval piety was strongly concerned for the welfare of the departed. These included death-bed and grave-side rituals, masses for the dead, month's and year's minds, All Souls Day, All Saints Day, relics, obituary lists, pardons and indulgences. If Chaucer's pilgrims had their own suspicions about indulgences, contemporary monks had their own problems, for obituary lists grew ever longer and far more time-consuming. Monasteries found it increasingly difficult to cope. The reform of Catholic ritual in 1614 simplified the system; but by that date the Protestant Reformation had already successfully challenged the medieval system.

VIII. THE REFORMATION AND ITS LEGACY

Within the British islands, the Protestant Reformation followed different courses. In Ireland, Catholicism remained the religion of the poor majority: Calvinism became the dominant theology of the Scottish Churches, and the

Anglican middle way became the established Church in England. Until the Reformation, both the dying person and his successors could hope to influence post-mortem destiny. With the Reformation 'The ritual ties connecting the living and the dead were severed' (Gittings, 1984: 40). After death, in the Reformed/Protestant view, all human intervention ceased.

When Protestants placed Purgatory out of bounds, then the funeral service lost half its effect: it could help only the bereaved and no longer the mourned' (Jupp, 1990: 2).

This represented a huge and far-reaching reaction against the Catholic tradition and its system of death-bed and grave-site rites, intercessions and indulgences for the dead, the chantry system, and days of commemoration. The British Reformation ended all these (Duffy, 1992; and Duffy, 2001). Calvinists forbad any human actions that could influence post-mortem prospects. The rubric in *The Directory* of 1644:

When any person departeth this life, let the dead body, upon the day of burial, be decently attended from the house to the place appointed for public burial, and there immediately interred, without any ceremony (quoted in Rowell, 1977: 83)

governed non-Catholic funerals in Scotland until the late 19th century.

Yet even Calvinists could be mindful of the social and secular role of funerals. *The Directory* (1644) advised that rituals avoiding commendation of the deceased,

shall not extend to deny any civic respects of differences at the burial, suitable to the rank and condition of the party deceased whilst he was living (Rowell, 1977: 83).

This tension had been foreshadowed by St Augustine—the tension between the (past) earthly status and (future) post-mortem status—and continues to cast shadows. Critics of Protestantism describe it as its own grave-digger, and this could particularly apply to its attitude to death and the afterlife. Davies has sought to understand contemporary changes in British funeral practice as a shift from 'prospective fulfilment of identity' to 'retrospective fulfilment of identity': a process whereby the focus of traditional funerals on the 'religious' future of the deceased has now shifted to their 'secular' past achievements (Davies, 2002). In retrospect, the Calvinist theology of funerals had helped provide the context for that direction.

In England, once the Elizabethan settlements had steadied the Church by the legal and civil disabilities placed upon Catholicism and Protestant Nonconformity, a more conservative tradition about funerals set in. The disputes within Edward VI's court produced two Prayer Books (1549 and 1552), as successive Protestant factions hardened at court. In the 1552

Prayer Book, there is no commendation of the soul, only the committal of the body to the ground, an emphasis close to that of Calvin's. A century later, with the Restoration of the Monarchy, the 1662 *Book of Common Prayer* was more of a compromise. This text held sway until 1928 (when Parliament rejected a revised *Prayer Book*), liturgical reform thus being delayed until the 1960s, by which time, in a vastly altered British society, many long-held beliefs, teachings and practices about death and the afterlife had changed.

IX. THE ANGLICAN DOMINANCE AND ITS DEMISE

The Restoration of the Monarchy in 1660 was followed by 160 years of Anglican dominance in the burial of the dead. The Church of England controlled the site, rite, mode and presidency of funerals. There were some Nonconformist alternatives: Baptists and Quakers, who had their own scruples about baptism, had to provide their own burial grounds. The rest had to have Anglican-led funerals in churchyards, to which dominance only the rise of the private cemetery movement after 1815 and the agitation of the Protestant Dissenting Deputies (until 1880) brought a finally effective challenge. By an Act of 1880, British people could also be buried without religious rites (Fletcher, 1974).

From the early 19th century on, changes in death beliefs and practices have been almost continuous. In a long term perspective, funeral practice has seen a shift away from the local, the parish, the family and the neighbourly to the dominance of commercial, medical and municipal interests (Jupp, 2006: 194–9) only to be challenged, in contemporary society, by the salience of individualistic, democratic and consumerist interests. The context of early 19th century change was the twin pressures of industrialisation and urbanisation. Nonconformist families, made more socially confident by capitalist prosperity and franchise extension, promoted their joint-stock burial grounds from the 1820s (Rugg, 1992), in an open challenge to the Anglican status quo. Class consciousness in burial practice and provision had a long history, especially in the cities since the Reformation (Harding, 2002), with which—unable to extend their burial ground holdings in a steadily urbanising society—the established Church could not cope.

In the 19th century, a series of burial scandals—of which the Resurrection men ('body snatchers') were the most notorious (Richardson, 1987; and Hallam, chapter sixteen this volume) but by no means representative—occurred. These were the consequence of increasingly restricted urban burial space, exacerbated by successive ravages of cholera in a society increasingly concerned with public health, and led to Parliamentary legislation effecting the closure of urban churchyards and burial grounds—the Burial Acts of 1850 and 1852 (Jupp, 2006). These burial grounds were predominantly owned by the Church of England. Their successors were cemeteries, locally owned and managed by local authorities. Local government authorities held no remit for theological interpretations of death and the dead. The essence of a publicly owned cemetery is the deposition and memorialisation of the dead, not their custody until the Day of Resurrection for reunion with their souls for Judgement.

Running both behind and parallel to the Anglican 'surrender' of its churchyards was a succession of changes in theological and popular attitudes to death and the afterlife which included the growing secularisation of suicide (MacDonald and Murphy, 1990); hesitant and then accelerating criticisms of the doctrine of Hell (Rowell, 1974; and Almond, 1994); the moderation and decline of Calvinism as one effect of the Evangelical Revival; an international missionary impulse that offered salvation in Christ to all people rather than just the elect, and which thereby encouraged a popular belief in Heaven characterised as the reunion of family members; and the salience of beliefs in the immortality of the soul (Barrow, 1986; and Hazelgrove, 2000). All these things contributed to a serious challenge of the traditional teaching of the Christian Churches whose dominance in funeral practice—the ritual point where official rite and doctrine met with public emotions and post-mortem hopes—was steadily being reduced from the commencement of the 19th century (Rowell, 1974; Wilkinson, 1978; and Jupp, 2006). In my estimation, the Church of England has not yet realised the extent of the influence it has lost (both institutional and pastoral) by the surrender of its churchyards.

X. CREMATION IN A SECULAR SOCIETY

Yet the burdens of cemetery provision, maintenance and finance proved a heavy one for local government. Some relief was sought in the Cremation Act 1902, which signalled the accelerating decline of the Church's role in disposal and helped to change its theological interpretation of death (Jupp, 2001). Modern cremation had first been seriously proposed by the French Revolutionaries and was later taken up by European doctors concerned for public health. In England and Wales, once local government had been allocated responsibility for the disposal of the dead, economic ways of providing land were to prove attractive. In 1874 Queen Victoria's surgeon, Sir Henry Thompson, founded the Cremation Society of Great Britain. As soon as *R v Price* (1884)[1] demonstrated that cremation was not illegal, the Society opened Britain's first crematorium (at Woking) and encouraged local authorities to realise the economic and public health advantages of cremation. Cremation's legality partially neutralised official Anglican

---

[1] *R v Price* (1884) 12 QBD 247.

attitudes in England and Wales, but in 1886 the Vatican prohibited cremation for Catholics (the anti-clerical factions of Catholic Europe plus the
influence of Freemasons were the major reasons for the Vatican's decision),
a ban that was only lifted in 1964.

Both for Protestants and Catholics, the act of cremation involved
symbolism that ran counter to traditional beliefs in the eschatological
resurrection of the dead human body. This was a more a cultural and
emotional response rather than a rational one. The Cremation Act 1902,
whilst allowing a conscience clause for Anglican clergy, further neutralised
clerical opposition. Cremation was promoted in principle by the Cremation
Society and in practice by local government. By largely abstaining from the
cremation movement, the Church lost its chance of influencing it. Between
the wars and particularly after 1945, local government invested heavily in
crematoria and the cremation rate first exceeded that of burial in 1968.

XI. COMPETING BELIEFS AND PRACTICES

Whilst the reasons for cremation's popularity are complex, the reasons for
its growing popularity intersected with several other developments, which
impacted upon religious attitudes. There was, first, a shift in the popular
imagination about the mode of life beyond death. Victorian Britain, like other
Western societies, became increasingly fascinated by spiritualism. Spiritualism
originated in 1848 when a certain Massachusetts family began to experience
what would later be called poltergeist activity. Being essentially DIY, the
spiritualist movement spread rapidly to Britain and to other countries. The
concept of contact with the dead through ouija boards, planchette and mediums, proved fascinating (Nelson, 1969). Alongside it there arose a scientific
interest in psychical research. The Psychical Research Society was founded
in 1882 and attracted many of the intellectual elite. Some Christian theologians, especially those among the modernists who sought to adapt traditional
doctrines to address the modern mind, privileged the immortality of the soul
above that of the resurrection of the body well before the First World War.

The second development was the experience of the First World War. The
complementary movement between the popular discourse about spiritualism and declining beliefs in the resurrection of the body was one of several
shifts accelerated by the experience of bereavements, both military and
civilian (Winter, 1995; and Bourke, 1997). Hallam (chapter sixteen this
volume) follows Richardson in relating the rise of cremation with a rise
in 'whole body donation' (Richardson, 1987: 260). For her, the change in
the 'social meaning of the corpse and its spiritual associations' depended
in part on the early 20th-century privileging of beliefs in the immortality of the soul over those in the resurrection of the body. The First World
War experience encouraged a resort to spiritualist mediums and revived

the most un-Protestant practice of praying for the dead. The Great War also hastened the further decline of belief in Hell and in a post-mortem Judgement (Wilkinson, 1978). This all served to remove religious sanctions from human mortality. Catholics could offer the 'upwardly-mobile' state of Purgatory, but Protestants could only offer Heaven or Hell.

When [Protestants] dropped Hell, Heaven was the only option left. No loss, no purchase. Once the Great War had locked Heaven's gate open, there was no risk after death. Once people could reject the very idea of an afterlife without reproof, there remained no risk in death (Jupp, 1990: 28).

Fear drained from death, to congeal more thickly around the prospect of dying and the consequences of bereavement.

Thirdly, the character of dying and of bereavement has been changing. Infant- and maternal-mortality began to decline from the last quarter of the 19th century. This shrivelled popular understandings of Providence (Chadwick, 1974) and of evangelical characterisations of the 'good death' (Jalland, 1996), in a demographic context changed by better health and diet, extended longevity and more wide-spread investment in insurance based on actuarial calculation (Prior, 1997). Increased medical interventions around the dying process have reduced family participation in the experience of dying, especially since the foundation of the National Health Service in 1948. In England and Wales, deaths in institutions surpassed home deaths for the first time in 1958–59. Seven-eighths of us die after our 65th birthday. Death in old age causes us few metaphysical problems, although its incidence, combined with advances in medical techniques, has helped give rise to the debate upon euthanasia (Jackson, chapter three this volume). It is only abnormal death—premature, accidental or violent death—that commonly raises for bereaved people acute questions of meaning. Untimely deaths consequently require more detailed and careful funeral rites to help families comprehend (in both senses) both the shock and the abnormality.

XII. IN CONTEMPORARY BRITAIN

In recent years, the balance has begun to swing back towards greater control and participation of dying people and their families in the funeral process through the growth of the hospice movement and the rise of consumerisation (see further the discussion by Scambler, chapter 10 this volume). As far as the experience of bereavement is concerned, the decline of the nuclear family and its neighbourhood networks have left a vacuum which a number of post-1950 bereavement support groups have arisen to help fill. Since the 1960s, the scholarly study of bereavement by, for example, Colin Murray Parkes, John Bowlby and Margaret Stroebe, has gone hand in hand with the growth of bereavement support groups like Cruse Bereavement Care, and a wide range of other support groups focussing on victims of such various events as road traffic accidents and cot deaths. The development of the hospice by Dame Cicely Saunders has pioneered new approaches for palliative care. Nicholas Albery founded the Natural Death Centre as a complement to Natural Childbirth practices, seeking to give those preparing for death far more control both over their dying and over their subsequent funerals. Late 20th-century concerns about the environment have encouraged both a movement towards natural or 'green' burial and an organised drive by the cremation movement to ensure that the cremation curbs its contribution to 'green-house gases'. The Environmental Protection Act 1990 stimulated greater filtration procedures at crematoria. In 2005, CAMEO (Crematoria Abatement of Mercury Emissions Organisation) was founded to effect a burden-sharing programme to reduce mercury emissions (largely from dental amalgam) into the atmosphere.

Whilst religious faith was the driving force behind the hospice concept, many other groups have interpreted death as a natural phenomenon, an approach which has appealed to a society where currently 10 per cent of people attend church monthly. Changing attitudes and practices in bereavement, in the dying process and in funeral rituals have all been affected by increasing secularisation especially as it affects Christian belief and practice. The latter includes the long decline in attendance at churches and Sunday schools, thus severely restricting the effective promotion of Christian teaching about death and the afterlife. The process of secularisation is exemplified by the Humanist movement, whose beliefs and practices about death and funerals are increasingly widely recognised as valid. Meanwhile, the course of secularisation is partly countered by the growth of the other major world faiths. The current controversy over open air Hindu funeral pyres is a sign of other faiths seeking to press their distinctive views about transmission to an afterlife. Hindu and Sikh communities in Britain have had to adapt traditional Indian procedures for funerals, including cremation, to meet British legal requirements (Laungani, 1996; and Firth, 1997).

The demise of traditional Christian beliefs about the afterlife is apparent from surveys. For example, in 1995, Davies and Shaw were commissioned by the Institute of Burial and Cremation Administration to survey popular attitudes towards the re-use of old graves—a policy which the Institute believed would solve the shortage of burial space in metropolitan areas. In total, 1603 people were interviewed (Davies and Shaw, 1995). The section on beliefs showed that 71 per cent believed in some form of life after death, whilst 29 per cent believed death was the end. The failure of the Churches' teaching and ritual ministries can be instanced when the interviewees were categorised by denomination and belief. Of those claiming Anglican identity, 32 per cent thought death was the end and 14 per cent believed in some form of reincarnation. Of those claiming Methodist identity, 30 per cent thought death was the end, and of those claiming Church of Scotland identity, 22 per cent. Of those claiming Catholic identity some displayed residual belief in the resurrection of the body (18 per cent) but 14 per cent believed death was the end, with 11 per cent believing in reincarnation. The Catholic shift had earlier been chronologically surveyed by Hornsby-Smith, who in 1991 charted one quarter as not believing in a life after death (Hornsby-Smith, 1991). He commented:

It seems that, for many ordinary Catholics, concepts such as eternal damnation or hell or the devil, are uncomfortable, unpleasant and inconvenient (Hornsby-Smith, 1991: 99).

In response to these popular shifts, certain Christian theologians have sought to reinterpret traditional beliefs, like J Hick (Hick, 1976), P Badham (Badham, 1978) and J Polkinghorne (Polkinghorne, 2002). At present their work is not as evident at parish level compared with the more widespread development of denominational liturgies to take wider account of causes and circumstances of individual deaths. These have included deaths of babies and children, suicides and victims of transport and terrorist death.

It should be emphasised that Christianity is robust in other continents. Secularisation is a British and European phenomenon (Davie, 2002). British society has entered a new stage where a variety of faith traditions—old and new—offers and develops their own death-ways. From the perspective of post-modernity, it is the collapse of the Christian dominance, both in organisation and in doctrine—whether Catholic, Anglican or Free Church—which has enabled the free-for-all in belief and practice about death. When all religious perspectives are considered valid, none can effectively claim uniqueness (Jupp, 2006: 196). Beliefs once considered heterodox—from ghosts to spiritualism, from reincarnation to psychical research—are now objects of both popular attraction and academic study. The increased competitiveness between beliefs can only be of benefit to truth.

People still feel the need to prepare for dying, to make sense of death, to mourn and commemorate their dead. Yet, with so many long-standing maps and signposts discarded, more Britons experience a need to create new ritual models for disposal (from natural or woodland burial to Humanist ceremonies); new ways of commemoration (from internet obituaries to brooches or fireworks containing ashes); and support networks in grief and mourning which former communities (of family, neighbourhood or Church) can not currently provide.

XIII. CONCLUSION

Funerals have a three-fold function: the disposal of the dead human body; the safe transmission of the soul to an afterlife; and the enabling of bereaved people and communities to adjust to their new roles in society. The three major religious faiths of the West affect how we face death because they teach that death is neither an accident, nor a punishment but is part of God's purpose in creation. Their funeral liturgies have always been constructed to show that the faith in which an individual lived and died is consistent with the religious tradition in words and symbols; the individual's faith and hope match those of the community and vice versa.

When, as at present, religious faith and sensitivity recede from family and wider social institutions and cultures, death becomes uncoupled from its traditional religious interpretations and the meaninglessness of individual deaths can increase. It is thus not coincidental that when as many as 30 per cent of Britons believe that this life is all we have, the funeral focus is switched to the character and achievements of the deceased, privileging biography over belief, or, in DJ Davies's phrase, 'retrospective' over 'prospective' fulfilment of identity (Davies, 2002). Where societies or sections within them acknowledge no credence or relevance of faith in an afterlife, commemoration rituals must also change their focus. Where there is no afterlife (and therefore no God upon whose memory or judgement to place reliance) the living and their successors must bear the burden of memory themselves. At family level, this may take the form of records, such as photographs, histories and genealogies, or material reminders, like photographs and keep-sakes. At national level, both secular and multi-cultural assumptions alike may be articulated in war and disaster memorials shorn of specific religious or afterlife reference.

Religious faith contains, in differing measures, convictions about the moral character and intentions of a creator God. Life for humans after death, then, has a specifically moral character, for which humans prepare in this life and in which post-mortem Judgement and sanctions play a major part. This is strong both in Islam and in traditional Christianity. Both the prospect of meeting God after death and of post-mortem moral sanctions impart an extra significance to earthly behaviour; for everything that we do in this life has an eternal significance, for ourselves and for others. Purgatory is a particularly optimistic concept because it offers a post-mortem system for moral improvement. Altogether, then, beliefs in post-mortem sanctions for moral behaviour, based upon moral understandings of the character of the Divine, can beneficially affect secular human behaviour.

A different kind of post-mortem influence upon secular life is also available. Certain religions believe in a dynamic form of life for the dead which has two-way effects. The dead can be aided by the prayers of the living (eg intercessions, indulgences), and the specially virtuous dead (the saints) can improve the efficacy of the prayers of the living. These supernatural helps for the living and for the dead can add an extra dimension to the maintenance and strengthening of both national identities (as in patron saints or mausolea; see Verdery, 1999) and family identities. Studies of cemetery behaviour in the United Kingdom and in Australia (Francis, Kellaher and Neophytou, 2005; and Bachelor, 2004) have demonstrated how commemoration of the dead helps maintain family (as well as religious) identity.

Secular societies, of course, must still grapple with meaning-making about death. Bereavement studies from the mid-1990s have shown how bereaved people have discovered, valued and maintained 'continuing bonds' with their dead. (This is understood popularly to be in contrast with the perceived purpose of funerals and of bereavement support as effecting 'closure' and enabling people to 'move on'.) Hallam *et alii.* (Hallam, Hockey and Howarth, 1999; and Hallam and Hockey, 2001) have demonstrated the increasingly wide roles allotted or attributed to the dead by the living, in experience and in material culture.

Finally, the guarantee of a post-mortem life that a religion provides its adherents is best undergirded not only by the support it gives people when they are dying, but in the attention that it gives to their bodies when dead. For example, when bodily resurrection is the understood mode of entry into the afterlife, the burial ground will usually be the site of the future resurrection. Rituals that celebrate the dynamic or latent life of the dead (pilgrimages to the shrines of saints; All Souls and All Saints days in both Scandinavian (Protestant) and Mexican (Catholic) cemeteries) not only emphasise the mutual care of the living and the dead, but also remind the living of the provisionality of human life, and reinforce the plausibility of religious beliefs. Conversely, the 'closed burial ground' (Warner, 1959) bears the coded message that there is no future for the dead and, by extension, for the living. The history of the Holocaust and of other modern forms of genocide reminds us of how the desecration of the living and the dead can be used to symbolise the destruction of specific social groups, their cultures and their beliefs. Ideally, religions should work for societies where care for the living is of a piece with care for the dying, and where care for the dead is consistent with survivors' beliefs about life in a new community beyond death.

The fact of mortality is undeniable. It continually prompts a search for meaning. The contemporary context includes the fragmentation of traditional Christian beliefs, the beliefs and practices of other world faiths, and the rise of secular Humanism. It includes new modes of support in dying, death, disposal and bereavement, which are powered, variously, by Government, charitable, environmentalist and voluntary group initiatives. It is difficult to discern how our responses to death in the 21st century will filter what is valid and valuable from the past or develop new rituals to match the new hypotheses about the meaning of death. This survey of the origins and developments in Christian doctrines and rituals is offered as a resource in the search for meaning and for solace in the fact of mortality, the prospect of death and bereavement, and the precedents for an afterlife.

END NOTE

I acknowledge with gratitude the kindness of Rabbi Professor Dan Cohn-Sherbok of the University of Wales Lampeter and of Mohammed Kassamali, Imam at the Husaini Islamic Centre at Peterborough, for their comments on earlier drafts of this chapter.

BIBLIOGRAPHY

Almond, PC (1994) *Heaven and hell in Enlightenment England* (Cambridge, Cambridge University Press).
Augustine, St (n.d. [1940]) *How to help the dead* (trans M Allies) (London, Burns & Oates).
Bachelor, P (2004) *Sorrow & solace: the social world of the cemetery* (Amityville, NY, Baywood).
Badham, P (1978) *Christian beliefs about life after death* (London, SPCK).
Barrow, L (1986) *Independent spirits: spiritualism and English plebeians 1850–1910* (London, Routledge & Kegan Paul).
Bennett, G (1987) *Traditions of belief: women, folklore and the supernatural today* (London, Penguin Books).
Bloch, M and Parry, J (eds) (1982) *Death and the regeneration of life* (Cambridge, Cambridge University Press).
Bourke, J (1997) *Dismembering the male* (London, Reaktion).
Bowker, J (1991) *The meanings of death* (Cambridge, Cambridge University Press).
Bremmer, J (2002) *The rise and fall of the afterlife* (London, Routledge).
Brown, P (1981) *The cult of the saints: its rise and function in Latin Christianity* (London, SCM Press).
Bynum, CW (1995) *The resurrection of the body in western Christianity, 200–1336* (Cambridge, MA, Harvard University Press).
Chadwick, O (1974) *The secularisation of the European mind* (Cambridge, Cambridge University Press).
Cohn-Sherbok, D (2003) *Judaism: history, belief and practice* (London, Routledge).
Colvin, H (1991) *Architecture and the after-life* (Newhaven, NY/London, Yale University Press).
Curl, JS (1993) *A celebration of death: an introduction to some of the buildings, monuments and settings of funerary architecture in the western European tradition*, 2nd edn (London, Batsford).
Daniell, C and Thompson, V (1999) Pagans and Christians, 400–1150 in PC Jupp and C Gittings (eds) *Death in England: an illustrated history* (Manchester, Manchester University Press) 65–89.
Davie, G (2002) *Europe: the exceptional case. Parameters of faith in the modern world* (London, Darton, Longman and Todd).
Davies, DJ (2002) *Death, ritual and belief: the rhetoric of funerary rites*, 2nd edn (London, Continuum).

Davies, DJ and Shaw, A (1995) *Re-using old graves: a report on popular British attitudes* (Crayford, Kent, Shaw & Sons).

Davies, WD (1965) *Paul and Rabbinic Judaism* (London, SPCK).

Duffy, E (1992) *The stripping of the altars: traditional religion in England c.1400–c. 1580* (New Haven, NY/London, Yale University Press).

—— (2001) *The voices of Morebath: Reformation and rebellion in an English village* (New Haven, NY/London, Yale University Press).

Firth, S (1997) *Dying, death and bereavement in a British Hindu community* (Leuven, Peeters).

Fletcher, R (1974) *The Akenham Burial Case* (London, Wildwood House).

Francis, D, Kellaher, L and Neophytou, G (2005) *The secret cemetery* (Oxford, Berg).

Gittings, C (1984) *Burial and the individual in early modern England* (London, Croom Helm).

Glasson, TF (1980) *Jesus and the end of the world* (Edinburgh, The Saint Andrew Press).

Hallam, E, Hockey, J and Howarth, G (1999) *Beyond the body: death and social identity* (London, Routledge).

Hallam, E and Hockey, J (2001) *Death, Memory and Material Culture* (Oxford, Berg).

Harding, V (2002) *The dead and the living in Paris and London. 1500–1670* (Cambridge, Cambridge University Press).

Hazelgrove, J (2000) *Spiritualism and British society between the wars* (Manchester, Manchester University Press).

Hick, J (1976) *Death and eternal life* (London, Collins).

Hornsby-Smith, M (1991) *Roman Catholic beliefs in England: customary Catholicism and transformations of identity* (Cambridge, Cambridge University Press).

Huntington, R and Metcalf, P (1979) *Celebrations of death: the anthropology of mortuary ritual* (Cambridge, Cambridge University Press).

Jalland, P (1996) *Death in the Victorian family* (Oxford, Oxford University Press).

Jupp, PC (1990) *From Dust to Ashes: the replacement of burial by cremation in England 1840–1967* The Congregational Lecture 1990 (London, The Congregational Memorial Hall Trust (1978) Ltd).

—— (2001) 'Virtue ethics and death: the final arrangements' in K Flanagan and PC Jupp (eds) *Virtue ethics and sociology: issues of modernity and ethics* (Basingstoke, Palgrave) 217–235.

—— (2005) 'Resurrection and Christian thought' in DJ Davies and LJ Mates (eds) *Encyclopedia of Cremation* (Aldershot, Ashgate) 353–358.

—— (2006) *From dust to ashes: cremation and the British way of death* (Basingstoke, Palgrave).

Lampard, J (2005) *Go forth, Christian soul: the biography of a prayer* (Peterborough, Epworth).

Laungani, P (1996) 'Death and bereavement in India and England: a comparative analysis' 1 *Mortality* July 1996 191–212.

Le Goff, J (1984) *The birth of Purgatory* (trans A Goldhammer) (London, Scholar Press).

MacDonald, M and Murphy, TR (1990) *Sleepless Souls: suicide in early modern England* (Oxford, Clarendon Press).

McDannell, C and Lang, B (2001) *Heaven, A history*, 2nd edn (New Haven, NY/ London, Yale University Press).

Malinowski, B (1954) *Magic, science and religion and other essays* (New York, Doubleday).

Morris, C (2005) *The sepulchre of Christ and the medieval west. From the beginning to 1600* (Oxford, Oxford University Press).

Nelson, GK (1969) *Spiritualism and society,* (London, Routledge and Kegan Paul).

Pearce, J (2005) 'Where we are with secular funerals' 71(3) *Pharos International* Autumn, 8–10.

Polkinghorne, J (2006) *The God of Hope and the End of the World* (London, SPCK).

Prior, L (1997) 'Actuarial visions of death: life, death and chance in the modern world' in PC Jupp and G Howarth (eds) *The changing face of death: historical accounts of death and disposal* (Basingstoke, Macmillan) 177–193.

Richardson, R (1987) *Death, dissection and the destitute* (London, Routledge & Kegan Paul).

Rowell, DG (1974) *Hell and the Victorians* (Oxford, Oxford University Press).

—— (1977) *The liturgy of Christian burial* (London, SPCK).

Rugg, J (1992) *The rise of cemetery companies in Britain 1820–1853*. Unpublished PhD Thesis (Stirling, University of Stirling).

Thomas, JH (1997) 'Life, death and paradise: the theology of the funeral' in PC Jupp and T Rogers (eds) *Interpreting death: Christian theology and pastoral practice* (London, Cassell) 56–66.

Thomas, K (1973) *Religion and the decline of magic: studies in popular belief in sixteenth- and seventeenth-century England* (Harmondsworth, Penguin).

Verdery, K (1999) *The political lives of dead bodies. Reburial and postsocialist change* (New York, Columbia University Press).

Vitebsky, P (1993) *Dialogues with the dead: the discussion of mortality among the Sora of eastern India* (Cambridge, Cambridge University Press).

Warner, WL (1959) *The living and the dead: a study of the symbolic life of Americans* 5 Yankee City Series (New Haven, NY, Yale University Press).

Wilkinson, A (1978) *The Church of England in the First World War* (London, SPCK).

Winter, J (1995) *Sites of memory, sites of mourning: the Great War in European cultural history* (Cambridge, Cambridge University Press).

Young, M (1988) *The metronomic society* (London, Thames & Hudson).

7

Purgatory: The Beginning and the End

FRANCIS WOODMAN AND JUDITH MIDDLETON-STEWART

The Christianisation of Europe continued apace but, as Le Goff has described, the growth of established Christianity exacerbated the problem of virtue and the monitoring of behaviour. There grew an awareness of the need for purgatorial process after death so that the Christian dead might be fit for Heaven.
(Peter Jupp, chapter six this volume).

I. INTRODUCTION

FROM ITS EARLIEST days, the Christian Church preached a message of salvation—eternal life hereafter with Christ (God) and all the saints. Obeying God's law, as interpreted by the Church, would ensure that on the Day of Judgement, the result would be eternal bliss in Heaven and not eternal damnation in Hell. However, this teaching raised as many questions as it answered: Who would do this judging? Was it the Old Testament God of vengeance or gentle Jesus, meek and mild? And if God and Heaven represented perfection, what chance did anyone have of gaining admittance? How bad could you be on earth and still stand a chance? As ever, the Church, finding itself in a hole, kept on digging and the doctrine of Purgatory was born.

This chapter looks at two English case histories from the middle of the 15th century. Both men believed in the Church's teaching as it then stood and both attempted to ensure their speedy admittance to Heaven when they died. That they went about it in different ways was due in part to their different social status but also their view of the world and of their role in it, both then and after death 'for eternity'.

The late Middle Ages had achieved a remarkable and powerful antidote to the fear of death by honing to perfection the doctrine of Purgatory—just as the reformers brought it crashing to the ground. The notion of Purgatory, a waiting room while one's soul was cleansed prior to claiming its place in Heaven, emerged early in the life of the Christian Church but, being a man-made solution to the fate of the soul after death, it took well over 1000 years to mature. St Augustine, in the 4th century, was probably the first to use the adjective 'purgatorial' in relation to the Christian experience, and he laid down certain parameters:

As for temporal pain, some endure it here and some hereafter, and some both here and there: yet all is past before the Last Judgement (Sayers, 1955: 55).

The idea that pain was experienced before and after death, but within definable time limits, was a novel approach which afforded some comfort to fellow Christians. The notion that repeated prayer was efficacious for the forgiveness of sins was added by Gregory the Great around 600, citing an example of 30 days' prayer in one case, similar to requests in the late medieval period for prayers to be said on the 30th day after death (Le Goff, 1984: 92–3). What was later to be named Purgatory was perceived as the middle ground—the *via media*. For the man and woman in the street, it meant that repentance for sins had to be made by the individual before their death. They were given a second chance, as it were, and it was their choice to take it or not.

Purgatory, in its simplest terms, gave the individual a final opportunity for repentance before death. The period of purgatorial trial replaced a far more terrifying ordeal, that of the Last Judgement, the iconography of which was drawn from quotations in both Old and New Testaments. By the late 12th century the word 'purgatory' was used to describe a middle way and, within 100 years of the establishment of the universities and 70 years of the foundation of the mendicant friars, Purgatory and intercessory prayers said by the living for the dead were well established within the Catholic Church. Purgatory was accepted as a Christian doctrine at the Council of Florence in 1439, and central to this was the absolute conviction that the length of time a soul spent there was influenced by the intercessions of the living. The more prayers that were said, the quicker the soul would be released to Heaven. This was reciprocal trading at its most beneficial, for those who prayed were left moveable goods sometimes amounting to no more than a couple of pence while others might be bequeathed plate, jewellery or apparel in the testament of the deceased, the testament being an ecclesiastical document proved in an ecclesiastical court.

Those who could, paid—those who could not, prayed; thus, the prayers of the souls above were enhanced by the living below. The prayers of the poor were especially efficacious and it was incumbent upon those that wished to be remembered after death and who could afford to put that remembrance into practice to ensure that hospitals and the sick, schools and scholars, the local church and its parishioners, would all offer prayers for the health of the souls of the dead. One only has to recall the seven corporal works of mercy—feeding the hungry, supplying drink to the thirsty, clothing the naked, visiting the sick, releasing the prisoner, housing the stranger and burying the dead—and relate these to bequests contained in the testaments of the late Middle Ages to understand the priorities (Middleton-Stewart, 2001). Food and drink, usually described as doles, were to be distributed to the poor at funerals; poor maidens were left marriage dowries; the gowns to be worn by the poor at funerals were for their perpetual use; and the torches held by the poor around the grave not only symbolised 'the light of the world', but were a scourge against the Devil. Hospitals and jails were provided with food and clothing for the inmates; the stranger at the gate was welcomed as a guest; and the funeral was attended by friends, neighbours and, of course, the ever-present poor. Ease of travel and communications might be accelerated by money being left to bridges and roads—and, on the coast, to the improvement of sea defences. Anything that came within the broad spectrum of 'love thy neighbour' was considered apposite in the testaments of the dead, for all these were adjudged charitable works.

It was the Mass, of course, which provided the focal point, and its celebration was at the centre of religious guilds and chantries (Duffy, 1992: 91–130). Religious guilds have been described as the original Friendly Societies. They catered for men and women of all ages, both rich and poor, and at their centre, there was the celebration of the Mass, during which the brothers and sisters of the guild would pray for the dead. These religious guilds provided sustenance for the widows and orphans of the dead, the aged and infirm, but should not be confused with trade guilds which only occurred in large or important towns and cities, or both, binding their members together under the title of their craft.

Chantries were specifically set up and endowed for soul prayers, the founder or founders stipulating exactly what duties they wished the chaplain or chantry priest to execute. Masses were often specified to run for a definite period of time and were called service chantries. They were frequently requested in what was called the last will, a legal document unlike the ecclesiastical testament. Lower down the financial scale, a testator might ask for prayers to be said by a stipendiary chaplain to run for three or six months. Service chantries would have cost the executors approximately £3 for half a year of prayer. Many wealthy service chantries were set up to run for up to 99 years, the overall responsibility left to feoffees nominated by the testator before death. Perpetual chantries, on the other hand, involved more carefully advanced planning. Here chantry founders would ask permission from the bishop of the diocese and the incumbent of the church in which the chantry was to be celebrated before they laid their plans. This was a foundation that was expected to endure for ever. Property comprised the core of the chantry's wealth and the chantry priest became the freeholder, responsible for the upkeep of the fabric and for the perpetual singing of masses for the soul of the founder. A chantry chapel could be built on to the exterior wall of a church, as was the Beauchamp chapel at Warwick. A popular setting might be at the east end of an aisle, enclosed by a parclose screen, for a chapel within which the chantry priest would 'sing for the soul' of the chantry founder, as at St Mary's church in Bury St Edmunds. Both these were a separate space apart from the main body of the church (Middleton-Stewart, 2001: 141).

Perpetual chantries, service chantries, religious guilds—all contributed to the plan and the elevation of the late medieval churches which can still be seen today, all owing an immediate debt to the doctrine of Purgatory. Hellfire and damnation had no part in this self-sufficient concept—the doctrine was regarded as an insurance against the unknown future.

II. RICHARD BEAUCHAMP, EARL OF WARWICK

Richard Beauchamp, Earl of Warwick, died at Rouen (Normandy) on April 30th 1439. He was 58. Beauchamp had made extensive provision for his tomb and chantry, planning almost 20 years in advance. Unfortunately, he made an almost complete mess of things.

Beauchamp had a long and distinguished career fighting for the Lancastrian Kings both at home and in France (Payne, 2003). A King's Councillor from 1410 and Captain of Calais in 1412, by 1439 he was military governor in France and Normandy. In Rouen Beauchamp oversaw the trial and execution of Joan of Arc, for whom he seemed to have some respect if not sympathy. He supervised the upbringing of the young Henry VI and played a vital role in maintaining the delicate political balance at court. His will was made some years before his death, apparently before his return to France. The war had turned sour for the English. Paris was abandoned following the desertion of Burgundy and crop failures at home led to famine.

Beauchamp made two advantageous marriages, having three daughters from his first marriage to Elizabeth Berkeley (died 1422) and a son and a daughter from his second, to Isabel Despenser. He was at the centre of a complex kin system, his five children having married into the Neville, Lisle, Roos, Latimer and Beaufort families. His eventual heir, Henry, and Henry's sister Anne were married in a classic brother-sister swap, Richard Neville marrying Anne while Richard's sister Cecily, married Henry. This extensive family would also surround Beauchamp in death, and fight thereafter.

Richard Beauchamp's Christian faith is undoubted. He made a personal pilgrimage to Rome and Jerusalem, returning in 1410, when others of his class might have paid another to go by proxy. He represented the English crown at the important church council at Constance in 1414. He founded two chantries, one at Guy's Cliffe (Warks.) in 1422, and another in his will at St Mary's Warwick, with yet more endowments to the religious houses at Elmley and Tewksbury. In the will the Earl's image in pure gold weighing 20 lbs was presented to each of the shrines of his 'patron' saints—Alban, Thomas of Canterbury, John of Bridlington, Edmund and Winefride. These saints will also figure in the decoration of his burial chapel.

Beauchamp's will is now lost but highlights were recorded at various times (Dugdale, 1656: 354–56). He directed his executors to carry out all the work for his burial chapel after his death. It might have been expected that work would have begun in his lifetime if for no other reason than to ensure it was done to his satisfaction. Beauchamp requested that wherever he died, his body should be brought back to England and laid in a 'clean' stone coffin placed next to his father before an altar in the south transept of his family church in Warwick. Then work would commence on a new building 'in such Place as I have devised (which is well known)', discrete from the church, placed against the south side of the choir and entered through a door in the south transept arm, directly in front of his temporary tomb. The four-year delay before any work actually happened is curious, as the various permissions necessary for the founding of the chantry were granted in the year of his death while the building work was subject to a contract in 1441. The delay would have been significant. By the time the chapel, glass, sculpture and tomb had been made, England had torn itself apart in civil war and the Yorkist Edward IV was on the throne. The chapel was only consecrated and the Earl's body interred in 1475, sometime after the murder of Henry VI and when England was temporarily peaceful.

The will established three trustees who would undertake its various provisions (Hicks, 1981). They would be funded from some 23 estates set aside for the purpose. Immediately upon the death of the Earl, 5,000 masses were paid for. The new chapel would be served by an additional four college priests, funded from an endowment worth £40 per annum. Initially, his three daily memorial masses must have been said at the south transept altar in full public view. After 1475, the masses took on a more private aspect. Who else would be there? The chapel is completely enclosed and entered only through one door. Once shut, there is no indication from within the main church that such a splendid building even exists.

The areas of interest here are what he asked for in his will by way of permanent commemoration and what he actually got. Both may reveal something of his beliefs and of those around him. There is also the complicated history and difficult legal situation of his executors. One thing is sure: Beauchamp intended his chantry masses to rise up to Heaven forever—'every day during the world' is quoted in the will. This should not be taken as evidence of his concern for his sinfulness, but as an expression of his unusual piety. It is notable that the most devout Christians appeared almost to over-indulge when it came to good works for the benefit of their souls. The eternal saying of masses and the consequent support for the

Fig. 1 *The Burial Chapel of Richard Beauchamp, Earl of Warwick (1382–1439), at Warwick.*

priesthood was what mattered, not how long the donor might have feared spending in Purgatory.

The chapel is grand and opulent even in its post-Reformation state (Cook, 1963; and Payne, 2003). Sufficient glass and sculpture survives to show that no expense was spared in the construction and decoration. Painted figures rise up the window jambs, while exceptionally expensive stained glass complemented the painted stone vaulting. The tomb rises upon a Purbeck base housing gilt-bronze figures, while the effigy of Beauchamp is similarly made of costly latten. The tomb alone cost about £700, while the total cost—£2,481 4s 7d—was the equivalent of the annual income of a substantial lord. The extra cost of enlarging the college buildings brought the total to £3,634.

Beauchamp's chapel combines a number of ideas of both Heaven and earth. The stained glass of the east window contains British saints of especial significance to the Earl and the Lancastrians. Commissioned by the trustees in 1447, it is the most expensive glass known from the 15th century. His patron saints stand in intercession. Above, the seraphim hold the musical notation for the Gloria, a theme picked up in the side windows and reflecting Beauchamp's expressed concern for the musical content of his masses. The window formally contained full-length images of Beauchamp, both his wives and his five children. The surrounding sculpture begins with God above the window apex, then the orders of Heaven with no less than 30 angels. There follow four female saints—Catherine, Barbara, Mary Magdalene and Margaret. In Beauchamp's mind, Heaven was an appropriately hierarchical place. This is reflected in his tomb.

It is quite clear that two things are going on in the decoration and fitting of the chapel. On floor level, we see the funeral, represented by the weepers surrounding the tomb. They are dressed in mourning but their identities are made clear by the heraldry beneath each figure. They represent the kin of Beauchamp with the Earl firmly centre stage and are arranged exactly as they would have been at the funeral in order of rank. Being on the side of the tomb chest the weepers literally support him. His widow is not shown; she was ill, did not attend the funeral and died some months later. At slab level, we see Beauchamp, eyes open, staring up to the vault and east window. Above is the Virgin Mary and beyond, to the east, God, the hierarchy of heaven and his intercessionary saints. The two events do not cross over. None of the weepers can see much above the floor, their partially veiled heads and down-cast eyes denying them the vision granted to Beauchamp. They perform the role that they undertook at his funeral although not here but in the original, temporary resting place. The portrayal of the weepers raises questions about who actually controlled the representation of the earthly event. Beauchamp's will stipulated that he should be depicted as a man—that is, not a lifelike portrait—dressed in armour. This much was completed by 1452, but as 'devised' by the trustees. The figure is in gilt-bronze, known as latten, a fabric of royal tomb figures. Beauchamp's is the only surviving example that is non-royal. His splendid Milanese armour and aristocratic attributes suggest that he envisaged his entry into Heaven in the same state he enjoyed on earth. Recently, it has been stressed that the hearse (frame) over the top takes the form of a carriage (Munby, 2002). It was designed to support the cloth placed over the tomb for the anniversary obit mass. Thus, it appeared even more like a grand carriage, quite literally transporting him to Heaven in all his finery. Beauchamp clearly expected to be in Heaven dressed as an earl, just as his intercessionary saints are attired as on earth. That is how we are able to recognise who they are. This is a complex and controversial aspect of all such tombs—do they display the deceased as on earth as a commemoration and for the benefit of the onlooker, or do they represent the expectations of the deceased in Heaven? The imagery of the Beauchamp tomb and the privacy of its setting strongly suggests the latter.

The delays evident in the building and fitting of the chapel were the result of a family feud, resulting in a series of court cases not unlike 'Bleak House' (Hicks, 1981). The problem lay with trustees who showed little sense of urgency while having their own economic problems, a widow terminally ill and three disputatious daughters who felt aggrieved. Though the chapel finally came into use in 1475, the land and inheritance disputes rumbled on until 1486, nearly half a century after Beauchamp's death.

The problem came from the Earl's two marriages. His first wife, Elizabeth, had three daughters, all of whom married great lords—Shrewsbury, Roos then Somerset, and Latimer. Then Elizabeth died. Beauchamp was determined to have a son and the chantry foundation at Guy's Cliffe was partly to pray for this intention. He soon married Eleanor Despenser, and then came the son and another daughter.

On the death of his first wife, Beauchamp started to set up a trust, partly to finance his intended burial chapel, but also to sort out the huge inheritance, confident that he would yet have one or more sons. The existing daughters later claimed that he promised to make sure that they were 'alright'. This was important especially as their mother, Elizabeth Berkley, was a considerable heiress in her own right. Her inheritance should go to them. In the event, the will of 1435 ignored the earlier daughters altogether, leaving some 23 estates temporarily to the trustees to finance the chapel, and everything else to his only son, Henry, who had been born to Beauchamp's second wife. By this time, the Warwick inheritance was worth £5,471 per annum. Only the Duke of York and the King were richer. As the heir was too young to take possession of his titles in 1439, no action was taken by the half sisters, but soon after his 21st birthday in 1446, young Henry died. He had taken possession of his estates, had married and had left an infant daughter. This was important, as the child could pass her inheritance to a future son. But this too was not to be. Most conveniently, the child died in 1449. Then the fight really began.

Throughout this period the trustees were slowly building and fitting out the chapel, but were constantly hampered by land disagreements and disputes with life tenants. Upon the child's death, the trustees had no hesitation in acknowledging Richard Neville, Earl of Salisbury as heir, based on his marriage to Anne, the only daughter from Beauchamp's second marriage. The legal argument was that Anne was a sister in 'full blood' to the previous heir, Henry. The half sisters were just that. However, the passing of the entire inheritance to Neville was challenged by the three half sisters on the basis that at least the Berkley inheritance of their mother should be split three ways between them. This challenge was further complicated by the inclusion of some of this land in the trust and the fact that no one seemed quite sure who would inherit what and where. Neville, however, used his considerable power at Court to frustrate the rightful claims of his sisters-in-law, and he saw off their husbands one by one. Somerset was blamed for the loss of the French war in 1450, accused of embezzlement, thrown into the Tower and finally cut down in St Albans in 1455. Latimer was declared insane, while Shrewsbury was killed in 1453 in the last battle of the Hundred Years War. But this did not stop their wives, who randomly seized estates and their revenues. Thus began decades of disputes, seizures and abortive settlements. The violent overthrow of the insane King in 1461, then of Edward IV and finally the murder of Henry VI did nothing to help the unstable economy, and law and order became especially fragile. Neville himself was killed in 1471, leaving his widow to fight on.

Throughout, the trustees showed a level of self-interest that did not encourage them to complete their task. The absence of a widow duty-bound to push ahead with her husband's wishes was a further hindrance. Given the intractable mess over land and income and a family at war in several senses, it is all the more extraordinary that Beauchamp's chapel ever happened at all.

III. JOHN BARET OF BURY ST EDMUNDS

Those who visited the exhibition entitled 'Gothic: Art for England 1400—1547' at the Victoria and Albert Museum in the autumn of 2003 may have left without making the acquaintance of John Baret. He was exhibit 331 (Marks and Williamson, 2003: 442). Baret was placed near the exit, a suitable resting place for a rotting cadaver. Stripped of his tomb, which remained in Bury St Edmunds, Baret's carved effigy, despite its grim representation, had lost its potency and its message. It was as though the putty-coloured limestone had merged into the hangings behind and the impact of his appearance and its message were lessened.

There are, and there were, multiple differences between him and Richard Beauchamp, the Earl of Warwick, the first personality in this chapter. But they present a double-bill, their wills itemising in minute and specific detail the pattern that their burial and obsequies were to take. Their wills may differ in form and substance, but the over-riding impression gained from each is of an undeniable faith and trust in their late-medieval religion and the belief that prayers and good works on earth would furnish them with a more comfortable end. Beauchamp, this able and cultured man, the third wealthiest nobleman of his day, chose to display his position, his connections and his undoubted wealth. His will gives us an excellent example of the time and labour expended on the creation of his tomb with its weepers representing his son, his daughter and other members of the Beauchamp dynasty. The private chantry chapel, built into the angle of the chancel and south aisle of their collegiate church of St Mary at Warwick, formed a fitting space within which this great servant of the Crown would be laid.

John Baret of Bury St Edmunds was a commoner, but a wealthy commoner. He lived in Suffolk at the very time that great riches were being made from draperies, but he had married well and could be described as a member of the parish gentry. This was certainly the status of his family in Cratfield, which lay to the east of Bury St Edmunds, and his relation, William Cratfield, had been Abbot of Bury Abbey from 1389–1414. Baret, who had no children, enumerated many other relations in his will as his heirs; some called Baret, some called Cratfield, indicating that this was a period during which many locative surnames changed to personal surnames. His relations spread out as far as Blythburgh and Southwold on the Suffolk coast, all of them leaving generous wills remembering their respective churches and local religious houses. A typically buoyant, socially acknowledged family of the period.

Fig. 2 *The tomb and image of John Baret in St Mary's Church, Bury St Edmunds.*

Baret's will, written in 1464 and proved on 2 May 1467, runs to 10,000 words (Tymms, 1850: 15–44). His shrouded, skeletal effigy had already been carved (a continental type of memorial popular in England at least since the 1420s) and his tomb and effigy were in place (Marks and Morgan, 2003: 94–5). Baret's inscribed shroud is written in Latin, a translation of which would read: 'Behold, now I sleep in the dust', and the stone scroll in his left hand is inscribed with words from the Office of the Dead:

O Lord, judge me not according to my deeds. I have done nothing worthy in Thy sight. Therefore I beseech Thy majesty that Thou, O God, shall blot out my iniquity.

At the far end, the tomb is inscribed with 'He that will sadly behold me with his eye may see his own mirror and learn for to die', and along the edge is engraved: 'For such as I am right so shall ye be'. This, in comparison to the effigy and the surroundings of Richard Beauchamp, is the commemoration of a simple and honest man who really does seem to have understood the meaning of death and decay. He left instructions to be implemented on the day and date he died; and his remission from Purgatory, the pardon which he had received from the Pope, was to be written on the tomb in some convenient place, 'that it may be read and known to exhort the people to pray for me'. To ensure his grave was cared for, the bearer of the paxbrede at St Mary's altar was to receive 8d per year.

Arrangements for his interment included a mass of prick-songs in worship of Our Lady at St Mary's altar at seven o'clock in order that Requiem mass could begin immediately after, to speed the time for the sermon. Master Thomas Harlow was to perform this task for 6s 8d and if unable to oblige, another cleric was to be chosen from Cambridge. Baret continued:

And my body to be buried by the altar of St Martin, named also Our Lady's altar, in St Mary's church at Bury, under the parclose of the return of the candlebeam before the image of Our Saviour, and no stone to be stirred of my grave, but a pit to be made under the ground-sill where Lady Schardelowe was wont to sit, and the body put in as near under my grave as may be without hurt of the said grave.

Baret, however, knew that there were plans afoot to extend the aisle in which his tomb was placed and he left adequate instructions for its re-positioning at a later date.

A funeral was the final chance for persuading people to pray for the soul by distributing food and clothes to the poor in the common dole. Baret, however, wrote: 'I will no common dole have'. In other words, he was planning his distribution of alms in great detail. At his interment there were to be five men clad in black in worship of the five wounds of Jesus, and five women in white in worship of the five joys of Mary, fulfilling one of the works of mercy—clothing the naked. Each poor man and poor woman in black and white, the contrast of darkness and light, were to have 2d and meat. Each mourner or 'weeper' held a torch of clean wax, the wax to be kept for a stock to light annually two tapers. The light given by the torches was believed to frighten demons away, and again contrasted darkness with light, interpreting Christ as the light of the world. Baret wrote that when his solemn dirge was kept, each poor man and woman there was to have 1d to pray for him, children were to receive 1d and others were to receive 2d. He followed with precision the favoured course of post-mortem celebrations so popular at the end of the middle-ages and he put into practice the seven works of mercy. Here he killed several birds with one stone by caring for the prisoners in the jail and for the sick in the town by feeding both with bread, meat and drink plus 1d each, while each leper in the town was to have 2d, and a loaf and 'halpeny'.

As he looked into the future in which he would play no part, Baret bequeathed 10 marks (£6 13s 4d in proper money) for the story of the Magnificat to be painted on the reredos and table in his chapel:

I will that the image of Our Lady that Robert Pygot painted be set up against the pillar next [to] the parclose of St Mary's altar with the base ready thereto, and in the middle of the base my candlestick of latten with a pyke to be set afore a taper

I have assigned unto five tapers belonging to the Nativity gild which stand aloft before the angels, with chimes to be set about Our Lady at the pillar.

The image of the Virgin against the pillar was to have a new crown of metal gilt as she stood within the housing of the reredos. Baret described the roof above his tomb:

[T]hree mirrors of glass to be set in the middle of the three vaults above my grave, which be ready with my other glass and diverse rolls with scripture.

This unique roof, decorated repeatedly with his monogram and multiple SS collars, the badge of allegiance to the house of Lancaster, is situated above the east end of the south nave aisle delineating the area of his chantry chapel below.

Baret has been credited with financing the superb angel roof in St Mary's nave (Haward, 1999: 52–65). He was certainly wealthy enough to have built not one private chantry chapel but several. Nevertheless, he opted to be buried and to be remembered in a side aisle. The chantry was to be served by a priest referred to as Saint Mary's priest, but as the chantry would not come into being until Baret's death, the priest had probably not been nominated at the time that Baret wrote his will. Lodgings for the chantry priest were to be found in Baret's house, which was to be divided in two, the priest 'to have it to him and his successors for ever'. This dwelling, which also housed Baret's workers and their looms, still stands close by St Mary's in what is now Chequers Square. The chantry priest was to receive a yearly pension for which he was to pray for Baret's soul at every meal, meat or supper and to say De Profundis and to rehearse the name John Baret openly, and everyone else to add: 'God have mercy on his soul'. In addition, Baret set up an obit or anniversary to be said annually on date of his death and also a seven-day celebration to be said on the weekday on which he died. To cover any other avenues of salvation that he had not explored, Baret commissioned the Candlemas gild, the gild of the Translation of St Nicholas and the gild of the Resurrection to remember his year day with a Mass and refreshment after.

In the abbey was the shrine of St Edmund who had been the patron saint of England until he was displaced by Edward III's favourite, St George, 100 years previously. At the end of 1433, the 12 year old Henry VI had arrived at the abbey for a visit which lasted four months. On his departure Abbot Curteis presented the young King Henry with an illuminated manuscript of 'The Life of St Edmund and St Fremund', the text by John Lydgate, monk of Bury and versifier to the nobility. Perhaps the monk on the right of the dedicatory miniature was Lydgate, in his day the pre-eminent English poet, unchallenged as a writer however turgid his verse may seem to modern taste. The boy King, who had been in the care of Richard Beauchamp of Warwick during his childhood, knelt to pray before St Edmund's shrine. Lydgate's friend was John Baret, who wrote in his will:

I give and bequeathe to St Edmund and his shrine my heavy piece noble which weigheth 20 ounces and my best heart of gold with angels and a ruby with 4 labels of white enamel, the said noble and the said brooch-heart of gold to be hanged, nailed and fastened upon the shrine on my cost by the advice of my executors where they and the feretories think and find a place most convenient, to the worship of God and St Edmund.

Baret disposed of his worldly goods with great care and in precise detail. He was anxious that his executors should complete St Mary's altar, at which his chantry was to be celebrated. The Risbygate, the most ruinous in the town, was to be repaired with freestone and brick, formed in an arch and embattled, and an image of Our Lady placed in a stone housing between arch and battlement. If brick was not good enough, calcyon and mortar were to be used after advice had been sought from Simon Clerk, the third master mason to be employed in the building of King's College Chapel. Finally Baret was determined that the timber cross before his house, acknowledging his belief in the Resurrection, should be built and supported on four posts as at the north Suffolk town of Eye ... 'or better', as he wrote in his will.

IV. CONCLUSION

The post-mortem provisions of these two men highlight a number of differences beyond their social status and wealth. The enactment of their respective wills is in sharp contrast; Baret made sure much was done before he died—Beauchamp did not. Baret's endowment is straightforward—cash and urban property—while Beauchamp's is almost unnecessarily complicated, to the point that it nearly did not happen. Beauchamp's intended trust land was feudal, and thus carried military responsibility that might end if the land was charitably entrusted. Twenty three estates might produce 250 knights and men, a sizeable number given that medieval armies were rarely over 5,000 men. England was at war and the King was reluctant to let such land be 'lost' to the Church. Great care had to be taken to get all the legalities in order. Land taken into a chantry foundation also became exempt from death duties, one of the most important sources of taxation in the Middle Ages. Hence Beauchamp's trustees, seemingly inexperienced or perhaps just inept, muddled along for 35 years before the Earl's wishes were eventually fulfilled. Baret's intentions were up and running almost from the day he died.

In addition, Beauchamp's failure to make proper legal provision for the funding reveals another side of life in the 15th century when the whole atmosphere of the period was one of illegality just under the surface—even the Lancastrian King was not technically legitimate in the eyes of many. Bending a judgement here, an inheritance there or refusing legal redress if it did not suit the King all seem to have been the order of the day. Was the King above the law? It all has a modern ring to it.

And then there is the contrasting nature of the two men's memorials. Beauchamp's tomb and sumptuous chantry represents a private world devoted solely to him and his salvation. It is almost selfish, but then his disregard for his elder daughters might be regarded in the same light. Unless the will is badly recorded, it lacks any provision for extended charity—no obit clothes or dole for the poor to attend his masses. Indeed the arrangement and access to the chapel would make that difficult. It is all about him. Baret on the other hand was a man of the community and his will involves his employees, the local poor and the good of the town in general. He wanted his name remembered by as large a section of the population as possible, as if being recalled was in itself a form of immortality. That this meant paying for it was not uncommon in the period. Hence, Baret stresses acts of charity to be continued after his death. This would get him remembered. Beauchamp appears to have made no such provision despite being infinitely richer. Even his children were to lose out.

Their common belief in the life hereafter and that time would be spent in Purgatory lies behind the actions of both men. Yet Baret had purchased a pardon for his sins from no less than the Pope himself. It is recorded on the tomb. If he had a 'Get out of jail free' card, what was his worry? Why bother with the masses, the chantry priests and the acts of charity? Either you believed in the pardon or you didn't. Baret's actions remain curiously contradictory.

In one respect, acceptance of Purgatory did turn the spotlight on the individual, who now faced a personal judgment at the point of death to decide the soul's immediate destination. That judgment took the form of a spiritual audit in which sins were balanced against good deeds (Rosemary Horrox, 1999: 110).

BIBLIOGRAPHY

Cook, GH (1963) *Mediaeval chantries and chantry chapels* (London, Phoenix House).
Duffy, E (1992) *The stripping of the altars* (New Haven, NY, Yale University Press).
Dugdale, W (1656) *Antiquities of Warwickshire* (London, Thomas Warren).
Haward, B (1999) *Suffolk medieval church roof carvings* (Hitcham, Suffolk Institute of Archeology and History).
Hicks, MA (1981) 'The Beauchamp Trust 1439-87', LIV Bulletin of the Institute of Historical Research 445–447.

Horrox, R (1999) 'Purgatory, prayer and plague 1150–1380' in PC Jupp and C Gittings (eds), *Death in England: an illustrated history* (Piscataway, NJ, Rutgers University Press) 90–119.

Le Goff, J (1948) *The birth of purgatory* (London, Scholar Press).

Middleton-Stewart, J (2001) *Inward purity and outward splendour: death and remembrance in the deanery of Dunwich, Suffolk, 1370–1547* (Woodbridge, Boydell).

Mumby, J (2002) 'Richard Beauchamp's funeral car' 155 *Journal of the British Archaeological Association* 278–287.

Payne, A (2003) 'The Beauchamps and the Nevilles' in R Marks and P Williamson (eds), *Gothic—Art for England 1400–1547* (London, V & A Publications) 219–333.

Rogers, N (2003) 'Regional production' in R Marks and P Williamson (eds), *Gothic—Art for England 1400–1547* (London, V & A Publications) 54–61.

Sayers, DL (1955) 'Purgatory: the doctrine' in DL Sayers (ed), *Dante's Divine Comedy 2: Purgatory* (Harmondsworth, Penguin) 54–61.

Tymm, S (1850) *Wills and inventories from the Register of the Commissary of Bury St Edmunds and the Archdeaconry of Sudbury*, reprint (New York, AMS Press) 1968.

8

Rites, Rights, Writing: 'Tintern Abbey', Death, and the Will

SARAH WEBSTER GOODWIN

[T]he dead are beyond harm. They cannot be hurt; neither can they have desires or welfare interests to be denied. In the absence of a belief in an afterlife, to regard someone (the same 'someone') as continuing in a state of 'being' after death (ie as a corpse) is problematic (Price, chapter twelve this volume)

I. DEATH, LAW, POETRY

IN AN EDITED collection on death's rights and rites, it might seem that poems would have no role to play. The focus would surely be on the status of death with respect to the law and to rituals: two bodies of collective knowledge and discourses that survive individuals and define a collectivity. But we know that it is a peculiar feature of Western European modernity that law and myth—once essentially a whole—evolved into distinct spheres, and that subsequently literature and the arts have performed some of the work once performed by myth as the vehicle of the law. Literature authorises the law by the means of narrative and emotion, cultivating sympathies and rationales on a broad scale such that peoples not only understand laws rationally but also embrace them as meaningful. As Oliver Wendell Holmes famously wrote: 'The life of the law has not been logic: it has been experience' (Ziolkowski, 1997: 5).

The corpse has one thing in common with both literature and the law: it points to life but isn't itself alive. As this edited collection suggests, the corpse is a provocation, a question, a sign that calls for interpretation. Its very muteness asks: What happened to me? Was my death wrongful? What is to be done with me? And what is to be done with my property? As we see in the chapters in this volume, the law is involved in the answers to all of these questions. They are also the stuff of many works of literature.

These questions are not all of the same order, and the chapters here address them in ways that sometimes differ in assumptions and method. The final question—What is to be done with my property?—takes on particular importance in contexts where the property is substantial. The last will and testament, which appears to be as old and hallowed as property itself—first as ritual, then later as text—became increasingly urgent in Britain during the period of industrialisation and increasing distributed wealth. This urgency worked itself out in countless ways: for example, in reformation of copyright and entailment laws, and even in legal challenges to primogeniture. At the same time, poets (including novelists and dramaturges) provided the 'myths, the narratives and imaginative scenarios that cultivated a broad base of support and understanding for the assumptions that underlay the evolving property and testamentary law. The concept of property itself is one of the foundations of legal thinking; to own something—whether land, objects, or intangibles—is not only to have rights over the use of it, but also to have the power to sell it or give it away. As Adams and Brownsword point out, the law exists because

group life must be regulated ... [I]f citizens wish to trade with one another, to buy and sell goods and services, there must be property rules and the ground rules for making exchanges need to be established (Adams and Brownsword, 2006: 7).

And it is fundamental to Western legal thinking that individuals may plan for the transfer of their property as they anticipate their death. This seems so commonplace to us as to be nearly transparent. And yet we know that such problematic matters as entailments, unjust wills, unconscionable heirs and intestate deaths provide the starting point for countless novels, shaping the reading public's conception of justice in response to the evolving laws. Where a will is contested, it is anything but transparent.

To suggest that literature prepares the way for new laws and then continues to cultivate our sympathies for them, is to imply that law and literature are complementary but also quite distinct cultural arenas. The differences may appear in stark relief when we consider the status of a poem as testament in contrast to a legal will. It is one of the tenets of post-modern thought—after Derrida and Lacan, elaborated by Kofmann and Bronfen (Kofmann, 1985; and Bronfen, 1992)—that art does the work of melancholia in revealing the death enacted in every utterance. Representation, in displacing the original, both resurrects it and kills it, turning it into a ghost or a trace of its former being, and thus an instantiation of death itself. Bronfen, responding to Kofmann, describes what we might call the relationship between poetry and death:

The creation of beauty allows us to escape from the elusiveness of the material world into an illusion of eternity (a denial of loss), even as it imposes on us the realization that beauty is itself elusive, intangible, receding. Because it is created on the basis of the same elusiveness it tries to obliterate, what art in fact does is mourn beauty, and in so doing it mourns itself (Bronfen, 1992: 64–6; see also Baudrillard, 1976; and Ernst, 1988).

Bronfen notes:

It is one of the central aspects of recent scholarship that deals theoretically and not just thematically with the issue of representations or figurations of death to emphasise the binding interrelation between writing and loss (Bronfen, 1991: 74; see also Goodwin and Bronfen, 1991).

Poetry, then, is essentially untenable because it reveals the untenable in language itself, even as it aims for a measure of immutability.

We can also see that a similar paradox holds for death rituals: for example, in the ways that tombstones mime the hardness of bones and stabilise the site occupied by the dead even as they also serve as a mental portal into their destabilising space (see Metcalf and Huntington, 1979: 99–109). Miller and Parrott (chapter nine this volume) describe in strikingly similar terms contemporary rituals of mourning that incorporate objects left behind by the dead: clothing, for example, is construed as temporary—it 'wears out'—in contrast to the permanence of jewellery. But precisely that durable quality can make jewellery seem hard and unforgiving: 'immutable, in a more abstract relation to the person'. Jewellery has 'become testimony to the irreconcilable'.

Thus, the very permanence of the object works both as an enduring monument and persistent reminder of loss. We might further explore the ways that the law's traditional inscription on 'tablets of stone' resembles tombstones in this regard: the stones, then, would attempt to render permanent what is constantly shifting within the context of lived realities. Irresolvable injustices would haunt these stones just as the dead haunt their graves, despite all of culture's multi-faceted attempts to secure an infallible and durable code of law.

It seems improbable, however, that the law performs such a dual work of representation with respect to death. Ritualistic and aesthetic representations both point to and radically question the grounds of their utterances. Can the law afford to destabilise itself in this way? Can it avoid doing it? Is the law, like poetry and monuments, subject to the force of utterance as both representation and destruction of the represented? It may be that testamentary law, the law of wills, provides precisely the site where we see this possibility most clearly. That is, the will, as a document, necessarily represents both the will of the individual—to the extent that it can be represented—and, indirectly but ineluctably, that person's death. The concept of property in Western culture is closely associated with notions of the individual and personal identity. All forms of property, tangible and intangible, covered by property law contribute to a person's identity—not only as it is perceived but also as he or she experiences and generates it—since the law covers not only land, objects and money but also ideas, works of art, expressions of the self. To will this property to others is necessarily to rehearse one's death. It is also, in some sense, to attempt to control or contain the loss that death brings: to attenuate the annihilation, to allow for some forms of survival. The testament, the public document, marks the place of death and of survival. As a legal act, it presumes that a will can be written, and that the text can suffice to convey the subject's will. Ratified by the law, witnessed, a kind of covenant, it prolongs the will and thus the subjectivity of its author. But it does so as an act of faith, not in a hereafter, but in a just legal system that values and indeed is founded upon the concept of the individual subject.

II. 'TINTERN ABBEY' AND THE DEATH OF THE SUBJECT

How might we then articulate the relationship, in modernity, of testamentary law and literature in regard particularly to death? Or, to narrow the question, how might literary works have helped to create a concept of individual subjectivity, of natural law, of the rights of the dead—despite the instability of all of these concepts—that would enable testamentary law to function effectively, to speak for the corpse, in a post-Enlightenment secular world? Posed in this way, the question leads us to the poets who gave voice to an emergent subjectivity during the late 18th and early 19th centuries. In 1798, Wordsworth's *Tintern Abbey* appeared at the moment historically when a modern subjectivity came into focus—indeed, as a major work of the Romantic canon, it was famously instrumental in shaping that aspect of modernity. Crucial to this subjectivity is a secular self-consciousness about the trajectory of one's own life, terminating in death. For the poet, religion no longer provides the consolation of a faith in an afterlife. The Western poetic tradition before Wordsworth had it that the poem survived the poet as a monument, a form or indicator of immortality, a verbal tombstone. But in *Tintern Abbey* Wordsworth shifts the role of the poem away from the status of monument to something more inter-subjective and dynamic as a model for the modern poetic response to death. *Tintern Abbey* aims at nothing less than extending the power of the poet's self, his subjectivity or will, beyond the reach of his own lifetime. The poem culminates in the poetic equivalent of a last will and testament. In turning away from religious faith, it aligns poetic powers implicitly with the secular force of law to extend subjectivity beyond the boundaries of death. At the same time, it provides a potent rationale and emotional context for the legal will as a powerful and pervasive document in a secular culture. It serves, thus, both as a general example of the dialogic relationship between law and literature in modern cultures, and as a specific moment in literary history with regard to concepts of property, inheritance and the will.

The will, *Tintern Abbey* seems to imply, is much more than a legal document; it is a statement that both represents the self that writes it and enacts the anticipated death of that self (provisionally, as fiction, but in some sense too as 'real,' in that it is inevitable, acknowledged and imminent). More than that, it creates and embodies the self even as it imagines its own undoing. The written self, in Wordsworth's reflections, is comprised of a series of memories and projections, presented in the narrative, poetic and linguistic systems that enable its representations and its survival, even as they also replace it, leaving it elsewhere. In this sense, and as a poem with a vast reach and influence since the early decades of the 19th century in Britain, it provides a model of post-Enlightenment secular thought about death rites and rights.

Scambler (chapter ten this volume) notes that though it is difficult to define 'modernity,' one pervasive feature of modern societies (*pace* Habermas) is the disjunction between the 'system' (economy, state) and the 'lifeworld' (private and public spheres). Scambler is primarily aiming to describe the present moment, but it is worth noting that *Tintern Abbey*, in my reading here, both represents and interrogates such a disjunction with implicit reference to the death of the subject. In other words Wordsworth asserts the poetic self as a kind of 'lifeworld' in response to the disjunctions imposed upon the self by the impersonal systems of the law and the economy. As Wordsworth wrote in another poem, 'The world is too much with us': by 'world', here, he meant the otherness of the modern, impersonal systems that Scambler argues invade and shape our experiences of death. At the same time, as will become clear, the poet relies on—and in some sense also inhabits—the law as a protected and protecting space. Perhaps like the mourning and memorial rituals described by Jupp, Miller and Parrott, and Hallam (chapters six, nine and sixteen this volume), poetry, for Wordsworth, provides a complement to the law, a more private and personalised, symbolic parallel world. But it does so without occupying an 'outlaw' position—on the contrary, it implies a necessary dialectic.

Tintern Abbey stops well short of referring explicitly to the law. Its narrative and meditative structure, however, imply powerful affinities between poetry and testamentary law. Poetry, in this paradigm, is thus a modern, civilising force. At the same time, *Tintern Abbey* argues for poetry's privileged relationship to wildness; both the wilderness of the non-human natural world and the as yet uncivilised wildness of the child before adult self-consciousness and constraints set in. Unlike the law, then, poetry works to release constraints, to return us to a fantasised wholeness of being that pre-exists the alienation of adult consciousness. Wordsworth posits here a dual and paradoxical role for poetry as both deep origin of the law and implicit challenge to it. In both of these roles, it proffers a modern answer to the anomie of death: art as the enduring monument to subjectivity, and as the extended reach of the subjective will into the lives of the survivors.

The poem rehearses the poet's death, and by representation also our own, even as it proposes a utopian vision in which desire and restraint, self and collective, wildness and law reconcile in the immutable wholeness of poetry.

This reading might seem far-fetched if it were not for recent scholarship that presents Wordsworth's lifelong relationship to the law. In his thorough and detailed study, Schoenfield refers to *Tintern Abbey* only in passing and argues throughout that Wordsworth's relationship with the law was ambivalent and complex (Schoenfield, 1996). Wordsworth, whose father and brother were both lawyers, engaged in two major legal struggles that lasted for years: the claims on his father's estate, and, later, his campaign for more protective copyright laws. Schoenfield traces exhaustively Wordsworth's engagement with the law in multiple arenas and shows that this engagement affected his metaphors as well as his themes in the poetry. Eilenberg, in a related study, details Wordsworth's extensive activism on behalf of copyright laws. As she points out, it was later in his life—from 1808 on—that Wordsworth lobbied for increased authorial rights, but this work became almost an obsession for him (Eilenberg, 1989). She notes that he drew explicit comparisons between copyright and monuments:

Copyright assumes not only the functions of epitaph but its ambiguities as well. It serves as a memorial to the work whose immortality it asserts. Attempting to compensate for the corruptibility of writing, it makes tacit admission of the frailty of words (Eilenberg, 1989: 368).

A reading of the poem as testament necessarily emphasises the closing verse-paragraph, in which the poet addresses his sister. The poem, it will be remembered, opens with a meditation on the rural scene before him and on its importance to him over the five years since he last visited it. Only in the concluding section do we learn that he is not alone and that his sister is there with him. Turning to her, he proposes that this scene should be as valuable to her in the future as it has been for him in the past:

Therefore let the moon
Shine on thee on thy solitary walk;
And let the misty mountain winds be free
To blow against thee: and in after years,
When these wild ecstasies shall be matured
Into a sober pleasure, when thy mind
Shall be a mansion for all lovely forms,
Thy memory be as a dwelling-place
For all sweet sounds and harmonies; Oh! then,
If solitude, or fear, or pain, or grief,
Should be thy portion, with what healing thoughts

Of tender joy wilt thou remember me,
And these my exhortations! Nor, perchance,
If I should be where I no more can hear
Thy voice, nor catch from thy wild eyes these gleams
Of past existence, wilt thou then forget
That on the banks of this delightful stream
We stood together

Alluding to her future loneliness and grief, then to his own future absence, before swerving away from it, the poet offers a legacy to his sister (and, by extension, to the reader). The imperative verb in the phrase 'let the misty mountain winds be free' establishes the mode of the will—though he characteristically softens it with a 'perchance' and a double negative later in the passage as he concludes the poem:

Nor wilt thou then forget,
That after many wanderings, many years
Of absence, these steep woods and lofty cliffs,
And this green pastoral landscape, were to me
More dear, both for themselves, and for thy sake.

The poet's legacy to his sister, then, is this particular landscape, in its value to him ('more dear') as he has articulated it in the poem: both as a particular place, and as a memory with particular powers.

The landscape's most striking qualities, in this legacy, are the tensions it represents between wildness and cultivation. Already in the passages quoted above the poet refers to 'these wild ecstasies' and to his sister's 'wild eyes', from which he catches gleams of his past. He contrasts that wildness with the more mature 'sober pleasure' he imagines her enjoying, when her mind

shall be a mansion for all lovely forms,
Thy memory be as a dwelling-place
For all sweet sounds and harmonies.

The contrast here is between a wild landscape—with the wildness it both meets and inspires in the younger witness—and, on the other hand, a more sober, mature, sheltered dwelling-place or mansion. This last metaphor for the mental estate he is willing her contrasts, in turn, with the 'lonely rooms' where, 'mid the din of towns and cities', he had previously turned to his memories of this place for sustenance. The shelter of the mind he proposes in the poem's final lines, then, offers something much more enduring and valuable than either the wild landscape or those indeterminate, transient rooms. It seems, paradoxically, to be a shelter *of* wildness as well as *from* it. What might that mean? In particular, what does it offer in the face of his death, so deftly invoked at the end?

Wildness is a leitmotif in the poem, but the treasured landscape is both wild and cultivated. It has often been noted that the poet's description of hedgerows as 'little lines of sportive wood run wild' works equally well as a metaphor for this poem itself. Wordsworth's luscious and playful enjambments and other manipulations of blank verse in the poem enact before our eyes and ears the kinds of running wild that he describes in the hedgerows. Verses throw vines over into neighbouring gardens; iambs merge into trochees just as orchards merge into copses; and everywhere wildness co-exists with order in a utopian connection of landscape and sky, nature and culture. The 'forms of beauty' described in the poem's opening verses, that will provide such a basis for later reflection and solace, are not terrifying in their sublimity, but are oddly domesticated. Early in the description, the poem refers to 'cliffs, which on a wild secluded scene impress/Thoughts of more deep seclusion'. Here the language approaches the sublime and would tend to lead us toward the deepest seclusion, the greatest wildness—our own extinction. But he turns instead to 'plots of cottage-ground' and 'orchard-tufts', which do not 'disturb/ The wild green landscape'. They do not disturb it because they blend into it, as the poem blends the rigors of iambic pentameter with spontaneity of feeling. In the contrast between wildness and domesticity in this setting, we find the metaphorical axis between nature and civilisation; between non-human, unself-conscious being and the self-aware subjectivity of the poet; between abstract death as the most extreme wilderness and consciousness as it manifests civilisation (or, to invoke more explicitly Freud's terms, between *das Unbehagen* and *die Kultur*). Poetry and law, it seems, both inhabit this very axis.

The poet ends his description of the landscape with an image that has long puzzled and occupied commentators: he makes note of

> wreathes of smoke
> Sent up, in silence, from among the trees,
> With some uncertain notice, as might seem,
> Of vagrant dwellers in the houseless woods,
> Or of some hermit's cave, where by his fire
> The hermit sits alone.

Here, again, he domesticates the landscape's wildness in an unexpected way, recalling 'vagrant dwellers in the houseless woods' and imagining a hermit by a cave. These two images of wilder habitation join the cottages and pastoral farms as a series of references to dwelling-places that anticipate and also contrast with the mental mansion he offers his sister in the poem's closing lines. In a scene where, as many commentators have noted, an abbey stands in ruins, occupied by impoverished, homeless people, he seems to feel viscerally that the wild landscape, in all its beauty, cannot offer up its gifts without the security of shelter, whether it be 'lonely rooms' or mental mansions.

Some commentators, noting these contrasts, have faulted Wordsworth for turning away from his more youthful politicised idealism and have seen this poem as a manifesto for that change. Others have defended him as being self-conscious here about the disappointments represented by the turn the Revolution had taken in France and the need for a new model of understanding in England (see Levinson, 1986; and McGann, 1984). What is particularly interesting about this debate is the way concepts of shelter and of vagrancy—poverty specifically as homelessness—form the axis. As Richey persuasively argues, this aspect of the poem is grounded in the poet's own extensive experience of homelessness (Richey, 1998). Orphaned young, he had for years lived a

rootless existence ... with no fixed residence or employment, living principally off the charity of friends as he sought to regain his bearings and find his place in society (Richey, 1998: 214).

Richey notes that we might expect the poet now to dwell upon his present contentment in finally sharing a home with his sister. Instead, he resists all allusion to the fact that they had finally realised this dream, and emphasises the more permanent dwelling-places of the mind, rendered more permanent and stable in the poem's monumentality.

What the poet thus offers his sister, in the form of a mental gift, is a *real* estate, in contrast to, but also emerging integrally from, the material lands and habitations before them. Viewing a site where enclosure has done its work and hedgerows mark property lines, he notes that those lines have 'run wild'. Taking the implications further, we might say that he posits poetry as a force in contrast to and even more powerful than the law. The law, as represented by property lines, must contain and demarcate; as represented by legal wills, it passes specified property on from the dying to the surviving. Poetry, in contrast, offers us the entire scene as a legacy for our *mental* lives, an immaterial gift that ignores property lines and incorporates wildness rather than constrains it. The law, again, is a system of representation that is itself constrained by its narrowly-defined relation with the material world. Poetry inhabits a more indeterminate zone, where the world is both immaterial and material: 'the mighty world/ Of eye and ear,—both what they half-create,/ And what perceive'. In doing so, poetry claims a privileged relationship with the subjectivity that half-creates and half-perceives the world. In one sense, the poem, too, half-creates and half-perceives the poet's subjectivity. Although, implicitly, the poet's self pre-exists the poem, it also comes into being in its verses—and thus achieves a measure of survival through them, independent of the body.

To sustain this particular power, however, poetry requires publication and the legal protection of copyright laws, so that any implicit critique of law here is informed, in turn, by the need for laws to establish poetic property (Eilenberg, 1989; and (Eilenberg, 1992). Further, the poem implies another kind of parallel between poetry and the law, one that complements and enlarges upon its testamentary function. Laws, traditionally, like myths before them, both reflect a culture's standards of behaviour and also shape them. Wordsworth makes a similar claim for the power of the landscape-scene he is bequeathing:

> Though absent long,
> These forms of beauty have not been to me
> As is a landscape to a blind man's eye:
> But oft, in lonely rooms, and mid the din
> Of towns and cities, I have owed to them,
> In hours of weariness, sensations sweet,
> Felt in the blood, and felt along the heart,
> And passing even into my purer mind
> With tranquil restoration:—feelings too
> Of unremembered pleasure; such, perhaps,
> As may have had no trivial influence
> On that best portion of a good man's life;
> His little, nameless, unremembered acts
> Of kindness and of love.

Here, too, poetry's landscape performs like and surpasses the law: it influences and shapes our moral behaviour, the poet claims, but it does so intrinsically, through the power of sympathy, rather than through the force of external authority. It surpasses the law to the extent that it passes here the litmus test of intrinsic value: the 'little, nameless, unremembered acts/ Of kindness and of love' are also unremarked, private, performed to observe not so much the letter but, more importantly, the spirit of the law. Later in the poem he reinforces the point, seeing

> In nature and the language of the sense,
> The anchor of my purest thoughts, the nurse,
> The guide, the guardian of my heart, and soul
> Of all my moral being

In and through poetry, then, we acquire the sensibilities that make us moral beings and that lead us to obey our highest calling.

This is the gift the poem thus offers by way of bequest. Its value is beyond estimate, but so is its cost. Wordsworth uses, explicitly, the language of gift and exchange in describing what he has drawn from this landscape as a memory from five years earlier. At that time, he tells us, nature, to him, 'was all in all', with 'aching joys' and 'dizzy raptures', 'a feeling and a love,/

That had no need of a remoter charm,/ By thought supplied' His experience of it was thus immediate, without mediation or reflection, unself-conscious. In the intervening years he has lost that capacity for immersion, for self-annihilation in the landscape, in the 'deep and gloomy wood'. And yet it seems it was precisely for that loss of self that it was valuable. He realises in retrospect that what he experienced then was what Freud would later term an oceanic feeling, a merging of the self with the world that is at the core of religious experience. The language the poem uses to describe this experience comes eerily close to a kind of death-in-life. He writes that 'we are laid asleep/ In body, and become a living soul', death-like, as we 'see into the life of things'.

If he has lost the unself-conscious relationship with nature, then, he has regained, paradoxically, the loss of self in this reflective/meditative mood that the memory of the landscape has empowered in him. The paradox is clear: to 'see into the life of things' one must in some sense still oneself, suspend one's own very life processes and allow oneself to merge with the 'deep power of joy'. 'Deep', like 'wild', is an adjective that recurs throughout the poem and accrues associations with a loss of self, akin to death, from the 'thoughts of more deep seclusion' in the opening verses, to the 'deep and gloomy wood' of his childhood, the 'sense sublime/ Of something far more deeply interfused' of his present meditation, to the 'far deeper zeal' of the poem's closing lines. The 'deep power of joy', metrically reinforced by that wonderful spondee, represents an imaginative return to the source of being; an annihilation of self that returns us to ourselves; a modern replacement for the ritualistic death by water. 'For such loss, I would believe/ Abundant recompense': in this famous phrase, Wordsworth summarises his poem and captures its logic. Losing his childish lack of self-consciousness, he would believe he acquires the gift of losing himself in private rituals of memory and meditation.

And then the crucial final step in the poem's logic: he is bequeathing this gift, this 'recompense', to his sister, and to subsequent readers. As we have seen, the poem turns to her, and in its final words asserts that

> these steep woods and lofty cliffs,
> And this green pastoral landscape, were to me
> More dear, both for themselves and for thy sake.

Here he expands exponentially on his claims. The private meditation, made public in the form of the poem and formal in the act of bequeathing, becomes a model and a rationale for a modern, secular, intrinsically compelling law, grounded in the individual subjectivity in dialogue with other subjects. Poetry, then, becomes a form of mediation between the now obviated role of myth and the modern function of law. And the testamentary moment is its proving ground, the context the poet's own death and will.

III. THE WILL AND THE LAW

One of my opening questions in this chapter was whether we might understand poetry and the law as occupying radically different positions with respect to death. As I noted, both ritual and art point to, and question, the grounds for their utterance. Law, in contrast, would seem to require a stable and unquestioning authority to be effective. One way we might read *Tintern Abbey*, however, is to see it as offering a rationale for the law that is based on a modern, post-Enlightenment conception of cognition and perception, and that foregrounds dialogue as its model. In the place of tablets of stone, we have a dynamic system of exchanges. In the place of assertions about the afterlife, we have a rational but also deeply-valued and emotion-rich conception of a subjectivity that is both constrained and sustained by the verbal systems that surround it. Law occupies one extreme of those systems, but it is not a stable, eternal extreme. Like poetry, it exists in dialogue, and it only works if the reader is moved through sympathy to live as a moral being and both to accept and to pass on the legacy.

One scholar has described the logic of *Tintern Abbey* as "astonishingly careless, in the sense of carefree" (Gravil, 2000: 8). Much is at stake in that freedom: the question is whether Wordsworth is turning away from or re-envisioning a revolutionary politics. Clearly, by 1798 Wordsworth had lost any sense that revolutionary change would bring a more just society to England. And yet he published *Tintern Abbey* in a volume of poems that is all but obsessed with matters of homelessness and property, and that chose a profound sympathy for the dispossessed over a poetic discourse of propriety. 'Carefree' hardly describes this poem. But it does serve as a kind of manifesto for individual freedom, for a subject whose greatest liberty is in the mind. As Friedrich Schiller wrote, 'Mein unermesslich Reich ist der Gedanke': thought is my immeasurable empire.

In locating his private memories on a continuum that projects into the future, with his own death strongly implied, Wordsworth opens himself and us to the possibility that the narratives we live and imagine inhabit a similar continuum, and that our private subjectivity takes on dimensions of permanence that are related—but not limited—to our material being. This chapter's epigraph quotes David Price, who has suggested that it is possible to see the being which once constituted the person as continuing to exist after death. Price (chapter twelve this volume) returns repeatedly to that question, in the context not of the will but of laws regarding the treatment of the corpse. In passing, he suggests the possibility that the self or the subject has a conceptual being that is not entirely limited to the biological life of the body (though, for his purposes, it remains attached to the body as corpse, and he would not give it status as a subject in the rational and legal sense). In many, probably most, human cultures before scientific method and logical reasoning came to define modernity, the notion that the self has a being that is more than organic seemed self-evident. Wordsworth, in *Tintern Abbey* and in many other poems, looks to poetic discourse for a way to understand human subjectivity beyond the life of the body. But it does not, as some might argue, posit a mode of being in opposition to the law, but rather complementary to it (see Binder and Weisberg, 2000: especially 3–21, for an extensive treatment of that distinction at that historical moment).

An essential question remains unanswerable in both the rational discourse of the law and the symbolic universe of poetry. What can be known about the subject's will from the written text? How do we know what the subject intended? It is doubtful, for example, that Wordsworth intended *Tintern Abbey* to be read as a will, since the testamentary resonances are all in the shadows of connotation and would likely have been unconscious. In a compelling essay on the relationship between wills and poems, Hancher discusses the difficulty in both legal practice and literary criticism of discerning the author's intentions (Hancher, 1998). He notes that judges interpreting wills must often, like literary critics, take a position regarding the degree to which they rely on presumptions about the author's intentions as they hand down practical decisions. The hermeneutics of the law, in this area, reflects fault lines that are surprisingly similar to those of literary criticism. How can we know what the dead author intended? What we have is the text. Do we allow 'external' evidence, and if so, how much? Is there such a thing, as some lawyers have argued, as 'plain words' in a will or a poem? As Hancher notes:

That is, jurists usually frame the dilemma of testamentary construction in terms of authorial intention versus verbal meaning (usually called 'plain words' or 'plain meaning'), rather than in terms of authorial intention versus judicial freedom (Hancher, 1998: 103).

How 'plain', in that legal sense, are words like 'hermit's cave', 'lonely rooms', 'mansion', or 'empire'?

Literary critics have the luxury of proposing interpretations that cannot and need not be practical, as Hancher points out. Judges, by contrast, must establish authoritative readings with practical consequences. And yet the logic underlying laws and legal systems may be challenged—I would argue, must be challenged, as the very process of dialogue that Wordsworth enacts as a model for democratic subjectivity. If our understanding of the modern, post-Enlightenment subject has moved towards placing ever greater emphasis on the self's constitution in discourses, in social contexts and in immaterial relations beyond the body, then surely we must also consider what that means for our laws surrounding the corpse and its subject—even if this appears to take us into conceptual realms that the law would previously have considered irrational, wild and out of bounds.

BIBLIOGRAPHY

Adams, J and Brownsword, R (2006) *Understanding law* (London, Sweet & Maxwell).

Baudrillard, J (1976) *L'échange symbolique et la mort* (Paris, Gallimard).

Binder, G and Weisberg, R (2000) *Literary criticisms of law* (Princeton, NJ, Princeton University Press).

Bronfen, E (1992) *Over her dead body* (New York, Routledge).

Eilenberg, S (1989) 'Mortal pages: Wordsworth and the reform of copyright' 56 *ELH* 351–374.

—— (1992) *Strange power of speech: Wordsworth, Coleridge and literary possession* (Oxford, Oxford University Press).

Ernst, G (1988) *La mort dans le text* (Lyons, Colloque de Cerisy, Presses universitaires de Lyon).

Goodwin, SW and Bronfen, E (1991) Introduction, in *Death and representation* (Eds Goodwin, SW and Bronfen, E) pp.3–25. (Baltimore, MD, Hopkins University Press).

Gravil, R (2000) 'Tintern Abbey' and the system of nature 6 *Romanticism* 35–50.

Hancher, M (1988) 'Dead letters: wills and poems' in *Interpreting law and literature* (Eds Levinson S, Mailloux S) pp.101–114. (Evanston, IL, Northwestern University Press).

Kofmann, S (1985) *Mélancolie de l'art* (Paris, Galilée).

Levinson, M (1986) *Wordsworth's great period poems: Four essays* (Cambridge, Cambridge University Press).

McGann, J (1984) *The romantic ideology: A critical investigation* (Chicago, IL, University of Chicago Press).

Metcalf, P and Huntington, R (1979) *Celebrations of death: The anthropology of mortuary ritual* (Cambridge, Cambridge University Press).

Richey, W (1998) 'The politicized landscape of 'Tintern Abbey' 95 *Studies in Philology* 197–220; Epscohost web site: http://web.ebscohost.com/ehost/pdf?vid=4&hid=114&sid=44a0d3ad–9b64–444c–aa58–a5178dcc24f9%

Schoenfield, M (1996) *The professional Wordsworth: Law, labor and the poet's contract* (Athens, GA, University of Georgia Press).

Wordsworth, W and Coleridge, S ([1800] 1968; 2nd edn 1991) *Lyrical ballads* RL Brett and AR Jones (eds) (London, Routledge).

Ziolkowski, T (1997) *The Mirror of Justice: Literary reflections of Legal Crises* (Princeton, NJ, Princeton University Press).

9

Death, Ritual and Material Culture in South London

DANIEL MILLER AND FIONA PARROTT

I. INTRODUCTION

THIS CHAPTER CONSIDERS the specifics of contemporary death culture in Britain. In this consumer society, the acquisition of goods is an important part of constructing and maintaining relationships with the living (Miller, 1998; 2001a). We argue that people continue to use these goods to forge personal and specific relationships to the dead. Consumption is increasingly directed towards the domestic environment, a place that is being developed as the foundation to many modern lives (Miller, 2001b: 1; Birdwell-Pheasant and Lawrence-Zuniga, 1999). Incorporating the dead as an informal part of the domestic environment has become a means of retaining personal relationships to the dead and a means of separating and divesting oneself of their presence.

The data is taken from an 18-month ethnographic study of households in South London, part of a larger project on the material culture of loss and separation which placed death and bereavement alongside other commonly experienced episodes of loss such as divorce, children leaving home, aging, illness and retirement. During fieldwork the focus on loss and separation expanded into a study of the location and management of memory (Parrott, 2007), and a consideration of the overall order of relationships between persons and things (Miller, forthcoming 2007). In this chapter we present photographs, clothes and jewellery as common objects used in rituals of bereavement, showing how the qualities of these things are used in quite different ways by different people. We observe how informal domestic rituals are used to enhance more formal and conventional death rituals such as the Christian funeral.

The case material is skewed towards middle-aged women; first, because it is women of this age who frequently take on the responsibility for preserving family memory and secondly, because photographs and clothing are domestic objects characteristically selected by women. In cosmopolitan

South London, where we found informants from every continent, these domestic death rituals also played an important part in the forging of complex ethnic identities.

II. ANTHROPOLOGY AND MATERIAL CULTURE

Anthropology typically highlights the cultural diversity and local particularity of our responses to death. Indeed, the most popular contributions to the anthropology of death and mourning are those that are seen as challenging psychological universals (eg Scheper-Hughes, 1992). Anthropologists tend to assume that peoples' responses to death depend on factors ranging from the belief in immortality to the degree of individualisation, none of which can be taken for granted. The concern with the degree of individualisation has characteristically been couched within a contrast between non-Western and Western death cultures, with various ethnographies illustrating peoples' concern with collective immortality versus personal immortality (eg Lienhardt, 1961).

Perhaps the most popular focus of anthropological research is ritual. Generalising from a great many studies, it seems that most societies have elaborate rituals of death that stretch out the death from a physical moment to a drawn out series of rituals of separation. A person who dies has many ties to the society to which they belonged and the restoration of the damaged social network requires time, collective participation and effort. In most cases, anthropologists describe an elaborate mortuary cycle through which the dead are gradually transformed from the specific individual to a generic ancestral figure. These themes are exemplified in recent collections on the anthropology of death, mourning and burial (such as Robben, 2004) and commentaries (such as Huntingdon and Metcalf, 1979).

Material objects play an important role in the way people reject the arbitrary, episodic nature of death, creating time for the requisite processes of detachment. Küchler's 2002 study of Malanggan, an object of tribal art from the New Ireland area of Melanesia, shows how these wooden carvings function to become the body of the dead around which rituals and ceremonies can be performed as many as 20 years after the death (Küchler, 2002). This highly elaborated 'body', composed of a complex arrangement of remembered images, allows the mourners to effectively distribute the obligations and land rights of the deceased. Afterwards, the smell of the rotting Malanggan is used to evoke the gradual decomposition of the social person.

It is a common finding that a material work of art or the destruction or exchange of goods (eg Kan, 1989; and Weiss, 1997) helps to separate the living from the dead in a series of appropriate stages in small-scale pre-industrial societies. This raises the question of whether there are analogous uses of material culture within our own society. Layne has carried out a study of the role of objects in bereavement among women who have suffered from late foetal or neo-natal loss (Layne, 2000; Layne, 2002; see also Taylor, Layne and Wozniak, 2004). These women find that the world of consumer goods is the most effective means of giving form to the personhood of the lost child and gaining recognition of their loss. The gradual disposal and putting away of the baby things they purchased in expectation of the birth provides the key way through which the parents relate to the death of the hoped for child. They may also continue to accumulate memorial goods such as jewellery and ornaments and include the deceased in gift giving rituals such as Christmas.

Considering the role of objects in death ritual in Melanesia and Euro-America we observe both the replacement of a person by an object and the use of things to create personhood. In short, the assumed dualism between what we would call subjects and objects hides a much more fluid relationship by which each produces the other. This is the founding premise of the approach to anthropology that we call 'material culture studies' (Miller, 2005) and which is exemplified by this chapter.

III. ETHNOGRAPHY ON A LONDON STREET

Our research expands upon these specific instances of the way material culture is used to mediate our relationship to death in Britain. As Hallam and Hockey, who have conducted an extensive historical review of the use of material culture in connection with death in Europe, observe,

[i]n the contemporary context, to wear the personal possessions of deceased relatives such as their watches, or to enshrine their clothing and cherish their photographs and letters, provides a means of coping with personal loss ... evoking that which they cannot replace and providing touchstones for inchoate feelings of grief (Hallam and Hockey, 2001: 19).

We aim to show more precisely the way objects such as clothes, jewellery and photographs are used as part of rituals of bereavement. The project on material culture and loss involved 100 households from a street in South London with a cross-section of council-owned, rented and privately-owned flats and houses. This street-based research strategy was designed to avoid the advance selection of people as tokens of sociological categories. In London the diversity one encounters increasingly fails to correspond with any given social category: for example, only 23 percent of the sample turned out to have been born in London, and a further 23 percent did not fit into any standard ethnic category such as White British, Afro-Caribbean or South Asian.

Over 18 months we approached, interviewed and spent time getting to know people informally in the home, attending family events where possible, and using local restaurants and pubs. Parrott attended the church on the street and a music playgroup but many informants were recruited by going door-to-door. Once the project had been presented and explained we received only eight blanket refusals to participate. We produced a database of digital photographs documenting interiors and specific objects, as well as transcripts and field notes for each household. In the final phase of the study, Parrott lived on the street sharing a house with informants. This helped to achieve the depth of encounter that characterises traditional anthropological methods of ethnography.

Our dialogues with informants involved tours of the objects in their homes and the recollection of objects in their parents' and former homes. Often this was the first time the person recalled events of bereavement through the stories of objects, their storage, display, circulation or disposal. Where we present individual narratives, these are not summaries of single interviews but thick, descriptive accounts based on the collation of information from multiple encounters.

IV. THE MATERIAL CULTURE OF DEATH AND BEREAVEMENT

If one set out to consider the form and consequences of material culture as part of a study of death and bereavement in contemporary Britain, then the most obvious focus of attention would be the cemetery. Recent literature on cemeteries shows the continuing importance of traditional rituals of burial and visiting, such as Francis and others' examination of various forms of funerary monuments in connection with the visiting patterns of different London communities (Francis, Kellaher and Neophytou, 2001; and Francis, Kellaher and Neophytou, 2005). However, recent work on cremation has also shown the creation of new opportunities for domesticating death ritual through the subsequent treatment of the portable funeral urn. This is increasingly brought back to the home rather than remaining within the boundaries of the cemetery (Hallam and Hockey, 2001: 93–100; and Kellaher, Prendergast and Hockey, 2005).

This chapter develops themes that emerged from these studies, namely, the increasing use of personal rituals and the sense that the domestic setting allows for the emergence of more private and individually meaningful forms of ritual. The difference is that we are, metaphorically speaking, following the urn back from the cemetery into the home. The material is organised by categories of artefact, beginning with photographs, followed by clothing and jewellery, and in an extended case study we compare the different uses made of these artefacts and cemetery visiting. As these case studies mainly involve women, we end with a comparison of men's rituals of remembrance. However, each case, in its micro-practice of death ritual, remains representative of the common potential for informal death ritual across the street study.

V. PHOTOGRAPHS

Beryl and Mary are two middle-aged women belonging to the congregation of the Anglican Church on the street that Parrott attended for the duration of the fieldwork. Beryl moved to England with her mother as a young child from Kingston, Jamaica. Her mother died shortly before the start of fieldwork. Mary's mother is Irish and her father is Nigerian, though she herself was born locally. Mary participated in the research eight months after her father died.

The death of their parents instigated an intense phase of active memorialising by Mary and Beryl. For Mary the process of taking photographs and videos began in anticipation of the bereavement, when her father's illness worsened. While it felt odd at the time, she wishes she had made more records, for 'nothing brings him so close as seeing him and hearing his voice'. Mary engaged a professional photographer for the Nigerian funeral in her father's village and the stone-setting a year later. She also took photographs at the funeral in the London church. These images were printed, packaged and sent to family and friends in both locations as a portable and appropriate form of transmittable memory. Although she has kept the videos to watch on her own, in time she wishes to copy and circulate these more widely.

Mary and her sisters did not wish the process of memorialisation to be restricted to the period of their father's illness and the funeral. They sorted and selected photographs from his past to give a much fuller picture of different aspects of his life. The funeral hymn sheet displayed a photo of her elderly father in traditional Nigerian textiles on the front and a photograph of him entering England in his hat and suit on the back, but the most complete memorialisation was produced through the creation of two photo albums tracking her father's life and all his important relationships. One remained in Mary's home; the other went to her mother's house and was made available to visitors.

Finally, Mary enlarged an imposing photograph of her father in traditional dress, before his illness, placing it on her mantelpiece so that his gaze presided over the front room. The selections framed an ideal and appropriate vision of her father, presenting him as, in her mind, he would have wished. Overall, photographs served to draw together a network of people in the United Kingdom and Nigeria, consolidating the formal events surrounding bereavement, the funerals and the stone-setting. While this formal ritual could potentially de-personalise the individual, returning them to the more generic status of ancestor, the photographs worked in the opposite direction, creating specific and personal mementos.

Beryl had intended to use photographs on her mother's funeral sheet. However, many of the plans for the funeral were not realised in time as she was working alone. Unlike Mary, Beryl was unhappy with the funeral. She felt let down by those who failed to attend and this left her feeling that due respect had not yet been paid. This was unfortunate, since great care is taken over the event in the Jamaican tradition where the success of the funeral acts to validate and acknowledge the life and acts of the person. This is particularly true of Jamaicans who have returned from living abroad, where the funeral tends to represent the culmination of a life consolidated through this ceremony of reincorporation in Jamaican soil (Horst, 2004). The inability of Beryl's mother to return to Jamaica due to her illness had already made the circumstances inauspicious. All these unresolved issues meant there was a premium on the potential of photographs, with their associated rituals of circulation and display, to mitigate the failure of the funeral, by suitably honouring her mother's life. This Beryl was able to do gradually over the following months.

Beryl wrote to relatives in Jamaica, posting them enlarged and hand-tinted black and white photographs of her mother, so that her image at least was able to return. By using two other photographic strategies of display, the framed photo and the album, Beryl was able to fulfil her need to create a 'tribute to my mother' in the semi-public space of the front room. A picture of her mother in her youth was selected for framing. Beryl located the spirituality of this particular photograph in its ability to convey her mother's 'inner beauty and generosity' through the beauty of her image. Although Mary framed an older portrait of her father and Beryl framed a young portrait of her mother, like many people, they used these photographs to reinstate a more desirable image of the deceased following an illness and unpleasant death. Beryl began to create a shrine around the framed photograph, buying and collecting additional objects, again referring to the arrangement as her 'tribute' to her mother. Along with the album, this helped her to elaborate upon the initial demands imposed by the funeral. Changing the lounge display through the seasons allowed her to renew her attentions to the memory of her mother. It also gave her a sense of order and control in dealing with her loss.

Whereas Beryl and Mary spent time displaying and distributing photographs they already had, other bereaved women on the street spent time trying to recover and accumulate photographs that were in the possession of other family or friends of the deceased. For example, Mrs Stone, another Jamaican migrant who lived on the street, continued to collect photographs from her daughter's family. This process extended the period of mourning years after her daughter's unexpected death from a hospital infection. While we commonly think in terms of people divesting themselves of objects associated with the deceased, as a material sign of the divestment of attachment, it is often quite the opposite process that dominates—one of accumulating, consolidating and ordering such objects. It is through accumulation that surviving relatives can gradually construct the proper abiding image of the deceased which they see as a mission bequeathed to them, what we call a 'labour of love'. Photographs, in particular, are associated with a quasi-ritual of declared intention and commitment to remember (see Edwards, 1999), often made as a kind of oath to oneself during bereavement.

In these cases, the use of photographs to move between formal rituals, as in funerals, and more informal and ad hoc rituals is also a means by which individuals mediate the complex issue of identity that comes with living in a Diaspora based in London. So Mary arranged a dual funeral here and in Nigeria, and Beryl is preoccupied with the failure of her mother to follow the idealised return to Jamaica that has become established for many Jamaican migrants. Yet other less obviously ethnic practices also shape the use of photographs in response to death and bereavement. For example, in the home of retired Irish publicans, the front room had become a gallery of wall-to-wall photographs, including graves and portraits of deceased regulars they adopted as 'family' as well as their actual family. The husband had arranged the display, while the wife kept those it depicted alive through the telling of stories. The use of objects in response to death and bereavement was the mode through which households on this London street enacted a range of cultural practices that were important to them.

VI. CLOTHING AND JEWELLERY

While photographs reproduce an image of the person, the material that once clothed their body can convey a relationship to the dead that uses other qualities and other senses, such as smell and touch, that complement the work of photographs (Ash, 1996). Returning to Layne's study of the things mothers use to memorialise their stillborn children and foetal loss, she discusses the special role played by clothes, with their specific qualities of softness and smallness intended to evoke babyhood. The selection and buying process turns them from general baby clothes into clothes destined for one's own child. The loss is all the more poignant because they were never worn. While these women cannot stroke the soft skin of a stillborn child, in grief they can evoke that experience through the touch and texture of these materials.

For Beryl, the presence of her mother's clothing was an altogether painful affair but she also gained considerable comfort from the closeness such ordinary objects left behind. In the first place:

[C]lothing is tactile you know, the memories are sort of, well the photograph is like a visual stimulus, but the clothes and particularly the socks that's got another dimension, it's almost like it's another level. I mean it's closer in a sense like I can hold your hand now, which almost brings her back, makes her more present.

But disposing of the most mundane and evocative clothing such as her mother's slippers allowed Beryl to slowly separate from that closeness. Eight months after her mother's death, Beryl sorted through her mother's clothing. First she disposed of the worn out clothing; secondly, rather than sending the less worn clothing to charity shops in the United Kingdom she parcelled up boxes to send to relatives in Jamaica, thereby contributing to her mother's vicarious 'return'. In the process, Beryl selected some more formal and well-cut dresses that had an outwardly aesthetic quality to provide her with a lasting memento of her mother's style. Unlike the deliberate saving of these more formal dresses, Beryl had some more painful decisions to make about wearing her mother's everyday clothing. Hoping for a recovery, Beryl had bought her mother some wool trousers to wear outside. Like the unworn baby clothes belonging to the mothers in Layne's work, the failure of these hopes made them particularly poignant objects. When Beryl desperately needed this warm clothing she described feeling extremely uncomfortable about wearing them, as if she was 'stealing from the dead'.

Neither the relationship to clothing nor to photographs occurs in isolation, each can help facilitate the use of the other. At one point she notes 'I couldn't just look at the socks and not at the photographs, photographs become much more important'. Over time Beryl transformed the presence of her mother in her life, from the disorder of being surrounded by everyday clothing to the creation of a photographic shrine. Similarly, formal clothing is often perceived to provide a suitable commemorative and transmittable object; one which may even be pictured in those same photographs. For example, Mary kept some Nigerian textile smocks like the one her father wears in the photograph on her mantelpiece; with the idea that together these objects conveyed a fuller sense of the whole person. In these lay practices, people exploit the differences between ordinary and formal or special clothing, and the contrasts between clothing and photographs constitute a trajectory of bereavement which becomes their way of 'dealing' with grief and memory.

For Mrs Stone, whose daughter died unexpectedly from a hospital infection, it is the constancy of jewellery that seems most appropriate for marking her continued relationship to her daughter. Unlike the clothing that reminds her of her daughter, such as the suit she bought for her wedding, she is not afraid of wearing the jewellery out. As she describes it:

She gave me this pretty little heart and I said: 'What have I to put this away for?' I said: 'I am going to be wearing this from now on'. I sleep in it, I bathe in it, I do everything in it. She's gone and I'm wearing it. So I've been wearing it everyday of my life. I don't take it off.

Wearing the heart shaped necklace was not an instant response. For a year after the death she kept it carefully in a box, the memories too raw for such things to be in close proximity, and only later did she think about the potential of this heart and chain as something that she could constantly wear.

These accounts stress the intentional reconstruction of object worlds, but material culture has its own potency that can disrupt such intentionality. As Hallam and Hockey point out, clothes found unexpectedly at the back of a wardrobe may create an unsettling reminder of the dead:

[I]n such instances, the potency of material objects as supplies of unwelcome memories exposes the shadow side of their domesticated role as malleable resources for more deliberate acts of memory making (Hallam and Hockey 2001: 105, 115).

Where possible, individuals such as Beryl and Mrs Stone are seeking to tame the traces of the dead, by sorting through the commemorative potentials of different genres of material culture such as clothing and photographs, and making them part of a range of formal and ad hoc ritual.

In the lives of each person, these materials are often creatively juxtaposed together in response to their particular bereavements. Often it is not one but a succession of deaths or separations that have an impact upon each other in creating that personal mode of memorialisation. The following extended case study illustrates this point, focusing on the contrast between the use of clothing and the use of the cemetery, which tends to be the primary focus of research on death and material culture in Britain.

VII. ELIA'S MEMENTOS AND CEMETERY VISITS

Elia's family originally migrated to the United Kingdom from Greece and there are elements of her story that would be recognised as characteristically Greek, but others that are simply characteristically Elia. Although narratives of bereavement have a significant place in Elia's corpus of storytelling, our account focuses upon three different types of material culture that are significant in her private practice, although they too feature in her interactions with others. Of these genres of material culture, the most successful form through which she domesticated the bereavement was clothing; the most painful and difficult to deal with was jewellery; and the most poignant was the cemetery. Using the reverse metaphor we can think of each of these forms as different places of memory, where each setting comes to objectify and shape different aspects of Elia's relationship to her bereavements.

Elia inherited many clothes from her mother, most of which had a double resonance, since they also had been made by her beloved Aunt Dimitra. At first she stored them in a box at the base of her wardrobe. Some she gradually and carefully gave away to others. The recipients had to be 'lovely' people as well as deserving. The origins of each item were made clear and they were expected to receive them with a sense of reverence.

After some 15 years Elia felt she could wear the clothes. At first she wore them alone in the house, then she started to wear them for special occasions.

It has to be a posh one, where I can carry it off. When everyone else is wearing £500 to £600 dresses I am wearing one of these.

For Elia the special value of this inheritance was evidenced by their ability to trump mere monetary value in the clothes of others. Now, she always wears something of her mother's or her aunt's when she goes to functions, whether a handbag, or a scarf. Such things bring the dead and living into immediate proximity. Through the clothes she can serve her mother: 'You find ways to bring her into social ways and family events, giving a good time to her'.

With the completion of this process has come the feeling that she no longer has to acknowledge the point of origin of an item when it is worn. Today she has assimilated through her wardrobe something of what was lost and mourned through the process of bereavement itself. That does not preclude explicit returns to rituals of bereavement in which clothes still evoke the sense of loss:

I would say to people: 'Would you like to see my mother's dress?', and there would be a showing. Sometimes I might look at them, but I would be crying. If I was on my own and I would be cuddling them and things like that, I would be crying for those two wonderful women, both for Aunty and for Mummy.

In Elia's case, jewellery is not as amenable to the same sense of gradual incorporation as clothing. Partly this reflects her particular sense of its materiality. Clothing changes and fades and can take on something of the corporality of its wearer. By contrast, jewellery stands immutable, in a more abstract relation to the person. This is enforced by its monetary value. While others see quite different qualities in jewellery, in Elia's experience, jewellery had become testimony to the irreconcilable.

Six weeks before her death, her mother set aside a diamond necklace for Elia. Within a month of the death, her father took it from her and gave it to an in-law with whom he wanted to keep in favour. Elia bore this hurt silently but never forgave him. She continued to sacrifice her time and energy to the family, despite which, in accordance with his view of tradi-tional gender roles, her father willed everything to his sons, making her feel that 'he did not acknowledge me as his daughter'. Against the advice of others he felt he had to abide by the Greek traditions of inheritance, tell-ing the men to 'look after her' but ignoring the fact that she was the one struggling financially. For Elia it is not the property, but the necklace, that is iconic of her bitterness. The pain was awakened when the engagement of a relative involved the transfer of one of the original diamonds. It took an intervention from the shades of her ancestors to reconcile Elia to attending the wedding in question.

One of the places where Elia can still give vent to her abiding sense of hurt is the cemetery, where we accompanied her on one of her visits (compare Francis, Kellaher and Neophytou for Greek Cypriot cemetery visiting (Francis, Kellaher and Neophytou 2005: 126–131)). Here she can express herself directly to the souls of the departed. She sits by the grave and asks aloud 'What did you do it for, Dad? Why did you do it to me?' She says she knows that in Heaven her mother is giving him a 'right telling off'. She loves the photos, which are an integral part of Greek gravestones. There is her aunt Dimitra:

[S]he always sends me off with a smile, she would say 'come along be happy darling, find happiness' and once I was up there and I actually sat on the stone and felt the love that they had for me and I put it into myself. I got all this love that they had, how they felt for me and I took it all on and I left the cemetery.

Elia puts on lipstick to visit the cemetery. Such things mattered a good deal to her relatives. Sometimes, when she has good news she will tell her deceased grandmother when she is in the kitchen. But when it's exceptionally good news, she feels she must come to the cemetery and tell her in person. While some view graves as a place for ritual and prayer, Elia feels this would get in the way of her personal relationships. She avoids any formal acknowledgement. For her this is a time to chat and quarrel and clean. Everything looks homely and cared for, as these Greek graves have the appearance of a carefully tended garden. Whatever she brings with her she leaves in peace, 'knowing that I am alive'.

In her experience of bereavement, the cemetery complements Elia's use of clothing. The cemetery is the place where her ancestors remain unchanged, where one can commune with them as they were in life. The cemetery is also a tragic space that reminds her that children can be taken away at an early stage and that death gives a perspective on life. By contrast, clothes are a medium through which her mother's and auntie's qualities become absorbed as part of her and part of what she can in turn give to her children and grandchildren. All of these genres act in complementary relation. The cold imperviousness of jewellery, the emotional porosity of stone graves, but above all the active permeability of clothes now embroidered with the ghosts of the departed that embrace you as easily as you can embrace them.

VIII. GENDER AND DEATH RITUAL

By choosing to emphasise the role of clothing and photographs, this chapter has emphasised genres of material memory often selected by women. Where women take on the task of organising family memory, the display of photographs as memory may come to be seen as a female activity. However, the men on the street also used objects in a variety of ways to mediate their experiences of loss. Sometimes these would seem characteristically male. For example Charles, an English man in his early forties, had a very strong bond with the men with whom he shared his highly-disciplined boarding school experiences. Two of these school friends have died, and between the remaining friends they have developed an annual ritual 'get together', based around drinking, that has something of the elements of a traditional wake. Indeed, he even referred to one funeral as having a certain 'Viking' quality to it. The camaraderie around drinking that is part of the subsequent memorial events does not represent a diminishing of respect but a variant of male bonding discovered around their shared loss and memories. In a similarly active but individual way, Jose, a Southern European man, remembers his father mainly through his wine-making, a process he learnt by watching his father as a child. Living in London, he will go to buy powdered grapes in the absence of fresh, in order to retain his link to this tradition. In both cases it seems these men use activities rather than objects per se, to find incorporating practices analogous with women's use of clothing described here. However, the distinction is by no means absolute and in other forms of loss, such as divorce, we have extensive examples of men using their separation from clothes (or sometimes just the clothing tastes of ex-partners) to mediate their separation from the former relationship.

Other genres such as books, record and CD collections and remembered music seem to appeal equally to both genders. However, there were several cases where men found music far more amenable to an active practice of memorialisation than photographs. Jack, an elderly Englishman, and Dave, a middle-aged Englishman, both played records to remember, respectively, their nephew and father. Significantly, Jack played a specific record for his deceased nephew, not on the date of his death but just before Christmas, to honour and give him a place in this celebration of family life. But rather than a male practice per se, these personal rituals are better seen as developing from their long-term love of music, seen in the quantity, quality and organisation of their record and CD collections.

IX. CONCLUSION

This chapter has considered how a range of ordinary domestic material culture is used to mediate people's relationships to the dead. Photographs, clothing and other genres such as jewellery and music are used to construct personal, individual rituals that may complement the more formal relationship to ritual prescribed by religious tradition.

By presenting individual case narratives, we have shown that it is better not to look for universal physical or symbolic properties of artefacts that would determine their use, but rather to think in terms of propensity and biographical experience. For Elia, the imperviousness of jewellery was a material quality that acted as a barrier to the way she used material forms to signify gradual change, separation and incorporation. By contrast, Mrs Stone found that a necklace that could be worn close to her heart was the single most poignant reminder of her daughter. In her case, the permanence of the material made it most effective. While Elia found clothing amenable to the gradual incorporation of her mother and aunt into her everyday life, Mrs Stone feared that the clothing by which she remembered her daughter would wear out. Both women considered the potential of each genre to enclose, to last or to fade but this did not mean they used them in the same way.

Individuals exploited the qualities of different objects to fulfil their specific commemorative needs. Beryl and Mary used the portability of photographs to distribute mementos across far-reaching diasporic networks from the United Kingdom, to Jamaica and Nigeria. Others used genres that already had particular relevance in their everyday lives to create informal private rituals, such as Jack's and Dave's incorporation of music into their much loved collections to commemorate their nephew and father. As part of the overall personalisation of ritual we can identify the influence of different backgrounds and cultures; from Beryl who was consumed by her mother's failure to follow the Jamaican ideal of return, or Elia who displayed a particularly Greek relationship to the grave which eschews formal religious prayer, to Jose, the Southern European, who struggled to continue to make wine in London in honour of his father. These ritual and material relationships with the dead become the way through which these heterogeneous ethnic and cultural identities are created and worked through.

Anthropologists have traditionally emphasised non-Western death ritual as central to the social construction of death, whereas the majority of work on death and bereavement in Euro-American societies has been dominated by psychology, counselling and psychotherapy (Valentine, 2006). It is possible to situate our research within the framework of attachment and loss. As Gibson suggests, clothing and photographs may be seen as exemplars of Winnicott's transitional objects (Gibson, 2004). However, we would emphasise that to understand these attachments to everyday objects and their use in informal ritual one must examine the wider social context of Euro-American society. That requires thinking in terms of the consumption surrounding events of death. In our consumer society, Layne shows how goods are used prior to the birth of a child to establish its social value at ever earlier stages. Thus, it is not surprising that in the event of late foetal or neo-natal death it is those same goods that are used to establish the subjective personhood of the lost child (Layne, 2000; and Layne, 2002). As Miller has shown in a previous study of shopping in North London, goods, including clothing, are used to create and sustain personal and familial relationships over considerable time periods (Miller, 1998). The same process is central to the way people deal with death.

Objects are employed to reconstitute the dead as subjects, that is, as highly specific and personal individuals. Such personalisation is particularly clear in the case of Mary's and Beryl's use of photographs, where framed images of their respective parents allow those people to continue to gaze over their living rooms. The same process of personalisation in these ad hoc informal rituals may be seen in the re-interpretation of formal ritual. Like many people, Mary used photographs to enhance the personal specificity of the funeral. Alternatively, Beryl used these informal rituals to extend the tribute paid by the funeral, and Elia creates her own informal rituals of cemetery visiting.

From a comparative anthropological perspective, we have seen that material objects extend rituals of bereavement beyond the event of death in a way analogous with the use of art objects and goods in non-Western societies. However, in other ways the conclusion is the opposite of those reached in the anthropology of death and mourning. In Robben's collection it seems that the problem of death in many non-Western small-scale societies is that people need to find ways of divesting themselves of the person that was amongst them, to allow these individuals to be reincorporated as a generic ancestral presence (Robben, 2004). This process may be sanctified through a long period of ritual activity that forms the funerary cycle. Our contemporary ideology requires the opposite task. Though we still make some use of conventional formal rituals, we are more concerned to find a means to retain the specific attributes of the dead; to make them personal and particular. Robben notes that anthropologists observing the elaborate mortuary rituals and ancestor worship among non-Western peoples often register their disappointment with Western death culture in terms of its apparently shallow, secular nature. Yet this omission is precisely that which helps retain the status of the dead as particular and personal.

BIBLIOGRAPHY

Ash, J (1996) 'Clothing and memory' in P Kirkham (ed) *The gendered object* (Manchester/New York, Manchester University Press) 219–224.
Birdwell-Pheasant, D and Lawrence-Zuniga, D (1999) *House life: Space, place and family in Europe* (Oxford, Berg).
Edwards, E (1999) 'Photographs as Objects of Memory' in M Kwint, C Breward and J Aynsley (eds) *Material memories: Design and evocation* (Oxford, Berg) 221–236.
Francis, D, Kellaher, L and Neophytou, G (2001) 'The cemetery: the evidence of continuing bonds' in J Hockey, J Katz and N Small (eds) *Grief, mourning and death ritual* (Buckingham, Open University Press) 226–236.
—— (2005) *The secret cemetery* (Oxford, Berg).

Gibson, M (2004) 'Melancholy objects' 9 *Mortality* 285–299.

Hallam, E and Hockey, J (2001) *Death, memory, and material culture* (Oxford, Berg).

Horst, H (2004) 'A pilgrimage home' 9 *Journal of Material Culture* 11–26.

Huntington, R and Metcalf, P (1979) *Celebrations of death: The anthropology of mortuary ritual* (Cambridge, Cambridge University Press).

Kan, S (1989) *Symbolic immortality: The Tinglit Potlatch of the Nineteenth Century* (Washington DC, Smithsonian Institution Press).

Kellaher, L, Prendergast, D and Hockey, J (2005) 'In the shadow of the traditional grave' 10 *Mortality* 235–250.

Küchler, S (2002) *Malanggan* (Oxford, Berg).

Layne, L (2000) 'He was a real baby with baby things: A material culture analysis of personhood, parenthood and pregnancy loss' 5 *Journal of Material Culture* 321–345.

—— (2002) *Motherhood lost: The cultural construction of miscarriage and stillbirth in America* (New York, Routledge).

Lienhardt, G (1961) *Divinity and experience: The religion of the Dinka* (Oxford, Clarendon Press).

Miller, D (1998) *A theory of shopping* (Cambridge, Polity Press).

—— (2001a) *The dialectics of shopping* (Chicago, Chicago University Press).

—— (2001b) Introduction in D Miller (ed), *Home possessions* (Oxford, Berg).

—— (2005) 'Materiality: an introduction' in D Miller (ed), *Materiality* (Durham, Duke University Press) 1–50.

—— *The Comfort of Things* (Cambridge, Polity, forthcoming 2007).

Parrott, F (2007) 'Now Where Did We Put Those Memories?' (Mais où a-t-on donc rangé ces souvenirs?) in *Grande-Bretagne Anthropologie at home, 2 Ethnologie Française* 305–312.

Robben, A (2004) *Death, mourning and burial: A cross-cultural reader* (Oxford, Blackwell).

Scheper-Hughes, N (1992) *Death without weeping: the violence of everyday life in Brazil* (Berkeley, CA, University of California Press).

Taylor, J, Layne, L and Wozniak, D (2004) *Consuming motherhood* (New Brunswick, NJ, Rutgers University Press).

Valentine, C (2006) 'Academic Constructions of Bereavement' 11 *Mortality* 1–22.

Weiss, B (1997) 'Forgetting your dead': Alienable and Inalienable Objects in Northwest Tanzania 70 *Anthropological Quarterly* 164–172.

10

Death on the Edge of the Lifeworld: the (Mis-)Appropriation of (Post-)Modern Death

GRAHAM SCAMBLER

I. INTRODUCTION

I T IS AN historical commonplace that while death is unavoidably part and parcel of the human condition, the actual circumstances in which people depart—whether or not for elsewhere—have been highly variable by time and place, even if eras and cultures have typically revealed distinctive patterns or structures. One dimension of this variation has been longevity, the life expectancy at birth enjoyed by those in contemporary developed societies being recent and exceptional. Another dimension is cause of death, the 'slow-dying' characteristic of many chronic degenerative conditions being a second feature of Western modernity (see Chau and Herring, this volume). Perhaps the most intriguing dimension, however—certainly for historians and social scientists—is the structural and socio-cultural context of death and dying. A brief discussion of the historically and geographically changing nature of death and of dying opens this contribution. It sets the scene for subsequent deliberations and the chapter's general thesis, namely, that some core structural and cultural changes around the 'social institution of death and dying' in the West in the modern era of the Occident have been under-analysed, even misunderstood.

This is followed by some sociological reflections on the general or 'ideal typical' features of the switch to 'modern society'. It is argued that one useful way of characterising conspicuously modern society is through an emphasis on growing social differentiation and a concomitant 'de-coupling' of the *lifeworld* (comprising the private sphere of the household and the public sphere or domain of contention and debate) from the *system* (comprising the economy and the state). A firm case can be made that among the sequelae of this de-coupling is a growing tendency for the system to penetrate and 'colonise' the lifeworld. This part affords a framework, in fact, for the analysis and conjectures of this chapter.

The third part of the chapter attempts an evaluation and revision of orthodox interpretations of modern dying. It is suggested that while much in these interpretations remains valid, insufficient attention has been paid to (i) 'some' structural properties of modern society, and to (ii) the 'post-modernisation' of Western culture. As this implies, credence is given to the concept of a post-modern culture, although the contention that Britain and other Western nation-states have become post-modern societies or entered a new capitalist epoch of post-modernity are roundly rejected. The conclusion consists of a few observations on the—increasingly vola-tile—relationship between structure and agency in connection with death and dying.

II. CHANGING PATTERNS OF DEATH AND DYING

Historical changes in life expectancy at birth are relevant in at least three respects: first, they show dramatic improvements in longevity from the earliest pre-modern to contemporary societies; secondly, they indicate the enduring nature of inter- and intra-national health inequalities; and thirdly, 'progress' is not inevitable. The best estimates of life expectancy in the earliest known human societies hover in the 20–30 age band, rising only to the 30–40 age band by the European Middle Ages. As late as the mid-19th century in England, the home of industrial capitalism, the figure had only reached the mid-40s. Data in 1871 that allowed for the calculation of gender differences revealed rather higher figures for women than for men. The 'leap' to a life expectancy at birth of around 75 years for men and 80 years for women in the England of the end of the 20th century reflects a remarkable change in approximately a century and a half. World Health Organization predictions for 2025 give a figure of 80 years for England (World Health Organization, 1998).

Globally, average life expectancy at birth now stands at 66, having risen over time from 48 in 1955. The geographic range, however, is considerable, with Sierra Leone's average of 34 at one end of the spectrum and Japan's 82 at the other. The WHO's predicted global average for 2025 is 73, with no country having an average life expectancy of less than 50 years (World Health Organization, 1998).

Intra-national variations, or inequalities, remain pronounced. This is not the place to go into detail, but it should be noted that almost all societies, past and present, have shown lower expectations of life at birth for those occupying lower social strata. This stratification of health has been pains-takingly documented in modern developed societies. In the United States, for example, there currently exists a 20-year gap in life expectancy between the most and least advantaged. In Britain the socio-epidemiological studies of Marmot and colleagues have revealed what they term a 'social gradient': data on both morbidity and mortality indicate that the lower an individual's occupational status, the more likely it is that he or she will become ill and experience a foreshortened life span (Marmot, 2006). Moreover this continues to apply—and with a now-predictable precision—even within seemingly narrow domains of work, like the staunchly middle-class civil service. Why there should be a social gradient remains a matter of dispute, although analysts readily agree on the importance of a mix of material, psycho-social and lifestyle factors (Scambler and Scambler, to be published 2007).

If there seems something ineluctable about health inequalities between and within nation-states, it needs to be recognised that gains in life expectancy at birth can be lost. The most vivid examples of this in the contemporary world are certain countries in Eastern European and beyond after the collapse of the Soviet bloc, and certain African countries after the advent of AIDS. In the Russian Federation, for example, life expectancy for men fell from 64 years in 1985–1990 to 58 years in 1994; for women the figure dropped less precipitously from 74 years to 71 years. Middle-aged men were the prime losers through this transition (Pearce, Griffin, Kelly and Miklelsen, 1997). In Uganda, where AIDS has become the main cause of death for young adults, life expectancy at birth had fallen from a peak of 56 years to 41 years by 1995–2000 (World Health Organization, 1998).

Interwoven with the undoubted general improvement of life expectancy at birth over time, and the endurance of health inequalities, is a changing pattern of causes of death. Consider once again the figuration of 19th-to-21st century England. The principal reason for the increasing life expectancy throughout the 20th century was the decline in deaths from infectious diseases: infant mortality in particular fell steadily from 1900. Conversely, the principal reason for the increase in heart disease, strokes and cancer—the degenerative diseases that comprise today's main causes of death—has been that individuals are increasingly likely to reach the older ages at which these typically, although not invariably, occur (Fitzpatrick and Chandola, 2000). This pattern is familiar through much of the developed world.

Enhanced longevity and a different pattern to causes of death, notwithstanding enduring health inequalities, have had significant ramifications for social institutions of death and dying. After all, between a fifth and a quarter of English deaths at the beginning of the 20th century were of infants, while death is now presumed to be a 'natural' conclusion to old age. Certainly, the shift from infectious to degenerative disease has typically extended what have been called 'dying trajectories'. Table 1, summarizing Lofland's influential comparison of pre-modern and modern death, reflects this (Lofland, 1978).

Table 1: Conditions Facilitating 'Quick Dying' in the Pre-Modern Era and 'Slow Dying' in the Modern Era

Conditions facilitating quick dying	Conditions facilitating slow dying
Low level of medical technology	High level of medical technology
Late detection of disease (or fatality producing conditions)	Early detection of disease (or fatality producing conditions)
Simple definition of death (eg cessation of heart beat)	Complex definition of death (eg irreversible cessation of higher brain activity)
High incidence of mortality from acute disease	High incidence of mortality from chronic or degenerative disease
High incidence of fatality-producing injuries	Low incidence of fatality-producing injuries
Customary killing or suicide of, or fatal passivity towards, the person once he or she has entered the 'dying' trajectory	Customary curative and activist orientation toward the dying with a high value placed on the prolongation of life

Two quick cautionary comments are in order, each concerning overly ready conceptualisations of 'old age'. First, it cannot, or should not, be assumed that the English experience of old age, death and dying is paradigmatic for all other developed and, more importantly, developing societies (Searle, 2000). And secondly, an important distinction has been drawn between the 'third' and 'fourth' phases of old age, the point being to emphasise that retirement from paid employment is far from synonymous with the disability and decline traditionally associated with old age—early old age needs to be differentiated from, say, post-75, late old age (see Laslett, 1996; and Gilleard and Higgs, 2000).

Mention should also be made of other shifts associated with the transition from the pre-modern to modern. It is often noted, for example, that whereas the death of a loved one, family member, friend or neighbour was once a familiar happening, and one dealt with in and by the community as a whole, the modern era has witnessed the progressive 'medicalisation of death', accompanied by its removal from the community or hospitalisation. The doctor and the hospital team are the new 'masters of death', it is said, of its moment as well as its circumstances; a claim addressed in detail in other chapters of this volume and one revisited later here. This change, it is suggested, has been associated with the modern denial of a—now demythologised and secularised—death, a denial to which death's near invisibility bears eloquent testimony (Ariès, 1983). Despite a discernible trend towards medicalisation/hospitalisation in England since the 1930s and 1940s, it is a view requiring qualification.

There is a sense in which death remains ubiquitous:

Most English people die in old age, out of sight, in hospital or nursing and residential homes. There are the all-too-frequent unseen deaths of the confused elderly, victims of strokes, or in coronary care or suffering from Alzheimer's disease. Meanwhile, virtually everyone has close friends, family or neighbours who have survived cancer treatment, a heart attack or HIV. Even these can say—however clean a bill of health their doctor has given them—that they have survived *so far*. Others with these conditions know their time is up, yet modern palliative care enables them to live actively at home and in the community for months or years. Death is nowhere to be seen, but it is everywhere. Death is no longer random, but it remains everybody's lot (Jupp and Walter, 1999: 278).

Moreover we shall encounter an argument later that death in our 'post-modern culture' is regaining some of its visibility, albeit in novel ways.

Death's medicalisation and hospitalisation, leading to its alleged denial, is related to assertions that death has become a taboo subject, despite the increasing salience of slow as opposed to quick dying. Evidence from studies a generation ago certainly implied both limited awareness of their situation on the part of the dying and a (rationalised) shying away from open communication of the facts on the part of doctors and other (mostly hospital) personnel (Cartwright, Hockey and Anderson, 1973). A more recent, and in many ways comparable, investigation, however, revealed a greater awareness in the terminally ill and a greater willingness to engage in open communication among doctors (Seale and Cartwright, 1994). But doctors do not always in the event behave as they either aspire to or predict for themselves (Taylor, 1988). The issue to which we shall return concerns the appropriateness or otherwise of incorporating what Glaser and Strauss famously called the 'open awareness context' (that is, health workers and patient each being aware that the latter is dying and acting openly on this basis) (Glaser and Strauss, 1965) into bureaucratic definitions of the 'good death'.

It might reasonably, if provisionally, be concluded at this point that in England and other kindred societies the transition from pre-modern to modern has brought enhanced longevity, associated with a new range of causes of death; a strong linkage of death with old age, even if this has involved a re-conceptualisation of old age; a shift from quick to slow dying; and a tendency for death to be displaced from the community to an assortment of institutions, implying a ceding of control by individuals, families and kin to health professionals. Some hints of divergence have been dropped, however, and these will be picked up again in light of the theoretically-oriented framework explicated in the next section.

III. A DE-COUPLING OF LIFEWORLD AND SYSTEM

It is neither possible nor desirable to give a precise date for the move from pre-modern (or traditional) to modern, since there is evidence of considerable inter- and intra-societal variation. It is not satisfactory either, of course, to leave things on the vague or nebulous side of imprecise. For some, modern implies post-ancient, for others the genesis of mercantilism or capitalism, while for others still it equates with a European modernity made manifest through the French Revolution and above all the Enlightenment of the late 18th century. Yet others emphasise the emergence of industrial capitalism in 19th-century England. The strategy here will be to define one central characteristic of modern or developed societies, as expounded by the German critical theorist, Habermas (see Habermas, 1984; Habermas, 1987; and Scambler, 2001).

Modern societies are held together by 'social integration' on the one hand and 'system integration' on the other. The former points towards symbolic reproduction and the latter towards material reproduction. The degree of societal differentiation characteristic of modern societies has at varying paces led to the delineation of four functionally distinct sub-systems: the *economy*, the *state*, the *private sphere* and the *public sphere*. Moreover there has been a fundamental de-coupling between the economy and state, comprising the system, and the private and public spheres, comprising the lifeworld. The sub-systems are interdependent: each is specialised in terms of what it produces but is dependent on the others for what it does not produce. The economy produces 'money', the state 'power', the private sphere (or household) 'commitment' and the public sphere (or arena of public debate) 'influence'. These products or 'steering media' are traded between sub-systems. To call on an example by Crook, Paluski and Waters,

the economy relies on the state to establish such legal economic institutions as private property and contract, on the public lifeworld to influence consumption patterns, and on the private lifeworld to provide a committed labour force, and itself sends money into each other subsystem (Crook, Paluski and Waters, 1992: 28).

But the steering media of the sub-systems are not equivalent in their capacities. With the progressive de-coupling of system and lifeworld, the media, and hence sub-systems, of the former have come increasingly to dominate the latter. Habermas writes in this context of a 'colonisation of the lifeworld' (Habermas, 1984). After the fashion of Marx's theme of 'commodification' and Weber's theme of 'rationalisation', the lifeworld has become increasingly colonised, that is, commercialised and bureaucratised.

What colonisation means, in effect, is that people's scope to determine the shape and direction of society through what Habermas calls 'communicative action', or the public use of reason, characteristic of the lifeworld, has become attenuated. Instead, people encounter each other as commercial and legal entities: more and more is decided, as it were 'for them' and 'behind their backs', as they find themselves on the wrong end of the means-to-end or 'strategic action' characteristic of the system.

Habermas insists that Weber, in writing of an 'iron cage' as the ineluctable product of modern rationalisation, conflates the 'logic' and the 'dynamic' of the processes he analyses. Lifeworld colonisation has indeed occurred, taking its toll of communicative rationality, but its occurrence was not preordained and its impetus might yet be arrested. It is a basic premise of Habermas's critical theory that commodification and bureaucratisation can be resisted, however difficult this may be in practice, and their instigators held to democratic account. He is not, let it be noted, anti-system, but rather opposed to system 'excesses' manifest as lifeworld colonisation. It is when that which is done in the name of economy and/or state, utilising the media of money and/or power, is no longer accountable to those in whose name it is done that unacceptable lifeworld colonisation is said to occur.

I have argued that the period beginning in the early to mid-1970s has witnessed changes in the nature of lifeworld colonisation in England and elsewhere (Scambler, 2002). Drawing on the French regulation school of political economy, I have contended that the changing logic of the regime of capital accumulation (of the economy) has occasioned a companion adjustment in the logic of the 'mode of regulation' (of the state). Another way of articulating this is to say that the balance between the economy's relations of class and the state's relations of command characteristic of the organised capitalism of the post-war period has shifted. In fact, in the disorganised capitalism since the 1970s, relations of command have ceded significant territory to those of class (quite contrary to premature announcements of their demise). Power and bureaucratisation, in Habermas' terms, have bent at the knee to money and commodification.

How does this important change, if the account is accurate, bear on the putative post-modernisation of English culture over the same period? There is an abundance of overlapping sets of properties of our contemporary culture to choose from in the published literature, and for present purposes the summary offered in Table 2 will have to suffice. Some points require emphasis here, however, because they pertain to the core thesis of this paper.

First, at the heart of post-modern culture is a recipe for 'relativised' *difference*, affording a wide-ranging and supposedly liberating choice of identities and narratives for self and others. Moreover there is no compulsion any longer for a chosen amalgam of identities and narratives to be commensurable. It is as if all of what Lyotard termed *grand* narratives, with their tired modernist baggage, have transmuted into post-modern *petit* narratives: you pays your money and you takes your choice (Lyotard, 1984).

But there's the rub for, secondly, this quite rapid displacement of a modern by a post-modern culture cannot be explained without reference to the

Table 2: Elements of the post-modern

Material
• Globalisation and the ascendancy of finance capital
• Decline of the nation-state and of national regulation
• Crises in post-war welfare states
• Diffusion of power
• Emergence of societies based on consumption not production
• Destandardisation of work
• Processes of class decomposition and dealignment
• Displacement of class by consumer identities

Cultural-aesthetic

- Post-modernism and the problematising of reality
- Dedifferentiation of value-spheres / deprivileging of science
- Tendencies to nihilism and fundamentalism
- Glocalisation in relation to culture

Rational

- Expiry of universal reason
- Termination of flawed Enlightenment meta-narratives
- Celebration of fragmentation and dissensus
- Intellectuals as interpreters not legislators
- New reflexivity

Methodological

- Polyphony and dialogue
- Decentring of authors' authority

system imperatives of economy and state, by class and command relations respectively. It is the re-invigoration of relations of class relative to those of command that provided the motor for change. Another way of characterising post-modern culture is as a vehicle for a class-induced culture-ideology of consumption more appropriate for disorganised than organised capitalism (Sklair, 2000). This is not to be determinist: culture need not have changed as in fact it did, although it is most unlikely that it would have changed in a manner dysfunctional for system imperatives. There is profit to be made out of *difference* and out of the relaxed multiplicity of identities and narratives that it allows and even legitimates. I have made a case elsewhere that what is popularly sold as culturally liberating is in fact merely 'disinhibiting' and, in its effects, profoundly neo-conservative: it pulls the rug from under the feet of those seeking a rationally compelling motivation for any progression from the *status quo* (Scambler, 2002; and Scambler, 2005).

So, thirdly, agency and culture alike are structured without being structurally determined. There is nothing overly disturbing about the ramifications of this sociological cliché. Neither agency, nor its correlates—like free will and rational action—are lost in processes of structuration; nor, indeed, are they conceivable without them.

And fourthly, a distinction needs to be drawn between the de-coupling of system and lifeworld in complex and highly differentiated modern societies and the colonisation of the latter by the former. It is hard to envisage a modern society in which much routine business is not conducted 'behind our backs' via steering media like money and power (the scope for the deliberative democracy of actual—if less so virtual—town meetings is limited); but this is possible without colonisation. Lifeworld colonisation occurs when democratic accountability is lost, that is, when this 'business' becomes unresponsive to the public reason and will. Important to any consideration of death in contemporary England is the degree to which the media of money (reflective of the sub-system of the economy and relations of class) and power (reflective of the subsystem of the state and of relations of command) have colonised the two sub-systems of the lifeworld, its private and its public spheres. It is to these issues that we now turn.

IV. A REVIVAL OF DEATH?

An influential challenge to the conventional wisdom that death has become taboo in modern society has been mounted by Walter (Walter, 1991). Walter considers a number of versions and critiques of the 'taboo thesis': (a) that there was a taboo, but that it is now disintegrating; (b) that death is hidden rather than forbidden; (c) that the taboo is limited to influential representations in the media and medicine; (d) that the loss of a coherent discourse within which death can be discussed has led to conversational unease; (e) that all societies must accept and deny death, with the result that illustrations to fit any thesis are readily accessible; and (f) that it is the modern individual, not modern society, that denies death. In a later contribution he develops his own thesis, suggesting that what he regards as death's revival is composed of two different strands. The first, a 'late modern' strand, is motivated by professional experts seeking control over death and dying. The second, a 'post-modern' strand, reflects the practical accomplishments of ordinary people seeking to express their emotions freely (Walter, 1994).

Professional expertise now extends beyond medicine to include palliative nurses, bereavement counsellors and so on. Under the influence of luminaries like Saunders (in the hospice movement), Torrie (in bereavement care), Lindemann, Bowlby, Murray Parkes and Worden (in grief counselling), sedatives and anti-depressants have been complemented if not displaced by the talking therapies. For Walter the modern, that is, the period invoked in the orthodox 'death as taboo' thesis recounted earlier, has seen death 'stripped of its public spectacle' to become 'a private, family experience'

(Walter, 1994: 23). Public discourses about death survive only in the form of medical texts, public health regulations, life insurance policies, the management of cemeteries and so on. Axiomatically, these discourses are

impersonal and unrelated to the private experiences of individuals who are dying or bereaved ... private experiences and public discourses do not tally (Walters, 1994: 23).

In short, there is a contradiction between private experiences and public discourses.

The late modern strand of death's revival aims to bridge the gap between private experiences and public discourses by the sponsorship and dissemination of knowledge that makes private experiences of death part of public discourses about death. In this way, experts exert control over their clients' private experiences. In bereavement counselling, for example, the trained expert, representing the public, recognises and legitimises the emotions of the bereaved whilst simultaneously protecting the public from these emotions by providing secure and secluded contexts for their expression.

The post-modern strand of the revival of death emanates from the lay populace. This strand rejects the professional preoccupation with stages and neatly delineated processes. Rather, it celebrates the heterogeneity of death, dying and bereavement and insists that people be permitted to die and grieve in their own ways and to give expression to their emotions as they see fit. The post-modern strand invites private feelings into the public sphere not so they can be controlled and legitimised by experts but to demand they be taken seriously in their own right. This articulation of diversity has the effect of challenging the public discourses of death and the cultural authority of the expertise underpinning them. Calling to mind a familiar cocktail of post-modern themes—difference, individualism, freedom, choice, self-identity and so on—Walter writes:

[T]he good death is ... the death that we choose. The good funeral is the funeral that uniquely marks the passing of a unique individual, and psychological manuals that prescribed stages of grief for mourners to pass through are now being discarded for an awareness of the infinite individual variations in the way people grieve (Walter, 1994: 2).

The post-modern strand to the revival of death is also present in the work of Seale, who argues that people tend now to appropriate psychological ideas, often with the aid of techniques culled from talking therapies, as 'cultural scripts' for understanding the torments of the inner-self and its relations to others (Seale, 1998). Mellor and Shilling, too, focus on the novel (post-modern) characteristics of what they, following Giddens's term 'high modernity'(Giddens, 1990) (a term I also favour over the more prejudicial 'late' modernity (Scambler, 2002)), although they accent costs over benefits (Mellor and Shilling, 1993). They contend that the reflexive deconstruction of public value-systems generally, including their ritualistic and bodily referents and practices ... has made strategies for dealing with death in high modernity ... precarious and problematic ... the desacrilization of our departure from the world is reflective of this general deconstructing process (Mellor and Shilling, 1993: 428).

In a more recent commentary on the revival of death, Arnason and Hafsteinsson offer a different view, one purporting to transcend Walter's division between the late modern and the post-modern (Arnason and Hafsteinsson, 2003). Their argument is that recent changes in the management of death and grief can best be grasped as aspects of permutations in governmental rationality. They concede that

something akin to a revival of death has taken place in the Western world during the last thirty years or so (Arnason and Hafsteinsson, 2003: 15).

But they evoke Rose's (Foucauldian) genealogy of 'subjectification' to emphasise meaning production (Rose, 1996).

Rose distances himself from those, like Giddens, who trace the rise of the individual to the societal transformation from pre-modern to modern, *Gemeinschaft* to *Gesellschaft*, mechanical to organic solidarity, and so on. Such transitions do not, for him, transform 'ways of being human by virtue of some "experience" that they produce' (Rose, 1996: 25). He rejects the presupposition implicit in such views of the continuity of human beings as the subjects of history, essentially endowed with the capacity for producing meaning. Devices for 'meaning production' are not delivered by experience; they possess their own histories. He links the concept of the genealogy of subjectification with that of 'governmentality':

[I]n the history of power relations in liberal and democratic regimes, the government of others has always been linked to a certain way in which 'free' individuals are enjoined to govern themselves as subjects simultaneously of liberty and responsibility.

And:

[T]he novel forms of government being invented in so many 'post-welfare' nations ... have come to depend ... upon instrumentalizing the capacities and properties of the 'subjects of government', and therefore cannot be understood without addressing these new ways (provided by the psychological complex) of understanding and acting upon ourselves and others as selves 'free' to choose (Rose, 1996: 12–13).

Walter's post-modern strand to the revival of death, attributing much to the insistent efforts of ordinary people to express their emotions overtly, is, in the opinion of Arnason and Hafsteinsson, 'not only to naturalize the need for emotional expression but misses sight of the effects of neo-liberal

governmentality' (Arnason and Hafsteinsson, 2003: 59). Bereavement counselling, the empirical focus of their narrative, is one of the means by which
neo-liberal governmentality exhorts its subjects to relate to themselves and
others as particular kinds of subjects.

In the concluding section I draw on the Habermasian framework delineated earlier to steer a course which learns and differs from each of these
positions on death's late modern/post-modern revival. The contested notion
of the 'good death' is deployed as an heuristic device.

V. THE GOOD DEATH

Death and dying in contemporary England are part past, part present and
part future: the past lives on and the future is anticipated and factored into
our understanding of the present. The constant re-working of the distinction between biological and social death lends additional support to this
observation. Concepts of the 'good death' have long been around (Jupp
and Gittings, 1999). Moreover they appear to show some similarity by time
and place:

> [S]ome ideals about dying well seem nearly universal: a death occurring after a
> long and successful life, at home, without violence or pain, with the dying person
> being at peace with his environment and having at least some control over events
> (Seale and van der Geest, 2004: 885).

In the period targeted here the 'good death' is an especially expeditious term
for any sociologist interested in death in England.

Walter's reference to a late modern strand in the revival of death strikes a
chord. If doctors can no longer quite be considered masters of the moment
and circumstances of death—indeed, their net loss of cultural authority
might be put down to a newly 'regulatory' as well as an increasingly 'marketised' state—there is no question that we are witnessing a bureaucratisation, and arguably a colonisation, of death through the mechanism of *audit*,
based on the often nebulous idea of evidence-based practice. The logical
end-point of this process is a set of definitive criteria of the good death
and the objective is its realisation. Consonant with the generic notion of
the 'expert patient', survey-based evidence of what dying people actually
want offers objectified and legitimised criteria of the good death that can
be translated into guidelines for dissemination. Arguably, another target
for bureaucratisation, as well as commodification, is the (re-)definition of
death in the face of new calls for the harvesting of organs (see Chau and
Herring, this volume).

Walter's post-modern strand is less resistant to examination, but
Arnason and Hafsteinsson's interpretation of Rose's Foucauldian analysis,
in my view, falls short as well. Certainly the late modern bureaucratisation/

colonisation of death at the bequest of relations of command seems relatively uncontroversial. The claim that a growing and individualised assertiveness on the part of the dying, caring and bereaved constitutes a (post-modern) mode of resistance, however, is less secure. To appreciate why, it is necessary to revisit the thesis rehearsed earlier that the post-modernisation of culture during disorganised capitalism is causally related to the resurgence of class relations relative to those of command (the associated emergence of a regulatory state is paradoxical but not contradictory). To reiterate, this is manifestly not to sanction any form of economic determinism. What passes too frequently in social scientific analyses as post-modern emancipation is more commonly a de facto 'disinhibition', and neo-conservative at that (Scambler, 2002; and Habermas, 1989). *Difference*, freedom, choice, self-identity and the rest are as much products of disorganised capitalism's consumer society, and therefore symptomatic of Sklair's culture-ideology of consumption, as they are windows of opportunity for personal initiative. It should surely not surprise us that what strikes us as natural is in fact social: after all, there are 'profits' to be made from *difference*, freedom, choice and self-identity.

But the solution is not Rose's or Arnason and Hafsteinsson's. Certainly the insights of Foucault applied by these analysts catch something of importance in the revival of death. The notion of governmentality warrants further explication in this respect. It refers to the 'conduct of conduct' or the 'government of government' and is distinct from *the* Government. It has to do with

how we govern and how we are governed, and with the relation between the government of ourselves, the government of others, and the government of the state ... It gives particular emphasis to issues of the government of human conduct in all contexts, by various authorities and agencies, invoking particular forms of truth, and using definite resources, means and techniques (Dean, 1999: 2–3).

Dean's own contribution is to argue that the concern to

govern through processes that are external to the formal apparatuses of political authority is to some extent reinscribed within a programme to reform and secure governmental mechanisms themselves, often by folding back the ends of government upon its instruments (Dean, 1999: 6).

Acceptance of such a thesis, he continues,

begins to make intelligible the reconfiguration of the social as a set of quasi-markets in services and expertise at the end of the twentieth century, of the governed as customers or consumers of such services and expertise, and explores the ways in which this is inflected with themes of community and identity.

This is alright as far as it goes. It is helpful, for example, in suggesting that 'authorities' and 'agencies' like medicine, nursing and bereavement counselling are now part of the government of government, if not of *the* Government. What is missing, however, is any sense that it is the resurgence of class relations—relative to those of command—that has provided the impetus for many of the processes commonly subsumed under the concept of governmentality. I have contended that the command relations associated with the new mode of regulation of the state and *appropriate* for disorganised capitalism, 'glossed' by (functionally equivalent) ideologies like neo-liberalism and the 'third way', have become both more diffuse and more penetrating or colonising of the lifeworld *on behalf of the class relations associated with the new logic of the regime of capital accumulation of the economy*. The changing relations of command might be 'characterised' with reference to governmentality, but can only be 'explained' with reference to the renewed vigour of relations of class (Scambler, 2002: 131). In their analyses of power, Foucault, Rose and others rightly emphasise its altered presence, but wrongly turn their backs on the continuing existence of only-too-real structures and perpetrators of power.

Returning to the idea of the good death in the context of death's revival in the era of disorganised capitalism and its culture-ideology of consumption/post-modernised culture, a number of theses worthy of further empirical examination arise.

The first of these hinges on one form of system colonisation of the lifeworld, *command colonisation*. In line with some of the accounts drawn on above, this recognises a trend towards the bureaucratisation of death via a prescriptive rhetoric of the good death. As Habermas, following Weber, notes, medical science is here deployed in the name of autonomy and democracy to take away autonomy and democracy, a ploy epitomised in the very concept of the 'expert patient' (Habermas, 1984). Notwithstanding the new-found deference of command to class relations, the latter have consolidated a more regulatory, interventionist 'surveillance state' with side-effects for the dying and their carers. This is a form of colonisation of the private sphere of the lifeworld. If governmentality characterises the *modus operandi* of this mode of regulation, it disguises the reflexivity of the state's power elite (Scambler, 2002).

The second thesis announces the other principal form of system colonisation of the lifeworld, namely, *class colonisation*. The tendency to commodify death has of course been apparent during each of the—liberal, organised and disorganised—phases of modern capitalism. It is likely that our regulatory and marketised state, itself substantially the issue of class pressure, will shepherd in, even insist on, new opportunities, or niche markets, for 'clients' or 'consumers' (formerly citizens) encouraged to anticipate either their own death or that of their loved ones (as well, of course, as insisting on the privatisation or re-commodification of the salient health services). It is self-evident, after all, that the more expensive the arrangements, rituals, ceremonies and adornments like coffins, the greater the love and loss. But there is much yet to learn from United States mentors here.

It is with reference to class colonisation, too, that new debates about just how to define contemporary death—conundrums alluded to in Table 1 and well rehearsed in this collection (see especially the discussion of Chau and Herring, this volume)—need to be framed. There is no denying the complexity of such definitional processes. To the extent that (re-)definitions are prompted by class-motivated, command-initiated calls for the more ready harvesting of organs, it is appropriate to think in terms of processes of colonisation. Colonisation could be said to have occurred if adjustments were made to the definition of death to facilitate commercial interests in the harvesting of organs in the absence of any real—as opposed to nominal, say parliamentary—mechanism of public accountability. Following in the footsteps of Weber and Habermas, it needs to be emphasised that medical, legal, even social scientific or humanistic, 'expert' judgement is no proxy for what the latter calls the public use of reason, the pivotal point again being the issue of tangible accountability.

The third thesis recalls the idea of *post-modern disinhibition*. In principal, post-modern relativised *petit* narratives permit a proliferation of cultural scripts, and thus a wider choice of ways to die and to mark death. Sometimes complementing, sometimes challenging, bureaucratic indicators of the good death, these mediated scripts in practice tend to favour what Seale terms 'confessional deaths',

in which terminally ill people fight, face and eventually accept their deaths, reconciling themselves with their loved ones, retelling and sometimes reconstructing personal biographies, presiding over their last days in a manner that is somewhat akin to that of a chief mourner at a funeral (Seale, 2004: 967).

At the other end of the spectrum, they tend to denounce dying alone, to take an example examined by Seale, as a form of 'bad death'. What appears as a new freedom to choose, as emancipatory, can in fact be the circuitous product of system colonisation via commodification (after all, the goal or end-point of capitalism is the commodification of everything) and/or bureaucratisation. To the extent that it is, people's choices contain elements of (class) 'exploitation' and (command) 'oppression'. Such a statement only seems controversial because, as ever, the social seems so natural, inevitable and proper (ie the ready accommodation of post-modern culture within the material auspices of the culture-ideology of consumption). This is not to deny the possibility, however, of genuine, if largely fortuitous, benefits of disinhibition.

Finally, reference must be made to *lifeworld resistance*. The dying or those 'left behind'—spouses or partners, offspring, siblings, friends, 'fans'—are typically more 'savvy' and reflexive than they are given credit for: exploitation and/or oppression are more transparent than is realised.

Often their agency is sufficiently structured, however, for them to deny or forego oppositional stances or engagement. The route to opposition in disorganised capitalism is no longer via class—if class relations are more relevant 'objectively', they are undeniably less so 'subjectively', that is, as a resource for personal and social mobilisation for change—but via the transference of antagonism from the 'enabling' to the 'protest' sectors of civil society (Scambler and Martin, 2001; and Scambler and Kelleher, 2006). Expressed differently, confusions, irritations and occasional rages around dying articulated in commonplace meeting places like shops and cafes need to be translated from the private to the public spheres of the lifeworld. This is essential if they are to gain effectiveness (ie to generate influence that can be brought to bear on the sub-systems of economy and state). This is a tall order.

Potentially important for lifeworld resistance in relation to issues of death and dying is the presence of the jury in the courtroom, an institution currently under sustained attack in England. Juries furnish a practical arena for deliberative democracy, and their displacement by expert 'knowledges' opens the door to extended command and class colonisation. It is fundamentally undemocratic for decisions on the harvesting of organs mentioned earlier, as well as on a host of other matters covered in this volume—like the rights of the dying and deceased and the 'body as property'—to be delegated to appointed experts, whether doctors, lawyers or academics.

Arguably, the social has been neglected in considerations of death, dying and bereavement, and most so in respect of the structural. With the emergence of modern society, the issues of lifeworld versus system and private versus public have become critical. Social differentiation has led to historically novel tensions. If, as Habermas (1984) argues, *a degree of* commodification and bureaucratisation are both inevitable and unobjectionable, colonisation is something else. And death, not least through its recent revival, is under threat of (further) colonisation. It is as important as it is difficult to acknowledge that this is a political matter, and it is in this context that many of the debates represented and commented on in the course of this multi-faceted text require to be understood.

REFERENCES

Ariès, P (1983) *The hour of our death* (Harmondsworth, Penguin).
Arnason, A and Hafsteinsson, S (2003) 'The revival of death: expression, expertise and governmentality' 54 *British Journal of Sociology* 43–62.
Cartwright, A, Hockey, L and Anderson, J (1973) *Life before death* (London, Routledge).
Crook, S, Paluski, J and Waters, M (1992) *Postmodernization: changes in advanced society* (London, Sage).

Dean, M (1999) *Governmentality: power and rule in modern society* (London, Sage).

Giddens, A (1990) *Consequences of modernity* (Cambridge, Polity Press).

Gilleard, C and Higgs, P (2000) *Cultures of ageing: self, citizen and the body* (Harlow, Prentice-Hall).

Glaser, B and Strauss, A (1965) *Awareness of dying* (Chicago IL, Aldine).

Habermas, J (1984) *The theory of communicative action* vol1: *Reason and the rationalization of society*. (London, Heinemann).

—— (1987) *The theory of communicative action* vol 2: *Lifeworld and system: a critique of functionalist reason* (Cambridge, Polity Press).

—— (1989) *The new conservatism* (Cambridge, Polity Press).

Jupp, P and Walter, T (1999) 'The healthy society: 1918–98' in P Jupp and C Gittings (eds) *Death in England* (Manchester, Manchester University Press) 256–282.

Laslett, P (1996) *A fresh map of life*, 2nd edn (London, Weidenfeld & Nicholson).

Lofland, J (1978) *The craft of dying: the modern face of death* (London, Sage).

Lyotard, J-J (1984) *The postmodern condition* (Manchester, Manchester University Press).

Marmot, M (2006) *Social determinants of health inequalities*. (Geneva, World Health Organization).

Mellor, P and Shilling, C (1993) 'Modernity, self-identity and the sequestration of death' 27 *Sociology* 411–431.

Pearce, D, Griffin, T, Kelly, J and Miklelsen, L (1997) 'An overview of the population in Europe and North America' 89 *Population Trends* 24–36.

Rose, N (1996) *Inventing our selves: psychology, power and personhood* (Cambridge, Cambridge University Press).

Scambler, G (2001) 'Unfolding themes of an incomplete project' in G Scambler and J habermas (eds) *Critical Theory and Health* (London, Routledge) 1–24.

—— (2002) *Health and social change: a critical theory* (Buckingham, Open University Press).

Scambler, G and Kelleher, D (2006) 'New social and health movements: issues of representation and change' 16 *Critical Public Health* 219–231.

Scambler, G, Martin, L (2001) 'Civil society, the public sphere and deliberative democracy' in G Scambler and J Habermas (eds) *Critical Theory and Health* (London, Routledge) 182–205.

Scambler, G and Scambler, S (to be published 2007) 'Social patterning of health behaviours' in A Scriven and S Garman (eds) *Public health: social context and action* (London, Routledge).

Seale, C (1998) *Constructing death: the sociology of dying and bereavement* (Cambridge, Cambridge University Press).

—— (2000) 'Changing patterns of death and dying' 51 *Social Science and Medicine* 917–930.

—— (2004) 'Media constructions of dying alone: a form of "bad death"' 58 *Social Science and Medicine* 967–974.

Seale, C and Cartwright, A (1994) *The year before death* (Averbery, Aldershot).

Seale, C and van der Geest, S (2004) 'Good and bad death: an introduction' 58 *Social Science and Medicine* 883–885.

Sklair, L (2000) *The transnational capitalist class* (Oxford, Blackwell).

Taylor, K (1988) '"Telling bad news": physicians and the disclosure of undesirable information' 10 *Sociology of Health and Illness* 109–132.

Walter, T (1991) 'Modern death: taboo or not taboo?' 25 *Sociology* 293–310.

—— (1994) *The revival of death* (London, Routledge).

World Health Organization (1998) *World health report* (Geneva, World Health Organization).

Part 3

Dealing with Bodies

11

'Hot' Homicides and the Role of Police-Suspect Interviews in the Investigation of Illegal Deaths

MARTIN INNES

I. INTRODUCTION

THIS CHAPTER EXPLORES the contribution of police-suspect interviews to the investigation of homicide, and more broadly how such interactions shape the ways that incidents of illegal death are defined and understood. In so doing it is organised to pivot around three principal claims. First, the majority of criminal homicides are 'hot' rather than 'cold-blooded' infractions of the criminal law. This is largely attributable to the nature of fatal interactions and the presence of toxic rage in response to a perceived threat to the perpetrator's fragile (usually masculine) identity. Secondly, this modal nature of homicidal interactions influences the police 'process structures' used to organise and systematise their response. Major crime enquiries are typically either 'self-solving' or 'whodunnit' investigations, with the former being more numerous than the latter. Finally, given the 'hot' nature of these crimes, police interviews with prime suspects often afford perpetrators and police alike an important sense-making opportunity, where what happened can be retrospectively reconstructed, informed by evidence from a range of sources. Consequently, suspect interviews retain an important role in the investigative and detective work performed by police, despite significant advances in the processing and analysis of physical evidence. These interviews can best be understood as co-productive transactions where a narrative account is negotiated and actively constructed by the participants.

The chapter commences with a brief overview of the key patterns and trends in criminal homicide in England and Wales. This is used to develop an understanding of the social organisation of the police response to such incidents. As will be shown, the circumstances and settings in which criminal homicides tend to occur exert a key influence upon the processes and systems that police enact. In examining the nature of the police work conducted, it is argued that establishing a conceptual distinction between how police 'investigate' a potential crime and how they 'detect' it may be useful. 'Investigative work' relates to those practices that police use to enquire into the circumstances of an incident in order to establish how it happened and whether it should be treated as a potential crime or not—what might be termed 'the howdunnit' question. In contrast, 'detective work' is more directly concerned with identifying a culpable prime suspect—the 'whodunnit' question—and assembling an evidenced case to prove that this person is responsible for causing the illegal death of another. Having developed this understanding of the form and functions of investigative and detective work, the chapter progresses to a more focused and detailed exploration of the role of police-suspect interviews. This is based upon an empirical case study of a suspect interview that highlights in particular the suspect's agency and shows how the police approach is constrained and structured by external requirements deriving from the broader legal process in which their work is situated.

The particular case featured in this chapter is drawn from an ethnographic research project on murder investigations conducted in a police force in Southern England in the late 1990s (Innes, 2003). In this study, observational fieldwork was conducted on five homicide enquiries in progress. This was augmented by interviews with police detectives and documentary analysis of 20 complete police case files, encompassing a range of different homicide and investigation types.[1] In focusing upon police-suspect interview encounters in the present discussion, as considered in more detail in the next section, the aim is to act as a corrective to previous accounts of police interviews that have tended to under-emphasise the agency of suspects and over-emphasise that of police. In the conclusion, some broader reflections about the nature of social reactions to death in the contemporary age are presented, together with a consideration of what the police investigative response to illegal death reveals about these.

II. DEATH AND CRIMINAL HOMICIDE

In 2005 there were 756 incidents classified as criminal homicides in England and Wales. It is now an orthodoxy of research on this topic that, in contrast to mass media depictions of fatal violence as taking place between strangers, the modal form of criminal homicide in England and Wales involves individuals known to each other in some way. It is also a crime with a certain masculine bias, in that males are over-represented as perpetrators, and,

---

[1] Readers seeking more background detail on the sample of cases and research design should consult the Methodological Appendix in Innes, 2003.

to a lesser extent, as victims (Polk, 1994; and Brookman, 2005). That there is not typically vast relational distance between participants in homicidal violence alerts us to the importance of the social and emotional dynamics routinely involved in fatal interactions. For, rather than such events taking place 'in cold blood', they are typically 'hot' impassioned acts, arising in emotionally charged circumstances.

Appreciating the significance of such emotional dynamics is vital to securing an understanding of some of the problems that police investigations have to resolve in manufacturing an authoritative account of who did what to whom and why. So, whereas mass media accounts of criminal homicide typically depict with clarity who is assigned to the victim role and who is cast as the perpetrator, the reality of criminal homicide is that such clear-cut assertions are artefacts of the work performed by police murder squad detectives. Some of these complexities inherent in homicide investigation work were alluded to by David Luckenbill in his classic study of homicide as a 'situated transaction' (Luckenbill, 1977). He showed how, in many of the cases in his sample, as the fatal interaction unfolded the roles played by the victims and killers in terms of who was the aggressor often reversed. In effect, the eventual victim often initiated the conflict that escalated to fatal violence. Developing this approach, J Katz found that the recourse to violence by one or other of the parties is frequently triggered not by some physical action, but rather a moral challenge or affront (Katz, 1988). The presence of this moral challenge is certainly a crucial ingredient in explaining the two main scenarios of criminal homicide in England and Wales: conflicts between young men in public settings; and violence enacted between domestic partners in the context of a deteriorating relationship (Brookman, 2005).

In his analysis of the role of masculinity in fatal violence, Polk identifies that one of the primary triggers for homicidal events is what he terms the 'defence of masculine honour' (Polk, 1994). This results from the need amongst young men to protect and defend their social identity and status when it is threatened, usually by other young males in public situations. The sequence of events in such incidents often involves one individual doing or saying something that can be read as a humiliating affront to the other. Not to respond to such a challenge would threaten the affronted male's sense of social and self-identity, and so in these incidents they invoke some form of response. If neither of the parties to the potential conflict backs down, then it can quickly move from a challenge and response, to a situation that increasingly locks the participants into a sequence of moves escalating to violence to resolve the conflict. From the police point of view, the sequence of moves and countermoves that occurs as the social interaction unfolds towards a tragic denouement means it is not certain who will end up dead, and notions of criminal intention are consequently rendered difficult to establish definitively.

The second key homicidal scenario relates to what, in police parlance, is referred to as 'domestic homicide.' Analysis of the recorded crime figures for homicide in England and Wales for the past decade reveals that approximately 45 per cent of all female victims and just under 10 per cent of male victims were killed by their present or former partner (Innes, 2003). As with the male-on-male interactions described above, in domestic homicides the implementation of violence can be understood as a form of social control, via which a destructive resolution to a humiliating situation is being sought. In such cases, there is often a sense of a deteriorating relationship, where one or other of the partners becomes consumed by what Websdale terms 'morbid possessiveness', coming to the conclusion that 'if I can't have you, then no-one can'. Fatal violence is thus enacted by the possessive partner as a 'solution' to what they perceive to be an unacceptable situation.

When defending 'masculine honour' the pivotal moment in such scenarios is, according to Katz, where humiliation transmogrifies into rage (Katz, 1988). This process of conversion does not happen all that frequently—people will often elect to bear the social stigma of humiliation—but when it does:

[P]ersons who become enraged must create the sensuality that makes them its vehicle ... assailants make themselves the object of forces beyond their control but retain the possibility of abandoning the process (Katz, 1988: 22).

In these types of fatal interaction, it is because the death of another may not initially have been the intended outcome, and because people act in an emotionally heightened state, that the interview in police custody is so important. As will be discussed in due course, it provides an occasion where the perpetrator of the fatal violence has to reconstruct his actions in order to account for what he has done. In so doing, he must try to make sense of a not very sensible line of action.

This sense-making function forms the core of the police role when responding to incidents of fatal violence. The 'hot-blooded' nature of the majority of such incidents introduces certain complexities and difficulties that have to be dealt with by police in terms of establishing who did what to whom and why. These complexities are of a different order to those involved in investigating more pre-meditated killings—where attention has to focus more upon identifying an unknown assailant. In the kinds of cases that are the explicit focus of this chapter, the identity of the assailant is often comparatively easily established by police. Indeed, in many such cases the killer self-incriminates (Innes, 2003). But what I have been trying to convey is that even where the killer's identity is apparent, there can be considerable complexity involved in producing an authoritative account that explains precisely what has transpired, and doing so in a manner that accords with the requirements and specifications of the criminal law. In the next section, I develop these themes by showing how the nature of the circumstances in which fatal violence tends to occur has a direct bearing upon how police organise their response to suspicious deaths.

III. POLICE INVESTIGATIVE AND DETECTIVE WORK

Given the social situations in which fatal violence is typically performed, it is perhaps not surprising to learn that the police are comparatively successful in 'solving' such crimes. An analysis of 10 years of statistical data between 1988 and 1997 revealed that the detection rate for criminal homicide in the United Kingdom hovers around the 90 per cent mark. Of course, a 'detection' is not the same as a conviction. About 40 per cent of all suspects for criminal homicide offences are indicted for and convicted of murder. But in only about 5 per cent of criminal homicide cases where a prosecution is undertaken are all suspects acquitted (Innes, 2003).

The social dynamics involved in the commission of fatal violence are also important in terms of understanding how the police response to such incidents is organised. Owing to the fact that the victim will frequently know his or her assailant, there will be a history of enmity between them and/or there may be witnesses to the violence, and therefore the majority of homicide investigations in England and Wales can be categorised as 'self-solvers' (Innes, 2003). In such cases, police are rapidly able to establish the basic contours of what has happened and who is responsible. Consequently, much of their actual work is focused upon unravelling the sorts of complexities outlined in the previous section about precisely who did or said what to whom and when, in order to construct a strong and detailed case for the prosecution.

Self-solving police investigations are manifestly less complex than the 'whodunnit' investigations that are launched by police where the identity of a prime suspect is less immediately obvious to them. Typically, self-solving investigations are also resolved much faster and demand fewer resources to service them than is the case for whodunnits. Indeed, there is an axiom amongst murder squad detectives that if you haven't identified a 'good suspect' within the first 48 hours of an investigation 'then you are in for the long haul'. However, the fact that they are less complex than whodunnit investigations, does not mean that we should dismiss the importance of 'self-solving investigations'. Nor should we make the mistake of glossing over the levels of painstaking detail that are routinely involved in self-solving police investigations. As I described in the earlier sections of this chapter, such incidents often involve their own complexities in terms of untangling a complex web of social connections, actions and reactions, rumours and innuendos which must be investigated in order to assemble an authoritative account about who did what to whom. In both self-solving cases and whodunnit enquiries, police will draw upon and be informed by information derived from a number of different sources, including 'contact trace materials', witness accounts, intelligence from police databases, and of course any suspect's account. The difference between these is that in the latter, whodunnit, form, reliable evidence is frequently harder to obtain and to validate in terms of its contribution to understanding what has occurred.

Recently, much attention has focused upon how advances in forensic science technologies have reconfigured the ways in which major crimes are investigated (Cole and Lynch, 2006; and Williams and Johnson, 2007). It is certainly the case that such developments—particularly in relation to the improving capacity to extract DNA profiles from minute traces of biological materials found at crime scenes, and the growth in the National DNA Database—have enabled police in the United Kingdom to solve some otherwise intractable crimes. Analysis of DNA has come to constitute an important method by which detectives can establish some form of connection between a suspect, a victim and a crime scene. However, it is important that we are not overly seduced by some of the more sensational claims made for such advances, and that we do not over-state the nature of the influence that such technologies have had upon investigative practice. Actually, in the majority of homicide cases in the United Kingdom, owing to the interactional circumstances in which they take place, DNA evidence does not play a pivotal role in the identification of suspects. Such materials may have a role in confirming aspects of the case for the prosecution that the police develop through other lines of enquiry. But in terms of the identification of a prime suspect, they are of significance for only a minority of the harder-to-solve 'whodunnit' homicide investigations. The reasons for this are quite simple. The collection and processing of samples from a crime scene that may contain DNA is a time-consuming business. Indeed, the full results of the analysis of physical materials from a scene can often take a number of weeks to become available to police. But as has already been discussed, because most homicides in the United Kingdom take place in public settings or involve participants who are intimately acquainted, in the majority of cases police tend to identify suspects and make sense of what happened much faster through the routine deployment of more established and traditional techniques. In the next section, the significance of one such technique that is highly valued by police themselves, the interview of a suspect in custody, is examined in some detail.

IV.   THE ROLE OF SUSPECT INTERVIEWS: A CASE STUDY

In the following extracts—taken from the police transcript of an interview with a man who had repeatedly stabbed his wife to death during their Sunday dinner and then fled the scene—a number of the themes and issues outlined in the introduction to this chapter are elaborated. The suspect starts with a rendition of the immediate context to the argument that arose between him and his wife and how he responded in a violent rage,[2]

S: [Victim name] told me dinner was in the kitchen, so I went and got it. We went and sat in the lounge. I tried making conversation with [victim name] but she wouldn't answer ... she said something I couldn't quite hear. She repeated it and I lost all control and I just stabbed her and I heard her say 'oh' and then we just attacked each other. I still had the knife in my hand and I keep repeatedly stabbing her and we tossed and turned and the next thing I know we're on the floor near the fire and then she said 'You're killing me' and then she said 'sorry' and I stopped after ... and I just couldn't, she held my arm and I was holding a knife toward her and I then just ran off ... She just made another snide comment ... I just ... had ... it was an unbelievable urge to hurt her.

It can be seen from this that the suspect has made a full and frank admission of responsibility to the police. Although it is difficult to establish how often suspects self-incriminate in this manner, there is substantial research evidence intimating that it may be a regular occurrence (Innes, 2003; Polk, 1994; and Brookman, 2005). This contrasts with a number of academic studies and the archetypal media representations of police interviewing, both of which have tended to gravitate around a notion that such interactions routinely involve skilled police questioning breaking down the resolve of a reluctant and recalcitrant suspect. But if the case study that is the focus of this chapter is representative of the majority of 'normal homicides'[3] that the police are called on to investigate, then there is a need to conceptualise their interviews with suspects in a different way: one that attends to the negotiated and collaborative ways in which police and their suspects co-produce an account of what has happened.

Furthermore, the extract above conveys a number of the key issues germane to understanding why people perform homicidal acts. From what the male suspect said, it is clear that he perceived a personal slight in his wife's actions and that he responded with an 'explosion' of frenzied violence. It is also interesting to note that he tried to invoke, albeit unsuccessfully, a notion of 'reasonableness' in his actions, even though what he did would be classed by most people as wholly unjustifiable. His first claim to this effect was that he was provoked when his wife would not respond to his attempts to initiate a conversation. Such a claim can be understood as attempting to mitigate guilt by establishing what Sykes and Matza famously termed a 'technique of neutralisation' (Sykes and Matza, 1957).

Although the suspect acknowledged that he initiated the violence, his statement 'we just attacked each other' seeks to convey to his interlocutors

---

[2] In the transcript: 'S' denotes suspect; 'P1' & 'P2' denote police interviewers.
[3] This is a deliberate allusion to Sudnow's concept of a 'normal crime' (Sudnow, 1965). That is, one possessed of the qualities that are viewed as typical for an incident of this type.

that the violence was not his alone. By preceding his account of the sustained nature of the violence he performed with a claim that they 'attacked each other', the suspect aims to provide an implicit justification for his failure to de-escalate his violence. The third claim for reasonableness in the suspect's initial account is where he describes the cessation of the assault when his wife cries that he is killing her. So, whilst he admits to being possessed of 'an unbelievable urge to hurt her', he also suggests that at the point where the gravity of his actions became evident, he responded in a reasonable manner.

What is not mentioned in this account, but had already been established by police through other lines of enquiry conducted with friends and relatives of the couple, was that there was a salient 'back-history' to the crime. Detectives working on the case had identified that the wife had been having an extra-marital affair and was in the process of leaving her husband. They had also been informed that the male partner had been violent towards his wife on several occasions. The detailed and extensive nature of the enquiries that police make when responding to suspicious deaths means that they frequently uncover 'discreditable' information of this kind about victims, their relations and witnesses. Sorting through such discreditable information can often be an important feature of interviews with suspects.

Having got the suspect to provide a brief account of what happened, the police officers conducting the interview prompted him to provide additional details about specific key points:

P1: I don't wish to dwell on it but do you remember anything about the comments she made to you and why it made you so angry ...?

The police officer's question here provides a good example of how in an interview they have to respond to information that may be partially revealed by the suspect. The suspect says that his wife 'made another snide comment' and the officer in his/her follow-up question has obviously identified this as important, as it is being suggested as the immediate provocation for the assault. Thus, in encouraging the suspect to develop his story around this particular point, the officer is seeking to anticipate an important decision in terms of constructing the prosecution case. He is trying to define the nature of the provocation, which in turn will influence how they define and classify the incident overall.

One of the principal concerns for all homicide investigations is seeking to establish whether these acts should be treated as murder or manslaughter. In law, in order for a case to be successfully prosecuted as murder, it must be demonstrated that not only did the named suspect cause the death of the victim, but that he intended and planned to do so. In the absence of mens rea or 'malice aforethought', the case will be one of manslaughter. Consequently, an important aspect of the homicide detective's work is searching for 'signifiers of intent'—specific actions performed by any suspect prior to the commission of the fatal act that can be construed as indicators that it contained some element of planning. In this case, as a result of the information gleaned from their interview with the suspect, in conjunction with their 'reading' of the scene of the crime and the distribution of physical evidence therein, the detectives were satisfied that this was not a premeditated act. Accordingly, the husband was subsequently charged with and convicted of manslaughter.

The data extracts around the issue of provocation exemplify how the police's approach to the interview interaction is structured by external considerations derived from the broader legal process in which their work is located. In seeking to establish the degree of provocation, they are working to fulfil the requirements of the law's definitions of murder and manslaughter and test the extent to which the specifics of the case that they are dealing with meet the law's standards. How they actually do this by deploying the disclaimer 'I don't wish to dwell on it' is especially interesting, as it subtly seeks to down-play the apparent significance of the line of questioning, when it is obviously consequential to the construction of the police's legal case. The suspect's reply to the question was as follows:

S: The content wasn't important ... just the way she said it. I had the knife in my right hand and I just turned round and pushed it in her ... I was just out of control, I mean the next 30 seconds were just a mad ... I just went mad and we were just fighting ... I was just stabbing her repeatedly ... I remember stabbing her in the chest and back. She was fighting back, trying to protect herself ... blood everywhere.

In this passage, the suspect starts to provide a more 'thickly' descriptive account of the physical dynamics of the assault. He acknowledges that the provocation did not warrant the reaction he gave it and then describes a frenzied and violent attack. He conveys a sense of both performing the acts but also being 'out of control'. This is an important passage in a number of respects. Firstly, it is starting to layer in more detail about the actions and reactions that occurred during the assault. The suspect recalls repeated stabbing and that the wounds he inflicted were both to the front and back of the victim. There is also a repetition of the claim that the victim was using violence, but this time he seems more willing to acknowledge that this counter-violence was an attempt to establish some protection.

Having established a full, frank and detailed admission for the commission of the crime, the detective then introduces a specific question, the relevance of which is elaborated by the second interviewer:

P1: You had one knife. Did you at any time stab her with the knife she was using?
P2: There are indications that both knives were used in the fight. Can you recall how they were used?

Here we can see an example of how police draw upon other sources of evidence in managing the interview. They had recovered two knives from the crime scene both of which had significant traces of the victim's blood upon them. By introducing this question, they are in effect challenging the suspect to render his account in a way that accords with the physical evidence the police have recovered at the scene of the incident.

In noting that in the first interview the suspect claimed that a 'snide comment' was the immediate provocation for the violence that he unleashed, the police focused upon getting the suspect to detail the actual crime and provide his account of what happened. In a second interview, once they had gathered, and had time to sort through material about the couple's marriage, they concentrated more upon getting the suspect's account of the deteriorating relationship. The picture that they developed was of a marriage coming to an end where the female partner was in the process of leaving the male, and the ongoing 'chronic' humiliation he felt switched to 'acute' and intense rage.

P2: Why is your marriage breaking up?
S: She doesn't love me … I'm just one of those wasters at the bar … I didn't want it to end, she wanted to. There's been a lot of problems this year for me … When we married I was the one who had to do all the changing.
P1: Was it your intention to kill her?
S: No, not to kill her. I didn't think she was dead when I left. I'm not making any excuses for what I did. There's no reason for it.

These final extracts from the interview are more personally oriented for the suspect than the previous ones, capturing how, in some circumstances and under certain conditions, the police interview is an opportunity to make sense of what has happened not just for the police, but for the perpetrator as well. There is a real sense in the above of an individual starting to piece together his act with its antecedent causes.

The reproduction of the interview transactions between the police and their suspect in this case is intended to illuminate two connected themes, both of which have tended to be glossed over in previous studies of police crime investigations and interview techniques. First, there is the extent to which the suspect is able to exert agency over how the interview interaction unfolds and how the account of the incident is constructed. This is not to deny the presence of an asymmetry in the power available to police interviewers when compared with that of their interviewees, for the former are undoubtedly in a dominant position. But rather, the point has been to clarify that the decisions taken by suspects about what to tell police (if anything) and when, do shape how the police's work is performed. As will be discussed in more detail below, there has been a tendency in some previous studies of the police's response to crime to over-state the power of the police (McConville and others, 1991). At the same time though, this empirical case study also captures the extent to which the conduct of the police's work is structured by the external requirements of the legal process.

V. DISCUSSION: MAKING SENSE OF DEATH

Police accounts of their response to incidents where illegal death is suspected, at least in terms of how they are rendered in mass media reports, generally suggest that their investigative function is simply and unproblematically concerned with illuminating the 'facts' and 'truth' of what really happened. Such rhetorical constructions belie the epistemological complexities of detective work. For police do not just uncover facts; they are in a very literal sense involved in '*constructing* a case for the prosecution', wherein information gleaned from various sources is employed as knowledge and evidence of how a past event occurred (Innes, 2003; and McConville and others, 1991). Thus, what are routinely and pragmatically treated as 'the facts' of a case are actually artefacts of police investigative method. In essence, the police investigative process is focused upon the production of what sociologists term 'a definition of the situation.'

According to the dictates of detective culture, the interview with a suspect in police custody is a pivotal moment in the conduct of an investigation, for it is an opportunity for police to test the strength and robustness of the case they are building with the person(s) who is the subject of their suspicions. By gauging the reactions of suspects to their evidence and inferences, police contend they can either confirm aspects of their case narrative, or acquire more information to assist them in developing further lines of enquiry. This emphasis by the police on the importance of interviews has informed a number of academic investigations into how these interactions are (or at least should be) accomplished. However, the majority of these earlier studies have provided only limited insights into the reality of the role of interviews in crime management processes, owing to their tendency to isolate interviews from other facets of police systems and practices (Watson, 1997; and Leo, 1996). So interviews have frequently been treated as the sole object of analysis, rather than being situated within a wider process that is in turn shaped by the rules, procedures and requirements of an adversarial legal process. Consequently, whilst previous studies have examined a variety of technical procedures that might enhance the validity and reliability of the interview process (Gudjonssen, 1992; and Milne and Bull, 1999), only limited consideration has been given to why police interviewers pursue certain lines of questioning and the implications for the processes of investigation and detection of the answers that suspects provide to these.

In her analysis of police interviews in Australia, relating to more routine crimes than homicide, Heydon identifies similar verbal exchanges to those described in the previous sections as evidence that the police endeavour to manipulate the suspect's account into one that accords with their own 'preferred' version of events (Heydon, 2005). But what her account lacks, focused as it is upon the application of formal conversational analysis techniques, is any consideration of how police influence may reflect the 'structurated' relationship that exists between a police investigation and the wider legal process (Innes, 2003). It is a structurated relationship inasmuch as the police investigation is responsible for producing the prosecutorial narrative and supporting evidence that constitute the focus for the legal decision-making that occurs at the judicial stage. At the same time, the law determines what counts as evidence for the police, how its validity and reliability is appraised, and, through the rules of evidence, regulates how such materials are to be gathered. Thus what Heydon's overly simplified conceptualisation fails to grasp is that an aspect of the police investigative function is formatting the available information and evidence in a way that coheres with the categories and requirements of the law's classificatory frameworks and procedures.

During the course of interview interactions conducted as part of their enquiries into suspected illegal deaths, police do seek to negotiate how a suspect accounts for his actions, but not for the reasons that Heydon implies (Heydon, 2005). Sometimes, police will directly challenge aspects of what a suspect says if these do not cohere with other evidence that police have available. On other occasions though, the nature of the influence that interviewing officers exert will be more subtle; concerned with formatting the suspect's account in a way that accords with the evidential requirements of the adversarial legal process.

Innes reports that in terms of the way in which they arrange the results of their lines of enquiry when investigating major crimes, police detectives draw upon specific narrative frames (Innes, 2003). These enable the evidence to be set out in a way that fulfils the requirements of an adversarial legal process and is persuasive to a jury. The narrative frames provide structured ways of telling the story of a crime that are based upon established conventions for crimes of a particular kind. These structured accounting frameworks are invoked because police have found that they are likely to fulfil the legally mandated requirements of the criminal justice process, whilst being persuasive to a jury to accept the police's version of events. These case narratives will obviously be moulded to reflect the situational specifics of individual incidents, but they tend to be underpinned by more basic and fundamental structures. So, for example, police case narratives about domestic homicides tend to be structured around fairly similar plots, motives, and sequences of events. These differ from the sorts of narrative employments that are used to describe and explain what happened in 'stranger murders', or other types of crime.

The concept of co-production is thus useful to this analysis in articulating how the accounts provided by suspects when being interviewed by police are often consequential to the narratives that police construct. In contrast to many previous accounts of police-suspect interviews that have emphasised the power of the police to shape how the interaction unfolds, the conceptual positioning adopted herein is intended to create a space in which the agency of suspects can be better appreciated. For, whilst police undoubtedly have more influence over the conduct of interviews than suspects, this does not equate to the latter having no influence. Decisions taken by suspects about what information to give to the police when being interviewed do have a bearing upon the subsequent conduct of the police investigation and the case narrative that is constructed. The latter consideration is especially apposite for the more 'mundane' types of homicide that have been the focus of this chapter, where it is comparatively commonplace for assailants to provide detailed accounts concerning the fatality (see also Innes, 2003). What the concept of co-production keys us into, then, is that whilst the police are ultimately engaged in the production of a definition of the situation, their ability to establish a valid and reliable, legally acceptable definition of what happened is contingent upon a number of sources of information, one of which is the suspect's own account. At the same time their own investigative and detective work is influenced by the requirements of the adversarial legal process which determines what material will count as evidence, and what is required for it to be viewed as valid and reliable.

VI. CONCLUSION

Rendering death meaningful seems to be one of the eternal preoccupations of the human condition. Police homicide investigations are one variant of how modern societies seek to explain the causes of unexplained deaths, where these are suspected to be attributable to the actions of another individual. As part of these enquiries, the interview with a prime suspect can contribute much to the police's understanding of what has transpired, and to their ability to develop an authoritative narrative setting out who did what to whom and why.

Due to the kinds of social situations in which fatal violence tends to occur, a significant proportion of all homicide suspects interviewed by the police make a full or partial admission. That suspects select this course of action has less to do with the persuasive powers of police interviewers than with the fact that the fatal assault was the outcome of an emotionally-driven explosion of violence. In fictional accounts of homicide, and the sorts of crimes that tend to be covered by journalists, the murder performed 'in cold blood' provides a useful dramatic device around which to construct a compelling story for an audience. However, the social reality of homicide and its investigation is in many respects not reflected in these dramatic accounts. The majority of homicides are more mundane and parochial, and the nature of the police work that is performed has less to do with investigators developing startlingly intuitive insights, than their painstakingly systematic reconstruction of events, based upon information derived from multiple sources. It is in such a context that the suspect interview becomes so significant to police detectives.

Previous accounts of police-suspect interviews have tended to focus upon the power of the police to shape the outcome, but in so doing, they have also under-emphasised the agency of suspects and the potential for their moves and counter-moves to shape the wider police investigation. In contrast, as described in this chapter, the interviews conducted in the context of homicide investigations into 'hot crimes' are often usefully conceptualised as co-productions. The interview in custody provides a vital opportunity for police to test, develop and refine the case narrative detailing their beliefs about what happened. As such, it is intimately connected to the fundamental social function of a police enquiry—to assemble an authoritative narrative that, framed by the conventions of criminal law, determines how a death is to be classified and what its causes are to be attributed to.

REFERENCES

Brookman, F (2005) *Understanding homicide in the UK* (London, Sage).
Cole, S and Lynch, M (2006) The social and legal construction of suspects 2 *Annual Review of Law and Social Science* 39–60.
Gudjonsson, G (1992) *The psychology of interrogations, confessions and testimony* (Chichester, Wiley).
Heydon, G (2005) *The language of police interviewing: A critical analysis* (Basingstoke, Palgrave Macmillan).
Innes, M (2003) *Investigating murder: Detective work and the police response to criminal homicide* (Oxford, Clarendon Press).
Katz, J (1998) *Seductions of crime: Moral and sensual attractions in doing evil* (New York, Basic Books).
Leo, R (1996) 'Miranda's revenge: police interrogation as a confidence game' 30 *Law and Society Review* 259–288.
Luckenbill, D (1977) 'Criminal homicide as a situated transaction' 25 *Social Problems* 176–186.
McConville, M, Sanders, A and Leng, R (1991) *The case for the prosecution* (London, Routledge).
Milne, R and Bull, R (1999) *Investigative interviewing: Psychology and practice* (Chichester, Wiley).
Polk, K (1994) *When men kill* (Cambridge, Cambridge University Press).
Sudnow, D (1965) 'Normal crimes: sociological features of the penal code in a public defender's office' 12 *Social Problems* 255–276.
Sykes, G and Matza, D (1957) 'Techniques of neutralization: a theory of delinquency' 22 *American Sociological Review* 664–670.

Watson, R (1997) 'The presentation of victim and motive in discourse: The case of police interrogations and interviews' in M Travers and F Manzo (eds), *Law in Action: Ethnomethodological and Conversation Analytic Approaches to Law* (Aldershot, Ashgate).

Websdale, N (1999) *Understanding domestic homicide* (Boston, MA, Northeastern University Press).

Williams, R and Johnson, P (2007) *Genetic Policing: The Uses of DNA in Police Investigations* (Cullompton, Willan).

12

Property, Harm and the Corpse

DAVID PRICE

I. INTRODUCTION

AMBIGUITY REGARDING THE body, and most especially corpses, pervades discussions and guidance with respect to medical and other uses of human-derived tissue. Such tensions and disparate standpoints have the capacity to create divisions between professional and lay, and public and private, practices and attitudes, exemplified perhaps in the organ retention inquiries of the previous decade (Price, 2003). Policy and practice have typically been led by pragmatic attitudes or utility-driven perspectives, or a blend of the two. Indeed, traditionally, practice has tended to drive policy (Price, 2000). Opportunities have, however, been created for the underlying principles of legitimate retrieval and use of body parts for such purposes to be made explicit, in measures such as the Human Tissue Act 2004. However, the proper balance between public and private interests, and harmful and non-harmful actions, remains elusive, with statutes displaying no transparent rationale or theoretical structure despite potential penal repercussions. Consent constitutes the cog of the 2004 Act, and most other analogous legislation, but its deeper function is shrouded in murkiness. Prima facie, though, consent reflects a liberal construct in this context, which this paper intends to analyse. Whilst the liberal paradigm cannot explicate the entire panoply of penal measures relating to the dead (see Herring, chapter thirteen this volume), it plausibly illuminates the consent basis of legislation relating to medical uses.

In my task, I draw very substantially upon the late Joel Feinberg's fine exposition of posthumous interests, but contend that it is necessary to be more specific about the essential character of such interests and how they become related to moral and legal protection (Feinberg, 1984; and Feinberg, 1985). Whilst his liberal philosophy relating to criminalisation is a compelling one, and despite his writings and thinking being repeatedly cited in the criminal sphere, it has been noted that his ideas and arguments are relatively seldom used in either detailed doctrinal analysis or practical problem-solving (Roberts, 2001: 173). I seek to tie up this analysis with a framework of property rights in disconnected or inanimate body parts, presented as a theoretical model. There has been considerable scepticism historically as regards property rights in human tissue, typically on grounds of depersonalisation and commodification, sometimes linked to a Cartesian perspective, which I will attempt to rebut. Indeed, it has been remarked that

[t]he suggestion that our bodies, or parts of them, are our property is one of the most contested in bioethics (Beyleveld and Brownsword, 2001: 171).

This paper is largely analytical but does seek to sketch a decision-making framework for the regulation of the usage of corpses for medical purposes, accommodating stresses between deceased 'persons' and their grieving relatives. As Wilkinson has stated, as regards research on, and disposal of, the dead,

[t]he responses in the first type focus on the devastating effects on the relatives and the responses in the second focus on the claims of communities over the bodies of those they believe to be their members. What the subjects themselves thought or might have thought has generally been either ignored or merely gestured at (Wilkinson, 2002: 32).

This paper seeks to partially address this lacuna. There is, however, substantial disagreement and a lack of consensus regarding the extent to which, if at all, such dead 'subjects' possess rights, or whether duties may be owed to them.

II. THE LIBERAL PARADIGM

Liberal philosophy is driven by notions of the human rights of individuals to determine and choose their own ends, and shuns the criminalisation of wrongs defined only by perceptions of the morality of conduct per se. It demands potential *harm*, or at least, and in Feinberg's view, *offence*, in order to legitimate the imposition of criminal sanctions. These exhaust the class of prima facie good moral reasons for prohibitions (although it is still necessary to establish, inter alia, that the infringement is sufficiently serious to justify the intervention of the criminal law). In Feinbergian terms, harm requires a 'setback to interest' in addition to *wrongdoing*, as a function of which consent nullifies potential harm. The ability to consent is recognised in moral philosophy as a central manifestation of personhood and individual autonomy. In a liberal context, it determines which harmful actions are 'morally indefensible'. Assuming the authenticity of a consent there will, for instance, be no offence committed under the Human Tissue Act 2004 where human tissue is stored and/or used for scheduled medical purposes, such as research. However, consent is not a pre-requisite for all the uses incorporated within the statutory regime; there are, for instance, exceptions with regard to existing holdings and to research using residual tissue from living persons, if approved by an ethics committee.

In the United States, one Congressman Moss once asserted that, regardless of the existence of consent, the practice of destroying human cadavers for vehicle safety research violated fundamental notions of morality and human dignity. Feinberg responded by stating that

a newly dead human body is a sacred symbol of a real person, but to respect the symbol by banning autopsies and research on cadavers is to deprive living human beings of the benefits of medical knowledge and condemn unknown thousands to illnesses and deaths that might have been prevented. That is a poor sort of 'respect' to show a sacred symbol (Feinberg 1985, p.75).

But 'disrespect' or 'indignity' is linked to acceptable and unacceptable use. The Nuffield Council on Bioethics stated that

[r]emoval of tissue from a corpse may constitute degradation unless it is either governed by a direct or indirect therapeutic intention or part of accepted funerary rites (Nuffield Council on Bioethics, 1995: para 6.29).

Acceptable uses are legitimate in principle but will infringe individual human rights in the absence of requisite consent. The use of the cadaver as a crash-test dummy in properly approved motor safety research for the prospective benefit of society would not be mistreatment of the corpse where consent was properly obtained, *if* this was considered a societally acceptable purpose (see also Herring, chapter thirteen this volume). The scheduled purposes set out in the Human Tissue Act 2004 are those deemed so appropriate. Whilst this is seemingly inconsistent with a wholly liberal construct, in the context under consideration here, the 2004 Act is an essentially permissive instrument. The wrongs are principally grounded in failures of respect for autonomy.

III. RIGHTS OF CONTROL

We must enquire, however, whence the legitimating authority of consent derives as regards the uses of the dead? Whose consent are we dealing with? Typically, it is the consent of relatives that looms largest, as can be seen in the organ retention controversies at Bristol and Alder Hey. Perhaps this stems, at least in part, from the fact that 'consent' is a concept with relevance principally to living persons. The Scottish Independent Review Group on Post-Mortem Tissue Retention recommended that the term 'authorisation' be employed in lieu, a proposal taken up in the Human

Tissue (Scotland) Act 2006, which lately came into force. But even if paren-
tal powers of proxy decision-making are non-contentious, the powers of
relatives of deceased adults are less transparently justified, as many commentators have observed (Mason and Laurie, 2001). In addition to which
there are potential conflicts with the wishes of now deceased 'persons'
formulated prior to death.

Indeed, lip service at least is commonly paid to the notion that the wishes
of the deceased person are of pre-eminent importance when considering
the use of the corpse for permissible purposes. Formally, the primacy of the
wishes of the (now) deceased person expressed prior to death can be seen in
the Human Tissue Act 2004 (including the Human Tissue Authority Codes
of Practice passed thereunder), in its forerunner the Human Tissue Act 1961,
in the Human Tissue (Scotland) Act 2006, and in most similar legislation
around the world. We need to interrogate and elucidate the provenance of
this pre-eminence in official policy, albeit that, in practice, healthcare professionals invariably defer to relatives in deciding whether to remove, store
and use human tissue from the corpse for purposes such as transplantation
and research (Wilton, chapter fifteen this volume). The notion of the consent of deceased persons is conceptually problematic. How can such wishes
exert any moral or legal sway once death has interceded and the individual
no longer exists? Even assuming that they can, what weight should such
wishes be assigned relative to other competing (living) interests?

IV. HARMING THE DEAD

Harris maintains that the dead are beyond harm (Harris, 2002). They cannot
be hurt; neither can they have desires or welfare interests to be denied. In the
absence of a belief in an afterlife, to regard someone (the same 'someone')
as continuing in a state of 'being' after death (ie as a corpse) is problematic
(Feldman, 1993; see also Chau and Herring, chapter two this volume).
Moreover, the moral status of any such 'being' is unclear. I shall, for present
purposes, assume that the deceased entity is not itself a being with moral
standing, notwithstanding that acts performed on the corpse have *meaning*
for still living individuals such as family members. The notion that the dead
themselves are beyond harm rightly appears incontrovertible to most, and
the law typically accords with such a view, exemplified in the approach of the
law of tort to deceased persons (see Hedley, chapter fourteen this volume).

A. Posthumous Harm

It is thus principally the formerly alive individual with whom we are cen-
trally concerned. Philosophy has had a hard time assessing whether acts

performed after death can morally connect to the once living person. As the Law Reform Commission of Canada asserted:

[T]he utter disregard of one's burial wishes, or the failure to honour one's express wishes on the post-mortem uses of one's body, lend credence to the claim that people have interests that survive their deaths and that they may be harmed when the interests are violated. What remains refractory is providing a coherent philosophical explanation of this intuition (Law Reform Commission of Canada 1992: 45).

The notion of 'posthumous harms' is unconvincing to many. Partridge, for instance, contends that the notion of interests surviving death is incoherent, as there is no one who can be harmed at the point that any wrongful setback of interest occurs (Partridge, 1981).

Feinberg, on the other hand, argues that a living person's interests may survive their death and where these are thwarted they are 'setback' and harm results if it is wrongfully caused (Feinberg, 1984). They are not mere 'public wrongs', as Partridge would have it. A convincing explanation of how even the causing of someone's own death may harm them has eluded most commentators, principally on the ground that, as Epicurus portrayed it, 'where she was, death was not, and where death was, she was not' (Lucretius 95–52 BC). Feinberg, however, observes that both death and developments after death are alike in coming into existence during a period when there is no longer a subject, and asserts that either death itself and posthumous events can both be harms, or neither can (Feinberg, 1984: 82). The most plausible explanation of how death itself may harm a person lies in the *deprivation* thesis, ie that death deprives a person of all the goods that they might otherwise have achieved (Nagel, 1979), and in so far as death precludes the ante-mortem person from achieving certain future-oriented desires, desire-oriented interests may be thwarted by events occurring by or after death. Desires as to the disposition of one's cadaver are future oriented and capable of being—*only* being—thwarted or implemented after death, ie when one has ceased to be.

B. Cause and Effect

The counter-intuitive concept of backward causation raises its head in this connection, and is the locus of the reservations of many commentators. As Waluchow remarks,

when I do whatever it is that sets back the interest of the ante-mortem person (perhaps I break the promise or violate the conditions of his will), I do not make it true that his interests *were* set back. Rather, I make it true that the interests he had are *now* set back. The setting back takes place now, not then. At most we can say that back then it was true that the interests were going to be set back (Waluchow, 1986: 731).

Indeed Pitcher contends that the occurrence of the post-mortem event makes it true that *even before* the person's death he was harmed—harmed in that the unfortunate event was going to happen (Pitcher, 1984: 187). He speaks of the casting of a 'shadow of misfortune' backward over the person's life. Li, however, distinguishes between the 'harm event' and the point at which an individual is 'harmed' *by* an event, and between 'potential' and 'actual' facts (Li, 2002). The ante-mortem harm, for our purposes, would connect to the thwarting of one's right to exercise control over one's corpse. There need be nothing awry or even counter-intuitive about such a view. We should merely take into account events occurring after death in determining whether the person's surviving interests were properly respected? This is congruous with Feinberg's notion of revaluing a person's interests after death before 'closing the tally on the person's life' (Feinberg, 1984: 83). Other actions and interventions may be required to realise an individual's ambitions, and whether they are achieved or not (eg organ donation) can therefore not be known until after their death.

However, it is maintained by some that posthumous interests can never be 'person affecting' (Harris, 2003b). No existing person is made 'worse off'. There is no change as between earlier and later physical states of either body or mind. Glannon similarly argues that if surviving interests are defeated, the overall goodness of a person's life may be affected but not the person him or herself (Glannon, 2001). However, from another perspective, the causing of harm need not be seen only in terms of some kind of *impactive* harm. Indeed, Glannon's assertion ostensibly emanates from his exclusive linking of harm to the person's wellbeing, which has an unavoidable experiential dimension. Pitcher challenges the notion that harm can only be seen in terms of an alteration in one's metaphysical state. Harm may be properly seen as a defeat of one's desires or preferences, although not conceived in terms of a solely hedonistic mental state (Kagan, 1992). Feinberg contrasts non-fulfilment of desires with mere non-satisfaction of desires, ie the achievement of objectives as contrasted with the psychological effect generated by such achievement (Feinberg, 1984: 84). The failure to fulfil one's desires therefore registers as causing harm in a nebulous way. Is there any reason, though, why, when a promise or obligation can only be fulfilled after death, we cannot say that the 'projected interest' of the formerly living person has been set back, and that harm has been thereby caused?

Legally, a breach of contract may occur even though no physical or financial loss accrued to the promisee (ie it is actionable per se). It might be objected that as a matter of law, rights and obligations typically terminate at death (see Hedley, chapter fourteen this volume). But although personal obligations could not be enforced *against* a dead person, certain promises owed *to* the person now deceased may still be capable of performance, and enforcement, after death. No explicit rationale is provided by the legal system for the notion that the posthumous thwarting of surviving interests may constitute harm to the previously living person, but there are various possibilities. This could even be viewed as the work of a legal fiction, just as, arguably, the right of a live-born child to sue in tort for the infliction of injuries resulting from an incident occurring before there was a legal person in existence so relies, at least in civil law jurisdictions (Kennedy and Grubb, 2000).

If we can overcome these conceptual and jurisprudential obstacles we will need to ascertain *what* interests are capable of being setback after death. Even if desires and wishes can potentially constitute surviving interests, not all desires or wishes can be linked to harms. Moreover, even if one accepts that there is a surviving interest in the attainment of certain aims after death, this may not translate unproblematically into a legal entitlement to protection. Feinberg insists that the thwarted desire which gives rise to harm be one in which the person has an 'investment'(Feinberg, 1984). But the individual no longer has any surviving welfare interests, and wishes regarding the uses or non-uses of one's corpse would not, at first glance, appear to be sufficiently weighty to become the subject of interests, and thus harm. Dworkin has offered the dichotomy between *critical* and *experiential* interests (Dworkin, 1993), which might appear to have some potential relevance, but once more these concepts do not map with ease onto protectable legal interests surviving death (Harris, 2003b).

C. Setbacks and Harm

I wish to suggest that we wrongfully setback surviving interests when we fail to respect the wishes of ante-mortem individuals regarding posthumous matters over which they have a right of control. We already respect people's wills as a matter of obligation, although we currently do not allow individuals to dispose of their own corpse. All possessions may be disposed of by the testator as he or she thinks fit, and as Brazier has graphically emphasised, as unfairly and inequitably as he or she determines (Brazier, 2002). Some would argue that this is not a matter of either moral or legal obligation to the decedent, but simply a mechanism to ensure the efficient and satisfactory transfer of assets and debts, and to ensure stability within society and the fulfilment of reasonable expectations. Similarly, some would argue that defamatory statements made posthumously merely defile the memory that those *living* have of the person. Callahan, for example, argues that obligations owed after death attach only to the heirs, not the ante-mortem testator (Callahan, 1987). As a matter of law, after death assets and liabilities become those of the decedent's estate. However, it is the estate of *someone*, namely 'of the person who once lived but who is now deceased'.

The most satisfactory way of conceptualising matters is similarly to regard the corpse as an entity in respect of which only the individual whose cadaver it now is had the right to assign and transfer, and to exclude others from doing so. We should not minimise the importance (possibly even spiritually inspired) of wishes as a reflection of the way that the person wished the book of their life to end, but, more fundamentally, it is simply *theirs* and no-one else's to dispose of; this is consistent with the preclusionary conception of property expounded by Beyleveld and Brownsword (Beyleveld and Brownsword, 2001). It is consequently submitted that we should extend the analogy with wills and view a person's corpse, or parts thereof, as *property* belonging to the formerly alive person. It is his or hers to control through the medium of consent (Price, 2005). The idea of matters over which one has a right of control can help delimit the liberal concept of 'harm' here. Whether one has a right to control one's confidences, one's privacy, etc, posthumously determines whether it is properly the subject of an interest surviving death—whether presently protected by law or otherwise—although these need not necessarily all be construed in property terms (see further, Herring, chapter thirteen this volume).

V. THE PROPERTY PARADIGM

The law has been traditionally reluctant to embrace the 'property paradigm' in this context. The 2004 Human Tissue Act eschews any such explicit classification of human 'relevant' tissue. Reticence to engage with an intrinsic property framework can also be inferred from the fact that the Act's proscriptions on trading are negated where certain work and skill has been applied to tissue resulting in it *becoming* 'property'. As this is presented as an exception to the norm, the 2004 Act seemingly snubs intrinsic property interests. Nevertheless, human tissue is capable of constituting property of one type or other at common law for various purposes, such as protecting the possessory entitlements of coroners engaged in post-mortem examinations, and of relatives or executors disposing of corpses, etc. And, as can be seen, the law even permits proprietary rights in human tissue to be acquired, by others apart from the tissue source, where work and skill has been applied to it. This was explicitly recognised only recently by Gage J in *AB v Leeds Teaching Hospital NHS Trust*.[1]

Antipathy towards the notion of property as it relates to parts of the body whilst the person is still alive, or even after death, seemingly emanates from the Kantian rejection of the notion of objectification of the body as a mark of disrespect. The Law Reform Commission of Canada stated:

Why, then, should bodies not be regarded as ordinary property? An important answer may be that notions of bodily property do violence to our concepts of

[1] *AB v Leeds Teaching Hospital NHS Trust* [2004] EWHC 644 (QB).

personal autonomy and human dignity. Property is traditionally associated with things, not with the human body. To equate the body with a thing is to dehumanize human existence; in the extreme, it suggests the repulsive notion that human beings may be owned. This answer hinges both on a thing-person dualism, and an inference that human bodily parts are reflective of our notion of self. Both are central to substantive objections to the buying and selling of human tissue (Law Reform Commission of Canada, 1992: 57).

This statement brings out the twin evils allegedly attaching to such objectification, *instrumentalisation* and *fungibility* (Wilkinson, 2003). But it is not credible to view such individuals as being treated *merely* as a means to the ends of others where the individual consents to, even requests, the activity or intervention. A vital aspect of being self-determining and choosing one's own ends is to be able to exercise control over one's body ie to be free from the controlling influences of others. Harris states that:

[r]espect for persons is widely regarded as the fundamental basis of any ethics involving human beings ... Respect for persons requires us to acknowledge the dignity and value of other persons and to treat them as ends in themselves and not merely instrumentally, as means to ends or objectives chosen by others (Harris, 2003a: 12).

The rights advocated inhere initially in the tissue source and not in others, and consequently notions of being 'used' or 'instrumentalised', and analogies with slavery, ring hollow. They are rights *in* not *over* the tissue source. Indeed, to *deny* property rights in cadaveric human tissue could arguably be seen to violate human dignity, as an expression of both empowerment and privacy. Furthermore, we are not concerned with whole living beings, where one may concede the difficulty of maintaining a conceptual dichotomy between the person and the 'thing'. Indeed, Kant regarded such a possibility as an impossible contradiction (Calder, 2006). Radin has opined that bodily parts may be too 'personal' to be property, and that we have an intuition that property necessarily refers to something in the outside world, separate from oneself (Radin, 1982). But she nevertheless concedes that it may be appropriate to call parts of the body 'property' after they have been removed from the 'system'. I would go further and submit that this does not depend upon the type of tissue involved ie which bits are 'self' and which are not.

A. Dualism

The property paradigm is frequently subject to criticism on account of its potential Cartesian inferences. Rao observes that the 'property' paradigm generates a fragmented relationship between the body and its owner—both literally and figuratively, the person 'inside' the body, in contrast with 'privacy', which creates an indivisible corporeal identity (Rao, 2000).

The exchanging and alienating of body parts is, to some, a reflection of Cartesian notions of the body as machine, separated from an incorporeal mind. Hacking, for instance, remarks that humans

are again becoming Cartesian because we now treat the body as an assemblage of replaceable parts, a veritable machine, exactly what Descartes said it was (Hacking, 2006: 13).

This is not, however, an issue resolvable purely on the grounds of the cogency of the dualist perspective. To suggest that to alienate parts of the body for worthy ends is supportive of the notion of a non-integrated person is unpersuasive. We can cogently 'give of ourselves' by donation of body parts, and are also able to assimilate and (re)integrate new body parts into our 'whole' being. The idea of a 'bounded' self, unable to be dis-aggregated or dis-integrated, is implausible. Even Kant accepted the justification for severing body parts for therapeutic ends. We are always more than the sum of our parts (Calder, 2006). To commodify is to *reduce* the body to its constituent parts.

B. Mine, Yours, Ours?

Joraleman and Cox (Joraleman and Cox, 2003) and Herring (chapter thirteen this volume) note that both property and embodiment can be interpreted in either individualistic *or* collective fashion. For instance, Giordano suggests that where the deceased's wishes are not known, the deceased's body may be regarded as 'belonging' to the relatives (Giordano, 2005). She alleges that we experience *some* others (the significant others) *as a part of ourselves*. It is nonetheless an 'other', rather than a wholly shared corpus, apart perhaps in cultures in which a collectivist philosophy, and maybe theology, applies to all bodies.

   This is not, of course, to deny that from the perspective of others, in particular grieving relatives, organs and tissues from the deceased are still identified emotionally, psychologically and spiritually with the formerly alive 'person'. They constitute part of the 'essence' of that individual, perhaps also explaining the 'instinctive recoil' of medical students encountering their first autopsies (Kass, 1985; and Hallam, chapter sixteen this volume). Medical training may indeed seek to inculcate a 'convenient' Cartesian psychology, to distance the individual from the physical being, to allow practices to be routinely carried out (Joralemon and Cox, 2003). The spiritual and emotional dimensions of this issue necessitate sensitivity of approach and inclusivity. However, although some commentators maintain that the 'self' may even survive death, symbolic power alone cannot change the ontological reality, albeit that relatives are often appropriately afforded decision-making powers post-mortem. Whilst accepting the important distinction between social and biological death, association and difficulties of psychological reorientation cannot (re)construct the self even if the person's identity lives, for others, after physical death has ensued (see Parrott and Miller, chapter nine this volume).

C. Commodification

The Law Reform Commission of Canada noted that for those who regard the body as simply a physical sub-stratum for the self, there seem few intrinsic impediments to tissue sales (Law Reform Commission of Canada, 1992). There is no basic moral objection to using the body to further the ends of the self. Since the body has only instrumental value, there is no reason either why that instrumental value should not receive a price. Conversely, for those who reject the mind-body dualism and equate the body with the self, human dignity permeates the entire human body and holds it priceless. This latter view binds to the other facet of the objectification critique, the fungible nature of property. To place a value on human beings is purportedly to deny their human dignity ie to regard the body as having a mere 'price'. The conflation of property and selling can once more be traced to Kantian roots (Wilkinson, 2003); a perception which, as we have seen, the 2004 Act itself regrettably does nothing to relieve. The conflation is nonetheless false. Property-based rights are quite coherent in this context, consistent with explicit restrictions on commercial activity relating to (eg transplantable) human materials. This is without prejudice to views as to whether commercial dealings in human tissue are permissible or otherwise. It has also been observed that, contrariwise, it is tempting for those who want to forestall a commercial market in organs to contend that bodies are *not* property. But such a stance makes it difficult to explain how then we can donate organs. As Childress has observed, if this is not my kidney, what right do I have to give it away? (Childress, 1989: 89). The Law Reform Commission of Canada asserted that the issue must be refined, to recognise that bodily parts may be property that carries the right of alienation, even if they cannot be property that carries a right to capital (Law Reform Commission of Canada, 1992). They are severable issues. The concept of property has never been synonymous with absolute rights (Christman, 1994).

D. Personality or Property

Laurie states:

A personal property paradigm could, in fact, serve an all-important role in completing the picture of adequate protection for the personality in tandem with other protections such as autonomy, confidentiality and privacy. However, the added value of a property model lies in its ability to empower individuals and communities and to provide the crucial continuing control over samples or information through which ongoing moral and legal influence may be exerted (Laurie, 2002: 316).

Beyleveld and Brownsword go further and argue that it is *necessary* to confer such control, on the basis that, in the absence of any objection to a use or where it held no utility for the owner, there would otherwise be no necessary presumption against use by others where this did not appear to be harmful to that person (Beyleveld and Brownsword, 2001: 188). This has particular poignancy as regards the dead, who are often considered 'beyond harm', a perspective that may underpin some of the historical practices in anatomy and pathology which have attracted censure. They continue:

Unless rule-preclusionary control is granted to persons to dictate legitimate uses of their bodies after death or removal, persons will be deprived of their legitimate expectation that their most sacred and private beliefs will not be trampled on after they die or have lost immediate control of the objects eliciting their concern. Thus, preclusionary control must be granted (Beyleveld and Brownsword, 2001: 188).

Privacy is a purely negative entitlement that guarantees security from governmental interference, whereas property possesses an affirmative dimension that enables purposive activity, although of course there are limits even to what one may do with one's own private property (Rao, 2000). It is the alienability or transferability of material that therefore typically invokes the property paradigm: what Grubb describes as 'dispositional powers' (Grubb, 1998). Many commentators divide body rights into personal rights and property rights, with personal rights being body rights that protect interests or choices other than the choice to transfer (Munzer, 1990).

The implications of the above, that a person's corpse represents the property of the ante-mortem person and thus subject to that individual's power of choice and right of control, is that consent should typically be acquired for permitted medical and scientific uses. A failure to respect such wishes harms that person, and this accounts for the potential penal sanctions imposed by the Human Tissue Act 2004 in this regard. However, one's surviving (posthumous) interests are different in both nature and texture from those same interests attaching when one was still alive, no matter how characterised. Rights to bodily privacy, for instance, are of a different nature and import when dead than alive, and are more easily overridden in the interests of others (see also Herring, chapter thirteen this volume). Indeed, prima facie the individual's autonomous wish that parts of the body be used for such purposes would be equally as compelling an interest as an expressed *objection* to the removal and use of parts for the same purposes. This would necessarily flow from a property-based approach where the power to alienate and to decline to alienate are two sides of the same coin. Harris contends that any such surviving interests to veto the use of the corpse for socially valuable ends are of minimal significance when weighed in the balance, and are very easily overridden by the requirements of the needy, as they are when the state permits compulsory autopsies for forensic ends (Harris, 2003b). Feinberg adopts an analogous view (Feinberg, 1985). It may be admitted that they are *more easily* overridden at least. An accommodation between private and public interests is unavoidable. But the property view would nevertheless generate a prima facie entitlement to control and transfer, albeit that this might be easily waived or delegated, and might in appropriate or exceptional circumstances, be overridden in the interests of others (Beyleveld and Brownsword, 2001).

Ironically, this is in some ways at odds with the regime incorporated in the 2004 Act, which contains *additional*, more extensive, consent obligations for certain uses regarding tissue taken from the dead than that taken from the living (there are no scheduled purposes excluded from the consent requirements as regards the former). It is often said that this is explained merely by the fact that the gravamen leading to the passing of the Act was the distress caused to relatives by the organ retention practices laid bare at Alder Hey, etc (Maclean, 2002). Maybe so, although the living can derive benefit whilst alive from the use of tissue in education etc, and are the beneficiaries of the treatment from which the (surplus) tissue derived. They could also be regarded as having given implied consent to such use, ancillary to the receipt of treatment. No such considerations attach to the deceased. In all instances, there is a context-specific balancing of private and public interests necessarily at play in the formulation of appropriate public policy.

VI. CONFLICT RESOLUTION

Wilkinson has written about the tension between the powers of deceased persons and their relatives to donate or withhold consent to donation (Wilkinson, 2005). He identifies four scenarios of potential conflict between such wishes and observes that the current position in both the United Kingdom and New Zealand (as in many other locations) is that the individual's refusal overrides the family's wish to donate and the family's refusal overrides the individual's wish to donate. He refers to this as the 'double veto'. This indeed reflects current practice (see Wilton, chapter fifteen this volume), although not the official policy embraced by the legislation alluded to above. He notes that it is nevertheless surprisingly hard to find any defence of this double veto in the literature, and suggests that it can be either defended on the basis of utility or on the grounds of rights. The former is problematic as a rationale in the light of the paucity of empirical evidence to support such a policy. Nevertheless, it is submitted to be much the more convincing rationale, in the light of the 'perception' of involved professionals (and many politicians) that a public relations backlash would ultimately result in even fewer organs being donated if such views were not respected (Wilton, chapter fifteen this volume). This contention is supported to a degree by public reactions in the light of the revelations emanating from Alder Hey and Bristol.

Wilkinson points out that arguments for giving one party a veto tend to undercut giving the other a similar veto, ie they tend also to support the primacy of that party's wish *to donate* (Wilkinson, 2005). For example, he notes that deference to family objection is usually stated to be founded upon respect for the feelings of relatives and their actual or potential distress. This argument would suggest that *wishes by relatives to donate* based on similar feelings should also generate a right to donate, whereas the deceased's objection will in fact invariably prevail both in policy and practice. He nevertheless maintains that it is quite coherent to say that an individual has a negative right of veto but no positive right to have organs and tissues taken after consenting. This is merely by dint of the fact that respect for a veto does not necessitate positive action by others for such wishes to be implemented. Healthcare professionals are under no duty to remove and use organs. There is therefore an important distinction here between negative (claim) rights and positive liberties, the former being obligatory and the source of duties, the latter being merely permissive. Wilkinson in fact opines that there may indeed be no cogent philosophical grounds for ceding any power of veto to relatives at all ie to 'trump' the deceased's positive wish. He does not, however, consider non-conflict situations, namely where the deceased has not explicitly stated his or her wishes. I intend to analyse these situations and then attempt to apply a Feinbergian analysis to my findings.

There are various regimes for organ and tissue donation but the primary distinction is between 'opting-in' and 'opting-out'—or presumed consent—regimes. Some would carp at the use of the notion of presumed 'consent' (Erin and Harris, 1999), an issue I will pass over for the present, because my main focus here is upon the potential role of relatives in this context. Relatives *can* be seen as the decision-making 'voice' of a deceased person for these purposes. This may be clearly seen in the proxy decision-making powers of parents on behalf of their deceased children who lacked decision-making competence at death. It is also transparent where the now deceased person appointed a relative or relatives to act as nominated representatives, as they are now able to do under the Human Tissue Act 2004, and in other jurisdictions such as Holland (Law of 24 May 1996). In other situations, one needs to differentiate opting in and opting out regimes, because their rationales are at variance.

In an opting-in regime, where the deceased remained silent, one may interpret this as lack of awareness, indifference or as deliberately leaving it to the family to decide. It is generally impossible to determine exactly what motives, if any, can be properly attributed to the deceased, but it is reasonable for a society to assign (proxy) decision-making responsibility to relatives. No such inference or assignment can reasonably be made in a presumed consent system, as silence in itself is then regarded, rightly or wrongly, as evidence of willingness to donate. In an opting-in system, contrariwise, silence is *not* typically regarded as evidence of an *un*willingness to donate. This is interesting, especially in view of the fact that reliably recording objections to donation is illusory in jurisdictions such as our own which lack a registry or an analogous mechanism of reliable, permanent recording. But, if silence is no cogent evidence of the deceased's wishes either way under such a regime, it is certainly not appropriate that silence should be treated as evidence that relatives have been implicitly empowered to decide *for themselves* whether to permit donation or not. Yet, this seems to be the inference, at least on the face of it, in many if not most jurisdictions of this genus. Giordano gleans such powers from the moral responsibility generated towards 'shared others' who can be regarded as 'part of' the relatives (Giordano, 2005). However, such proprietorial claims have been previously rejected. In addition, to assume *personal* dispositional rights to authorise use of the body for medical purposes from a mere right/duty of disposal of the body (and associated possessory entitlements relating thereto) is an unwarranted inference and non sequitur. In any event, Giordano recognises that there are grounds to respect the express wishes of deceased persons as regards the use of (their) corpses (Giordano, 2005). Do these dissipate if not brought to fruition in the explicit articulation of wishes? She rejects the role of relatives as the best interpreters of the deceased's wishes, solely on the pragmatic ground that identifying the appropriate relative to this end is difficult. But such arguments are not only ostensibly over-stated, they cannot override the moral basis for the deceased's entitlements.

If it is indeed properly a question of a *proxy* decision being elicited, then a substituted judgement standard should be applied, as is obligatory by law in Germany for instance, even if in many circumstances this may be tantamount to no more than an educated guess. The hierarchical ordering of relatives for consent purposes in the 2004 Act is seemingly consistent with such an approach, with those prima facie closest to the deceased making the decision. However, the system ought, in that event, to be flexible enough to permit or facilitate the admission of (better) knowledge from other sources, including relatives further down the pecking order, as to the deceased's wishes. Liddell and Hall in particular have drawn attention to this lacuna (Liddell and Hall, 2005). In a presumed consent regime too, where the deceased remained silent on this issue prior to death, the family's views would not seem to carry weight in their own right, as such silence is evidence of a willingness to donate. However, information might legitimately be sought from relatives to supplement existing knowledge of the deceased's wishes, rather than the relatives' own views per se, and this is made explicit in certain jurisdictions (see eg France's Circular DGS/DH/ EFG No 98-489 of 31 July 1998).

Where the deceased objected to organ removal and use for therapeutic ends, but such objections were ignored, or where relatives' wishes were not appropriately respected, close relatives might well be deeply wounded. This potentially invokes the other pillar of the liberal paradigm supported by Feinberg: *offence*. 'Offence' is a detrimental mental, experiential state, and is a concept with an 'expressive character', which distinguishes it from harm. Whilst he argues that it is reasonable to use the criminal law to protect persons from wrongful offence to themselves (such as some nuisances), he observes that where deep personal affronts are concerned, the individual is outraged by conduct aimed at another, ie it is impersonal. The offended party does not think of him or her self as the victim. Feinberg, however, recognises that if a person's own impersonal moral outrage is to be the ground for legal coercion and punishment, it must seemingly be by virtue of the principle of legal moralism, to which the liberal is adamantly opposed (Feinberg, 1985: 68). He therefore emphasises that

[t]he offense-causing action must be more than wrong: it must be a *wrong* to the offended party, in short a violation of *his* rights.

It is here that Feinberg's concept of *profound offence* comes into view. He states that profound offence offends because the conduct that occasions it is believed to be wrong, it is not believed to be wrong simply because it offends someone. The offence is parasitic on the harm done to the now deceased. Thus, we are not dealing with wounded feelings per se. Regarding a scenario where a woman's dead husband's face was smashed to bits during a scientific experiment conducted in the absence of consent, he comments:

Her grievance is personal (voiced on her own behalf) not simply because her moral sensibility is affronted (she has no personal *right* not to have her moral sensibility affronted) and she cannot keep *that* out of her mind, but rather because it is *her* husband, and not someone else. In this quite exceptional kind of case, the personally related party is the only one whose rights are violated, though many others may suffer profound offense at the bare knowledge (Feinberg, 1985: 69).

The relationship is crucial and, coupled with the natural inclination of parents or spouses in particular to feel they have failed in their duty if they have not properly 'protected' their children/partners after death, this explains the deep wounds inflicted on many relatives by some of the organ retention practices recently revealed. This not only provides support for criminal sanctions, but also for the availability of a civil action for relatives who have suffered as a consequence (see Hedley, chapter fourteen this volume).

Feinberg maintains that profound offence warrants the intervention of the criminal law even when 'the moralistic case is severed from their argument' (Feinberg, 1985: 69). Relatives are themselves potentially wronged by such conduct as a product of their decision-making functions on behalf of the deceased. No 'wrongful offence' can, however, arise where the relative's objection was at odds with the wishes of the deceased. There is no right there that is overridden.

VII. CONCLUSION

This paper has sought to test the coherence and justificatory basis for the consent model adopted by regulatory regimes governing human tissue use, conceived in liberal terms.

It is submitted that the instinctive view that we can harm a person after their death has been shown not to be mere intuition masquerading as morality, but intuition based upon sound moral principles. The emphasis upon the wishes of the tissue source evidences a moral and legal right to control such tissue even after death. It has been suggested that property rights provide the explanatory power underpinning such rights of control. Relatives of adult deceased persons have a 'default' decision-making role in lieu of direct evidence of the deceased's wishes. Space does not permit much in the way of analysis of the *weight* that should be afforded the wishes of the tissue source. However, it would seem entirely legitimate to mandate both flexibility as regards the pre-requisites for the assignment of such interests and, in instances where the public interest is extremely compelling and weighty, potentially even to allow the corpse to be used for various ends in the absence of consent (eg a Caesarian section performed upon a dead woman who was pregnant, to enable the birth of a viable child). The debate should move to focus on this issue.

REFERENCES

Publications

Beyleveld, D and Brownsword, R (2001) *Human dignity in bioethics and biolaw* (Oxford, Oxford University Press).
Brazier, M (2002) 'Law and regulation of retained organs: the legal issues' 22 *Legal Studies* 550–569.
Calder, G (2006) 'Ownership rights and the body' 15 *Cambridge Quarterly of Healthcare Ethics* 89–100.
Callahan, J (1987) 'On harming the dead' 97 *Ethics* 341–352.
Childress, J (1989) 'Ethical criteria for procuring and distributing organs for transplantation' 14 *Journal of Health Politics, Policy and Law* 87–113.
Christman, J (1994) *The myth of property* (New York, Oxford University Press).

Dworkin, R (1993) *Life's dominion* (London, Harper Collins).

Erin, C and Harris, J (1999) 'Presumed consent or contracting out' 25 *Journal of Medical Ethics* 365–366.

Feldman, F (1993) 'Some puzzles about the evil of death' in JM Fischer (ed), *The Metaphysics of Death* (Stanford, Stanford University Press) 307–326.

Feinberg, J (1984) *Harm to others* (Oxford, Oxford University Press).

—— (1985) *Offense to others* (Oxford, Oxford University Press).

Giordano, S (2005) 'Is the body a republic?' 31 *Journal of Medical Ethics* 470–475.

Glannon, W (2001) 'Persons, lives, and posthumous harms' 32 *Journal of Social Philosophy* 127–142.

Grubb, A (1998) 'I, Me, mine: bodies, parts and property' 3 *Medical Law International* 299–317.

Hacking, I (2006) 'The Cartesian body' *BioSocieties* 1, 13–15.

Harris, J (2002) 'Law and regulation of retained organs: the ethical issues' 22 *Legal Studies* 527–549.

—— (2003a) 'Consent and end of life decisions' 29 *Journal of Medical Ethics* 10–15.

—— (2003b) 'Organ procurement: dead interests, living needs' 29 *Journal of Medical Ethics* 130–134.

Joralemon, D and Cox, P (2003) 'Body values: The case against compensating for transplant organs' 33 *Hastings Center Report* 27–33.

Kagan, S (1992) 'The Limits of well-being' in E Paul, F Miller and J Paul (eds), *The good life and the human good* (Cambridge, Cambridge University Press) 169–189.

Kass, L (1985) 'Thinking about the body' 15 *Hastings Center Report* 20–30.

Kennedy, I and Grubb, A (2000) *Medical law*, 3rd edn (Oxford, Oxford University Press).

Laurie, G (2002) *Genetic privacy* (Cambridge, Cambridge University Press).

Law Reform Commission of Canada (1992) *Procurement and Transfer of Human Tissues and Organs*. Working Paper 66. (Ottawa, Law Reform Commission of Canada).

Li, J (2002) *Can death be a harm to the person who dies?* (Dordrecht, Kluwer Acadamic Publishers).

Liddell, K and Hall, A (2005) 'Beyond Bristol and Alder Hey: the future regulation of human tissue' 13 *Medical Law Review* 170–223.

Lucretius (95–52 BC) *De Rerum Natura*.

Maclean, M (2002) 'Letting Go ... Parents, Professionals and the Law in Retention of Human Material after Post Mortem' in A Bainham, S Sclater and M Richards (eds), *Body Lore and Laws* (Oxford, Hart Publishing) 79–90.

Mason, J and Laurie, G (2001) 'Consent or property? Dealing with the body and its parts in the shadow of Bristol and Alder Hey' 64 *Modern Law Review* 710–729.

Munzer, S (1990) *A theory of property* (Cambridge, Cambridge University Press).

Nagel, T (1979) *Mortal questions* (Cambridge, Cambridge University Press).

Nuffield Council on Bioethics (1995) Working Party Report *Human Tissue: Ethical and Legal Issues* (London, Nuffield Council on Bioethics).

Partridge, E (1981) 'Posthumous interests and posthumous respect' 91 *Ethics* 243–264.

Pitcher, G (1984) 'The misfortunes of the dead' 21 *American Philosophical Quarterly* 183–188.

Price, D (2000) *Legal aspects of organ transplantation* (Cambridge, Cambridge University Press).

—— (2003) 'From Cosmos and Damien to Van Velzen: the human tissue saga continues' 11 *Medical Law Review* 1–47.

—— (2005) 'Human Tissue Act 2004' 68 *Modern Law Review* 798–821.

Radin, M (1982) 'Property and personhood' 34 *Stanford Law Journal* 957.

Rao, R (2000) 'Property, privacy, and the human body' 80 *Boston University Law Review* 359–460.

Roberts, P (2001) 'Philosophy, Feinberg, codification, and consent: A progress report on English experiences of criminal law reform' 5 *Buffalo Criminal Law Review* 173–253.

Waluchow, W (1986) 'Feinberg's theory of "preposthumous" harm' *Dialogue* **XXV** 727–734.

Wilkinson, S (2003) *Bodies for sale* (London, Routledge).

Wilkinson, T (2002) 'Last rights: the ethics of research on the dead' 19 *Journal of Applied Philosophy* 31–41.

—— (2005) 'Individual and family consent to organ and tissue donation: is the current position coherent?' 31 *Journal of Medical Ethics* 587–590.

Legislation

Human Tissue Act 2004.

Human Tissue (Scotland) Act 2006.

13

Crimes Against the Dead

JONATHAN HERRING

I. INTRODUCTION

THE GREAT BRITISH public are terrified of being the victims of crime (Farrell and Gadd, 2004)—perhaps understandably so—but they probably think that at least after death, crime will be no more. Unfortunately not. There are an impressive number of offences in English and Welsh law that can be committed against corpses.

The purpose of this chapter will be to consider the crimes that can be committed against dead bodies in England and Wales. It will start by outlining the range of offences, and then consider the potential justifications for these. It will be argued that the current law is seriously deficient. First, there are a number of glaring gaps in the coverage of the criminal law. In particular, the desecration of corpses as part of racial or religious hatred or for sexual purposes is inadequately dealt with by the current law. Secondly, there is no coherent approach to the nature of the wrongs that are committed when the bodies of the dead are maltreated. This means that the offences lack a clear conceptual foundation.

II. CRIMES AGAINST THE DEAD: THE OFFENCES

The following does not purport to be a complete list of the offences against corpses, but it includes the most significant ones.

A. Offences Connected with Burial

There is no denying that the law on burial is in a mess. Even the Government admits it. The 2004 Consultation Paper on review of the law on burial by the Home Office explains:

The law relating to burial (including exhumation and the disturbance of human remains) is not to be found within a single statute or coherent body of legislation.

It has evolved in a piece-meal fashion in response to the social and public health
concerns of the day, with little apparent regard for setting the broad framework
for the provision of burial facilities, determining service standards, or regulating
burial practice or procedure (Home Office, 2004: 3).

Looking into the law of burial the technically-minded lawyer may be for-
given for thinking she has died and gone to Heaven. Nothing can be stated
without extensive caveat, and even then, with a due degree of hesitancy. It is
not surprising that the Home Office has indicated that the time has come to
reform burial law and that responses to its consultation paper have broadly
favoured changing it. In the meantime the Department of Constitutional
Affairs has produced a *Guide for Burial Ground Managers*, perhaps in
recognition of the complexity of the law (Department of Constitutional
Affairs, 2005).

Despite the myriad of regulations, only a few will lead to a criminal
sanction if breached. The main offences connected with burial are the
following:

   (i) Section 25 of the Burial Act 1857 makes it an offence to remove or
       otherwise disturb buried human remains without legal authorisation.
       This may be the offence committed by those who removed Gladys
       Hammond's corpse from a graveyard in October 2004, apparently
       as part of a campaign about animal welfare (BBC Newsonline,
       2006a). Authorisation in the case of land consecrated by the Church
       of England is in the form of a faculty from a Diocesan Consistory
       Court, and in the case of other land, a licence from the Home Office.
       The Home Office will normally grant a licence to move a body for
       personal reasons if the burial ground manager, the grave owner and
       the next-of-kin are in agreement and there are no known legitimate
       objections (Home Office, 2004: 12).
  (ii) The Cremation Act 1930 prohibits the cremation of human remains
       anywhere except in a crematorium (White, 1993). This caused
       problems in one case where a man created a funeral pyre to burn
       his father's body, in line with Sikh practices. According to media
       reports, the police permitted this on humanitarian grounds (BBC
       Newsonline, 2006b).
 (iii) The Local Authorities' Cemeteries Order 1977 (LACO) creates cer-
       tain offences in local authority cemeteries. The activities prohibited
       include causing a disturbance or nuisance in a cemetery, and activi-
       ties which interfere with a grave. The offences appear to be designed
       primarily to ensure good public order and to preserve the appropri-
       ate atmosphere of a cemetery.
 (iv) A large set of offences are also found in part 1 of schedule 2 of
       LACO. These include burying people in a cemetery without the per-
       mission of the burial authority, or burying a body at an inappropriate

depth. These offences do not carry a high penalty: the maximum is a £1000 fine. The consultation on the Home Office's reform proposals indicated that the most common of these offences is people interring ashes in a cemetery overnight, without proper authorisation (Home Office, 2004: 47).

(v) LACO allows burial authorities to impose regulations governing their grounds. It explicitly permits the authorities to prohibit 'the interring or scattering of cremated human remains in or over a part of the Cemetery set apart for the use of a particular religious body' (article 5(6)). Where such a prohibition has been issued then, it is an offence to inter or scatter without the authorisation of that religious authority.

(vi) The courts have been highly creative in finding common law offences to deal with the problems of disturbances of graves. Most of these offences were found in the 19th century, when concerns over 'grave robbing' were at their height. They include:

- Unlawfully removing a body from a grave *R v Lynn*[1];
- Disposing of a body for dissection without lawful authority *R v Cundick*[2];
- Executors or close relatives of a deceased person failing to bury him or her if they could afford to do so *R v Vann*[3];
- Unlawfully disposing of a body with intent to prevent an inquest *R v Stephenson*[4]; *R v Godward*[5];
- Exhuming corpses for indecent display (Nuffield Council on Bioethics, 2005: paragraph 7.13).

These offences are rarely used nowadays.

B. Preventing the Lawful Burial of a Corpse and Obstructing a Coroner

These two offences are useful for the prosecution when the indications are that the defendant was with the body of the deceased, the body having been found in the defendant's house or car, but there is insufficient evidence that he or she caused the death (eg *R v Sullivan*[6]). The more commonly used offence is preventing the lawful burial of a corpse. Oddly, it was only confirmed comparatively recently that that such a crime existed. In *R v Hunter*[7] the Court of Appeal confirmed that the offence did exist, although

---

[1] *R v Lynn* (1788) 100 ER 394 (**KBD**).
[2] *R v Cundick* (1822) 171 ER 900 (**KBD**).
[3] *R v Vann* (1851) 169 ER 523 (**KBD**).
[4] *R v Stephenson* (1884) 13 QBD 331.
[5] *R v Godward* [1998] 1 Cr App R (S) 385 (**CA**).
[6] *R v Sullivan* [2003] EWCA Crim 806.
[7] *R v Hunter* [1973] 3 WLR 374.

it had to rely on a reference in a textbook (Russell, 1964: 1420) which itself referred to a comment on an unreported case (*R v Young*[8]) in a 1788 judgment (*R v Lynn*). The Court of Appeal noted that a charge for the offence had not been laid in modern times. Although since *Hunter*, the offence has been used fairly frequently, still much uncertainty surrounds its definition, including whether it is necessary to show that the body has been hidden and whether the prosecution needs to show an intention to prevent a burial or some other form of blameworthy state of mind.

The case law has not clarified the essential wrong at which this offence is targeted (Hirst, 1996). A number of alternatives have been suggested in the case law. Cairns, LJ in *R v Hunter*, in supporting the sentence of three years, explained that the offence had caused serious distress to the relatives, who had not known what had happened to the victim for four months. In *R v Swindell*[9] the offence of prevention of a lawful burial was justified on two grounds. First, it was said to be an offence against public order. Secondly, it was said to be a grave offence because it resulted in evidence being destroyed and was therefore an offence against the due administration of justice. In *Attorney-General's Reference (No. 90 of 2005)*,[10] a man punched his wife on the jaw. She later choked on her blood as a result of the punch. He then purchased a freezer, and over the course of the next few days cut his wife into pieces and placed her in it. He was sentenced to two years for the manslaughter and to three years for the prevention of the lawful burial. The Court of Appeal refused to find the sentences unduly lenient. Notably here, the sentences indicate that what he did to the body after the death was regarded as more serious than the killing. But the case also raises questions about the nature of the offence. The 'prevention of the lawful burial' was hardly a full description of the wrong he had done. It was the desecration of the body, rather than the prevention of the burial, which was attracting the sentence, but as we shall see, there is no specific offence dealing with maltreatment of bodies.

C. Property Offences

Can taking a corpse or part of a corpse be regarded as theft? Or can damaging a corpse amount to the offence of criminal damage? This all turns on the hotly disputed question of whether the law recognises our bodies as property (Dworkin and Kennedy, 1993; Matthew, 1995). Gage, J in *AB v Leeds Teaching Hospital NHS Trust*[11] recently accepted that the law is uncertain and unclear. The safest thing that can be said is that there

---

[8] *R v Young* undated, referred to in *R v Lynn* (1788) 100 ER 394 (**KBD**) *Lynn*.
[9] *R v Swindell* (1981) 3 Cr App R (S) 255 (**CA**).
[10] *Attorney-General's Reference (No. 90 of 2005)* [2006] EWCA Crim 270.
[11] *AB v Leeds Teaching Hospital NHS Trust* [2005] QB 506 (QB).

are some respects in which the body can be treated as property and other respects in which it cannot. The traditional rule has been that there is no property in the human body. This has been understood to represent the common law, although explicit authority for the proposition is, in fact, limited (Magnusson, 1998).

In relation to corpses, the Court of Appeal in *Kelly*[12] held that:

... parts of a corpse are capable of being property ... if they have acquired different attributes by virtue of the application of skill, such as dissection or preservation techniques, for exhibition or teaching purposes.

In fact, the Court of Appeal in *R v Kelly*[13] went further and suggested that parts could become property if they attracted a 'use or significance beyond their mere existence'. This had happened in that case as the body parts had been preserved and used as specimens. In *Dobson v Northern Tyneside Health Authority*[14] reliance was placed on the view in *Doodeward v Spence*[15] where Griffith, CJ stated:

when a person has by lawful exercise of work or skill so dealt with a human body or part of a human body in his lawful possession that it has acquired some attributes differentiating it from a mere corpse awaiting burial, he acquires a right to retain possession of it, at least as against any person not entitled to have it delivered to him for the purposes of burial.

These cases leave undecided what kind of skill must be exercised on a body-part in order for it to acquire the nature of property. The exercise of skill in dissection or preservation may well be sufficient. There are media reports of a man who damaged a corpse exhibited as part of the *Body World* exhibition being charged with criminal damage (BBC Newsonline, 2002).

The Human Tissue Act 2004 does nothing to address directly the question of who owns bodily material. Section 32(9) refers to human material which has become property by the application of human skill, but gives no guidance as to when human material can become property, and if so, who owns it. The implication of the section is that generally human material is not property.

D. Necrophilia

Extraordinarily, there was no specific offence of engaging in sexual activity with a corpse until section 70 of the Sexual Offences Act 2003 was

---

[12] *R v Kelly* [1999] QB 621, page 629.
[13] *R v Kelly* [1999] QB 621 (**CA**), **page 629**.
[14] *Dobson v Northern Tyneside Health Authority* [1996] 4 All ER 474 (**CA**).
[15] *Doodewood v Spence* (1908) 6 CLR 406 (High Court of Australia), page 749–750.

passed (Cook and James, 2002). The offence was a fairly late addition to the Bill and was subject to quite some debate in the House of Lords (Hansard, 2003). It creates an offence of sexual penetration of a corpse, and states:

> (1) A person commits an offence if—
>   (a) he intentionally performs an act of penetration with a part of his body or anything else,
>   (b) what is penetrated is a part of the body of a dead person,
>   (c) he knows that, or is reckless as to whether, that is what is penetrated, and
>   (d) the penetration is sexual.
> (2) A person guilty of an offence under this section is liable—
>   (a) on summary conviction, to imprisonment for a term not exceeding 6 months or a fine not exceeding the statutory maximum or both;
>   (b) on conviction on indictment, to imprisonment for a term not exceeding 2 years.

There are a number of points which are worth making about this offence. The first is its sentence. The offence of rape carries a maximum sentence of life imprisonment. This offence has a two-year maximum sentence. This indicates that it is regarded as, relatively speaking, a minor offence. It carries the same maximum sentence as voyeurism, for example. The second point is that unlike the other offences involving penetration in the Act, which require proof that the anus, vagina or mouth of the victim were penetrated, this offence only requires proof that a part of the body was penetrated. A penetration of a wound on a corpse could fall within the definition of 'penetration of a corpse'. One explanation for the breadth of the offence may be that there is no 'fall back' offence. In the case of a live person, penetrations other than of the anus, vagina or mouth can be charged as straightforward sexual assaults or common assaults. There would be no such alternative in the case of corpses. Nevertheless, it is a little odd that the term a 'sexual penetration' has one meaning for live people and another for corpses. The definition also means that sexual behaviour with corpses that does not involve penetration is not caught by the offence, and indeed may not amount to any offence. It is unclear why sexual behaviour that involves a penetration of a corpse is more serious than other sexual contact of a corpse. For example, is the sexual violation any worse if a defendant gives a male corpse 'oral sex' than if he puts his finger into a corpse's ear for sexual reasons? Yet the current law criminalises the 'aural sex', but not the oral. Clearly, the need for penetration means that the legal definition of necrophilia is narrower than that used by psychiatrists (Rosman and Resnick, 1989).

A third point concerns the mental element of the offence, which is that the defendant knows or is reckless that he has penetrated a corpse. This could be problematic. Consider this scenario: a man is attacking a woman, intending to rape her. In the struggle he places his hand over her mouth. He realises that she loses consciousness, but does not realise that she has, in fact died. He then has sexual intercourse with her. This could not be rape, because he would not have raped a live person, and it would not fall into the definition of sexual penetration of a corpse unless he knew that the woman had, or might have, died. The only available charge would be an attempted rape, which does not appear to be a satisfactory result.

A final point is that the offence is only committed if the touching is sexual. Section 78 of the Sexual Offences Act 2003 states:

penetration, touching or any other activity is sexual if a reasonable person would consider that—
(a) whatever its circumstances or any person's purpose in relation to it, it is because of its nature sexual, or
(b) because of its nature it may be sexual and because of its circumstances or the purpose of any person in relation to it (or both) it is sexual.

This makes it clear that the touching can be treated as sexual on the basis of a person's intention, even if the act would not appear sexual to the casual observer. The offence would therefore be committed if a mortician or pathologist penetrated a corpse for sexual purposes, even if as 'part of an autopsy' or in preparation for burial.

E. Human Tissue Act 2004

The Human Tissue Act 2004 (hereafter 'HTA') was passed following outcries at the way in which human material was retained for research purposes without adequate consent at Alder Hay and other hospitals (see Wilton, chapter fifteen this volume). The purpose of the Act was to provide a legislative framework for taking, storing, and using human bodies, organs and tissue (Department of Health, 2004: paragraph 5).

The Act creates a number of criminal offences, the most significant of which are the following:

(i) *Failure to Obtain 'Appropriate Consent'*
   Section 5 states:
   (1) A person commits an offence if, without appropriate consent, he does an activity to which subsection (1), (2) or (3) of section 1 applies, unless he reasonably believes—
   (a) that he does the activity with appropriate consent, or
   (b) that what he does is not an activity to which the subsection applies.

Unfortunately this offence requires much unpacking. It relates to conduct defined in the first three subsections of section 1. These are:

(1) The following activities shall be lawful if done with appropriate consent—
  (a) the storage of the body of a deceased person for use for a purpose specified in Schedule 1, other than anatomical examination;
  (b) the use of the body of a deceased person for a purpose so specified, other than anatomical examination;
  (c) the removal from the body of a deceased person, for use for a purpose specified in Schedule 1, of any relevant material of which the body consists or which it contains;
  (d) the storage for use for a purpose specified in Part 1 of Schedule 1 of any relevant material which has come from a human body;
  (e) the storage for use for a purpose specified in Part 2 of Schedule 1 of any relevant material which has come from the body of a deceased person;
  (f) the use for a purpose specified in Part 1 of Schedule 1 of any relevant material which has come from a human body;
  (g) the use for a purpose specified in Part 2 of Schedule 1 of any relevant material which has come from the body of a deceased person.
(2) The storage of the body of a deceased person for use for the purpose of anatomical examination shall be lawful if done—
  (a) with appropriate consent, and
  (b) after the signing of a certificate—
    (i) under section 22(1) of the Births and Deaths Registration Act 1953 (c. 20), or
    (ii) under Article 25(2) of the Births and Deaths Registration (Northern Ireland) Order 1976 (S.I. 1976/1041 (N.I. 14)), of the cause of death of the person.
(3) The use of the body of a deceased person for the purpose of anatomical examination shall be lawful if done—
  (a) with appropriate consent, and
  (b) after the death of the person has been registered—
    (i) under section 15 of the Births and Deaths Registration Act 1953, or
    (ii) under Article 21 of the Births and Deaths Registration (Northern Ireland) Order 1976.

The Act governs 'relevant material.' Under section 53 of the HTA, relevant material is defined to include tissue, cells and organs of human beings, excluding gametes, embryos outside the body, hair and nail from a living person. Cell lines are also excluded by virtue of section 54(7), as is any other human material created outside the human body, for example through manipulation of DNA.

The offence in section 5 is not committed if there is appropriate consent. Consent must be given to the storage or use for the particular purpose in question. There are special rules about consent in relation to children and incapacitated adults, which we will not go into here. But in the case of deceased people, consent or non-consent of the deceased can come from three sources: the deceased; an appointed representative; or the person in closest qualifying relationship to the deceased.

To summarise, the offence arises where a person does an act under section 1(1)—(3) such as removing bodily material from a deceased person, and if he does so without consent and without a reasonable belief in consent. However, a person's act is made lawful by section 1 of the HTA if he is acting for a 'schedule 1' purpose. The schedule divides these purposes into two parts. We shall see why shortly:

PART 1
1. Anatomical examination.
2. Determining the cause of death.
3. Establishing after a person's death the efficacy of any drug or other treatment administered to him.
4. Obtaining scientific or medical information about a living or deceased person which may be relevant to any other person (including a future person).
5. Public display.
6. Research in connection with disorders, or the functioning, of the human body.
7. Transplantation.

PART 2
8. Clinical audit.
9. Education or training relating to human health.
10. Performance assessment.
11. Public health monitoring.
12. Quality assurance.

The following can be done with appropriate consent for any of the twelve purposes:

(i) the storage of the body of a deceased person (excluding anatomical examination)–
(ii) the removal from the body of a deceased person of any 'relevant material' of which the body consists or which it contains.

The following can be done with appropriate consent for a purpose in part 1 of schedule 1:

the storage or use of any 'relevant material' which has come from a human body.

The following can be done for a purpose in part 2 of schedule 2, even without consent:

the storage or use of any 'relevant material' which has come from the body of a deceased person.

It should be noted that there are special provisions dealing with the storage of bodies for anatomical examinations (HTA, section 1(2), (3); see Wilton, chapter fifteen this volume).

The section 5 offence raises a number of issues. First, the defence of 'reasonable belief' is important. It means that if, for example, a doctor was convinced by a written document that a patient had consented to the use of her body but in fact that document was forged, the doctor could not be prosecuted.

Secondly, there is an ambiguity which unfortunately strikes at the heart of the offence. As we have seen section 5(1) states:

A person commits an offence if, without appropriate consent, he does an activity to which subsection (1), (2) or (3) of section 1 applies

Section 1(1) opens:

(1) The following activities shall be lawful if done with appropriate consent—
(a) the storage of the body of a deceased person for use for a purpose specified in Schedule 1, other than anatomical examination

The ambiguity arises in a scenario where a person is storing the body of deceased person for a purpose not listed in Schedule 1 (eg to turn a body into a private art exhibit). Whether this is an offence or not turns on the meaning of 'an activity to which subsection (1) applies'. In section 1(1)(a) for example, is the activity simply the storage of a body of a deceased person, in which case the defendant would be guilty? Or is the activity 'storage of a deceased person for a Schedule 1 purpose', in which case the defendant is not guilty of the offence under section 5?

The Department of Health describes the offences in these terms: 'removing, storing or using human tissue for scheduled purposes, without appropriate consent' (Department of Health, 2005). This would appear to suggest that if the actions are done for a purpose not included within schedule 1 then there is no offence committed under the HTA, although there may be some other criminal offence (eg theft). If this is correct, as seems likely, it must be questioned whether there is much sense in making doctors guilty of an offence if they remove tissues from cadavers for research without consent, while people who remove bits of bodies for prurient interest would possibly not be guilty of any offence.

Thirdly, it is worth noting that under section 50, a prosecution of the section 5 offence can only be brought in England and Wales with the consent of the Director of Public Prosecution.

Fourthly, the maximum sentence for this offence is three years, regarded as very high by some, but thought by the Government to be appropriate in the most flagrant of breaches (Price, 2005: 809).

(ii) A False Representation of Consent
It is an offence under HTA section 5(2) for anyone to falsely represent that there is 'appropriate consent' or that an activity does not require consent for the purposes of the Act, if the person knows the representation to be false, or does not believe it to be true.

(iii) Failure to Obtain a Death Certificate.
It is a criminal offence under HTA (2004) section 5(4) for someone to store or use a body for anatomical examination without a death certificate. There is a defence for someone who believes that there is a death certificate or that s/he is doing something not covered by the Act.

(iv) Using or Storing Donated Material for an Improper Purpose.
A person who uses or stores donated material commits an offence unless it is done for one of the following purposes:

- the purposes detailed in Schedule 1;
- medical diagnosis or treatment;
- decent disposal;
- for purposes specified in regulations made by the Secretary of State.

There is a defence under section 8 of the HTA if a person reasonably believes that he or she was not dealing with donated material.

(v) Analysis of DNA Without Consent
An offence is committed under section 45 of the Act if a person has any bodily material intending to analyse its DNA without 'qualifying consent'. A defence is available if the results are to be used for an 'excepted purpose' (e.g. detection of crime).

(vi) Trafficking Human Tissue For Transplantation
There are offences in section 32 connected with the selling or trafficking for human tissue for transplantation.

(vii) Unlicensed Activities
Carrying out licensable activities without holding a licence from the Human Tissue Authority is an offence under section 25. There

are also lesser, related offences under section 16, such as failing to produce records or obstructing the Authority in carrying out its powers or responsibilities.

(viii) Possession of Anatomical Specimens Away from Licensed Premises
Section 30 of the HTA creates an offence of having an anatomical specimen anywhere other than premises where an anatomy licence is in force, without proper authorisation.

F. Outraging Public Decency

No doubt some forms of desecrating a corpse could amount to the offence of outraging public decency; a common law offence. In *Clark*[16] a woman who left a newborn infant's corpse on open view in a public place was found to have outraged public decency and committed the offence of public nuisance. In *Gibson*[17] a man used freeze-dried embryos to make a pair of earrings, which he displayed in an art gallery. This was found to outrage public decency. This suggests that the display or use of corpses in an outrageous way in public would amount to the offence.

III. GAPS IN THE CRIMINAL LAW

Having summarised the main offences against corpses, I will now seek to examine some of the main gaps in the coverage of the criminal law in this area.

The law is remarkably lax on the disposal of bodies. Apart from cremation, over which there is some restriction, executors can do with a body or its remains pretty much as they please in private, unless they are acting under the HTA (White, 1993). They can bury the body in a garden, put it in their loft, eat it, give it to an artist (BBC Newsonline, 2006c), plastinate it (Walter, 2004) or display it, although the Human Tissue Authority has stated that in the future, a licence may be required for the public showing of corpses less than 100 years old (BBC Newsonline, 2006b).

The law also shows a lack of respect for the deceased's wishes about what should happen to his or her body after death. For instance, if a devout Muslim man dies, making it clear that he wishes to be buried in accordance with Islamic tradition, there is nothing to prevent his son, a recent convert to Christianity, from arranging a burial in accordance with the rites of the Roman Catholic Church. Not only is there nothing stopping the son, there is nothing the Muslim man could have done in advance to prevent his son from doing this.

---

[16] *R v Clarke* (1883) 15 Cox 171 (CA).
[17] *R v Gibson* [1990] 2 QB 619 (CA).

There are no offences which specifically deal with the desecration of graves motivated by religious or racial hatred (see eg BBC Newsonline, 2004b), nor is there a general offence of desecrating a corpse. We have seen that sexual acts with corpses short of penetration are not criminal. Nor are other acts of desecration. Most notoriously, the wrapping of a Muslim woman's corpse with bacon appears not to have been an offence (BBC Newsonline, 2004a). The investigation into that behaviour also uncovered a man who took a huge number of photographs of corpses and desecrated a body by writing with marker pen on it. It is possible to argue that there are some old common law offences that could be resurrected to deal with discretion cases. There is one unreported case of a clergyman being convicted of the offence of 'mutilating a corpse' after he cut off the genitals of corpses (referred to in Nuffield Council on Bioethics, 2005, paragraph 7.13). The Nuffield Council Report also suggests that there is an offence of 'offering indignities to the remains of a body' (paragraph 7.13). However, the authority supporting the existence of these offences is very slim and one cannot be at all confident that they exist.

John Spencer characteristically outlines the inadequacies of the current law. He notes that the HTA:

will make punishable, with substantial prison terms, doctors, medical research-workers and similar enemies of society who, without appropriate consent store or use bodies or parts of them in the course of activities such as medical research, medical treatment and training doctors ... they will leave unpunished, as before, those who mutilate or desecrate human bodies for other and less savoury ends; such as black magic, perverted sexual pleasure, malice, or a desire to shock or offend (Spencer, 2004: 9).

IV. JUSTIFYING CRIMES AGAINST THE DEAD

First year criminal law students are often taught that a crime is made up of a harm to a victim and blameworthiness of the defendant. This is over simplistic but, as a basic rule of thumb, correct. Key to understanding an offence is an appreciation of the wrong it is seeking to tackle. The identification of the wrong is important for two particular reasons. First, it provides a justification for the act to be viewed as criminal. We need to be sure that the harm caused by the act is sufficiently serious to justify a criminal sanction (Husak, 2005). Secondly, the wrongfulness of the act is important in establishing the limits of the offence. We can only define an offence correctly if it is clear which wrong the offence is intended to target. Without such knowledge there is a danger that the offence will be too broadly drafted and capture conduct which should not be criminal, or too narrowly defined and will fail to convict people who do the relevant wrong.

Having, albeit in very bare outline, emphasised the importance of discovering a justification for a crime, we can now turn to look at the arguments that might be put forward to justify certain acts to corpses being wrongful, so as to support criminalisation (see also Price, chapter twelve this volume). It is not my aim to fully assess the strength of each of these grounds, but rather to point out what a criminal law based on this wrong might look like.

A. The Wrong Against the Dead Person

Perhaps the instinctive reaction to a case involving some kind of mistreatment of a corpse is that there has been a wrong to the dead person. However, the notion of wronging the dead is not straightforward. After all, being dead, the person cannot feel pain and has no interests that can be set back. She therefore cannot be harmed (Callahan, 1987; and Harris, 2002). Indeed, many philosophers have claimed that even death itself cannot be regarded as a harm (see the discussion in Li, 2002).

Of course, there are others who are adamant that the dead can be harmed (see eg Berg, 2001; Glannon, 2001; and Grover, 1989). One justification for arguing that one can wrong the dead is to say that we generally care about what happens to us after we die and how we will be remembered. We view lives as a story and are legitimately concerned with how the story ends (Kotre, 1995). Indeed some people take great efforts and spend substantial amounts of money to ensure that they are remembered well after they are dead, for instance by creating works of art that will outlive them or by donating to causes which will build a memorial to them. Why else are some donors keen to have buildings named after them?

This, then, can lead to an argument that we have interests while living about what happens when we die. What happens to us when we die can therefore harm the interest we have while alive in how our dead bodies are treated. Feinberg put it this way:

All interests are the interest of some persons or other, and a person's surviving interests are simply the ones that we identify by naming *him*, the person whose interests they were. He is of course at this moment dead, but that does not prevent us from referring now, in the present tense, to his interests, if they are still capable of being blocked or fulfilled, just as we refer to his outstanding debts or claims, if they are still capable of being paid. The final tally book on a person's life is not closed until some time after his death (Feinberg, 1984: 83).

So when a person is 'wronged' after death, this is not a wrong to the corpse but a wrong to the live person they once were (Steinbock, 1996; and Boddington, 1998)

Accepting for the moment an approach along the Feinberg lines, it may be questioned how grave a wrong is done to a deceased if their corpse is maltreated. Most people are happy for their body to be cremated or buried and left to decompose. Does this not indicate a lack of genuine concern on their part as to what happens to their bodies? Indeed, Feinberg indicates the kind of interests that are most likely to be infringed as

the desire to maintain a good reputation ... the desire that some social or political cause triumph, or the desire that one's loved ones flourish.

Yet traditionally the criminal law has not been used to protect these kinds of interests. You can harm the reputation of a good person while alive, or reduce someone to poverty without infringing the criminal law.

Feinberg developed the strongest argument in favour of seeing the interests of the deceased as justification for the criminal law (Feinberg, 1984). This emphasises the interests that the individual had when living that they be treated in a particular way after their death. Where, therefore, the act significantly thwarts the interests while alive of the deceased (eg if they were treated after death in a way which they would have strongly objected to if alive), this could amount to a sufficiently strong wrong to justify the intervention of the criminal law.

B. The Wrong Against the Dead Person's Relatives/Friends

An alternative argument is that maltreating a corpse is a wrong to the relatives and friends of the deceased as they suffer distress at seeing their loved one treated in such a way. The difficulty with relying on this argument is that the criminal law does not normally punish the causing of emotional harm alone unless that leads to a psychological injury. The reasons for the law's reluctance are obvious: we are prone to say spiteful, unpleasant, hurtful things regularly and to criminalise them would be to over-extend the law.

An alternative argument is that the relatives have some kind of right to control how a corpse is treated and an infringement of this right is a wrong. Brazier suggests that the right to respect for family life could be used here. She explains:

The image of the newly dead person remains fixed in the minds of most bereaved families. Mutilation of the body becomes a mutilation of that image. Reason may tell the family that a dead child could not suffer when organs were removed. Grief coupled with imagination may overpower reason. Families grieve differently just as they live their lives differently. Respect for family life requires respect for such differences (Brazier, 2002: 560).

As Brazier also points out, a number of religions, especially Judaism and Islam, require respect for the integrity of the dead body (see further Jupp, chapter six this volume). To ignore those wishes is to infringe the rights to respect for religious belief under Article 9 of the European Convention on Human Rights. She explains the seriousness of the issue:

> Relatives of people whose organs were removed without consent have expressed to me fears that at the Resurrection their beloved husband or father will not be resurrected because he was not buried whole. Or he will endure eternity disfigured and disabled. It is easy to mock such beliefs from an atheist, agnostic or 'liberal' viewpoint. The pain such a belief must produce is acute and life-destroying (Brazier, 2002: 561).

The point introduces a broader one. It indicates that the separation of the interests of the deceased and of the relatives may be inappropriate. We have a community of individuals who have a collective interest in seeing that their dead are buried in accordance with the rituals and traditions of that community. Brecher writes:

> although dead, we do not cease entirely to be members of a particular community; and it is on that account that the dead can be said to have interests (Brecher, 2002: 113).

In a similar vein, Giordano argues that

> [w]e experience some others (the significant others) as a part of ourselves. Even once the loved person is dead, she or he continues to be, in some important way 'my daughter' or 'my father'. This person belongs in some sense to the significant others (Giordano, 2005: 471).

The argument here is that our lives and bodies are not isolated but are in relationship with others, and our links of love, friendship and community continue after death (see further, Miller and Parrott, chapter nine this volume). The relatives' rights, therefore, arise from a recognition of the importance of the bonds which persist after death. An act which shows a lack of respect to those socially important bonds could be said to amount to a sufficiently grave wrong to justify criminalisation.

C. The Wrong Against Morality

It can be argued that it is legitimate to render criminal an act which is illegal simply because it is immoral. Where, therefore, the treatment of a corpse is seen as infringing a fundamental moral principle, then the act can be outlawed. Again, this is an issue which has been much debated amongst jurisprudes and it is not possible to do justice to the sophistication of the argument here.

Perhaps the best-known proponent of such a view is Lord Devlin, who argued that society can use the criminal law to protect fundamental moral values (Devlin, 1965). Society is entitled to defend itself against moral decay and disintegration in order to protect social order. The difficulties with this approach are well-known; not least that it was used by Lord Devlin to criminalise same-sex sexual behaviour. Modern day supporters of a Devlin-esque approach suggest that where Devlin may have gone wrong was his insistence that it did not need to be shown that the behaviour was actually morally wrong, but rather that it was regarded as being wrong. It is understandable why Devlin took the approach he did, as it would be difficult to prove that something is 'immoral'. But without such a requirement, his approach can justify a society criminalising all kinds of behaviours to protect itself from so-called moral disintegration. George argues that

[a] concern for social cohesion around a shared morality can justify some instances of the enforcement of morals, but only if that morality is true (George, 1993: 71).

The difficulty lies, of course, in establishing what morality is true.

D. Disgust

It can be argued that actions, sights or deeds which create disgust among reasonable members of the general public can be criminalised. The notion of disgust is intended to be a strong one. If you leave your house, you can expect to see, hear and smell all sorts of horrible things, but you should be protected from that which is disgusting. Of course, this too is problematic. People are disgusted by things at which they should not be. In one infamous British case, the disgust of a member of the public at seeing two men kissing justified their arrest and conviction (*Masterson v Holden*[18]). Singer, a respected philosopher, has recently argued that any disgust we might feel about a person having sex with an animal is illogical, and so as long as there is no cruelty involved, the act should not be regarded as criminal (Singer, 2000).

If this is the basis of legislation, it is important to note its limits. It would need to be shown that the behaviour reached a high level of disgust and that there was no countervailing good.

---

[18] *Masterson v Holden* [1986] 3 All ER 39 (QBD).

E. A Wrong Against Public Interests

Another argument is that the use of the criminal law in relation to corpses can be justified in relation to the living. The fact that we know that on death our bodies will be protected from various wrongs saves us the expense and worry that wewould otherwise have in ensuring that our bodies were looked after in the way that we wanted. This is clearly applicable in some situations. Berg argues in favour of law protecting confidentiality even after the death of the individual because otherwise the living would be deterred from disclosing confidential information to their doctors (Berg, 2001). Similarly, it might be thought that a person who is terrified of having their organs removed upon death might avoid medical treatment towards the end of their life. We have an interest in ensuring that our bodies will be respected after death and might experience fear and distress otherwise (Wilkinson, 1992).

Criminal offences against corpses might therefore be justified if it could be shown that without them, people would act in ways which would harm the public interest. The image of the newly dead person remains fixed in the minds of most bereaved families.

F. Public health

The treatment of corpses does raise some wider public interests. The most obvious is in relation to public health. The sanitary disposal of corpses is necessary to prevent the spread of diseases. There is little dispute over the legitimacy of this ground, providing the threat to public health is shown to be sufficiently serious.

V. REFORMING THE LAW AGAINST CORPSES

Any attempt to reform the criminal law on corpses should start by considering which, if any, of the justifications above are an acceptable basis for the intervention of the criminal law. The offence should be tailored to meet that specific wrong. Many of the current offences suffer from the fact that the wrong at which they are directed is unclear. A good example is the offence in section 5 of the Human Tissue Act 2004. Where material is taken from the deceased without appropriate consent, what exactly is the wrong (Price, 2005)? It cannot be directed solely to the interests of the deceased because the wrong is committed even where it is far from clear that the deceased would have objected to the behaviour. Nor is it to the relatives, because where the deceased has made her/his wishes clear, the material can be retained regardless of the relatives' wishes. In the Parliamentary debates, it was asserted that the principle behind the statute was the right to control one's bodily material. Perhaps the best explanation for the offence is that it is in the nature of a property offence, with the property being taken without the consent of the person who has authority to determine whom it belongs to (Price, 2005). Yet the common law has been adamant that there is generally no property in the corpse and the Act appears to support that view. The lack of clarity over what is the wrong at which the offence has been directed will cause great difficulty for the courts when they must interpret the offence and seek to define its limits.

Views will differ on which, if any, of the wrongs mentioned above should be sufficient to justify criminalisation. Indeed, it might even be concluded that none of them are sufficient. I would argue that there should be criminal offences created to protect the corpse from being treated in a way which interfered with the deceased's wishes, as per the Feinberg reasoning. The easiest way to define such an offence would deal with disrespectful treatment of the deceased on the basis of his or her sex, sexuality, race or religion. An offence should also be created to protect the rights of the family or community of which the deceased was a part, where the deceased's body was treated in a way which showed a lack of respect for the racial, ethnic or religious culture of the group. Finally, there should be offences directed to the protection of public health interests.

VI. CONCLUSION

This chapter has sought to provide an overview of the main crimes that can be committed against the dead. It has also shown that there are a number of different interests which could claim to require protection under the criminal law. It is submitted that the current law fails to articulate clearly the interests it is seeking to protect. For many of the offences, it is unclear whether the wrong is one to the deceased, to the relatives, or some kind of public wrong. This also leads to the law being complex and unclear.

It has been argued that there are major gaps in the law. The fact that it appears that whoever draped the body of a dead Muslim woman in bacon committed no offence, and that sexual behaviour with corpses that does not involve penetration escapes punishment, is unsatisfactory, especially given that less serious maltreatment against corpses is prohibited.

The criminal law on corpses desperately needs clarifying. The start of the debate must be to ascertain the wrong(s) done when a corpse is maltreated, and the severity of the wrong(s). Only then can a coherent law be produced.

REFERENCES

Publications

BBC Newsonline (2002) 'Man charged after corpse show damage' 27 March 2002
BBC Newsonline (2004a) 'Desecrated body family could sue' 6 April 2004.
BBC Newsonline (2004b) 'Arrests after graves desecrated' 4 April 2004.
BBC Newsonline (2006a) 'Hammond police discover remains' 3 May 2006.
BBC Newsonline (2006b) 'Body parts shows to need licence' 15 May 2006.
BBC Newsonline (2006c) 'Funeral pyre starts legal wrangle' 12 July 2006.
Berg, J (2001) 'Grave secrets: Legal and ethical analysis of post mortem Confidentiality' 34 *Connecticut Law Review* 81–122.
Boddington, P (1998) 'Organ donation after death' 15 *Journal of Applied Philosophy* 1–13.
Brazier, M (2002) 'Retained organs: Ethics and humanity' 22 *Legal Studies* 550–564.
Brecher, B (2002) 'Our obligations to the dead' 19 *Journal of Applied Philosophy* 109–119.
Callahan, J (1987) 'On harming the dead; 97 *Ethics* 341–352.
Cook, D and James, S (2002) 'Necrophilia: Case report and consideration of legal Aspects' 5 *Medical Law International* 199–205.
Department of Constitutional Affairs (2005) A *Guide for Burial Ground Managers* DCA 62/05 (London, Department of Constitutional Affairs).
Department of Health (2004) *Human Tissue Act 2004: Explanatory Notes* (London, The Stationary Office).
Department of Health (2005) *The Human Tissue Act 2004* (London, Department of Health).
Devlin, P (1965) *The enforcement of morals* (Oxford, Oxford University Press).
Dworkin, G and Kennedy, I (1993) 'Human tissue: Rights in the body and its parts' 1 *Medical Law Review* 29–45.
Farrell, S and Gadd, D (2004) 'The frequency of the fear of crime' 44 *British Journal of Criminology* 127–132.
Feinberg, J (1984) *The moral limits of the criminal law. Harm to others* (New York, Oxford University Press).
George, R (1993) *Making men moral* (Oxford University Press, Oxford).
Giordano, S (2005) 'Is the body a republic?' 31 *Journal of Medical Ethics* 470–475.
Glannon, W (2001) 'Persons, lives and posthumous harms' 32 *Journal of Social Philosophy* 127–142.
Grover, D (1989) 'Posthumous harm' 39 *Philosophical Quarterly* 334–353.
Hansard (2002–03) *House of Lords Debate*, Vol 694 9 June 2003, col 83.
Harris, J (2002) 'Law and regulation of retained organs: The ethical issues' 22 *Legal Studies* 237–249.
Hirst, M (1996) 'Preventing the lawful burial of a body' [1996] *Criminal Law Review* 96–101.
Home Office (2004) *Burial Law and Policy in the 21st Century: The Need for a Sensitive and Sustainable Approach* (London, Home Office).

Husak, D (2005) 'Criminal Law Theory' in M Golding and W Edmundson (eds), *Philosophy of law and legal theory* (Oxford, Blackwell Publishers) 107–121.

Kotre, J (1995) *White gloves: How we create ourselves through memory* (New York, WW Norton and Co).

Li, J (2002) *Can death be a harm to the person who dies?* (Amsterdam, Kluwer Law International).

Magnusson, R (1998) 'Proprietary rights in human tissue' in N Palmer and E McKendrick (eds), *Interests in Goods* (London, Lloyds of London Press).

Matthew, P (1995) 'The man of property' 3 *Medical Law Review* 251–270.

Nuffield Council on Bioethics (2005) *Human Tissue: Legal and Ethical Issues* (London, Nuffield Council on Bioethics).

Price, D (2005) 'The Human Tissue Act 2004' 68 *Modern Law Review* 798–821.

Rosman, J and Resnick, P (1989) 'Sexual attraction to corpses: a psychiatric review of necrophilia' 17 *Bulletin of American Academy of Psychiatry and Law* 153–163.

Russell, W (1964) *Russell on Crime*, 12th edn (London, Stevens).

Singer, P (2000) 'Heavy petting' in *Nerve* at: http://www.nerve.com/opinions/singer/heavypetting/main.asp

Spencer, JR (2004) 'Criminal liability for the desecration of a corpse' [2004] 6 *Archbold News* 7–9.

Steinbock, B (1996) *Life before birth: The moral and legal status of embryos and fetuses* (Oxford, Oxford University Press).

Walter, T (2004) 'Plastination for display: a new way to dispose of the dead' 10 *Journal of the Royal Anthropological Institute* 603–627.

White, S (1993) 'An end to DIY cremation?' 33 *Medicine, Science and the Law* 151–159.

Wilkinson, P (1992) 'Last rights: the ethics of research on the dead' 19 *Journal of Applied Philosophy* 31–41.

Legislation

Burial Act 1857 (20 & 21 Vict, c 81).

Cremation Act 1930.

European Convention on Human Rights 1950.

Human Tissue Act 2004.

Local Authorities' Cemeteries Order 1977 (SI 1977/204).

Sexual Offences Act 2003.

14

Death and Tort

STEVE HEDLEY

I. INTRODUCTION

'Tort' covers a variety of claims. They are usually claims for compensation, brought by someone who has suffered harm, against someone else who is alleged to have been responsible for that harm. The harm is usually personal injury of some kind, although other types of harm are recognised (eg, injury to reputation or to property interests) and the responsibility usually takes the form of a 'duty of care', that is, a legal duty to act with reasonable care and skill to avoid harming the interests of others (also called a duty to avoid 'negligence'). For current purposes, we can say that most tort cases concern personal injuries allegedly caused by negligence, although for completeness we need to mention injury to reputation or 'defamation' (ie 'libel' or slander'), interference with proprietary interests ('trespass to land', 'negligent damage to property' and 'nuisance') and other sorts of economic injury (including, in restricted circumstances, 'purely economic loss').

How does death matter in all of this? There are really two questions, the first rather easier to answer than the second:

1. What effect does the death of one party to a tort dispute have on that dispute?
2. Does it make any difference whether the death was caused by the other party, and/or was a consequence of the injuries the dispute was about?

The second question really only arises in the context of personal injury actions—in theory someone might die through indignation on being libelled, but in practice these things don't happen—and will be considered later.

II. THE FIRST QUESTION: THE EFFECT OF DEATH ON TORT ACTIONS

The modern position, established since 1934, is that tort actions have a life of their own, and do not die with either of the people involved in them. Put more formally:

[O]n the death of any person ... all causes of action subsisting against or vested in him shall survive against, or, as the case may be, for the benefit of, his estate (Law Reform (Miscellaneous Provisions) Act 1934, section 1(1)).

This reversed the early common law rule that *actio personalis moritur cum persona*—'a personal action dies with the person'. In other words, it terminates automatically on the death of either claimant or defendant. From the early medieval perspective, of course, the old rule made quite a lot of sense: common law was then concerned not so much with reaching a fair resolution of each dispute as with preventing extra-judicial resolution through feud or vendetta. From that perspective, the death of one of the parties constituted the end of the dispute.

The modern rule—that rights of action usually don't die with either of the people involved, even if they are 'personal' rights—is therefore the opposite of the medieval rule. But the change is not quite as important as it sounds. What the modern rule does is to ensure *survival* of rights of action. If, at the instant before death, there was a right to sue, then that same right is available after the death. But the right does not expand or grow. By and large, nothing that occurs after the claimant's death can be regarded as a legal wrong to the claimant: nothing that happens to their body can be an 'injury'; and they no longer have any property or other assets to be taken from them. This branch of the law therefore pays little heed to dignity or respect for the deceased, as discussed by Price (chapter twelve this volume; the criminal law is different, see Herring, chapter thirteen this volume). Again, dead people aren't regarded as blameworthy, and so a case that the defendant was responsible for some harm or other will have to be based on the defendant's pre-death behaviour. The effect of death is that all the rights and liabilities accumulated up to that point are transferred to the deceased's estate, to be sorted out by the executors or administrators. It is really just a more subtle application of the medieval approach, allowing property disputes to continue (because, after all, *someone* must own the property in dispute), but closing down more 'personal' disputes—not with the abruptness of the medieval rule, but nonetheless quite firmly. The old attitude still applies in very 'personal' disputes: actions for injury to reputation terminate with the death of either party (though this aspect of the 1934 Act has been criticised for failing to include other torts protecting merely dignitary interests, such as false imprisonment); and claims for 'exemplary damages'—meant to call attention to outrageous breaches of duty—do not survive the death of the claimant.

The general effect of death on tort claims, therefore, is to crystallise the claim at that point. Any claims which existed immediately before the death remain in existence, and must be resolved as part of the process of administering the deceased's estate. Death neither increases nor reduces one's liabilities: it simply draws a convenient line under them.

III. THE SECOND QUESTION: WHAT IF THE DEATH *IS* THE INJURY COMPLAINED OF?

What is the response of the law of tort where the very complaint being made is that the defendant's conduct resulted in the death?

In the early days of the common law, the maxim *actio personalis moritur cum persona* applied, regardless of whether the death was the very thing complained of. This sounds ludicrous to modern ears, but was more understandable in the light of the purposes of tort law at that date. If one of the parties to a dispute was dead, then there was no longer a dispute for the common law to resolve. If the death didn't seem fair or just, well, death rarely was.

The law was not completely helpless, however. If a particular person could be identified as responsible for the death, then a plea of felony could be made, resulting in official action against the killer. Sometimes the official response included an order for reasonable compensation, to prevent the dead man's relatives taking more drastic measures (Baker, 1979: 411–13). There was also the curious doctrine of the deodand, by which a physical object which had caused a death was forfeit, a process which sometimes meant that the deceased's relatives received a share of the thing's value (Sutton, 1997; and Baker, 1979: 322). But all of these processes were increasingly exploited for the benefit of the officials involved in them, depriving the victim's family of any financial remedy. The procedures in cases of feud quietly evolved into something resembling modern criminal law, being confined to cases of murder and manslaughter, and with the killer being punished not for the injury to others but for breach of fealty owed to the King. All his assets were forfeit, but they went to the King and not to the victim's family. And the profits of the deodand were quietly appropriated for the officials involved. So by 1600, the *actio personalis* maxim governed completely: death of either party to personal injury litigation terminated it; and causing the death of another was not a ground for civil action.

Change did not come until the 1840s, when the spread of the railways across Britain led to an increasing number of injuries and deaths. The fact that injured railway passengers could sue, but dead ones could not, became something of a public scandal. Inventive lawyers revived the antique action for a deodand, which in its 19th-century form no longer permitted forfeiture of the railway engine involved in the death, but allowed juries to impose fines on the railway companies—which they did with enthusiasm. This situation was then skilfully used by the Chief Justice of the day as a bargaining chip, promoting a Bill to abolish deodand as anachronistic, but insisting that the price of reform was the introduction of personal injury liability on more modern lines (Kostal, 1994: 289). The result was the Fatal Accidents Act 1846, which created a cause of action in favour of the dependants of the deceased. The basic principle having been conceded, later reforms were less controversial. Abolition of the *actio personalis* rule in all but a handful of cases was effected in 1934, and the dependency action has since been restated and broadened.

So by the time the modern rule—that tort actions survive the deaths of the parties to them—was introduced, a great many decisions as to the function and scope of tort law had already been made, and were not lightly to be disturbed. In principle, from 1934 onwards, the death of the claimant could be regarded as an injury for which compensation could be given. But the wording of the statute does not encourage this—'the damages ... shall be calculated without reference to any loss or gain to his estate consequent on his death'—and the rules on damages ensure that any such claim comes to nothing (Law Reform (Miscellaneous Provisions) Act 1934, section 1(2)). There is an exception for funeral expenses. Death of the claimant is only rarely a ground for increasing damages, and frequently a ground for reducing them. If it is asked: 'What price does tort put on a life?' the answer is in the region of £0. The only substantial claim allowed is that of dependent relatives, who can demand at least part of the income stream they would have received had the death not occurred.

The tort lawyer's attitude to death was therefore established well before the massive expansion of claims which occurred over the 20th century, and the result of which is so much a matter of political debate today. Personal injury actions in the early 21st century in fact overwhelmingly focus on very particular sources of injury: injuries at work, on the roads and through negligent health care together account for over 95 per cent of all claims. Official and unofficial insurance arrangements ensure that claims proceed in a routine manner. The people supposedly in dispute with one another actually have very little to do with the process: the claim proceeds in much the same way whether claimant and defendant are alive or dead—indeed, the defendant is in practice almost invariably an insurance company, and so was only 'alive' in a rather technical sense in the first place. (In road accident cases, the defendant is nominally the driver whose driving caused the accident, although in practice this individual has little to do with the processes that follow.) The court's response to the accident can only consist of an award of money, and the decisions on whether an award is payable and if so how large it should be, depend on relatively abstract rules, which only occasionally mention death as a special case.

A. Death: Liability

The classic statements of negligence liability make no special mention of death. Indeed, such statements are classic precisely because they ignore irrelevant particulars and focus at precisely the right level of abstraction. So, as each new class of tort students learns, the duty on the defendant in negligence cases goes like this:

You must take reasonable care to avoid acts or omissions which you can reasonably foresee would be likely to injure your neighbour. Who then, in law, is my neighbour? The answer seems to be—persons who are so closely and directly affected by my act that I ought reasonably to have them in contemplation as being so affected when I am directing my mind to the acts or omissions which are called in question (*Donoghue v Stevenson*[1]).

Death is therefore one of a range of things which might 'injure your neighbour' or 'affect' him or her. It is obviously at the higher end of seriousness in that regard: creating a risk of accidental death, even a quite small one, makes it 'likely' that your 'neighbour' will be 'affected' by your conduct. Accordingly, the range of people you 'ought reasonably to have … in contemplation as being so affected' can be quite broad, and can include people who wouldn't normally have any hope of a claim against you.

So when the claimants' lawyers look back on a chain of events that ultimately led to a death, they are looking for a defendant who ought reasonably to have foreseen the possibility of injury, and who then acted in a manner which was insufficiently careful in the light of that possibility. Does it matter that death resulted? It matters in the sense that serious injuries are taken more seriously: defendants are expected to think further ahead if serious injuries are possible; more care is expected of them; and defendants receive less sympathy if they argue that the loss was too 'remote', that is, too unlikely a prospect to contemplate before the event. But there is no great difference in attitude in death cases and cases of serious injuries. Indeed, while in practice it is hard to avoid completely, nonetheless the courts will be adamant that these cases are not to be judged with hindsight. The question is not how we view the facts now that we know a death has resulted, but how the defendant should have viewed them before the event, when injury was a mere possibility. Death is therefore special in this context because it is an exceptionally severe consequence, with an unfavourable prognosis. However, the rules on damages then take most of that significance away, reducing most claims by dead claimants' estates to very low figures indeed.

---

[1] *Donoghue v Stevenson* [1932] AC 562 (HL) 580, Lord Atkin.

B. Death: Damages—Claims by the Estate

As to the calculation of damages for death, a brief introduction to damages generally is necessary. Early 19th century damages law left the ascertainment of the precise sum in these cases to juries, which were forbidden to give a reason for their verdicts. While the trial judge or appeal court might strike down an apparently unreasonable award, this was relatively rare. But over the late 19th and early 20th centuries, judicial willingness to go along with high awards distinctly lessened. The causes are not very clear, but almost certainly included the increasing number of claims, the practical impossibility of concealing from the jury whether the claim was to be met by insurers, and the increasing democratisation of juries as a result of universal suffrage. Whatever the cause, by the 1930s a jury was only summoned in a personal injuries case if an exceptionally strong case to that effect was made to the trial judge, which rarely happened. Later cases changed 'rarely' to 'almost never' (see especially *Ward v James*[2]).

Assessment was therefore left in the hands of the trial judges, who in the early years felt free to be almost as inscrutable as juries, simply awarding a sum or sums under very broad heads such as 'pain and suffering' or 'loss of income'. Again, appeal courts would only rarely hold any award to be unreasonable. In time, however, a more systematic approach was adopted. The turning point was in 1970, where the Court ofAppeal laid down that precise itemisation of each award was mandatory (see *Jefford v Gee*[3]; *George v Pinnock*[4]). It was increasingly recognised that efficient dispute resolution involved minimising court hearings, and that predictability of result was far more valuable than any supposed benefit from allowing individual judicial scrutiny of each case. In the light of those considerations, the modern law aims at greater and greater precision. Personal injuries claims boast a 99 per cent settlement rate, unusually high for any area of contested litigation, and which would be quite impossible if individual judges were able to differ sharply on the amounts they could award.

In the modern law, while of course any loss suffered by the claimant in consequence of the defendant's tort may be itemised and proved (as 'special damages'), the courts expect the 'general damages' for personal injury to fall under these five heads:

1. Pain and suffering
2. Loss of the amenities of life
3. Loss of future earnings
4. Loss of earning capacity
5. Future expenses

---

[2] *Ward v James* [1966] 1 QB 273 (CA).
[3] *Jefford v Gee* [1970] 2 QB 130 (CA).
[4] *George v Pinnock* [1973] 1 WLR 118 (CA).

The last three items are 'pecuniary' items, meant to represent as accurately as possible sums lost or bills incurred as a result of the injury. The first two 'non-pecuniary' items are attempts to capture the injury to feelings entailed by the accident, and bear no relationship to any other sum of money involved in the facts. The relative size of the 'non-pecuniaries' usually depends on the severity of the case. Where the injury is medically relatively trivial—so the injury is largely to the claimant's dignity and sense of well-being—the 'non-pecuniary' sum may constitute the bulk of the award. At the other end of the scale, say where a high-earning claimant comes out of the accident as a quadriplegic requiring constant care, then the figures for loss of earnings and for future expenses will be very large, and the figure for non-pecuniary loss, while substantial, will be nowhere near as great.

To get an idea of the value put on life itself, we need to look at the items one by one:

(i) Pain and Suffering

The court asks how great the pain was, what its quality was, and how long it lasted. These figures are largely conventional. While ultimately a court might resolve such a case by gut feeling, the first resort of lawyers and judges is past precedent. As a matter of theory, this head of damages is rather unprincipled, the more glaringly so as greater and greater efforts go into refining the other heads. The sums

could be multiplied or divided by two overnight and they would be just as defensible or indefensible as they are today (Cane, 1993: 139).

Some writers insist that there must be a genuine attempt to ascertain how much pain the particular claimant is or has been in, suggesting that otherwise the entire exercise is a sham. Others, including a significant number of trial judges, are aghast at any emphasis on individual suffering, because they imagine it will lead to increasing protestations by claimants that they are in agony—protestations which in some cases the judges suspect to be merely strategic. However, this general lack of satisfactory theoretical backing is not usually seen as a reason to cut back on these damages. On the contrary, the Court of Appeal recently increased them substantially, on the ground that insufficient allowance for inflation had been made in the past (*Heil v Rankin*[5]). Statute provides that the knowledge that the accident has shortened the claimant's life is to be reflected in the award for pain and suffering. (Administration of Justice Act 1982, section 1(1)). The Act also abolished 'loss of expectation of

---

[5] *Heil v Rankin* [2001] QB 72 (CA).

life' as a distinct head of damages. This had previously been an entirely conventional, free-standing sum (*Benham v Gambling*[6]).

The death of the claimant, however, is not seen as attracting generous damages here. On the contrary, death is seen as terminating any suffering involved, and damages for pain and suffering are given only for the period between the accident and the death. It follows that no damages at all are awarded under this head in a case where death instantaneously follows the defendant's negligence, or if the accident instantaneously rendered the claimant unconscious, and death ensued without consciousness ever being regained. It has also consistently been held that even the most painful death does not in itself attract an award for pain and suffering: the last few moments of mental agony and pain are in reality part of the death itself, for which no action lies under the 1934 Act (*Hicks v Chief Constable of South Yorkshire Police*[7]).

This can be seen as mildly paradoxical: ordinary pain and suffering merits compensation, whereas an agonising death does not. A possible resolution of the paradox is that an ordinary award can be seen as a sop to bruised feelings, whereas a dead person is incapable of having their feelings so mollified; no sum of money will make any difference to how they feel, so the courts may as well give nothing as something. There is probably some truth in this, though it invites the question of why awards for pre-death pain and suffering survive to the estate at all, as the same could be said of those—*by the time the damages are paid*, they can do nothing to alleviate the feelings they are supposed to compensate for (for an example of such an award see *Watson v Willmott*[8]). But issues of that sort cannot really be resolved on any principled basis until we first have a principled basis for assessing pain-and-suffering damages, which the lawyers do not have, and suspect that no one else does either.

(ii) Loss of the Amenities of Life

This head attempts to compensate for the fact that the injury did not simply inflict pain but also deprived the claimant of opportunities for enjoyment of life. The court therefore asks the extent to which the accident lowered the claimant's emotional quality of life, and in particular whether the injury prevented or interfered with the claimant's hobbies, sex life, social life, or ability to relax.

This award also is highly reliant on past precedents, and in most situations is in practice part of the same enquiry as for ascertaining pain and suffering damages—if indeed the two are distinguished from one another at all. For some limited purposes, the two *are*

---

[6] *Benham v Gambling* [1941] AC 157 (HL).
[7] *Hicks v Chief Constable of South Yorkshire Police* [1992] 1 All ER 690 (CA).
[8] *Watson v Willmott* [1991] 1 QB 140 (QB).

distinguished. So, claimants who are in a persistent vegetative state as a result of the accident receive no damages for pain and suffering because, so far as the court can tell, they aren't in pain, but they have received substantial sums for loss of amenity because this represents a genuine loss, whether or not the claimants are aware of it (*West and Son v Shepherd*[9]). However, this 'logic' has never yet been used to justify an award in respect of a period after death (see Grubb, 2002: 7.11). Death marks the end of any compensatable loss of amenity.

(iii) Loss of Future Earnings

Earnings lost as a result of the injury are usually assessed on a multiplier-multiplicand basis, that is to say the court multiplies two figures:

- The multiplicand, consisting of a 'typical' year's earnings of the claimant—usually taken to be his/her earnings in the year immediately preceding the accident; and
- The multiplier, which is meant to reflect the number of years over which the loss will be suffered. The multiplier will be lower than the actual number of years involved: a claimant who suffers a five-year drop in earnings is over-compensated by a multiplier of five, as the damages will consist of a lump sum received considerably before the lost wages would have been paid. The multiplier therefore reflects not only the length of time over which the injury persists, but also a discount for the early receipt of the money. There is also some attempt made to reflect hypothetical future contingencies, such as (in the claimant's favour) lost chances of promotion and (on the defendant's side) the chance of other accidental injury.

The calculations here have become increasingly sophisticated, as pro-claimant or pro-defendant lobbyists are able to point to systematic bias against them. In particular, the rather impressionistic approach, in the earlier cases, to selection of the multiplier was convincingly shown to favour defendants (because the courts tended to over-estimate contingencies which might have reduced the claimant's income for other reasons), and as a result the courts are now directed to official tables for the calculation of multipliers, which incorporate actuarial data on income and age (formal provision for the use of these 'Ogden Tables' is made by the Civil Evidence Act 1995, section 10). Ferocious battles between rival lobby groups routinely occur over the size of the discount for early receipt, currently set at 2.5 per cent (Damages (Personal Injury) Order 2001). The Court of Appeal regards itself as free to depart from this figure where sufficient cause is shown (*Warriner v Warriner*[10]). There are

---

[9] *West and Son v Shepherd* [1964] AC 326 (HL).
[10] *Warriner v Warriner* [2002] EWCA Civ 81.

currently moves towards allowing the court to avoid much of the problem by encouraging the award of a tax-free annuity (a 'structured settlement') rather than a lump sum in damages.

The effect of the claimant's death on the future earnings claim has followed a convoluted path. In 1962, the Court of Appeal considered such a 'lost years' claim, where but for the accident the claimant would probably have been in remunerative employment, but on the facts as they stood was expected to have died. They ruled that there was no claim for earnings in those 'lost years': while the loss was genuine enough in purely financial terms, an award of that sum would not correct this injustice. A dead man does not feel any better, or even any richer, by being presented with a large sum for lost wages (*Oliver v Ashman*[11]). However, this reasoning was rejected as being over-simplistic by the House of Lords in 1980. The deceased does indeed not suffer a loss in any real sense, but his/her dependants do, and awarding a sum for earnings in the 'lost years' compensates for that loss (*Pickett v British Rail Engineering Ltd*[12]). As a result, the court should calculate the extent of the wages lost, then deduct from it the bare minimum cost of living for the same period, which, on the logic of this claim, is an expense which the claimant has saved as a result of the accident—on the calculation of this saved expense see especially *Harris v Empress Motors Ltd*[13]. The resulting figure, calculated on a multiplier-multiplicand basis, is payable as damages. Opinion was divided on whether this award of 'wages in heaven' was fair. In 1982, Parliament ruled that while the injustice to dependants implicit in the earlier approach was real enough, it did not arise where those dependants could make a claim of their own under the Fatal Accidents Act 1976 (considered below). Accordingly, the 'wages in heaven' claim can only be made by a live claimant, this head of claim terminating with his/her death (Administration of Justice Act 1982, section 1(2)).

(iv) Loss of Earning Capacity

This head of damages, which is less relevant for present purposes, only arises where there is a substantial loss of earnings which is not amenable to the multiplier-multiplicand approach—typically where a young claimant of uncertain prospects is rendered unemployable by the effects of the accident. Even in a case such as that, the modern tendency is to apply the multiplier-multiplicand measure on the assumption that the claimant would, but for the accident, have earned the national average wage. Death of the claimant terminates such a claim.

---

[11] *Oliver v Ashman* [1962] 2 QB 210 (CA).
[12] *Pickett v British Rail Engineering Ltd* [1980] AC 136 (HL).
[13] *Harris v Empress Motors Ltd* [1983] 3 All ER 561 (CA).

(v) Future Expenses

Medical care and other expenses attributable to the accident are recoverable as part of the award. Where such needs are long-term, they are reduced to damages on the same multiplier-multiplicand basis as has already been discussed. The calculations are simplest when all such services are likely to be paid for by the claimant. The damages then reflect the likely cost. Increasingly, the courts are according monetary value to care given on a voluntary basis: where the necessary care will be provided by family members, a figure for the value of that care may be included in the damages (eg, *Housecroft v Burnett*[14]). It is not yet entirely clear whether that sum, when paid, belongs to the victim or to the carer (Grubb, 2002: paragraph 6.65). Clearly, the main effect of death on this head of damages is to limit it: dead people do not require medical care.

In summary, therefore, personal injury damages law places a value of £0 on each life involved. Technically speaking, damages are not awarded for the death, but for the injury suffered. The fact that the injury resulting from the defendant's conduct proves fatal is not in itself a compensatable item, though (anomalously) a defendant who caused a death is liable for reasonable funeral expenses. The damages

shall be calculated without reference to any loss or gain to his estate consequent on his death, except that a sum in respect of funeral expenses may be included (Law Reform (Miscellaneous Provisions) Act 1934, section 1(2)(c)).

The inclusion of these expenses is anomalous, because the cost of a funeral is merely an accelerated expense—the deceased's estate would eventually have had to pay for a funeral anyway, whatever the defendants had or had not done. In other respects, the claim is limited to losses already suffered at the instant before death, and no further damages are recoverable for the period after death. The claimant no longer experiences pain or suffering, is taken to require nothing further for loss of the amenities of life, will not miss the wages that will not be earned, and will have no expenses in the future. So the overall effect of the death is to benefit the defendant rather than the claimant. This approach may seem striking at first glance, but it is in fact merely a none-too-surprising consequence of focussing on compensation alone. If it is said that tort seems incapable of expressing outrage at an unnecessary death, or of inflicting just punishment on those who caused it, the answer is that expressing outrage and inflicting punishment are not recognised goals of tort law. Where tort would be open to criticism in its own terms would be if the dependants of the deceased did not receive just compensation. To that question I now turn.

---

[14] *Housecroft v Burnett* [1986] 1 All ER 332 (CA).

C. Death: Damages—The Dependency Claim

The main claim today remains the one introduced in 1846, though it has been restated and slightly expanded since. Briefly, if someone dies as the result of a tort, and if at their death they had one or more dependants, then those dependants acquire a cause of action against the tortfeasor for the value of the dependency. Not all dependants can sue in this way—the statute (the Fatal Accidents Act 1976) has a precise list of which relatives can sue, although today it's a pretty extensive list.

The dependency claim is unique as far as I know, and certainly has some non-standard features. The claim belongs to the dependants, not to the deceased person, although it is administered through the deceased's estate. It arises only where the deceased would have been able to sue if he or she had survived, and is defeated by any defence that would have been good against the deceased. In particular, if the deceased was r per cent responsible for the accident, the dependency claim is reduced by r per cent (Fatal Accidents Act 1976, section 5). In principle each dependant has an individual claim for their lost part of the dependency, although the statute says that all of the claims are to be handled together by the executor (Fatal Accidents Act 1976, section 2). It takes a purely factual criterion—the amount of income which would have been paid but for the defendant's misconduct—and substitutes a legal right to its continuance. This 'dependency' bears no necessary resemblance either to any right of maintenance the dependant could legally have demanded from the deceased, or to the amount they can demand when the deceased's estate is divided up. The build-up of case law reveals a gradual expansion of the concept of the 'dependency'. The courts have been prepared to include and to estimate a dependency which they imagine would have come into an existence later if the death had not occurred (*Taff Vale Railway Co v Jenkins*[15]). Moreover, the courts have since the 1970s begun to hold that the 'dependency' need not consist of money—so the death of a family member not in employment leads the court to assess the value of their services at home, which sum is then the basis of a dependency (eg *Hay v Hughes*[16]; accidents in the home are rarely the subject of tort actions, so these claims are relatively infrequent).

The statutory list of dependants of course mirrors the legislators' concepts of what a family looks like. The original 1846 list included only the deceased's spouse, parents, grandparents, step-parents, children, grandchildren and step-children. The 1976 list, now in force, seeks to be more inclusive, including all descendants and ascendants of the deceased, as well as brothers, sisters, uncles and aunts, and their children (Fatal Accidents

---

[15] *Taff Vale Railway Co v Jenkins* [1913] AC 1 (HL).
[16] *Hay v Hughes* [1975] QB 790 (CA).

Act 1976, section 1). Children treated by the deceased as part of the family are also included. Marriage is still of some significance under the detailed rules, but no longer has commanding status: illegitimate children have the same entitlement as legitimate, and anyone cohabiting 'as the husband or wife of the deceased' receives the same rights as a spouse, provided that the cohabitation had lasted at least two years (Fatal Accidents Act 1976, section 1(3); for some of the difficulties involved in the cohabitation provision, see *Kotke v Saffarini*[17]). The recent introduction of civil partnerships included modifications to the 1976 Act, so that civil partners have the same rights as spouses, and relationships can be established through civil partnership as well as by blood or by marriage (Civil Partnership Act 2004, section 83). The live question today is whether the list continues to serve a purpose, or whether it could simply be abolished. The Law Commission wants to bring in a general clause which would allow any person actually or potentially dependent on the deceased to bring a claim (Law Commission for England and Wales, 1999: paragraph 3.46).

Traditionally, the claim was strictly for money lost: the 'dependency' was financial only, usually calculated on a multiplier-multiplicand basis. It included the anomalous claim for reasonable funeral expenses. But not a penny more was allowed for emotional pain. However, the narrow traditional conception of the claim has not proved satisfactory to all, and various rather ad hoc compromises have been introduced. If the widow of a deceased man remarries and her new husband is a wealthier or more generous provider, then on this narrow conception the dependency will be very low or even non-existent: the death has not caused the widow a significant financial loss. Therefore, a common tactic by defence counsel in the early 20th century was to parade the more attractive claimant widows before the court, to support an argument that a future profitable re-marriage was very likely (the 'cattle market' approach, as it was known). Outrage at this manoeuvre eventually led to a change in the law in 1971, so that the actual or potential re-marriage of a claimant widow is ignored (Law Reform (Miscellaneous Provision) Act 1971, section 1, now consolidated into the Fatal Accidents Act 1976, section 3(3)). The absence of any provision for non-financial loss was addressed in 1982, when legislation allowed for the claim to include a sum for 'bereavement', not corresponding to any financial loss. This is currently set at £10,000 (Damages for Bereavement (Variation of Sum) (England and Wales) Order, 2002). If the deceased was married, the sum belongs to their spouse; if he or she was an unmarried legitimate minor, it belongs to both his or her parents; if an unmarried illegitimate minor, then to her mother; otherwise, the sum is not claimable (Fatal Accidents Act, 1976, section 1A, inserted by the Administration of Justice Act 1982, section 3). This is obviously a little arbitrary, but then so would be any suggested replacement formula.

---

[17] *Kotke v Saffarini* [2005] EWCA Civ 221.

So, in summary, the injury done to those left behind by the death is seen as interference with their 'dependency', an unusual sort of a right to say the least. While, as I have shown, the tendency has been to expand the rights available here, nonetheless the rate of expansion has been slow. Are there any other avenues open to those who had been close to the deceased, before he or she was deceased?

D. Death: Damages—Secondary Nervous Shock Claims

A relatively unexplored route, though it is becoming more well-known, is to track the emotional effects of the death and to see which of their consequences can constitute actionable wrongs. This can take the court down strange doctrinal alley-ways (see particularly *AB v Leeds Teaching Hospital NHS Trust*[18]). The older, and to lawyers most familiar, route to liability here is the law of 'nervous shock'. A nervous shock claimant has to show that they have suffered an injury, which usually consists of showing that they have a recognised psychiatric disorder, such as post-traumatic shock disorder (PTSD). A claimant with such an injury, who can show that it resulted from the activities of the defendant, will then have to show that this was in breach of a duty owed by that defendant. This is relatively easy if the claimant was foreseeably at risk from the defendant's activities: if any reasonable person could have seen that carelessness by the defendant posed a risk of injury to the claimant (by reason of their physical or emotional proximity to the deceased), then a duty is owed, and the negligent defendant is liable for any injuries which result. That is the easy case, where the claimant is a 'primary victim' of the defendant's activities. The more difficult case is where there never was any danger to the claimant, but rather to someone else of psychological significance to the claimant. The claimant's shock results not because they were themselves in danger but because of what they see or hear, whether the deceased's injuries occurred before their very eyes, or in another sufficiently shocking way. Such 'secondary victims' are often allowed to recover damages, but under very restrictive rules.

So where a death occurs as the result of the defendant's negligence, and the claimant's reaction to this death can be regarded as a psychiatric injury, then liability can be established, provided that the injury is sufficiently direct. 'Directness' for this purpose is not at all well defined, although it is agreed that the main factors are directness of perception (seeing someone being mangled to death is more shocking than reading that they have been mangled to death) and directness of relationship (the death of your child is more shocking than the death of a stranger). The current law tries as far as possible to treat shock as one injury with special features rather than as

---

[18] *AB v Leeds Teaching Hospital NHS Trust* [2004] EWHC 644 (QB).

something wholly distinct from the rest of negligence law. The results are not, however, altogether satisfactory, and the law is in constant development as the judges flit from one awkward compromise to another.

As to injury, the current approach is that injury is sufficiently established if there is a recognised psychiatric condition. Quite apart from any changes in legal attitude (and the courts tend to make major innovations here on a regular basis) the definition of 'injury' will fluctuate with whatever psychiatric knowledge can be brought to bear on the particular case—the law shows a deference to medical knowledge which it shows only patchily in other contexts (see Jackson, chapter three this volume; and Chau and Herring, chapter two this volume). PTSD is now a sufficiently well-established condition to count as an 'injury' for this purpose, and most nervous shock cases are variants on this. But borderline cases are not uncommon. In the case of *Vernon v Bosley (No 1)*,[19] for example, the Court of Appeal had the unedifying task of deciding whether a father's reaction to the loss of his daughters by drowning constituted 'pathological grief disorder' (an injury for which he could be compensated) or was 'merely' a severe grief reaction (not an injury, and so not compensatable). The objections to this approach are obvious: the knowledge that a sum in the order of half a million pounds hung on the precise label the courts placed on his mental state cannot have assisted his recovery. Further, it posed substantial temptations, which the father did not resist to the courts' satisfaction: success in his personal injury action depended on showing that his condition was severe and long-lasting, whereas success in his family proceedings depended on showing the reverse—and a comparison of the evidence in those two separate actions made sorry reading indeed (see *Vernon v Bosley (No 2)*[20]). The line drawn is plainly not satisfactory, but the courts currently see no other possibility short of holding that 'mere' grief is actionable, which for them would be a step too far.

As to directness, the criteria are reasonably well established: how direct was the claimant's perception of the death? What was it that they actually perceived? Did they know the victim before the accident, and if so, did they care very much about what happened to him or her? These tests are easy enough to apply and the law seems relatively stable. The worry is, of course, that it is all nonsense, that it takes psychiatric commonplaces about who is likely to suffer shock, and turns them into moral injunctions. No doubt someone who suffers PTSD over a death they did not see, and/or whose victim they did not know, is unusual, but it is not clear how they can be stigmatised as a person of 'insufficient psychological firmness' and therefore undeserving of compensation (the requirement that the claimant demonstrate 'the customary phlegm' or come up to 'a normal standard of

---

[19] *Vernon v Bosley* [1997] 1 All ER 577 (CA).
[20] *Vernon v Bosley (No 2)* [1999] QB 18 (CA).

susceptibility' derives from *Bourhill v Young*[21]). This is only one step away from saying that they should buck their ideas up and stop whingeing, which would not usually be seen as an appropriate response to a sufferer from a recognised disorder. For this reason, there is almost universal agreement amongst academics that the 'directness of perception' criterion should be abolished, though the 'directness of relation' criterion has rather more defenders.

In these 'nervous shock' cases, courts here are uncomfortably caught between two realities, one psychological and the other political. The psychological reality is that the injury caused by the death of a loved one is as real as any of the injuries the courts are more used to dealing with, and no legally valid reason for treating it less generously has been discovered. The contrary belief held by the legal system in the past represents not ancient wisdom but pre-scientific ignorance, deriving largely from an exaggerated fear of 'compensation neurosis'. The competing political reality is that giving full weight to the seriousness of such psychological injuries would cause a major storm, in the course of which the judges would be trenchantly criticised for encouraging a 'culture of compensation'. But the uneasy middle course the judges have followed is not really satisfactory from any point of view. The continual resort to psychiatric concepts is a particularly glaring example of buck-passing—no doubt there are arguments both for and against psychiatric recognition of 'pathological grief disorder', but none of them have to do with whether compensation should be paid to the sufferer. No doubt the line will continue to be blurred for quite a while yet.

IV. CONCLUSION

As a generalisation, therefore, the effect of death in a tort action is to wind it up, enabling a firm line to be drawn under the liabilities and the matter to be settled on the basis of how things stood at the instant before death. This is so even where the death of the claimant was itself the fault of the defendant, although in that case the deceased's relatives may argue that they have suffered a fresh injury, in the form of damage to their economic 'dependency' or (possibly) nervous shock.

In some ways this is surprising, shocking even. It can certainly lead to surprising results. Suppose the defendant's negligent driving results in the death of a 30-year-old adult, who had been a high earner with good prospects of promotion. As a result of the accident, however, the victim dies without ever regaining consciousness. If it turns out that this 30-year-old had dependants, the claim will probably be in the millions; if not, the claim will be limited to the cost of torn clothing and other property damaged in

---

[21] *Bourhill v Young* [1943] AC 92 (HL).

the accident, plus a reasonable sum for funeral expenses. Viewed in terms of the defendant's moral culpability, this makes little sense. But then it is a very long time since the law of personal injury was an exercise in morality, if indeed it ever was.

Fatal Accidents Act 1976

Sections 1 and 1A are reproduced here. These texts were inserted by the Administration of Justice Act 1982, section 3. [Square brackets] indicate amendments currently in force.

1. Right of Action for Wrongful Act Causing Death

(1) If death is caused by any wrongful act, neglect or default which is such as would (if death had not ensued) have entitled the person injured to maintain an action and recover damages in respect thereof, the person who would have been liable if death had not ensued shall be liable to an action for damages, notwithstanding the death of the person injured.

(2) Subject to section 1A(2) below, every such action shall be for the benefit of the dependants of the person ('the deceased') whose death has been so caused.

(3) In this Act 'dependant' means—

    (a) the wife or husband or former wife or husband of the deceased;

  [(aa) the civil partner or former civil partner of the deceased;]

    (b) any person who—

        (i) was living with the deceased in the same household immediately before the date of the death; and

       (ii) had been living with the deceased in the same household for at least two years before that date; and

      (iii) was living during the whole of that period as the husband or wife [or civil partner] of the deceased;

    (c) any parent or other ascendant of the deceased;

    (d) any person who was treated by the deceased as his parent;

    (e) any child or other descendant of the deceased;

    (f) any person (not being a child of the deceased) who, in the case of any marriage to which the deceased was at any time a party, was treated by the deceased as a child of the family in relation to that marriage;

  [(fa) any person (not being a child of the deceased) who, in the case of any civil partnership in which the deceased was at any time a civil partner, was treated by the deceased as a child of the family in relation to that civil partnership;]

(g) any person who is, or is the issue of, a brother, sister, uncle or aunt of the deceased.

(4) The reference to the former wife or husband of the deceased in subsection (3)(a) above includes a reference to a person whose marriage to the deceased has been annulled or declared void as well as a person whose marriage to the deceased has been dissolved.

[(4A) The reference to the former civil partner of the deceased in subsection (3)(aa) above includes a reference to a person whose civil partnership with the deceased has been annulled as well as a person whose civil partnership with the deceased has been dissolved.]

(5) In deducing any relationship for the purposes of subsection (3) above—

(a) any relationship [by marriage or civil partnership] shall be treated as a relationship by consanguinity, any relationship of the half blood as a relationship of the whole blood, and the stepchild of any person as his child, and

(b) an illegitimate person shall be treated as the legitimate child of his mother and reputed father.

(6) Any reference in this Act to injury includes any disease and any impairment of a person's physical or mental condition.

1A. Bereavement

(1) An action under this Act may consist of or include a claim for damages for bereavement.

(2) A claim for damages for bereavement shall only be for the benefit—

(a) of the wife or husband [or civil partner] of the deceased; and

(b) where the deceased was a minor who was never married [or a civil partner]—

(i) of his parents, if he was legitimate; and

(ii) of his mother, if he was illegitimate.

(3) Subject to subsection (5) below, the sum to be awarded as damages under this section shall be [£10,000].

(4) Where there is a claim for damages under this section for the benefit of both the parents of the deceased, the sum awarded shall be divided equally between them (subject to any deduction falling to be made in respect of costs not recovered from the defendant).

(5) The Lord Chancellor may by order made by statutory instrument, subject to annulment in pursuance of a resolution of either House of Parliament, amend this section by varying the sum for the time being specified in subsection (3) above.

REFERENCES

Publications

Baker, J (1979) *An introduction to English Legal History*, 2nd edn (London, Butterworths).

Cane, P (1993) *Atiyah's Accidents Compensation and the Law*, 5th edn (Cambridge, Cambridge University Press).

Grubb, A (ed) (2002) *The Law of Tort* (London, Butterworths).

Kostal, R (1994) *Law and English Railway Capitalism 1825–1875* (Oxford, Oxford University Press).

Law Commission for England and Wales (1999) *Claims for wrongful death* LAW COM No 263 (London, Law Commission).

Sutton, T (1997) 'The deodand and responsibility for death' 18 *Journal of Legal History* 44–55.

Legislation

Administration of Justice Act 1982.

Civil Evidence Act 1995.

Civil Partnership Act 2004.

Damages (Personal Injury) Order 2001 (SI 2001/2301).

Damages for Bereavement (Variation of Sum) (England and Wales) Order 2002 (SI 2002/644).

Fatal Accidents Act 1846 (9 & 10 Vict, c 93)

Fatal Accidents Act 1976.

Law Reform (Miscellaneous Provisions) Act 1934.

Law Reform (Miscellaneous Provision) Act 1971.

15

An Anatomist's Perspective on the Human Tissue Act

JOANNE C WILTON

I. INTRODUCTION

MOST MEMBERS OF the public, and especially patients, seem to believe that a practising doctor should have a thorough understanding of human anatomy. Indeed, many consider the study of anatomy to be one of the most basic and important subjects for medical students, helping to lay the foundations for all future learning and medical practice. The medical profession itself has also debated this subject (Sritharan, 2005). How to best achieve this anatomical understanding is a perennial, contentious and unresolved subject of debate in the various medical schools throughout the United Kingdom ('Anatomy Teaching: the cruellest cut of all' is a conference that was held in March 2007 at the Royal College of Surgeons to discuss just such issues). Whilst some establishments tend towards the use of plastic models and computerised images, with little or even no access to cadaveric material, most encourage an appreciation of three-dimensional anatomy through the investigation of cadaveric human material. Timetable constraints and curriculum pressures mean that most medical students do not themselves actually dissect, but the majority of students do study prosected material prepared in advance by prosectors and Dissecting Room (DR) technicians, and some—including Cambridge students—undertake significant active dissection of human cadavers.

This chapter explores the impact of recent legislation governing the provision of resources for the study of anatomy using cadaveric material. It outlines some of the problems being encountered by anatomists in both the legislation and its implementation. Additionally, the impact of the legislation on those working with cadavers and on the recently bereaved is considered. We start with a brief contextual historical overview of cadaveric procurement processes, and of the contribution of public as well as expert opinion in instigating legal reforms associated with the storage and use of human tissue.

II. A BRIEF HISTORY OF THE STUDY OF HUMAN ANATOMY IN EUROPE

Dissection of cadaveric material has traditionally been considered the preferred method of studying anatomy for doctors in training and, of course, for anatomists. Galen is perhaps the most famous ancient anatomist, although the religious and social taboos in the 2nd century BC restricted most of his findings to research into the anatomies of the dog and the Barbary ape. Indeed, until medieval times, such taboos restricted the study of anatomy in Europe to the dissection of animals, the Roman Catholic Church dominating the moral codes authorising scientific research and investigation. Only in the 14th Century were investigations based upon the dissection of human bodies established in the University of Bologna. Thereafter, anatomical dissection of human material continued to be carried out only spasmodically, and then as a secretive underground activity, although the authorities tended to ignore the practice. Eventually, recognised teachers of anatomy in some major European centres such as the Universities of Bologna and Montpellier, and the Medical School at Venice were licensed to make a public dissection of a human body annually. Vesalius (1514–1564), considered to be the first modern anatomist, was licensed by the decree of a Paduan judge in 1539 to dissect executed criminals.

A. The procurement of Cadavers for Anatomical Study in Great Britain

What was happening in Great Britain during this period? In England, in 1540 a Royal Charter from Henry VIII first licensed human dissection—a painting by Holbein in the Barber-Surgeon's Hall records the fact—and subsequently Thomas Vicary published the first work on anatomy written in English (Vicary, 1577). John Caius was later appointed lecturer in anatomy at the Barber-Surgeon's Hall in London, but on founding his own college in Cambridge, he obtained a Royal Charter from Queen Elizabeth I permitting the Master and Fellows of Caius College to take the bodies of two criminals that had been executed in Cambridge each year to be used for the purposes of anatomical dissection. Interestingly, a clause in the Charter made it compulsory to have a solemn funeral of the subjects dissected, to be attended by Master, Fellows and students of the whole college. This is far more than would have been be afforded executed criminals in England at the time, and indicates a recognition of respect afforded to the 'donor', regardless of his/her history. Later, John Hunter FRS (1728–1793), a famous anatomist and pathologist, was known to have spent many hours preparing anatomical dissections, from which the techniques of chemical fixation of material allowed him to keep specimens.

The Royal Charters and decrees of city councils restricted the number of bodies made available for anatomical dissection annually. Quite clearly demand outstripped supply, and whilst England, particularly London, became a world centre for medical teaching, the procurement of bodies for anatomical dissection again became an underground and secretive activity. It is clear that obtaining the exhumed bodies of the recently interred for dissection as part of the study of anatomy was endemic across the country. The law did not recognise the removal of a body from the grave as a crime—since a body was not property (see Price, chapter twelve and also Herring, chapter thirteen this volume)—so long as the grave was not desecrated nor was any shroud or jewellery removed from it. The 'resurrectionists' were well aware of this loop-hole, and elaborate procedures were adopted to ensure that it protected their activities. The trial of Burke and Hare in 1828 for procurement of murdered bodies for anatomical dissections brought about a public outcry (Bailey, 2002). In the same year, a select committee reported on the question of how to regulate the acquisition of bodies for dissection, and despite substantial opposition, the Anatomy Act 1832 was passed.

This Act required that anyone intending to practise anatomy, usually only one or two persons at each institution, must obtain a licence from the Home Secretary. In doing so, these licensed teachers were responsible for the proper treatment of all bodies dissected, for the facilities used (which were also licensed) and for regular reports to the Inspector of Anatomy, who therefore knew of the whereabouts of every body being dissected in Great Britain and Ireland. There were two major conditions, namely that the licensed teacher of anatomy in the lawful possession of a body might permit it to undergo anatomical dissection provided that (i) no relative objected, and (ii) the person had not left a request in writing that their body was not to be dissected. However, the Act also allowed access to corpses unclaimed after death—those dying in prison, in the workhouse or in hospitals—and the Act was seen blatantly to discriminate against the poor. This perception of an elitist attitude was reinforced in the 1920s, when the then Inspector of Anatomy, responding to anxieties that insufficient bodies were available for anatomical dissection because of the declining number of workhouses, ruled that bodies from mental asylums should be made available to anatomists in return for a fee to the institution's officials.

The regulatory framework until 2006 was based on the 1832 Act, supported and updated by the passing of the Human Tissue Act 1961 and the Anatomy Act 1984 with further Anatomy Regulations in 1988. Since then, those working in anatomy departments throughout the country have found this statute and its administration to be effective, fair and well administered. The regulatory framework had a number of key features whereby Her Majesty's Inspector of Anatomy (HMIA) inspected all premises in which anatomical specimens and bodies for anatomical examination were kept, as well as inspecting record keeping and disposal practices. Embalming, storage, dissection and teaching of prosected specimens could only occur on licensed premises. Bodies could only be obtained after an adult had requested that his or her body be used after death specifically for anatomical dissection. Authority to examine the body expired after three years from the date of death, and the licensed teacher was committed to ensuring that the subsequent disposal was in accordance with the wishes of the deceased, or next-of-kin, wherever practicable. Body parts could only be retained for separate study with the express (signed) permission of the donor and the agreement of the relatives. Those persons who were licensed by the 1984 Act were also responsible for record keeping associated with all anatomical practices and these records had to be kept for five years following the disposal of the last part of the body. The respectful use, treatment and disposal of cadaveric material were a mainstay of the Act.

B. Art and Pathology: Disrespect and Scandal

Throughout the 1990s, there was increasing public concern over the treatment of bodies in the United Kingdom. In part this concern was due to a general disaffection with the NHS treatment of the dead and dying reported largely in the local media, but mainly due to a series of high-profile exposés widely discussed in the national media. The level of respect afforded to the dead body by public institutions became an issue.

In 1997, the then HMIA, Dr Laurence Martin, was instrumental in the conviction and imprisonment for nine months of the sculptor Anthony-Noel Kelly.[1] The artist had made casts of human body parts obtained from the Royal College of Surgeons to display as part of an exhibition in 1997. The prosecution case was based upon the theft of the specimens, and the consent of donors to such use for imagery purposes was not an issue. Consent, however, became an issue. The desirability of guidelines on the use of images of recognisable bodies without consent was discussed by the press itself, in the context of images of the recently deceased body of Diana Princess of Wales in August 1997.

There was a further public outcry following the revelation in the late 1990s that pathologists at Alder Hey Hospital in Liverpool had, over a number of years, removed and/or stored tissues following the post-mortem investigations of children, without the consent of their parents. This was followed by a similar scandal in Bristol, again concerning tissues from children (Maclean, 2002). In the absence of a convincing explanation from the medical establishment, these emotive issues garnered huge publicity and resulted in a far-reaching and much-publicised inquiry, which in its report recommended amendments to the Human Tissue Act 1961. Shortly

---

[1] *R v Kelly* [1998] 3 All ER 741 (CA).

afterwards in 2002, but this time in front of a live audience and on television, Gunther von Hagens executed a piece of performance art when he dissected Peter Meiss in a public human dissection—the first in London since 1832. The legality of this act was uncertain, but is likely to have influenced an enquiry and subsequent report (Department of Health, 2003) into the import and export of human tissues.

The government felt compelled to act quickly to re-establish trust and respect for a floundering medical profession—the Human Tissue Act 2004 and the Human Tissue (Scotland) Act 2006 were born. Interestingly, in light of the impact of this legislation on anatomy, there is little evidence to show that these scandals influenced the donor registers for anatomical dissection—the relationship between potential donors (and subsequently their next-of-kin) and the anatomy departments throughout Great Britain was (and remains) a good one.

III. HUMAN TISSUE ACT 2004

In 2004, a new Human Tissue Act was passed, governing England, Wales and Northern Ireland (Scotland has its own Act), and came into effect on 1 September 2006. It attempted a complete overhaul of relevant legislation, repealing entirely the Human Tissue Act 1961, the Human Tissue Act (Northern Ireland) 1962, the Anatomy Act 1984, the Corneal Tissue Act 1986 and the Human Organs Transplants Act 1989, as well as schedule 9, paragraph 7 of the National Health Service and Community Care Act 1990, schedule 4, paragraphs 8 and 9 of the Human Fertilisation and Embryology Act 1990, and schedule 1, paragraph 92 of the Health Authorities Act 1995. The Act sets up a Human Tissue Authority (HTA) as an arms-length body to oversee legislation. The HTA licenses and inspects a number of activities which include: post-mortem examinations and the removal and, separately, the storage of post-mortem material; anatomical examination and the storage of anatomical specimens; transplantation; storage of material from a living person; and the public display of material from a deceased person—this latter activity being of particular relevance to museums, where the Act requires that there be a licence to exhibit material less than 1000 years old. There is prohibition on: removing, storing or using human tissue without consent; DNA 'theft'taking and testing DNA without consent; organ trafficking; and the storage of tissue or organs for purposes either prohibited or not stated in the individual licence (see Herring, chapter thirteen this volume, for a fuller discussion). Penalties of up to three years' imprisonment and/or a fine for each unsanctioned activity are specified. Anatomy constitutes a relatively small component of the HTA's regulatory responsibilities, but the new Act has proved far-reaching for those people working with human anatomy specimens in England, Wales and Northern

Ireland. All activities relating to the procurement, storage, use, disposal, imagery and display of human tissues obtained from live or dead donors must now be licensed by the HTA. Such conduct without a licence could be deemed illegal and lead to criminal sanctions (see Herring, chapter thirteen this volume).

Having recently passed and set up the Human Fertilisation and Embryology Act 1990, with its Code of Practice and a regulatory authority (the Human Fertilisation and Embryology Authority: HFEA) to administer activities in laboratories and hospitals throughout the United Kingdom, it is clear that the government used this as a model in devising the Human Tissue Act 2004, and setting up the HTA in 2006. Whether this has been helpful or not remains to be seen. However, it certainly speeded up the process between the first discussions in 2002, to full implementation in 2006. Those applying for a licence are required to comply with the published Code of Practice issued for each sector by the HTA (eg for Anatomy see Human Tissue Authority, 2006a; 2006c). There are also published guidelines for completing the application forms, again appropriate to each sector. Whilst Designated Individuals (DIs) (one for each licence) are named on the licence, they are not the licence-holders; these are invariably institutions or departments. This is a departure from the practice for anatomy under the previous Human Anatomy Act where an anatomy department would typically have at least two individual licence-holders. The HTA as a new body is likely to change its codes and guidelines as best practice dictates. However, it is already envisaged by the Department of Health (Department of Health, 2004; 2006) that the HTA remit will expand through a merger with the HFEA to form a single Regulatory Authority for Tissues and Embryos (RATE), possibly by 2008. In addition to:

replacing the HTA and the HFEA in regulating all functions relating to the whole range of human tissue—blood, organs, tissues, cells, gametes and embryos, RATE would also take over from the Medicines and Healthcare products Regulatory Agency (MHRA) the responsibility for the regulation of the donation, procurement and supply of blood and blood products (HTA, 2006b).

This is a massive and diverse regulatory load.

Although broadly welcomed by the (interested) public and the majority of the medical community, some scientists have been less positive—the Wellcome Trust and Cancer Research UK have implied that the changes went too far and might jeopardise medical teaching and research in the future (BBC news report, 30 August 2006). The HTA licence requires that a single DI is responsible for all activities associated with tissues obtained under the licence; that is the procurement, storage, use and disposal of all the tissues obtained, and includes its use in diagnosis, teaching and research. This list may cover the activities of many individuals within a number of laboratories (in the pathology sector for example) or teaching (anatomy sector), where the conduct of the students has also to be accounted for. The Code of Practice requires regular audit of all these activities, and a complete paper trail, which means an increase in administration costs for many institutions. The extent of the responsibility for such a wide range of activities by individuals covered by the licence being channelled through a single person, the DI, might be perceived as daunting, especially given the prospect of potential criminal liability and/or failure of licence renewal. There is a risk that the DI (or other researchers) might avoid not only activities clearly prohibited by the Act, but also those that could conceivably be prohibited by the Act, leading to an unduly cautious interpretation. There is also concern that the Code of Practice is more far-reaching than the Act itself, and that some activities not prohibited by the Act may not be sanctioned by the HTA. For example, it appears to be forbidden to take and use images of cadaveric material from those bodies that were consented under the old Act (1988), even though image taking and using is not prohibited in the new Act of 2004. Thus, the HTA requires that specific consent be obtained, which was neither required nor obtained previously, and that all images must have a paper trail.

A. The Act as it Affects Anatomy Teaching

Familiarity with the workings of this new Act is necessarily very limited, as it only came into effect on 1 September 2006 (four months prior to this chapter being written). However, what follows is based on the experiences of myself and several colleagues working in most of the anatomy departments in England, Wales and Northern Ireland during the period leading up to the Act coming into effect and its first four months of operation. Most anatomy departments require a licence for the procurement and storage of anatomical specimens, the carrying out of anatomical examination, the storage of a deceased body or relevant material (ie prosected specimens) which has come from a human body for use for a scheduled purpose (ie anatomical examination), and its final disposal. The HTA published its Code of Practice in July 2006, after approval by the Secretary of State for Health and Parliament in April 2006. Anatomy departments and medical schools were required, when applying for their licences, to show that their activities complied, as far as possible, with the demands of the Code. The closing date for applications was 31 August 2006, for those wishing to continue their activities in anatomy departments; those submitted successfully were granted provisional 'deemed' licences by the end of December 2006.

The application form for the new HTA licence asks a series of exhaustive questions, and the applicant is required to provide substantive information to the HTA of the extent to which a department's activities comply with the requirements of the Act. There are three distinct sections: information about the DI and licence-holder; information about the establishment; and a compliance report. The compliance report itself comprises four categories: consent; governance and quality systems; premises, facilities and equipment; and disposal. For each, the applicant must assess and evaluate their performance against HTA standards. Over and above issues of donor consent, disposal, and the suitability of an individual to be responsible for all matters pertaining to anatomical dissection in a specific site, the HTA licence additionally involves health and safety, information regarding staff training and the implementation of standard operating procedures for all activities in the licensed premises.

The submitted compliance reports are, at the time of writing, in the process of being examined in detail to ensure that applications were meeting the criteria stipulated in the Code of Practice for Anatomical Examination. This process will be completed by April 2007. Full licences will then be issued with (or without) conditions attached. Any conditions attached to a licence will have a time limit for attainment. There might also be site visits by representatives of the HTA, which are likely to be risk-based and not be mandatory. Thus, if the HTA assessors consider that the licence application indicated insufficient compliance with the HTA guidelines, it will be more likely to get a site inspection. As most anatomy establishments have a record of previous inspections under the former Anatomy Act, it is likely that the first site inspections will concentrate upon those other non-anatomy sectors covered by the Act and not previously regulated.

There have been two major concerns from my colleagues involved in anatomical examination and teaching.

(i) Increased Costs.

The first concern is fiscal. The HTA requires that a licence fee be paid annually, and that a licence will be repealed if it is not paid. Under the Anatomy Act 1984 there was no requirement to pay for a licence application, no annual fee, and no payment required for inspection. Under the new Act, each department, regardless of the number of bodies used and stored for anatomical dissection, must pay an annual fee of £6000 and the costs of the possibly bi-annual inspections. There has been no discussion of how such figures have been calculated, nor recognition of the size and use of anatomical specimens by different institutions. The Presidents of the Anatomy Society of Great Britain and Ireland and of the British Association of Clinical Anatomists wrote jointly to the Chair of the HTA on behalf of anatomy teaching establishments in England, Wales and Northern Ireland in October 2006. They asked for details of how this fee level had been arrived at, in view of the fact that the income derived would be three to four times greater than the costs of running HMI Anatomy's inspectorate. They also asked (i) why *all* activities licensed on 1 September 2006 were charged the same fee and not according to the costs of regulating each sector as previously had been stated would be the case, and (ii) why anatomy did not receive a discount for being regulated previously as did some tissue banks for human use. The Chief Executive replied to the letter but did not offer any satisfactory explanations. However, he did state that the £6000 fee paid in 2006 was for this year only and that subsequent fees would be based upon the assessment of the real cost of regulating each sector. The threatened demise of human anatomy dissection and prosection in some medical schools will become more likely as a result of the increased costs incurred.

Additionally, there has been a considerable increase in the administrative load for most establishments, especially in the period immediately prior to the submission of the licence application. Whilst it is clearly desirable that the HTA ensures that best practice is adopted in all establishments where cadaveric material might be used and stored, a marked increase in workload for some individuals in the short-term has been generated where there was previously no evidence that any problems existed.

(ii) Loss of Anatomical Regulation in a Large Regulatory Structure.

A second very different, and slightly uncomfortable, change is that having been used to liaising with the office of HMIA, most recently Dr Jeremy Metters or his secretary, directly, the HTA has made no provision for a similar office. The HMIA was able to give advice quickly to bequeathal secretaries, licensed teachers, prosectors and dissection room staff, and indeed he knew most of us by name. Perhaps more importantly for those of the public contemplating body donation but not knowing who to contact, the human voice at the end of the telephone, was invaluably reassuring. It is yet to be proven whether such enquiries will be dealt with as promptly or as knowledgeably by the new Authority.

The requirement for regular audits of all these procedures will be more than some establishments have previously been used to. With regard to staffing, for instance, complying with the HTA Code of Practice appears to necessitate more training of DR technicians and bequeathal secretaries than is current practice (for instance, in dealing with the recently bereaved, and writing and monitoring of standard operating procedures). However, the HTA seems remarkably unaware of existing practices in this area. For example, the Institute for Anatomical Studies (IAS) has long been aware of the paucity of appropriate training across the country for the relatively few individuals concerned compared with the larger numbers of medical staff, pathologists and technical staff associated with consent, procurement, use and storage of pathological specimens. Within the majority of anatomy departments, which are running expensive facilities on diminishing departmental budgets, with costs exacerbated by the new licence fee, there is no spare funding available for recruitment of extra staff, or for specialised on-site training. The IAS, which runs two meetings a year, provides a very useful forum for discussion by the relatively few DR technicians, secretaries and prosectors from across the country. Additionally, when DR technicians require additional training it is usually provided bespoke at the appropriate establishment (with the trainer or trainee as the host), so that costs can be minimised essentially to travelling expenses and overnight accommodation. It is perhaps surprising that the HTA does not guide establishments towards these helpful resources. Nor does it draw attention to other useful documents, such as *Care and Respect in Death: Good Practice Guidance for NHS Mortuary Staff* from the Department of Health.

B. Consent of the Donor and Relationships with the Next-of-Kin

A number of reports such as those from HMIA (Metters, 2003), the CMO (Chief Medical Officer, 2001), and reports following the Alder Hey (Redfern, 2001) and Bristol (Kennedy, 2001) enquiries made it clear that non-consented acquisition and storage of human organs was common practice throughout the country. The extent of the influence that these reports had upon the development of the Human Tissue Act 2004 and on the Codes of Practice published by the HTA is not clear, but the principle of informed consent rightly underpins the Act, and is key to the licensing of all sectors. For quite some time now, anatomy departments have been informing potential donors and their next-of-kin of the need to ensure that written consent exists in their documentation, and that the family is informed of their wishes. Each school or department produced an information pack containing a form of some description for the donor to complete. The HTA requires that the forms be witnessed and that a register of potential donors be kept by the institution, a procedure most schools had adopted some years previously. Significant differences, howeve, have arisen in two areas as a result of the new Act. First, the donor can opt to allow the department to keep their body, or parts thereof, indefinitely, and secondly explicit permission must be provided to allow images to be made of their dissected remains. Anatomists, unlike clinicians, do not have a person-to-person relationship with donors. We are dependent upon individuals contacting us through a variety of means, by telephone, letter, and increasingly by email. The potential donor is then sent a booklet of information and consent forms for his or her anatomical dissection, retention of parts, whether images might be taken and desired means of body disposal. Having read and hopefully understood the information, the donors complete the requisite forms in the presence of a witness who is also required to sign the forms. Whilst DIs and bequeathal secretaries are happy to answer any queries, we can only do this when contacted by the donors or their witness, be they next-of-kin, executor, friend or medical professional. We must take on trust that there has not been coercion to sign, and that the donor is fully cognisant of what they have agreed to. The DI must be assured that appropriate consent has been obtained and that the paperwork confirms that. If there is a subsequent query by next-of-kin regarding the acceptance of a body for anatomical dissection, the DI can then use 'reasonable belief' as defence against litigation (section 5 Human Tissue Act 2004). Potential donors and their witnesses can of course contact us for more information at any time, but rarely do so. It is usually about 15 years before registered potential donors actually become donors following their death, and it is unusual for there to have been any recent personal contact. However, we then must speak to next-of-kin and executors, often under very difficult circumstances, and a relationship of trust needs to develop rapidly between them and the receiving institution. Paradoxically, more time is spent with these people than the donors, and it is important that this continues. Whilst the donor may well opt for cremation, it is often the next-of-kin who requests that we allow them to collect the ashes for scattering in an appropriate setting.

Most establishments have some form of memorial or committal service and inform the next-of-kin (unless they do not wish it) of the time that their family members will be remembered. At the memorial stage, any jewellery or personal objects are re-united with the body prior to disposal, again an action that recognises 'their possession' by the now dead body (Price, chapter twelve this volume). Many next-of-kin like to be informed in advance so that they can go to a place of solitude as an act of remembrance at the same time as the service. Any eulogies presented by students during such services are available to next-of-kin should they wish to receive them. These respectful sentiments are valued by the next-of-kin, but also, perhaps especially, by the students and staff who have worked with the bodies prior to their disposal. Elizabeth Hallam (chapter sixteen this volume) discusses the significance of ritualised practises of disposal and memorialisation to anatomists and medical students, and some of the student eulogies written for, and spoken at, the committal services are very moving. For example, the tribute written and read by a first year medical student at the committal service at Cambridge University in June 2006 includes:

When we first entered the dissection room we saw humans, people, but as we increased our knowledge of anatomy, they became muscles, vessels and nerves. It is easy to forget the humanity of the situation. The very same bodies that passively teach us anatomy have themselves taught, loved, and lived. Now we have time to reflect and once again see our cadavers as human beings.

We should take time to thank the friends and families. In order to dissect these bodies we have taken a step back from relating to the emotions of their loved ones, for whom the process of mourning for their relatives has been interrupted by the grand gesture of donation.

It is important, then, that we have this time to reflect, and say goodbye to the 50 people who have made this all possible for us; who have in some oblique way allowed the passage of knowledge from one generation to the next. We say good-bye to the bond we have developed over the past eight months through the little human touches we have seen: a scar, a pacemaker, an artificial knee: all signs of who these people were, and whom their relatives knew and loved.

Our cadavers had shown the foresight to commit their bodies to a cause that is so worthy: the gift of their endowment spreads through the benefit it brings to the patients we treat in our future careers. Their gesture is selfless; they receive no reward in life, so that in death they help so many. We will always be grateful for this. Hopefully we have done them justice in our commitment to the subject. (reproduced with permission)

I am aware from correspondence and telephone conversations that events around the delayed funeral often help the next-of-kin to complete their bereavement process (see also Miller and Parrott, chapter nine this volume).

However, the new Act, via the Code of Practice, appears to diminish the role of the next-of-kin. The HTA explains in paragraphs 45–7 that the DI, or deputy, does not need to have the permission of the next-of-kin to accept the body of a donor registered after 1st September 2006. In paragraph 47, dealing with tissues obtained from deceased adults, the Code of Practice states:

If the family or those close to the deceased person object to the donation, for what-ever purpose, when the deceased person (or his/her nominated representative— see below) has explicitly consented, clinicians should seek to discuss the matter sensitively with them. They should be encouraged to accept the deceased person's wishes and it should be made clear that they do not have the legal right to veto or overrule those issues.

This guidance ignores the fact that the anatomy establishments are of course completely reliant upon the next-of-kin or executors, and the maintenance of a good relationship with them is paramount. Thus, the next-of-kin or executors, inform DIs or departments that a donor has died and of the whereabouts of the body, and register the death prior to the DI being able to make a decision as to acceptability of the donation. There is no possible acceptance without this first informative act. Additionally, HTA guidelines state that departments should allow a maximum of six days between the day of death and the delivery of the body for embalming, although previously many departments accepted refrigerated bodies as long as 10 days after death. Indeed for bodies not kept in refrigerated conditions, the advice is that only three days should elapse, unworkable in many rural situations, and likely to result in rejection of an otherwise suitable bequeathal. To ensure acceptability, urgent action by the next-of-kin is required at what is almost invariably an emotionally charged time for them. Although never mentioned, caring next-of-kin would like to believe that their donating relatives will not be violated, and the time taken to talk to next-of-kin during the informing/acceptance process, thereby forming a short personal relationship, is very important. There is perhaps an act of faith between the donor's next-of-kin and those invisible people on the end of the telephone: their relatives are in good hands, and their altruism is recognised. Whenever a body is accepted, letters of thanks are sent to next-of-kin or their executors, and an offer to be kept informed of committal services *and any written material associated with them* is also made. Many next-of-kin take up this option of receiving such information (such as the eulogy reproduced above). A letter of thanks also goes to those relatives or executors who have informed us of the death of a potential donor who, for whatever reason, we have been unable to accept. So, whilst the 2004 Act and the HTA, through its requirements for compliance or guidance notes, do not require such efforts to be made, a system of best practice has developed in the anatomy departments that appears to be neither recognised nor mandatory.

Whilst most of the paperwork associated with accepting a body is organised between the accepting institution (in practice the DI and/or bequeathal secretary) and the next-of-kin or executor, and is covered prior to the acceptance of a body, the failure of the doctor signing the death certificate to also complete form HTA(A2) often delays institutions in informing the HTA of acceptance. It can take some effort and time (up to weeks) before the doctor can be encouraged to complete the form, and seems like a disrespectful act, not by the student or the department, but by the medical profession itself. Sadly, the HTA does not yet appear to be aware of the practical implications of requiring this paperwork. The delay may be a reflection of the difficulty in defining both the time and the cause of death (see Chau and Herring, chapter two this volume), although the same doctor must have completed the death certificate. Thus, prior to acceptance, the DI or designated deputy must confirm that the donation is acceptable. There is a number of clinical conditions the presence of which means acceptance is prohibited, usually in order to protect staff and students/dissectors. These include any forms of dementia not proven to be of vascular origin (to ensure that donors that might have prion disease are not accepted even if undiagnosed), or forms of septicaemia where *Clostridium difficile* might be implicated. We are therefore attempting to discern the truth from relatives and medical staff, but of course are not able to use the methods discussed in this book by Martin Innes in police interviews. I sometimes wonder whether the delay in completing form HTA(A2) by the doctor who signed the death certificate is due to the fact that in contrast to the easy verbal assurance over the telephone that there is no apparent transmissible disease, signing such a document is perceived as more difficult—longer-lasting. That element of respect we extend to the dead is not always reflected in the medical profession's respect of their role in our acceptance of the bodies of their recently departed patients.

C. The Altruistic Donor

Who are the donors? As discussed earlier, over the last 3000 years, anatomical examination has largely been practised on executed convicts, or unclaimed bodies—and this remains the case in many countries, including the United States and Russia. However, it has now been the practice for some time, that in Great Britain, donation for anatomical examination would be exclusively the last and altruistic act of a competent adult. Despite a common belief that most donors are those that cannot or do not want to pay for funeral expenses, most donors are white, often middle-class and donate from an abiding respect for the medical profession—often having had direct or close personal experience of medical help. Based upon the information given to us regarding the preferred cremation and committal services of the donors, very often their religion is stated as Church of England; there are also many agnostics, atheists and humanists, and a few (recently) practising Roman Catholics. It is very rare that anatomy departments receive a donation from practising Jews, Hindus, Sikhs or Moslems or from the West Indian communities (although there are a *few* more registrations of intent to donate, indicating again our reliance upon the explicit consent of next-of-kin). This means that the bodies used in dissection rooms do not reflect the community in which future medical (or dental) students will practise, nor the cultural make-up of the typical student cohort. Is there a continuing role for the altruistic act of body donation? (see also Jupp, chapter six this volume).

D. Working in the Dissecting Room

An area that is rarely acknowledged is the emotional resilience of those accepting telephone calls from the recently bereaved (usually bequeathal secretaries and DR technicians), and in preparing and embalming the body immediately after it has entered the facility (DR technicians). It is rare that undertakers or mortuary staff will clean a body if it is not to be viewed by the next-of-kin, and the state of the body is unknown to DR staff until receipt. This can be quite shocking and stressful. DR staff work in teams that rarely total more than three individuals, and often there is a lone technician dealing with the body. So people have to develop their own coping strategies and cannot necessarily rely on team support.

The HTA rightly reinforces the responsibility of anatomical institutions to maintain respectful attitudes towards the cadavers and cadaveric tissue at all times. This is easily accomplished where members of DR staff are involved, but the attitude of students, and especially post-graduate course participants, is less easily monitored. My experience is that there is a natural and easy respect paid towards entire cadavers by students studying anatomy (whether they are medical, dental or science students); indeed, an element of affection comes into play. Bodies are not identified by their names (until the committal service), an anonymised numbering system being created by the local institution, but many groups of students able to dissect bodies will give a name to their cadaver. There is often discussion as to the appropriateness of the name, but it is always done with respect and with a degree of affection. Students viewing large prosected specimens will be very aware of the idea that there is a 'person' present. However, when material is used that is relatively small—an organ for instance, such names are never used, nor even considered, and the relationship is colder, more abstract, though still a respectful one. A heart shown as a prosected specimen will be referred to as 'the' heart by students and invariably by teaching staff, but when seen on a cadaver, even when dissected, will often be referred to as 'his' or 'her' heart. This idea of retained possession and personhood seems to be accepted without introduction or definition. Perhaps it is intuitive, but typically only when there is a perception of completeness.

This abstraction of the body from body parts, especially those very small isolated parts used in pathology and histopathology, might in part explain the puzzled reactions of the pathologists in Alder Hey and Bristol to the collections of tissue they had acquired over a period of years. The judge in the Kelly trial in 1997 acknowledged that the work done by creating a prosected specimen rendered a value to the body, making the receiving institution 'owners' rather than 'holders' of the specimen. Might, perhaps, pathologists have been credited with a similar assumption that such additional value extended to their practices under the 1961 Act? It is disappointing that the new Act of 2004 does not explicitly state that the work (or the extent of that work) of anatomists or pathologists on bodily material can render it property that can be owned (see also Price, chapter twelve this volume). One might argue that the time used in dissecting a specimen is a very difficult and more time-consuming craft than that of examining a tissue under a microscope, which nonetheless is regarded as property.

There is anecdotally a widely-held belief that there is a dark humour associated with coping strategies for those working in dissection rooms and prosectoria, and has been the subject of some interesting papers where the depersonalisation of the future patient by medical students has been examined (eg, Penney, 1985; and Hafferty, 1991). This has not been my experience; indeed it is a long way from the experience of most of my colleagues, and is contested by a number of authors (eg, Sukol, 1995).

Students in the DR are very much influenced by the attitudes of the staff around them. If the DR and teaching staff are respectful, and do not use derogatory language, then the students are likely to replicate such dignified attitudes. Moreover, there is evidence of student abreactions to peers who transgress the line to black humour (Druce and Johnson, 1994). There must of course be an element of detachment, but this does not mean that there needs to be silence. Most anatomy lecturers cultivate an atmosphere of enthusiastic interest, enquiry and respect. Students I have worked with, regardless of the course they are studying, are informed that all the bodies they will see as prosected specimens and may dissect, are those of consenting donors. Medical students might also be aware that the bodies they are dissecting are those that not so long ago were patients, or that one of their future patients might be so impressed by their doctor's treatment or attitude or empathy that they might register as a donor for future medical students. There is a suggestion that there is a shared experience between donor and future doctor; certainly some of the eulogies written by students reflect this type of relationship.

That fully consenting donors are used informs a respectful attitude from the students, but it also means that the donors have given their explicit permission for their bodies to be dissected in such a way. This sets up an implicit relationship between the student and the donor: students are not being asked to commit violent acts, but are being given the opportunity to learn by the donor, their 'silent teacher' (see also Herring, chapter thirteen this volume).

The Human Tissue Act 2004, perhaps because of its origins, does not seem to fully appreciate the subtleties of these interactions.

IV. IS THERE A FUTURE FOR ANATOMICAL DISSECTION IN THE UK?

The impact of technology upon medical imaging means that more doctors are able to visualise more of the human body to identify diseased organs, ischaemic tissues, or broken bones. More medical staff will need to be able to interpret these images than before, so the need to appreciate the three-dimensional anatomy of our bodies is perhaps more important than it was in the past. In my opinion, the role of cadaveric dissection remains at the forefront of medical education. Our doctors need to be aware of the concept and extent of variability, which extends to body structures as much as it does to circulating glucose levels. The dissection of a body also provides an introduction to death and its consequences, and to the necessity of professionally separating the person from the body appropriately (Johnson, 2002). The new HTA ensures that best practices are adopted, that consent of the donor is sought and recorded, and that there has been discussion of this wish with another—the witness. Additionally, it considers the premises and their fitness for purpose, and that staff are working in a safe and appropriate environment. However, it does all this at a cost, and one that might be prohibitive for some medical schools. Moreover, in its application by the HTA, much of the sensitivity, good-will and good practice generated prior to the 2004 Act might be at risk, largely because the anatomy sector is such a small part of the HTA's current remit, and is likely to be a smaller proportion in the future. Let us hope that such financial, economic and bureaucratic constraints do not prevent this valuable experience being extended to our future clinicians, doctors, dentists and allied health professionals.

REFERENCES

Publications

Bailey, B (2002) *Burke and Hare: the year of the ghouls* (London, Mainstream Publishing).
BBC News 30 August 2006 see [news.bbc.co.uk/1/hi/health/4944018.stm]
Chief Medical Officer (2001) 'The Removal, Retention and Use of Human Organs and Tissue from Post Mortem Examination' (Norwich, The Stationery Office).
Department of Health (2003) *The Import and Export of Human Body Parts and Tissue for Non-therapeutic Use*. A code of practice' Department of Health Gateway ref 1167 (Norwich, The Stationery Office) (Downloadable version: www.dh.gov.uk/assetRoot/04/07/11/35/04071135.pdf).
Department of Health (2004) *Report on reconfiguring the Department of Health's Arm's Length Bodies*. Department of Health (Norwich, The Stationery Office).
Department of Health (2006) *Review of the Human Fertilisation and Embryology Act:* Proposals for revised legislation (including establishment of the Regulatory Authority for Tissue and Embryos) Cm 6989. (Norwich, The Stationery Office).
Department of Health–Modernising Pathology Team (2006) *Care and Respect in Death: Good Practice Guidance for NHS Mortuary Staff* (London, Department of Health).
Druce, M and Johnson, MH (1994) 'Human dissection and attitudes of preclinical students to death and bereavement' 7 *Clinical Anatomy* 42–49.
Hafferty, FW (1991) *Into the valley: death and the socialisation of medical students* (London, Yale University Press).
Human Tissue Authority (2006a) Human Tissue Authority Code of Practice—Anatomical Examination (HM Government).
Human Tissue Authority (2006b) New Chair of HTA and HFEA Appointed www.hta.gov.uk/newsroom/media_releases.cfm
Human Tissue Authority (2006c) Human Tissue Authority Licensing Information www.hta.gov.uk
Johnson, MH (2002) 'Male medical students and the male body' in A Bainham, SD Sclater and M Richards (eds), *Body Lore and Laws* (Oxford/ Portland OR, Hart Publishing Ltd) 91–103.
Kennedy, I (2001) *Learning from Bristol: The report of the public inquiry into children's heart surgery at the Bristol Royal Infirmary 1984–1995*. Cm 5207 (Norwich, The Stationery Office).

Maclean, M (2002) 'Letting go … parents, professionals and law of human materials after postmortem' in A Bainham, SD Sclater and M Richards (eds), *Body lore and laws* (Oxford/ Portland OR, Hart Publishing Ltd) 79–90.

Metters, J (2003) *Isaacs report: the investigation of events that followed the death of Cyril Mark Isaacs* (Norwich, The Stationery Office).

Moore, W (2005) *The knife man: blood, body snatching, and the birth of modern surgery* (New York, Random House Inc).

Penney, JC (1985) 'Reactions of medical students to dissection' 60 *Journal of Medical Education* 58–60.

Redfern, M (2001) *Report of the Royal Liverpool Children's Inquiry: Summaries and Recommendations* (Norwich, The Stationery Office).

Sritharan, K (2005) 'The rise and fall of anatomy: Anatomy nearing extinction or set for a come back?' 13 *Students' British Medical Journal* 332–333.

Sukol, RB (1995) 'Building on a tradition of ethical consideration of the dead' 26 *Human Pathology* 700–705.

Vicary, T (1577) *A profitable treatise of the Anatomie of mans body* (London, Henry Bamford).

Legislation

Anatomy Regulations 1988 (I 1988/044).
Corneal Tissue Act 1986.
Health Authorities Act 1995.
Human Anatomy Act 1984.
Human Fertilisation and Embryology Act 1990.
Human Organs Transplants Act 1989.
Human Tissue Act 1961.
Human Tissue Act (Northern Ireland) 1962.
Human Tissue Act 2004.
Human Tissue (Scotland) Act 2006.
National Health Service and Community Care Act 1990.

16

Anatomical Bodies and Materials of Memory

ELIZABETH HALLAM

I. INTRODUCTION

THIS CHAPTER EXPLORES how the deceased human body becomes a material of memory in anatomical practices, together with the materials that are deployed in memorialising donors to medical schools.[1] Memorial forms are discussed here in terms of the visual and tactile processes of learning anatomy, and in terms of memorial inscriptions created for donors. In addressing these issues in Scotland from the 19th century to the present, this chapter builds on anthropological studies of relationships between death, memory and material cultures (Hallam and Hockey, 2001)—a set of concerns also shared by Miller and Parrot (chapter nine this volume). The contemporary context of the research is characterised by intensified public concern about the treatment of the corpse in medical settings, as well as fascination with the cadaver in controversial exhibitions such as Gunther von Hagens' *Body Worlds/Körperwelten*, which have been viewed by millions of visitors world-wide (cf Walter, 2004a; and Walter 2004b). Recent media coverage has highlighted concerns about a national decline in numbers of donated bodies (*The Guardian*, 2006). Issues of legality and rights with regard to the bodies/body parts of deceased persons have featured strongly in recent public discussions. The Human Tissue Act 2004 and the Human Tissue (Scotland) Act 2006 regulate the removal, storage and use of human organs and tissues from the living and the dead, as well as focusing on the securing of donors' consent for these uses (see Herring; Wilton; and Price, chapters thirteen, fifteen and twelve, all this volume).

Focusing on the social relations of anatomical bodies and their associated materials of memory, this chapter is based on ethnographic and archival

---

[1] The generous help of Margaret Moir, Easter Smart, Ian Stewart and the staff and students in the Department of Anatomy, University of Aberdeen, has made this research possible. Permission to conduct the research was kindly granted by HM Inspector of Anatomy for Scotland and the Licensed Teacher of Anatomy at the University of Aberdeen.

research in one particular context—the Department of Anatomy[2] at Marischal College, University of Aberdeen, in the North East of Scotland. Anatomy has been located in Marischal College since the early 19th century and there is a rich accumulation of archival, museum and visual-image collections that have grown in relation to the teaching of this subject. This discussion draws upon textual records, as well as observations, informal interviews and conversations.[3] It begins with an account of processes by which bodies were acquired for dissection in Aberdeen following the Anatomy Act 1832. It traces these through the 19th century and then examines the rise in bequests of bodies in the mid-20th century. The forging of anatomists' social networks as means to secure donations is discussed. The ways in which memories and memorials are constituted in the context of these social relations are then considered. Addressed in subsequent sections of the chapter are processes of anatomical memory making through dissection as well as modes of inscription that constitute the memorial significance of the name in a service of remembrance, a memorial book and a cemetery memorial.

II. BODIES OF THE 'UNCLAIMED'

The provisions of the Anatomy Act 1832 made it lawful for unclaimed bodies in hospitals, prisons and other institutions to be given over for anatomical examination, and for people to direct that their bodies be employed for this purpose. Rather than relying on supplies of executed criminals and bodies obtained by other means, as in cases of taking from graves, anatomists were now supposed to have a legal supply of cadavers for teaching medical students (Richardson, 2001). Teachers of anatomy were required to obtain a licence from central government and an Inspector of Anatomy was appointed to oversee the activities of licensed teachers in England and Wales and in Scotland.

In Aberdeen, during the year following the Anatomy Act 1832, a Parochial Burying House or Funeratory was established. This was managed by a committee composed of the Provost and Magistrates, as city officials, along with the teachers of anatomy and surgery, overseen by Her Majesty's Inspector of Anatomy for Scotland. Notes in the Committee's records from 1846 explain the perceived need for the Funeratory:

It was found in practice that great inconvenience and public excitement were produced by the removal of bodies direct from the places of death to the Schools of Anatomy (MSU1332/4/1, 1846: 1).[4]

---

[2] The Department of Anatomy is currently part of the School of Medicine.

[3] Interviews and conversations have been conducted with those teaching and learning anatomy, the organisers of the Memorial Service and the Chaplain to the University. Further study would benefit from interviews with donors and their relatives.

[4] These records remain under restricted access at the discretion of the University's Licensed Teacher of Anatomy.

Indeed, in Aberdeen there had been a fierce public demonstration of opposition to the treatment of cadavers in a private anatomy theatre when it was destroyed by fire in January 1832 (Richardson, 2001; and Pennington, 1994). When the Funeratory was instituted in 1833 such houses were, according to its Committee,

made use of as houses of reception where dead bodies may lie for 48 hours after death, open to the inspection of friends or relatives, who may claim and bury them thence (MSU1332/4/1, 1846: 1).

If bodies remained unclaimed the Superintendent, who was resident at the Funeratory, would arrange their removal to anatomy schools by porters. After dissection, each body would be buried, and this was, again, arranged by the Superintendent. The Committee regarded the Funeratory as a benefit for many, as an

advantage accruing to poor persons who are often compelled to live in the room in which a dead body is lying, and to the public in cases of severe epidemics (MSU1332/4/1, 1846: 1–2).

Of importance to medical schools was the

supply of bodies for anatomical purposes … obtained without the cognisance of any, save the Committees of management of Funeratories and the Offices appointed by the Act (MSU1332/4/1, 1846: 2).

This aspect of discretion, or the maintenance of low public visibility, was one that continued to concern the Committee until it was reconsidered during the mid-20th century, with significant effects that are discussed later in this chapter.

Throughout the 19th century, the Funeratory in Aberdeen received the bodies of paupers from poor houses, hospitals, asylums, a house of refuge and private dwelling-houses in the city. A register was kept, assigning a number to each body, noting the person's name, age and sex, their last place of abode, date and place of death, date of removal from the Funeratory, the relative who claimed the person or, if the body remained unclaimed, the anatomy or surgery teacher's name, the date the body was sent to the school and, finally, the date of interment (MSU1332/4/3, 1843–1944). Those who had drowned in rivers, the sea, and the harbour were also recorded, sometimes unnamed, as were unknown deceased infants. Bodies were claimed by spouses, parents, siblings, sons, daughters and other relatives or, in the case of unknown infants, by the Procurator Fiscal. The documentation procedure of the Funeratory thus kept a written trace of the movements of these persons from death to burial. It formed a record of either social relatedness after death or of detachment and abandonment with regard to the poorest in the city.

Once claimed by teachers in anatomy and surgery in Aberdeen, each body was kept for about four to six weeks prior to burial at Footdee near the city's harbour, and, after 1860, in Nellfield Cemetery in the city centre. During the early 20th century there were continued concerns about local perceptions, such that further care was taken in the removal of bodies to the Funeratory. The Committee required the transportation of bodies in 'such a manner that will not wound local feeling' and with the use of a 'proper hearse etc' (MSU1332/4/1, 1914: 197). The place of burial again transferred in 1921 to Trinity Cemetery, also in the city centre, the ground having been obtained on the condition that its purpose would not be marked at the site. During the century following the 1832 Act, then, the supply of bodies remained low in relation to anatomists' perceived teaching needs, and throughout this period there continued a strategy of seclusion with regard to acquisitions and burials of those bodies. Throughout the 19th century, subjects were obtained from within the city. Then, as numbers became particularly low in the second decade of the 20th century, bodies were sought from a wider geographical area in North-East Scotland. In 1914, the Funeratory Committee considered extending its reach further North to Orkney and Shetland, and from the 1930s to the 1950s, arrangements were also made to transfer bodies from England (MSU1332/4/1).

III. BODIES OF DONORS

Addressing the pattern of body acquisition for anatomical purposes in Britain from the 19th century onwards, Ruth Richardson has shown that until the war in 1914–18, bodies for dissection were obtained under the Anatomy Act 1832 from hospitals, prisons, workhouses and asylums (Richardson, 2001). These were 'unclaimed' rather than donated bodies. Then, during the 1930s, the number of people bequeathing their bodies gradually began to rise and this rising trend was most marked from the mid 1940s onwards. Since the Second World War, Richardson argues, there has developed a 'culture of medical donation' including whole-body donation for dissection, as well as organ and blood donation (Richardson, 2001: 419). Richardson suggests that the rise in whole-body donation was related to the rise in the popularity of cremation, which, she argues, indicates a change in the 'social meaning of the corpse and its spiritual associations' (Richardson, 2001: 260). In addition to the 'growing disbelief in the spiritual coherence of the corpse', Richardson points to a 'more benign public view of scientific medicine' as a leading factor in the rise of donation (Richardson, 2001: 260). In Scotland, however, during the 1950s, a much slower increase in bodies donated for dissection in comparison with England was observed (*Scots Law Times*,

1958). The general shift to bequests requires examination in specific social contexts to show how it took place especially through the forging of connections between anatomists, other professionals, potential donors and their relatives.

In Aberdeen, anatomists began to discuss the issue of bequests in the early 1940s. The Funeratory Committee was eager to acquire more subjects from within the city and HM Inspector of Anatomy for Scotland at the time

referred to bequests which had been made by friends of his own and others and indicated he thought a good deal could be done in this direction if the requirements were actually known (MSU1332/4/1, 1942: 308).

By 1945 Robert Lockhart, Professor of Anatomy, claimed that there was 'too much secrecy' about the matter and suggested that 'more publicity should be given to the University requirements' (MSU1332/4/1, 1945: 315). The Committee's strategy was to increase public awareness of its work by cultivating a wider network of sympathetic contacts. To this end, the Presbytery in Aberdeen was approached and a minister invited to join the Committee. During the early 1950s, this minister, Reverend Ricketts, conducted the recently inaugurated annual service held in the Dissecting Room of the Anatomy Department prior to the burial or cremation of bodies. The Funeratory Committee was also re-named with the view that the new name, the Anatomy Act Committee, would be more conducive to 'public interest and support' (MSU1332/4/1, 1955: 347). This was approved in 1958, the year that an appeal for bequests of bodies was launched in the local newspaper.

This cultivation of contacts and dissemination of media messages generated correspondence between anatomists and potential donors. Letters from the 1960s and 1970s reveal aspects of these unfolding dialogues, and they point to the key intermediaries through whom anatomists extended their call for donations (MSU1332/4/4/17). The Anatomy Act Committee had been circulating information about the procedures of donation to solicitors in the region and had also considered a similar circular for churches and Hospital Boards. Doctors and solicitors in Aberdeenshire and a minister in Inverness sent indications to David Sinclair, Professor of Anatomy, about their patients, clients and parishioners who had expressed wishes to bequeath their bodies. Intentions to donate came from people who had no surviving relatives as well as from those with relatives who were in sympathy with the bequest. It is notable that donors often expressed the desire to make a bequest together with a relative (such as a mother with her daughter) or spouse. This relational aspect of decisions to donate is also evident in the making of decisions to reverse a previous bequest. In the case of one woman in 1972, her declared intention to donate was withdrawn when she was widowed and planned to remarry, her son and daughter objecting to the bequest. In another case a bequest was framed in terms of sympathy with others sharing a similar vocation. The potential donor, a first aid teacher, wrote:

As I have no affiliation to any religious body, the act of burial means nothing to me. I would feel a sense of completion if I know that some hard pressed teacher of first aid or anatomy teacher could get some use out of my bones when I have finished with them (MSU1332/4/4/17, 1969).

It was such relationships and dialogues that formed the process of making a bequest to the Department of Anatomy. By 1970, anatomists in Aberdeen reported that the number of donations received was exceeding the number required, and 800 people had made written statements of their intention to donate (MSU1332/4/1, 1970: 39).

In a study of donors' attitudes conducted in the early 1990s in medical schools in London, a significant factor in many decisions to make a bequest was knowing someone who had donated or who intended to donate (Richardson, 1995). Social relationships between donors are also significant in the Aberdeen context, as are the cultivation of contacts between potential donors, anatomists and their associates. The process of donation is currently co-ordinated and managed by the Anatomy Bequests Administrator in the University's Department of Anatomy. The Administrator is the person who receives enquires and advises on procedures for potential donors, as well as co-ordinating the arrival and disposal of bodies. She maintains an archive of completed donors' bequest forms that began in 1965. The Administrator is thus a central figure in the practice and the on-going social relations of donation: she participates in matters personal and legal, emotional and bureaucratic, mundane and ceremonial. To make a bequest a person will contact the Administrator and will be periodically in communication with her until the time of death, at which point the Administrator manages the bequest via the person who is in lawful possession of the body—in many cases, the donor's next-of-kin. Donors to the Department of Anatomy in Aberdeen, who are mostly from the region, have registered their bequests between four and 34 years prior to their deaths. In this setting, the average length of time between the declaration to donate and the death is about 16 years.[5] From the perspective of the Administrator and Licensed Teacher of Anatomy, donors will usually initiate a bequest when they are sorting out their wills, and when bodies are taken into the Department they usually range in age from their late 50s to over 100. Members of a family often wish to make a donation together and relatives tend to be disappointed in cases where, for example, both parents have planned to donate and only one of them is accepted at the time of death.[6] The donation of the body is part of a

---

[5] According to a pilot study of bequests conducted in 2005 by the Licensed Teacher of Anatomy, University of Aberdeen.

[6] Donors are informed that a body cannot be accepted in a number of circumstances, including when a person has had particular diseases.

person's anticipation of the end of life. Yet, as the bequest is often registered some years prior to this, donors will often contact the Administrator to advise her of any changes in, for example, their wishes or next-of-kin. The Administrator records these personal intentions and social connections via the documenting systems required for bequests.

In the event that a donated body is accepted, with the consent of the person in lawful possession of the body, the deceased is taken directly from the place of death to the Department of Anatomy by undertakers.[7] If a donor dies in Aberdeen and the Department of Anatomy is organising the transportation, the funeral director's firm employed since the 1920s conducts this work. Alternatively, donors from outside the city will usually be transported by local undertakers. The body must arrive in Anatomy within a specified number of hours after death to ensure its preservation. Between the time of death and delivery to Anatomy, however, a viewing of the person in a chapel of rest at an undertaker's premises is sometimes arranged by relatives with advice from the Licensed Teacher of Anatomy. Thus a body will arrive in Anatomy as a deceased person who is still part of the social relationships sustained in life; this is a very different body to those of the 'unclaimed' who were socially isolated at the point of death.

The mid-20th century shift from the deployment of 'unclaimed' to donated bodies was a significant aspect of changes in the social relations and cultural practices of anatomists. As we have seen there was a forging of professional relationships with solicitors, ministers and the local press to recruit assistance in the task of encouraging bequests. The bequest-making process also entails on-going connections between anatomists, donors and their relatives. Anatomists took a leading part in cultivating the social relations of bequests from the mid-20th century and an important dimension of these relations was the formation of means by which donors would be remembered. The following sections of this paper explore the ways in which anatomists have instigated and participated in memorials as practices, in the case of a memorial service, and as material objects, in the form of a memorial book and a cemetery memorial. Before addressing these, however, there is a discussion of the Dissecting Room, in Aberdeen University's Department of Anatomy, as a site of memory making—not in terms of the memorialising of particular persons and their lives, but with regard to the engagement of memory in the generation of anatomical knowledge.

IV. REMEMBERING IN THE DISSECTING ROOM

Dissecting rooms have been perceived amongst anatomists and medical students as places where essential knowledge of the human body is acquired,

---

[7] Bodies were delivered direct to the Department of Anatomy, rather than going to the Funeratory, by the late 1960s.

and where significant impressions are retained, informing future practice. Sinclair's analysis shows how medical knowledge is developed in multi-sensory ways involving sight, touch, and hearing (Sinclair, 1997). It is in the dynamics of visual and tactile engagement with a range of dissections, models and diagrams that anatomical knowledge is developed (Hallam, 2005; and Hallam, 2006). The Dissecting Room is a place of transforma-tion for medical students, as they are confronted by the body after death, learning from it over a period of about eight months and retaining powerful memories of it.

Since the 19th century, there has been a strong emphasis on practical anatomy as the main learning method where students dissect a cadaver themselves. From the 1860s onwards, Aberdeen anatomists stressed that visual access to the interior of the human body was paramount for each student, as it encouraged them to investigate for themselves. Students were advised 'not to trust to the word-knowledge obtained from lectures or books', to move away from 'word-knowledge' and to build up their anatomical knowledge from the 'actualities' of the body revealed through careful dissection (Struthers, 1899: 232). The subordination of words learned by rote in favour of learning through touch and observation high-lights the significance of the students' own embodied senses in developing their knowledge of anatomy. Although considerable changes have taken place in medical education throughout the 20th century—with a reduc-tion in the time students dedicate to anatomy, as well as on-going debates amongst anatomists about the role of dissection (eg Ellis, 2001; McLachlan and De Bere, 2004; and Older, 2004)—in the Department of Anatomy at Aberdeen there is a continued emphasis on the value of learning with the use of cadavers. Dissection was conducted by students until September 2003, when there was a move toward teaching with prosections (already dissected material).

Students learn with what are referred to as 'embalmed subjects'. Upon arrival at the Department of Anatomy the deceased person, the donor, will have been embalmed and prepared by technicians for the Dissecting Room. Significantly, the name of the person is not disclosed within this setting. Given that the name confers personhood and individuality (La Fontaine, 1985), removing it would signal the reverse of this. Instead of their name the deceased person is given a number. As the Licensed Teacher of Anatomy explained, there are only two occasions when a donor's name is used in the Department: when the body arrives the name is replaced by a number and when it leaves the name is given back to the number (Interview, July 2006). Numbers become unique identifiers for each body and this mode of anonymity underlines the transforma-tion of a person into a cadaver. Richardson argues that corpses used in medical education are traditionally 'depersonalized and biography-less' (Richardson, 2001: 418). The replacement of name with number is an important part of this transformation, as recognition of a body as a particular person can, from anatomists' point of view, interrupt the process of learning anatomy.

In the Dissecting Room and in the adjoining Anatomy Museum students are encouraged to develop 'anatomical skills' through 'practical experience'. The first of these skills is

being able to visualise in the mind's eye and feel with an examining hand the body structures as they lie beneath the skin.

This training of eye and hand is meant to develop the student's capacity to visualise in three dimensions, and to remember, 'how parts of the body are put together and how these components work' (Learning Guide 2002–03). These forms of visualisation are central to the development of students' anatomical knowledge. What is remembered by students, then, is not a person but an anatomical body. Memory of that body is formed through detailed manual and visual exploration. Learning in the Dissecting Room thus generates embodied forms of memory, similar to what Connerton describes as incorporating practice. He argues that our bodies 'keep the past ... in an entirely effective form in their continuing ability to perform certain skilled actions'. By performing particular actions and movements 'habitual skilled remembering' develops so that it becomes 'sedimented in the body' (Connerton, 1989: 72). Memory of the anatomical body may take this form where repeated handling and visual scrutiny of the dissected cadaver cultivates the anatomical skills that are incorporated by the body of the student. In the context of the Dissecting Room, then, the de-personalised cadaver has a significant role in forming students' memories of the anatomical body. Students will later hear the names of these bodies as, once moved out of the Dissecting Room, the 'embalmed subjects' are given back their names in spoken acts of remembrance during a memorial service. However, this subsequent memorial disclosure of donors' names does not enable students to retrospectively associate the individual names with the actual bodies that they had encountered in the Dissecting Room. In this respect students' memories of the donor might remain as an anatomical body rather than as a named person.

The following sections of this chapter examine the anatomical memorials—a complex of linked sites, practices, and material objects—instituted by anatomists in their networks of social relationships, especially with the relatives and friends of donors. The three memorial forms discussed, a service, a book and a cemetery memorial, are relational in the sense that they have emerged as part of particular social relationships and, in their composition and focus on material inscriptions, they relate to one another, and, indeed, to further memorials. Of particular significance here is the name and its rendering in spoken words and in manuscript.

V. THE MEMORIAL SERVICE

The Memorial Service to acknowledge those people who have donated their bodies to medical science is held each year at King's College Chapel in Old Aberdeen. The Service is held primarily for the close friends and family of approximately 30 donors, but the Anatomy staff also regard it as significant for themselves and for their students. Attended by about 300 people, the annual Memorial Service on the first Thursday in May is one of the largest events in the Chapel's calendar. The family and friends of donors, indeed all in attendance, are sent letters of invitation by the Licensed Teacher of Anatomy. Relatives who attend include spouses, siblings, daughters, sons, and (usually adult) grandchildren. Nurses sometimes attend for donors who have died without relatives in residential homes. For the large majority of donors, there will be a person present who knew them in life and who will hear their name read out, a gesture that is to 'witness' the name, for the hearing and viewing of a person's name are the central memorial acts of the Service.

The Anatomy Bequests Administrator, in the Department of Anatomy, takes a leading role in the organisation of the Service. She communicates with donors' next-of-kin, undertakers, staff and students in Anatomy, HM Inspector of Anatomy for Scotland and the Chaplain to the University—a minister of the Church of Scotland—who leads the Service. Until recently, the service was held at the time when donors were to be cremated or buried. At the conclusion of donors' time in the Dissecting Room, a maximum of three years, coffins are ordered from the undertakers and donors are then transported in hearses for cremation at Aberdeen Crematorium or burial in the city's Trinity Cemetery. The cremation service, held on the day of the Memorial Service, is also led by the University Chaplain and attended by staff in Anatomy along with HM Inspector of Anatomy for Scotland.[8] Funeral expenses are met by the University except when donors request the return of their remains to their family for private burials. Since 2003 a change in the timing of the Memorial Service, in relation to the return of donors' remains for disposal, has taken place. The Service is now held in the May following the death of the donor, a time that does not necessarily coincide with the disposal of the body. The latter can now happen one to two years after the Memorial Service, at which time the next-of-kin will either request the Crematorium to arrange the scattering of ashes, or they collect them for scattering in a place that is personally meaningful, such as a family grave. As the Memorial Service and the final disposal of donors' remains may now take place at different times, for relatives and friends

---

[8] Currently the large majority of donors are cremated, with only one or two donors preferring burial. The burial service at Aberdeen's Trinity Cemetery, conducted by the University Chaplain, is attended by staff in Anatomy.

of donors there are two significant moments following the death—the Memorial Service and, later, the disposal of remains.

Initiated in Aberdeen in the early 1950s, the Memorial Service was the first of its kind to be held in Scotland (Interview, July 2006).[9] It was initially held in the refurbished Dissecting Room in the Department of Anatomy and, although it was attended primarily by staff and students, relatives of donors were admitted, as many had expressed the wish to be present (Fyfe, 1987). The inception of the Service was part of practices in anatomy that, during the 1950s, paid increasing attention to the attitudes and intentions of donors. Notable in this respect was the observance of donors' requirements for their burial. For example, some donors supplied their own coffins and specified the place for the return of remains for burial or for the return of ashes. Care was taken with the requests of donors and the mourning practices of relatives. For example, following one Catholic donor's wishes, a rosary was buried with him. Another donor had arrived in Anatomy accompanied by a wreath sent by mourners and in this case the remains were later returned with a second wreath. The Memorial Service developed in this context of increased communication between anatomists, donors and their relatives.

By 1972 the Memorial Service had been relocated to the Chapel at King's College and it was then led by the Chaplain to the University. This relocation may have corresponded with a shift in emphasis to encourage the attendance of more donors' relatives and friends. From the current Chaplain's perspective, she has inherited a 'tradition' which she now continues through her own participation in the Service (Interview, August 2006). As a minister of the Church of Scotland she presents the Service with 'Judeo-Christian overtones', as this is considered to be consistent with the broad beliefs of donors. The Chaplain is aware that most people attending might not be 'religious', and the intention is to create a service that is 'very open' and not exclusive. The Chaplain describes the 'main essence' of the Service as a 'thanksgiving for what we have been given in life and death', to express 'gratitude to God as well as for the huge gift of the body to anatomy', and to signal the 'hope of eternal life'. The Chaplain also aims to create a setting in which people can grieve, or say goodbye, and she gives a message to both the bereaved and students that the 'value of life continues after death' (Interview, August 2006).

Following the entry of donors' relatives and friends into the Chapel and the seating of students, the Memorial Service begins with a procession of councillors from city and region, senior members of the Department of Anatomy and University and HM Inspector of Anatomy for Scotland. The Memorial Book, on display on a table at the entrance of the chapel, is

---

[9] The Memorial Service in Aberdeen also formed a model for the Service of Thanksgiving first held in 1982 for the donors to medical schools in the University of London (Tinker, 1998). I would like to thank Peter Jupp for this reference.

open to show the names of the donors commemorated in the Service. The entrance to the Chapel is through the Antechapel, which is the University's War Memorial, commemorating the names of hundreds of men associated with the University who died in the First and Second World Wars. The names are carved into the wood panelling around the walls and are recorded in the Book of Remembrance set into a recess. During the time of the Memorial Service, then, there is a convergence of memorials—for donors to Anatomy and for men who died in war—both operating through the inscription of the name.

During the Service there are several readings from scripture by a medical and a science student while the address of the Chaplain forms the Service's emotionally heightened phase when the names of donors and their places of residence are read aloud. This is an important point of recognition for donors' relatives and the first time that students will have heard the names. The Chaplain's address in 2006, as on previous occasions, gave special consideration to the name:

As we have listened to the long list of names, we allow those names to resonate in this place. There is something very special in a name (Chaplain's Address, May 2006).

Addressing relatives, the Chaplain defined the name as a source of memories of a person during their lifetime. To express the gratitude of students toward donors, the Chaplain also read part of a speech that medical students at Dundee University had written for one of their own memorial occasions. This speech underlined the value of the human body as a source of knowledge:

Our silent teachers, as that is exactly what they were, provided us with a text that no book could duplicate, no series of lectures could match and no computer could simulate ... the donation of one's body to medicine literally becomes the gift of life ... We will never forget their generosity, and be forever humbled, indebted by their final gracious gift (Chaplain's Address, May 2006).

Here the memorialising of the donor for their relatives and for students is conducted through the reading of the name and by reflection upon the meaning of the name. While relatives of donors are prompted to remember a person's life via their name, students remember the 'silent teacher' whose body is other than a text, and is not conveyed in words.

VI. THE MEMORIAL BOOK

In the entrance corridor of the Department of Anatomy at Marischal College, there are two memorial books on display in a locked glass-fronted case (Figure 1). The case is built into the wall, framed in oak and lined with dark red velvet. A brass plaque on the inner frame carries the inscription: 'This book records in gratitude the names of those who bequeathed their

Fig. 1 *The Memorial Book in the entrance corridor of the Department of Anatomy, Marischal College, University of Aberdeen. Photograph: Norman Little.*

bodies for the advancement of medical science'. The case allows the viewer to see the two dark blue and green covers of the books that are embossed with gold tooling and lettering. The front cover of the most recent book, entitled *In Memoriam*, is visible and, behind this, the spine of the older book which reads *The Book of Memory*. The contents of the books are concealed and protected, as the case has to be unlocked before the books can be opened and read. Thus the books, as memorial objects, remain on permanent display while their written contents are periodically viewed. When opened, each right-hand page is assigned to a consecutive year and shows the names of donors who died in that year, alongside the place each person was associated with, usually the place of death. The occasions when the Memorial Book is opened are specifically framed as acts of remembrance, when people related to a donor visit the Department of Anatomy to see that person's name, and during the annual Memorial Service. Through its inscription the Book becomes a focus for personal acts of memory making, and it is also central to the collective memorial occasions.

The Memorial Book was established in 1966. In the context of the Anatomy Act Committee's discussions regarding the numbers of bequests, and the issue of publicising the need for bequests, Denis Dooley, then HM Inspector of Anatomy for Scotland, suggested that

a Book of Remembrance could be purchased which would then be kept in the Anatomy Department as a form of memorial and to which the public could have access (MSU1332/4/1, 1966: 26).

Such a Book was obtained by David Sinclair, the first names were recorded in 1966, and it is currently maintained by the Anatomy Bequest Administrator. She organises the writing of donors' names by a person skilled in calligraphy. An anatomist and a photographic technician in the Department have entered names in the past and, since 1999, the names have been written by an art teacher (now retired) from an Aberdeen school that was attended by several Aberdeen anatomists. As the exclusive memorial inscription of a donor's name, these words carry considerable significance for relatives. If a donor's next-of-kin is unable to attend the Memorial Service, due to illness or geographical distance, the Administrator makes a copy of the inscribed name from the Memorial Book and sends it to them with the Order of Service. In recent years, then, the Memorial Book has also become a series of distributed inscriptions kept by relatives in Scotland, Canada and Hong Kong. In its material form, and in its single-page copies, the Book memorialises persons deceased and at the same time has the potential to maintain connections between the Department of Anatomy and the relatives of donors.

From the point of view of anatomists, the inscription of donors' names forms a record of gratitude expressed for each bequest. The Book operates as a memorial for individual persons but it also situates individuals in relation to a wider culturally valued process, the 'advancement of medical science'. The memorial inscription operates in a number of ways. It records the name of a person alongside the name of the place that was significant to them in life. A person retains, therefore, a connection with a place in which they had lived and at the same time they are memorialised in a place of anatomical learning. On each page of the Memorial Book individuals are also memorialised as part of a group of persons whose commonality is the act of their donation. Single dates of death are not recorded here; rather the memorial inscription subsumes individual deaths beneath the commonly shared year of death. Furthermore, each page in the Book, marking another year that passes, constitutes an ever-growing community of donors. Yet for the donors' relatives and friends the inscribed name retains the unique features of the person whom they knew, providing the material from which memories of a life can be generated and renewed.

VII. THE CEMETERY MEMORIAL

The Memorial Service and the Memorial Book are also linked to the University of Aberdeen's Anatomy Memorial in the city's Trinity Cemetery (Figure 2). The Memorial is set on a high plot of land, which is reserved for the burial of donors. Facing into the cemetery with the sea behind, the Memorial features a prominent dedication: 'In memory of those who gave their bodies for the increase of knowledge and the advance of medicine'.

Fig. 2 *The Memorial in Trinity Cemetery, Aberdeen, 2005. Photograph: Elizabeth Hallam.*

These words run across the full breadth of the Memorial, spanning its left and right arms. On the central panel is a plaque carrying a further inscription:

'Their name liveth for ever. The people will tell of their wisdom and the congregation will show forth their praise' Ecclesiasticus 44.

While the first inscription is legible at a distance, the second is rendered on a smaller scale and has to be approached from the shallow steps that lead to the upper platform of the Memorial. An impression of austere simplicity is conveyed. The spatial orientation of the Memorial is significant, as, in its elevated position, it creates definition for the third of an acre of uninterrupted ground that extends before it. This is for the exclusive use of the Department of Anatomy and, while donors are buried there, its grass remains unmarked with any individual headstones. The Memorial thus operates as a collective marker that registers the presence of donors, whilst preserving their anonymity.

   The Memorial's materials are very much in sympathy with the headstones in the cemetery, which are predominantly granite, but its lack of personalised decoration stands in marked contrast—it is both part of and distinct from the collectivity of graves. While the Memorial is devoid of personal names, the inscription draws attention to the significance of the name and its remembrance through the quotation from Ecclesiasticus. This collective memorial, like the Memorial Book, emphasises one central gesture in the lives of those buried—that they gave their bodies—and it links this gesture to the powerful narrative of medicine's advancement and claims regarding the growth of knowledge. Despite the collective emphasis and lack of individuated features, the Memorial has become, in practice, a focus for personal gestures of remembrance. In this respect the metal letters composing the Memorial's predominant inscription have been pressed into service as resting places for small floral tributes. In 2006, visitors had left, for instance, daisies at the letter W in the word *who*, an artificial rose at the O of *bodies*, and a Christmas basket of flowers was also hooked onto the word *knowledge*. Relatives also sometimes scatter donors' ashes at the Memorial.

The history of the Cemetery Memorial, like the Memorial Book, is related to anatomists' efforts to create positive public visibility for anatomical research, to express gratitude to donors and their relatives, and to encourage future donors. During the 1960s there was a considerable increase in bequests and in 1968 David Sinclair, Professor of Anatomy, raised the issue of a memorial with the Anatomy Act Committee. At this time, Sinclair pointed out, many donors were being cremated but there was still a considerable number preferring burial. However, at Trinity Cemetery the 'ground in which they were interred was not marked in any way as indicative of who lay there' and so Sinclair suggested that 'some form of headstone be instructed and erected' (MSU1332/4/1, 1968: 33). HM Inspector of Anatomy for Scotland informed the Committee that a memorial was also being considered in London, taking 'simple forms such as a Garden of Remembrance' (MSU1332/4/1, 1968: 33). That other medical schools were planning a memorial was considered encouraging, although, by 1974, the Memorial completed in Aberdeen was still regarded as the first of its kind in Britain (Letter, 19 March1974).

In fashioning the Memorial, anatomists in Aberdeen were keenly aware that relatives were concerned about where donors were buried and that they wanted to visit the place of burial. In 1972 Sinclair explained the concern:

in recognition of our great indebtedness to those who bequeath their bodies and to their families who permit us to make use of them, we instituted a Book of Remembrance ... and this is much appreciated by relatives and friends (Letter, 19 June 1972).

However, Sinclair continued, it was felt that Trinity Cemetery should 'carry some visible recognition of its purpose and of our gratitude to those who are buried there'. Furthermore, this was an issue that

comes particularly to mind at the time of the Annual Service, when we [anatomists] are approached by relatives who wish to know where the donors are buried, and are often considerably distressed when we are obliged to tell them there is no commemorative stone or memorial (Letter, 19 June 1972).

On the reoccurring occasion of the Memorial Service a dialogue between anatomists and donors' relatives was forming and it was through these interactions that plans for the Cemetery Memorial began to emerge.

During the early efforts to establish a memorial it was discovered that the ground at Trinity Cemetery had been originally given in 1921 'on the condition that no reference to its use was made' and that there should be 'no memorial of any kind' (MSU1332/4/1, 1969: 36); Letter, 10 November1969). Sinclair investigated this, obtained permission to erect a memorial and also raised funds for it, utilising finances from the previous sale of the Funeratory, together with contributions from the University and the City.[10] By 1970 designs for the Memorial, on what was regarded as a difficult sloping site, were considered by the Anatomy Act Committee. Surviving sketches suggest that various memorial forms were initially envisaged, including crosses, headstones, a pillar, a sculpted wreath and praying hands. The guiding principles of the design, however, were that it 'should not be one which should attract particular attention and ... it should be a simple form'. Consideration was also given to the inscription, which 'should be in the same terms as the Memorial Book in the Department' (MSU1332/4/1, 1970: 41). A 'general inscription' was anticipated, however, that excluded any 'individual names' (Letter, 10 November 1969).

To realise the Memorial along these lines a successful approach was made to staff at the Scott Sutherland School of Architecture in Aberdeen. By June 1972, formal designs were presented by the architect W Coutts Youngson. He proposed a 'simple silhouette' with the central feature standing as a

wall designed to present a bold inscription in metal roman capitals, a small bronze plaque and a base or platform for a piece of symbolic sculpture which might be acquired in due course (Letter, 8 June 1972).

The 'symbolic sculpture' was never fully realised (though a human figure was selected from invited proposals by students at Gray's School of Art in Aberdeen). So, as the Memorial came to be made in practice, its textual inscriptions have emerged and remained its predominant features.

Thirty four years ago the Memorial was devised 'to commemorate the goodwill and public spirit shown by those who bequeathed their bodies' (Letter, 20 March 1974). It remains active in the sense that it is visited, and people leave flowers and also sometimes scatter the ashes of donors there. In the past year the Memorial has been 'rededicated', in a service led by the Chaplain to the University, after extensive cleaning and planting. The current Licensed Teacher of Anatomy explained in a University press release that a 'service to rededicate the Memorial to those who have

---

[10] In 1921 Trinity Cemetery was managed by the Incorporated Trades. It is now maintained by the City Council but the University of Aberdeen is responsible for the Memorial.

given their bodies for the advancement of medicine and science' was to be held in October 2005 at Trinity Cemetery. The public statements from the Department of Anatomy surrounding this service were to express gratitude for the bequests made by more than 2200 people since the 1920s. They also highlighted the changes in medical science—in clinical practice, teaching, learning and research—whilst underlining the continuing

> need for students to learn the structural organisation of the human body, for which the human body itself still provides the primary, and most valued, means of learning (Press release, 18 October 2005).

Here the message is that while medicine inevitably changes there is a crucial continuity: the need for donated bodies, or what the anatomist David Sinclair termed 'invaluable gifts' (Letter, 19 March 1974).

VIII. BODIES, NAMES AND MEMORIALS

Histories of anatomy and the treatment of the body after death in Britain are, as Richardson has shown, fraught and controversial (Richardson, 2001). This chapter has sought to discuss the social relations of anatomy and the memorial practices entailed in the treatment of anatomical 'subjects' in the North East of Scotland following the Anatomy Act 1832. The shift from the acquisition of 'unclaimed' bodies to the rise in donation in the mid-20th century is traced here in the context of anatomists' professional connections with solicitors, doctors, ministers, civic and institutional officials, and the local press. It is through these intermediaries, and in dialogue with potential donors and their relatives, that bequests were generated. The social status of anatomical 'subjects', or cadavers, is of particular significance, as these subjects have transformed over the last century from socially disconnected bodies to deceased persons that are enmeshed in ongoing social relationships. These relationships are registered in the making of memorials. Here the names of persons are particularly significant. The donor's name is not disclosed in the Dissecting Room, as the process of learning and remembering anatomy proceeds through repeated tactile engagement with a depersonalised cadaver. This generates embodied forms of memory that are central to students' knowledge of anatomy. However, the name is returned to the cadaver as it moves out of the spaces of anatomy towards final disposal. This reconstitutes the cadaver as a person to be remembered and it takes place through the spoken word in the Memorial Service and the inscription in the Memorial Book. The Cemetery Memorial reiterates the significance of the name without disclosing individual names, and marks the place of burial with a collective message. This inscription articulates gratitude for the giving of bodies in relation to a narrative of the advancement of medicine. These memorials are interconnected in the social relationships through which they emerged and in the forms that they have taken—especially as materially significant inscriptions. Anatomists' participation in these memorial practices is part of the process of expressing gratitude for, and of inviting further, donations. The memorials in this respect are active in the remembrance of donors and in the cultivation of further social relationships that help to sustain the practice of anatomy.

REFERENCES

Archival Sources

Chaplain's Address (May 2006) Memorial Service, King's College Chapel, University of Aberdeen.

Learning Guide (2002–03) *Learning guide to systems 1 practical anatomy*, University of Aberdeen.

Letter (10 November 1969) David Sinclair, Department of Anatomy Records, University of Aberdeen.

Letter (8 June 1972) W. Coutts Youngson, Department of Anatomy Records, University of Aberdeen.

Letter (19 June 1972) David Sinclair, Department of Anatomy Records, University of Aberdeen.

Letter (19 March 1974) David Sinclair, Department of Anatomy Records, University of Aberdeen.

Letter (20 March 1974) David Sinclair, Department of Anatomy Records, University of Aberdeen.

MSU1332/4/1 (1856–1977, with notes c 1844–1847) Anatomy Act Committee Minutes, 2 volumes, Special Libraries and Archives, University of Aberdeen.

MSU1332/4/3 (1843–1944) Register of bodies brought to the Parochial Burying House, 2 volumes, Special Libraries and Archives, University of Aberdeen.

MSU1332/4/4/17 (1965–1972) Anatomy Act Committee Records, Special Libraries and Archives, University of Aberdeen.

Press release (18 October 2005) from the Department of Anatomy, University of Aberdeen.

Interviews

Interview (July 2006) with the Licensed Teacher of Anatomy, University of Aberdeen.
Interview (August 2006) with the Chaplain to the University of Aberdeen.

Published works

Connerton, P (1989) *How societies remember* (Cambridge, Cambridge University Press).

Ellis, H (2001) 'Teaching in the dissecting room' 14 *Clinical Anatomy* 149–151.

298   *Elizabeth Hallam*

Fyfe, FW (1987) 'In memoriam. RD Lockhart' 155 *Journal of Anatomy* 203–208.

Hallam, E (2005) 'Anatomy museum: Anthropological and historical perspectives' in A Semedo and J Teixera Lopes (eds), *Museus, discursos e representações* (Porto, Edições Afrontamento).

—— (2006) 'Anatomy display: Contemporary debates and collections in Scotland' in A Patrizio and D Kemp (eds), *Anatomy acts. How we come to know ourselves* (Edinburgh, Berlinn).

Hallam, E and Hockey, J (2001) *Death, memory and material culture* (Oxford, Berg).

La Fontaine, JS (1985) 'Person and individual: Some anthropological reflections' in M Carrithers, S Collins and S Lukes (eds), *The category of the person. Anthropology, philosophy, history* (Cambridge, Cambridge University Press).

McLachlan, JC and De Bere, SR (2004) 'How we teach anatomy without cadavers' 1 *The Clinical Teacher* 49–52.

Older, J (2004) 'Anatomy: a must for teaching the next generation' 2 *The Surgeon: Journal of the Royal Colleges of Surgeons of Edinburgh and Ireland* 79–90.

Pennington, C (1994) *The modernisation of medical teaching at Aberdeen in the nineteenth century* (Aberdeen, Aberdeen University Press).

Richardson, R (1995) 'Donors' attitudes towards body donation for dissection' 346 *The Lancet* 277–279.

—— (2001 [1988]) *Death, dissection and the destitute* 2nd edn with a new afterword (London, Phoenix Press).

Scots Law Times, October 11 1958.

Sinclair, S (1997) *Making doctors: an institutional apprenticeship* (Oxford, Berg).

Struthers, J (1899) 'The progress of the medical school' in P J Anderson (ed), *Aurora borealis academica. Aberdeen university appreciations* 1860–1899 (Aberdeen, Aberdeen University Printers).

The Guardian, January 30 2006; July 4 2006.

Tinker, E (1998) 'An unusual Christian Service: for those who have donated their bodies for medical education and research' 3 *Mortality* 79–82.

Walter, T (2004a) 'Plastination for display: A new way to dispose of the dead' 10 *Journal of the Royal Anthropological Institute* 603–627.

—— (2004b) 'Body worlds: clinical detachment and anatomical awe' 26 *Sociology of Health and Illness* 464–488.

Legislation

Anatomy Act 1832 (2 & 3 Will IV c 75).
Human Tissue Act 2004.
Human Tissue (Scotland) Act 2006.

Index

Aberdeen, Memorial Service at, 288–90
Aberdeen University
    Department of Anatomy, 280, 283, 285,
      286, 290–92
    Memorial Books, 290–92
    Dissecting Room *see* Dissecting Room,
      Aberdeen University
    War Memorial, 290, 292
abnormal deaths, 109
Abraham, Biblical figure of, 98
act/omission distinction, 38, 49, 52
actio personalis moritur cum persona rule,
    242, 243, 244
Adams, J, 134
advance decisions/directives, 78
afterlife
    and Christianity *see* afterlife, Christian
      perspectives
    Jewish beliefs, 96
    moral issues, 112
    resurrection as understood mode of entry
      into, 113
afterlife, Christian perspectives
    Christ's death and resurrection, 96,
      99–101
    demise of traditional beliefs, 110–11
    Jewish origins, 98–9
AIDS, as cause of death, 165
Albery, Nicholas, 110
Alder Hey hospital, body organ retention
    scandal, 101, 201, 211, 212, 264, 270
amenities of life, loss of
    damages claims, 248–9
analgesia, and palliative care, 44
anatomy, 8–9
    cadavers, procurement for study (Great
      Britain), 262–4
    future of anatomical dissection, in UK,
      276–7
    history, in Europe, 262–5
    Human Tissue Act 2004
      altruistic donor, 274
      anatomy teaching, affecting, 267–70
      consent of donor, and relationships
        with next-of-kin, 270–74
      Dissecting Room, working in,
        274–6
      see also Human Tissue Act 2004

NHS treatment, disaffection with, 264–5
specimens, possession away from
    licensed premises, 230
Anatomy Act 1832, 263, 280, 282, 296
Anatomy Act 1984, 263
Anatomy Act Committee, Aberdeen, 283,
    291, 294, 295
Anatomy Bequests Administrator, 284
ancestors, beliefs on death, 96
Anderson, Jill, 64, 65–6, 67, 72
Anderson, Paul, 65, 66, 67
Anglican Church, 105, 106–7, 110
ANH (Artificial Nutrition and
    Hydration), 50
ante-mortem harm, 204
anthropology
    and ancestors, beliefs on death, 96
    comparative perspective, 160
    and Judaism, 98
    and material culture, 148–9
    non-Western death rituals, 159
Aries, P, 25
Arnason, A, 173, 174–5
artefacts, symbolic properties *see* objects,
    and death rituals
Artificial Nutrition and Hydration
    (ANH), 50
artificial ventilation, 50
assisted dying
    Assisted Dying for the Terminally Ill Bill
      2005, 58, 68–71, 72
    Assisted Dying for the Terminally Ill
      Committee, 40
    carers' participation, 60
    House of Lords Select Committee, 39, 40,
      41, 45, 68
    see also euthanasia
assisted suicide
    criminalising carers, 60–62
    legal availability, 58–9
    and right to be helped to commit
      suicide, 85–7
see also assisted dying; euthanasia; suicide
atheists, and funeral rituals, 97
Augustine, Saint, 102, 105, 118
Australia, non-voluntary euthanasia in, 47
autonomy, and right to die, 79, 84, 89
autopsies, 208